Shakespeare and Child's Play

Shakespeare wrote more than fifty parts for children, amounting to the first comprehensive portrait of childhood in the English theatre. Focusing mostly on boys, he put sons against fathers, servants against masters, innocence against experience, testing the notion of masculinity, manners, morals, and the limits of patriarchal power. He explored the nature of relationships and ideas about parenting in terms of nature and nurture, permissiveness and discipline. He wrote about education, adolescent rebellion, delinquency, fostering, and child-killing, as well as the idea of the redemptive child who 'cures' diseased adult imaginations.

'Childness' – the essential nature of being a child – remains a vital critical issue. In *Shakespeare and Child's Play*, Carol Chillington Rutter analyses a range of recent performances on stage and film, among them:

Penny Woolcock's *Macbeth on the Estate*
Julie Taymor's *Titus*
Kneehigh's *Cymbeline*
Greg Doran's *A Midsummer Night's Dream*
Declan Donnellan's *The Winter's Tale*.

This timely study shows how these performances use Shakespeare's insights in order to re-examine and rethink these emotive issues in terms of today's society and culture.

Carol Chillington Rutter is Professor of English in the Department of English and Comparative Literary Studies, University of Warwick. She is author of *Enter the Body* (2001).

For my daughters Bryony and Rowan, whose lives I watch prepared 'For more amazement', and for Harry, 'Dear life', the boy who got away.

Shakespeare and Child's Play

Performing lost boys on stage and screen

Carol Chillington Rutter

Routledge
Taylor & Francis Group
LONDON AND NEW YORK

First published 2007
by Routledge
2 Park Square, Milton Park, Abingdon, Oxon OX14 4RN

Simultaneously published in the USA and Canada
by Routledge
711 Third Avenue, New York, NY 10017

Routledge is an imprint of the Taylor & Francis Group, an informa business

© 2007 Carol Chillington Rutter

Typeset in Baskerville by
Bookcraft Ltd, Stroud, Gloucestershire

British Library Cataloguing in Publication Data
A catalogue record for this book is available
from the British Library

Library of Congress Cataloging in Publication Data
Rutter, Carol Chillington.
　　Shakespeare and child's play: performing lost boys on stage and
　　screen/Carol Chillington Rutter.
　　p. cm.
　　Includes bibliographical references and index.
　　1. Shakespeare, William, 1564–1616 – Characters – Children.
　　2. Shakespeare, William, 1564–1616 – Stage history. 3. Shakespeare,
　　William, 1564–1616 – Film and video adaptations. 4. Boys in literature.
　　5. Childhood in literature. 6. Children in literature. I. Title.
　　PR2992.C4R87 2007
　　822.3'3–dc22　　　　　　　　　　　　　　　　　　　　　2007022682

ISBN13: 978–0–415–36518–5 (hbk)
ISBN13: 978–0–415–36519–2 (pbk)
ISBN13: 978–0–203–01658–9 (ebk)

Contents

Plates

Preface

I want to begin with three images that help me lay out my project in this book, all of them pictures of boys, children at play, and Hamlet: a production photograph, a book illustration, and a memory caught like a snapshot in the mind's eye.

The production photograph is from 1948. In it, a lad lies sprawled on the floor gazing hard at something as though he's watching TV. But clearly, the technology doesn't exist. He's surrounded by courtiers in nineteenth-century Ruritanian uniforms; the cavernous room is heavy with funereal black swag drapes and only gloomily illuminated by candelabra massive enough to light a cathedral. The child himself, prone at the feet of the queen who could be the young widow O'Hara from *Gone with the Wind*, looks like her mascot, a little 'ape', a miniature version of the adults, in an elaborately frogged jacket and white gloves. His face is shining with excitement. The players have arrived at Elsinore! They're bringing the place to life with a play! And the kid, looking at *The Murder of Gonzago*, is clearly enthralled. Who is he? Nobody. Just a child – peripheral. (In this photograph by Angus McBean of Michael Benthall's *Hamlet* at the Shakespeare Memorial Theatre he's practically out of the frame.) He's one of the supernumerary 'unnamed parts' listed in the castlist (far down the programme after Claire Bloom's Ophelia, Paul Scofield's Hamlet, Diana Wynyard's Gertrude[1]). But if he's nobody, he's also Prince Hamlet's double, as the scene's blocking, captured in McBean's photograph, shows. While the keen-eyed boy looks at the Player King on the dais (stage left), Prince Hamlet fixes his look on the 'player king' occupying his father's throne (stage right): both 'boys' stretch out on the floor; alert; symmetrical studies in black and white; the little boy somehow the residual trace, the ghost, of the child who was Hamlet. At the end, it's this little boy who is Elsinore's lonely survivor. As corpses are removed, he'll sit ignored, sobbing.

Plate 1 'The play's the thing' in Michael Benthall's 1948 *Hamlet*. As the Prince (Paul Scofield, centre) observes one 'player king', the boy (Timothy Harley, far left) watches another. (*Source*: Angus McBean photograph. By permission of the Shakespeare Birthplace Trust.)

My second image is actually a pair of silhouettes composing a symmetrical diptych. It's a black-on-black wood engraving illustrating the Cranach Press *Hamlet* (1930), the work of Edward Gorgon Craig – actor, director, scenic designer, puppeteer (and illegitimate son of the age's greatest actress, who started her career playing Mamillius, Ellen Terry). On the left-hand page, a classically-inspired, austerely modernist adult Hamlet stands gazing down at a skull, lightly touching it where it rests on a half-column plinth. On the facing page, the composition, bodies and roles are reversed. Yorick is alive! A medieval figure jigging with animation in a plumed cap and long skirts held up to show the bells on the tips of his flowing sleeves, the jester is fooling, is playing to Hamlet – but a Hamlet who nowhere appears in Shakespeare's play. Hamlet here is a child, sitting at Yorick's feet, gazing up, entranced.

Gordon Craig's engraving could be the illustrated caption to my third picture, an image that suddenly surfaces from memory to fix itself in Hamlet's mind's eye. In Shakespeare's 5.1 the banished Prince, returning

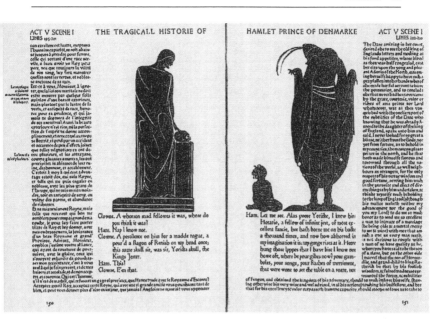

Plate 2 'Alas poor Yorick'. Illustration by Edward Gordon Craig from *The Tragedie of Hamlet*, text edited by John Dover Wilson (Weimar, 1930). By permission of the Henry E. Huntington Library.

home to Elsinore via (an odd route) the graveyard, pauses with his friend Horatio to question a man at work: 'Whose grave's this, sirrah?' And: 'How long hast thou been a grave-maker?' (5.1.115, 138). The second question is answered with a mnemonic: 'I came to't,' replies the Grave-digger, 'that day our last king overcame Fortinbras … the very day Hamlet was born': 'thirty years' (5.1.141, 144, 158). The first is answered with an object. Hamlet is handed a skull; a skull, says the Gravedigger, that has 'lain in the earth three and twenty years'. 'A whoreson mad fellow's it was … a mad rogue … This same skull, sir, was Yorick's skull, the King's jester' (5.1.168–9, 171, 174, 175–6). As though catching in the throat of the play, the Gravedigger's line stops words. And time. Cradling this latest mnemonic, all that remains of Yorick, Hamlet, wonderingly, is overwhelmed by an absent past flooding into his present, and an absent self. For the ghost of childhood is drawn out of the grave with the skull: 'I knew him, Horatio – a fellow of infinite jest, of most excellent fancy. He hath borne me on his back a thousand times … Here hung those lips that I have kissed I know not how oft' (5.1.180–5). That 'I' who 'knew him', 'kissed' him, 'rode on his back' twenty-three years ago was a boy no more

than seven years old; a boy, son of a warrior king, who, in this memory, is
at play with a surrogate father of gibes and gambols and love (the court
jester being, of course, a travesty king). By comparison, how remote the
real father feels, dead only two months – 'nay, not so much, not two'
(1.2.138) – but significantly distanced, buried in that armour from thirty
years back that remembers what he wants remembered, his victory over
Fortinbras (but not what else happened that day, his son's birth); that
makes him in death a martial icon, paternity unadmitted; and makes him
too, when he returns, a revenant from a hopelessly redundant antique
past. What does the child in Hamlet make of such remembering?

Remembering his own childhood, Hamlet remembers other childhoods. He knows the story of King Herod. He seems to have seen the story
acted (by a player who 'out-Herod[ed] Herod', (3.2.14)). So he's witnessed
the slaughter of the innocents, watched all those infants murdered before
his eyes. Then, too, he knows 'Aeneas' tale to Dido' (2.2.448), the story of
the fall of Troy. He knows what happened to the boy Astyanax, Hector's
child, Troy's heir, thrown from Ilium's last standing tower. And little
Polydore, Priam's youngest son: his throat cut, his body dumped. And
Ascanius: Aeneas's child – saved! Rescued from Troy's flames, Ascanius
appears safe (it seems) in Dido's Carthage on Dido's lap, until he's
snatched by Venus, who substitutes her own boy-child, Cupid, in the
Trojan's place, to wreak havoc on Dido's heart. And with all these
remembered children, who show how costly childhood is for children,
Hamlet is somehow 'remembering' the boy, Will Shakespeare: the lad in
the Stratford grammar school learning his Virgil, the boy in the Guild Hall,
perhaps (like Robert Willis in Gloucester[2]) standing between his father's
legs watching the players perform the medieval mysteries, perhaps for the
last time before Protestant church reformation silenced them.

The children suggested by these images are the subject of this book.
I'm looking at boys: as children remembered, storied, imagined, fantasised; as children in relation to adults but sturdily themselves, anarchically
upsetting settled narratives; as peripheral children, watching, witnessing;
as children at the centre of the tale, doing, acting; as children belonging to
a classical, early-modern, or post-modern present, re-performing that
present to another present; as children at play, theatrically at work, doing
performance work for Shakespeare's playtext, on Shakespeare's stage,
and, in subsequent performances, on ours: all of them telling stories that
reframe the stories we tell about ourselves.

The children Shakespeare scripted are the best refutation I know of the
argument advanced forty years ago by the historian of *mentalités*, Philippe
Ariès, and taken up by Lawrence Stone, that the idea of 'childhood' was

unknown in early modern European culture and that parents were affec-
tionless because 'the very high infant and child mortality rates' made it
'folly to invest too much emotional capital in such ephemeral beings'. Children, Stone theorised of an emotionally miserly, pre-sensitised yet self-
interestedly curious culture, were 'little animals', 'smelly and unformed' at
that, merely 'toys to divert the mind';[3] 'expendables', wrote Ariès; a child
'such an unimportant thing, so inadequately involved in life'[4] – arguments
rehearsed much more recently by Patricia Fumerton who cites 'the
"mereness" of the child' in early modern culture, placing children among
what the Elizabethans and Jacobeans found to be 'trivial', 'ornamental'.[5]
But as Shakespeare shows, Stone, Ariès, and Fumerton were, quite simply,
wrong.[6]

And so was Marjorie Garber. 'There are very few children in Shakespeare's plays,' she wrote in *Coming of Age in Shakespeare*. She saw these 'few
children' as 'terrible infants', thought 'we' are 'relieved' when they 'leave
the stage' and suggested, rather bizarrely, that it may 'be no accident that
almost all go to their deaths'.[7] But Garber's 'few' counted only little
Martius in *Coriolanus*, Mamillius in *The Winter's Tale*, Macduff's 'egg' in
Macbeth, and the princes in the Tower in *Richard III*. That is, she left out of
the reckoning most of Shakespeare's parts for children, another fifty or so:
Lucius and Aaron's baby in *Titus Andronicus*; the 'history boys' of *Henry VI*:
Talbot's John, York's Rutland, Lancaster's Edward, Somerset's Rich-
mond, baby Edward at the end; Clarence's son and daughter in *Richard
III*; Don Armado's Mote in *Love's Labour's Lost*; Mistress Page's William
and Parson Hugh's school of scholar 'fairies' in *The Merry Wives of Windsor*;
Arthur in *King John*; *Henry VIII*'s baby Elizabeth; *The Taming of the Shrew*'s
transvestite Bartholomew, 'wife' to Christopher Sly; Titania's changeling
child (if he's brought on stage in *A Midsummer Night's Dream*) and beardless
Flute, just right for Thisby; Francis the drawer in *1 Henry IV* and Falstaff's
page in *2 Henry IV* – the same, who, older in *Henry V*, goes to the French
wars with Nym and the rest; Benedick's boy in *Much Ado*, Brutus's in
Caesar, Troilus's in *Troilus and Cressida* and Mariana's in *Measure for
Measure*; Capulet's child (too young to be a bride in *Romeo and Juliet*); *Henry
V*'s baggage boys; *Hamlet*'s Player Queen; the boy choristers in *As You Like
It*'s Forest of Arden; Banquo's Fleance, *Macbeth*'s 'cream-faced loon' (a
'lily-livered boy'), and the weird infant prodigies that surface in the
witches' cauldron; *Pericles*'s Marina and *The Winter's Tale*'s Perdita, first
babies, then girls; anonymous pages – like the extra in *Richard III*. Then
there are the notional or symbolic babies: the one Julietta 'groans' with;
the one Cleopatra nurses; the one Joan of Arc, at the stake, pleads; the
one Helena, big bellied, promises in answer to Bertram's riddle; the one

Doll Tearsheet threatens to miscarry. And finally, the off-stage children: Antigonus's three daughters, Cleopatra's 'unlawful' brood; the Nurse's Susan (along with all the other 'hopeful issue' of the house of Capulet, dead in childhood). Keith Thomas tells us that in early modern culture children 'were ubiquitous'.[8] They were in Shakespeare, too. Far from being trivial in his writing, they are central, constitutive of adult projects. Simultaneously the embodiment of the future the adult plans but knows he will not live to see and the nostalgic recollection of the adult's innocent past, children in Shakespeare are stubbornly material, getting in the adult's way. But they are also ghosts, hauntings.

What counts as a 'child' in Shakespeare – and in this book? The Elizabethans inherited from the Greeks various models for thinking of man's life as a sequence of 'ages'.[9] Ptolemy, conceiving an astrological typology, plotted seven ages to correspond to the seven planets, the scheme Jacques elaborates in *As You Like It*'s 'All the world's a stage' speech where childhood starts with 'the infant, / Mewling and puking in the nurse's arms', proceeds to 'the whining schoolboy ... creeping like snail / Unwillingly to school', and finishes up with the youth, the adolescent 'lover' writing 'a woeful ballad / ... to his mistress' eyebrow' (2.7.139, 143–9). Framing a different, biological, model, Aristotle theorised three phases of life – growth, maturity, decay – which Henry Cuffe, in *The Differences of the Ages of Man's Life* (1607), reckoned by numbers, seeing childhood lasting until age twenty-five: infancy took the child to three or four; boyhood to nine or ten; 'our budding and blossoming age' to an age Cuffe left unspecified, and finally, 'youth' brought the child to adulthood.[10] Beyond bare numbers, ritual, too, marked the stages of childhood. By Elizabethan custom, lads were 'breeched' – taken out of 'petticoats' and put into doublet and hose – aged about seven. As infants in robes they'd been sexually undifferentiated from girls; breeches were clothes that marked their physiology, signified them as men-in-the-making. By Elizabethan statute, apprentices were bound until they were twenty-four, and were not permitted to marry until then, the end of apprenticeship marking the move into adulthood. For lads like Shakespeare's Flute in *A Midsummer Night's Dream*, it was 'a beard coming' (1.2.44) that meant they'd attained manhood. 'Childhood', then, was an elastic concept for Shakespeare's contemporaries. If they frequently failed to distinguish the 'boy' from the 'youth', that was not, as C. John Sommerville observes, because they 'recognized no difference', but because 'To them, childhood was a gradual ... process'.[11] But however Shakespeare's contemporaries calculated childhood, demographically, there were a lot of children underfoot: by the end of the seventeenth century, the under-fifteens in

England constituted more than 30 per cent of the population.[12] If we make the likely guess that in the professional London acting companies all the sharers (normally eight or so players) had apprentices attached to them (while the hired men didn't), and that the sharers made sure their playwrights wrote parts for the boys – it being their responsibility as masters to ensure their apprentices stage time in front of spectators – we'll see not only that many more parts were played by children on Shakespeare's stage than our theatre allows for but also that the demographics of the early modern stage-world reproduced more or less exactly the demographics of the world-at-large.

This book began its life in today's theatre, with small things that snagged my spectatorly memory: a filthy child rising from the dead on a blasted heath; a lad throwing snowballs; a baby nuzzled by a bear; a birthday boy spinning a top; a little man, dressed like his dad, dancing with the queen, his mother, like children do, his feet on top of hers; swaggering youths flourishing weapons that, like the hand-me-down clothes they were wearing, were too big for their backs; a toddler in a photograph, knickers drooping, twirling on a beach; a schoolboy dropping his books; a child kissing a corpse – and that lad, abandoned in Elsinore, left to his tears. It gathered more 'looking' in the cinema: a kid staring out of a paper-bag mask; a pack of feral street-children roaming a blighted inner-city housing estate, kids lost in, lost to modern consumerist culture who haunt the adults who've lost them; big-eyed babies; a small boy witnessing atrocity. Wanting to think about these 'snags', these children in contemporary re-performances of roles written by Shakespeare, and to offer close analyses of them as 'subsequent performances', this book attempts also to recover some sense of Shakespeare's 'original' children, their cultural contexts, their narrative work, their early modern theatrical lives. Reading Shakespeare's children in their time and ours, I'm asking questions about the cultural location and valuation of children (then, now), what stories we tell in and of them; whether children can tell their own stories; wondering what we 'mean' by children in Shakespeare – and what children in Shakespeare 'mean' by us.

Interested everywhere in performance, my chapters are interested, also, in books; indeed, my chapters are book-ended with books: early modern books, books that locate the 'pastness' of the early modern child's past (grammar school texts and classroom anthologies; herbals; a 'how-to' manual for monarchs; the Elizabethan Book of Common Prayer; an encyclopaedia of animals; the chronicle history of the kingdom; conduct books). And books that think about the child in the present: a Shakespeare script; life-writing from a child survivor; a play composed of stories

told to a child about a child; a post-modern, dystopian first-person narrative of growing up – and making it (just). Ovid appears here; and
Erasmus, Elyot, Brinsley, Mulcaster. But so do Anthony Burgess, Martin
McDonagh, and Uzodinma Iweala. Their books offer parallel texts for
reading and watching Shakespeare's children at play as well as sources
informing my own spectatorship. There is always, I want to say as I finish
writing, so much more to be said.

  To begin with, my opening chapter makes two sweeps across London in
January 1559 and in October 1593, observing Elizabethan children at play
as a kind of cultural 'trailer' before turning to Shakespeare's earliest plays,
the *Henry VI* trilogy, to see them offering a near-complete anthology of parts
for boys that the playwright would continue to rewrite for the rest of his
career, and the sites – domestic, political, emotional, theological – they
would occupy as subjects and objects. I also stake out my double project:
this is a book about our own culture's performances on stage and screen,
performances that put our conflicted responses to the emotive issue of the
child squarely in view. It's about how we (actors, directors, designers, film-
makers, spectators, cultural makers and consumers) position the child to
perform cultural work, to play out preoccupations, anxieties, fears, aspirations, dreams and desires. Laying down a marker for the rest of the book, I
end this chapter looking briefly at two recent Shakespeare productions that
open up precisely these current performance issues.

  Chapter 2 looks at education and instruction, what the child must learn
(the basics of literacy, the alphabet) and what duties he must perform
(witnessing, remembering, retelling). Focusing on the schoolboy Lucius in
Titus Andronicus, this chapter thinks about classical education and the Elizabethan grammar school, about the books the child brings on stage,
about Ovid and the instruction offered in the *Metamorphoses* (*Titus*'s
parallel text), about exercises in rhetoric that teach boys to 'become'
women, about stories that are told that fashion Rome to itself and its Elizabethan heirs. It looks, too, at education's failures: the delinquent 'boys'
Chiron and Demetrius. For little Lucius in Rome, the core curriculum
he's assigned is to 'look like a child', that is, both 'to look with a child's
eyes' and 'to be physically a child'. That curriculum becomes not just the
content but the mode of production in Julie Taymor's *Titus*, a film that
takes 'looking like a child' as its major premise and project as it rethinks
Shakespeare's atrocity play as a story of child witness. *Titus* opens in close-
up on a child's eyes, sees the story almost entirely from the child's point of
view, and ends with that child walking away – while another child fixes his
unblinking look on the camera. Tracking the child's part, offering a close
reading of this film, I suggest that in Taymor's *Titus* 'looking like a child'

ultimately offers a saving perspective, opening a space for cultural impro-visation, for 'play', that just might 'save' Shakespeare's *Titus Andronicus* for the recuperations it imagines possible in its final theatrical moments.

In *Titus*, Lucius survives; in *The Winter's Tale*, Mamillius doesn't. That irony is terrible not least because whereas Lucius's assignment as a child is simply to 'learn' of the living and to 'talk' of the dead, Mamillius's is to stand placeholder for enduring patriarchal fantasies that are bound up in adult nostalgia for escape into perpetual childhood, a state of being 'the boy eternal'. Mamillius's assignment is to provide the antidote to adult-hood, medicine for hurt minds; to 'cure thoughts' that 'would thick' the adult's 'blood'. Then he dies – sickened by the grown-ups. Chapter 3 examines the language of desire and longing that frames this 'medicinal' child and endows him with meaning in Sicilia – and it traces this language through Gerard's *Herbal*, Elizabeth's *Boke of common praire*, and Topsell's *Historie of Foure-footed Beastes*. But it also looks intently at 'childness' performed, at Mamillius at play, and finds that recent directors of *The Winter's Tale* are asking tough questions about the crisis of paternity this play stages, about masculinity and power, fathers and violence, the adult habit of constructing tales that work to cover up catastrophic wrongs or to mythologise the mistakes they make as something else – and tough ques-tions, too, about the play's 'happy ending'.

My final chapter looks at *Macbeth*, a play that conducts a war on chil-dren, Macbeth needing to destroy the 'seeds of time' in a futile attempt to control the future he both wants and wants different. In Fleance, Banquo's boy, Shakespeare rewrites John Talbot from *1 Henry VI*, a warrior child, apprenticed to his father to learn the martial art of slaughter, who serves to test male codes of valour, principally the 'acceptable' practice of wasting the future by killings its children. But Fleance is more than a boy-soldier; he's the one fingered by the Witches – 'Banquo's issue' – as Scotland's future king. So how does a child get training for that job? To answer, I offer King James's treatise, *Basilikon Doron*, as a parallel text to Shakespeare's Scottish play. But I see, in perfor-mance, directors much less interested in testing 'the king-becoming graces' than in exploring, via *Macbeth*, contemporary formulations of evil and of fear – and using children to conduct that exploration. In Max Stafford-Clarke's *Macbeth*, set in Idi Amin's Uganda, child conscripts performed atrocities; in Penny Woolcock's television film *Macbeth on the Estate*, the witches were kids.

The children of this book are mostly invisible to criticism. Perhaps with good reason. Children, as Keith Thomas reminds us, are 'like women': they're 'what anthropologists like to call a "muted group"', their 'own values, attitudes, and feelings' 'largely excluded from the official record'.[13] Like his women's roles, the parts Shakespeare wrote for boys (and in the all-male Elizabethan playhouse, of course, all his children's parts were played by boys[14]) are comparatively 'muted': that is to say, they don't have many lines; they aren't prominent in the written record we call the 'playtext'. But then, that playtext is merely the residue, the shards of a much bigger thing, the performance.[15] And it's in performance that Shakespeare's children achieve highest visibility, tell a story beyond the text – like the sobbing boy in Elsinore – in a voice that speaks performatively, through the body. In scenes where Shakespeare's adults do the talking, his children do the playing.

Preparing children to achieve public presence and voice was something Shakespeare's contemporaries took very seriously. Equally, they expressed hopeful ambitions for the future of their children. Instructing his son on the raising of his son, William Cecil, Lord Burghley, advised him to 'Bring thy children vp in obedience and Learning, yet without austeritie, praise them openly, reprehende them secretly: giue them good countenance, and conuenient maintenance.'[16] The ambition Shakespeare's Coriolanus expressed for his boy Martius was a life informed with nobleness, a life 'To shame unvulnerable'; a life of steadfast constancy offering a fixed point for others to steer by, 'Like a great sea-mark standing every flaw/And saving those that eye thee' (5.3.72–5). Hoping to raise heroes, however, men like Burghley knew they had to be realistic of their chances. After all, childhood's origins were hardly auspicious, hardly predictive of gracious success. 'The first male child' born on earth, they remembered, was 'Cain' (*King John*, 3.4.79).

The ambitions which early modern culture expressed for its children are ones post-modernity still entertains, grapples with, contests, refashions, turns to different ends. These are ideas that Shakespeare keeps before our eyes, helps us think through. As for Shakespeare himself: in my opening chapter I argue that he was a playwright who observed children very closely. Watching Shakespeare watching, and watching myself watching Shakespeare: this constitutes my double project in this book.

Notes

1 In Benthall's production, Scofield alternated Hamlet with Robert Helpmann; Scofield is seen in the photograph.
2 For a transcription of Willis's childhood memory of watching a play in Booth Hall, ca. 1570, see Audrey Douglas and Peter Greenfield (eds), *REED: Cumberland, Westmorland, Gloucestershire*, London and Toronto, 362–4.
3 See *Family, Sex and Marriage in England 1500–1800*, London, 1977, 105, 116, 177.
4 See *Centuries of Childhood*, Robert Baldick (tr.), London, 1962, 39.
5 See *Cultural Aesthetics*, Chicago, 1991, 218.
6 Historians who have offered revisions of Ariès and Stone include Linda Pollock, *Forgotten Children*, Cambridge, 1984; Ralph Houlbrooke, *The English Family 1450–1700*, Harlow, 1984; Keith Thomas, 'Children in early modern England', in Gillian Avery and Julia Briggs (eds), *Children and Their Books*, Oxford, 1989, 45–77; and Keith Wrightson, *English Society 1580–1680*, London, 1998. Childhood appears to be gaining new and important critical visibility in Shakespeare studies. See Kate Chedgzoy, Susanne Greenhalgh, and Robert Shaughnessy (eds), *Shakespeare and Childhood*, Cambridge University Press, 2007; and see the work Chedgzoy flags up in recent doctoral dissertations which will no doubt issue in publications: Edel Lamb, *The Children's Playing Companies of Early Modern London: Childhood, Theatre and Identity, 1599–1613*, Queen's University of Belfast, 2005; Stephen Kavanagh, *Shakespeare and the Politics of Childhood*, Trinity College Dublin, 2006; and Marie Rutkoski, *The Mouths of Babes: Children and Knowledge in English Renaissance Drama*, Harvard, 2006.
7 *Coming of Age in Shakespeare*, London, 1981, 30.
8 'Children in early modern England', 48.
9 I'm depending here on Bruce Smith's excellent *Shakespeare and Masculinity*, Oxford, 2000, 71–5.
10 Quoted in Smith, 74.
11 See *The Discovery of Childhood in Puritan England*, Athens, Georgia, 1992, 15.
12 I owe this statistic to Keith Thomas, 51.
13 'Children in early modern England', 47–8.
14 Focusing here on parts for boys, played by boys, I am ignoring entirely parts like Rosalind and Viola, written for the cross-dressed male actor who is frequently called a 'boy' and is, in early modern terms – *vide* Cuffe, for whom boyhood lasts to age twenty-five. In our terms, however, s/he is more accurately thought of as a young man.
15 I argue this at greater length in *Enter the Body*, London, 2001, xiv–xv.
16 'The counsell of a Father to his Sonne', 1611, STC2 4900.5.

Acknowledgements

In Holinshed we read of the army of experts and advisers – 'midwiues, rockers, nurses' – mobilised to attend an early modern birth, to bring the child into being. I have that narrative much in mind as I record my gratitude to the many friends and colleagues who helped bring this book into being.

My colleagues at Warwick constantly stimulate my thinking and make my life in the university a pleasure – and meaningful. Tony Howard, Peter Mack, Thomas Docherty, Jonathan Bate, Cathia Jenainati, Teresa Grant, Paul Prescott, Paul Allen and Susan Brock read chapters, asked questions, found information, set me right when I was drifting, and, in their own teaching and research, give me models of practice, ways of re-imagining how we write about theatre, history, performance, and the cultural moment. I want to thank Tony in particular – who always knows what I'm talking about even when (or especially when) I don't.

I'm grateful to a wider circle of collaborators – for that's how I see them – who share their work with me and who constantly encourage mine (sometimes down the telephone in the small hours of the morning): Barbara Hodgdon, Skip Shand, Marion O'Connor, Tony Dawson, Jim Bulman, Robert Shaughnessy, Michael Dobson, Reg Foakes, Paul Edmondson, Stanley Wells, Kate Chedgzoy, Boika Sokolova, Jorie Woods, Péter Dávidházi, Richard Rowland, Bill Worthen, Charles Edelman, Peter Smith, and Peter Holland. Rowland, Dávidházi, and Bulman read multiple drafts of my chapters and sharpened both the writing and the scholarship with their perceptive interrogations; Smith handed over loads of production files; Woods gave me a line of inquiry I needed just when I needed it; Holland read the manuscript cover to cover; Shand commented on everything I threw at him and put formative things my way: he arranged for CBC (Canada) to provide me with a documentary, *Uganda's Haunted Children*, he sent me *Beasts of No Nation* to ponder, and he gave me permission to finish: 'This book,' he wrote, 'is ready for the grown-ups.'

Invitations in recent years to give papers at the International Shakespeare Conference (Shakespeare Institute, University of Birmingham), the Shakespeare Birthplace Trust, the International Shakespeare in Performance Colloquium, and the Roehampton Shakespeare's Children/Children's Shakespeares conference have offered me opportunities to present preliminary versions of this work. I thank my hosts on those occasions: Peter Holland, Robert Shaughnessy, Susanne Greenhalgh, and Paul Edmondson. Parts of Chapters 2 and 4 first appeared in an earlier form in *Shakespeare Survey* 56 (2003) and 57 (2004) as 'Looking Like a Child – or – *Titus*: The Comedy', 1–26, and 'Remind Me: How Many Children had Lady Macbeth?', 38–53.

But while gadding to conferences is enormous fun and intellectually productive, it's the day-to-day business of engaging with students that I find does most to provide a nursery for my work. At Warwick, I'm blessed with challenging, articulate, argumentative, thoughtful students, both undergraduates and post-graduates, who, passionately interested in Shakespeare and performance, influence everything I do. Here, I want to record my debt to those whose work has directly entered this book via conversations and their own writing: Irene Musumeci, Bronia Evers, Naomi Everall, Jonny Heron, Harriet Mann, Ben Fowler, and Nicoleta Cinpoes.

As always, the librarians of the Shakespeare Birthplace Trust (Sylvia Morris, Head of Library, Helen Hargest, Madeleine Cox, and Rebecca Roberts) provided tireless support: their particular genius is to give you not just what you asked for, but what you should have asked for. I appreciate their expertise, their generosity, and above all, their patience. Also I want to credit, at the Trust, the hugely informative and entertaining conversations I've had with Roger Howells, and the photographic work of Malcolm Davies. Additional photography was supplied by Chris Wright and Charlotte Wright; and image manipulation by Andrew Maddison: for their wizardry, my thanks.

I'm fortunate, in this book, to have had direct input from a number of directors and actors who produced the work I'm writing about: Terry Hands, Declan Donnellan, Nick Ormerod, Simon Russell Beale, Sinead Cusack, Harriet Walter, Richard Pasco, Judi Dench, James Hayes, Greg Doran, Tony Sher, and Emma Rice. I thank you – and hope that, in some small way, my writing honours the performances you gave.

Near the beginning of my research, Perry Mills, Head of Sixth Form and a quite remarkable English teacher, invited me in to King Edward's

School for Boys, Stratford upon Avon, and allowed me to 'play' with his students. The result was the Thisby Project: an investigation of the intersection between text and performance, the grammar school student and the early modern curriculum, the boy player and the (female) part he played. Our experiments turn up in Chapter 2. The lads were stars – in trousers and skirts: James Butt, James Cottriall, Matthew Cowen, Ben Darlington, Alex Feys, Jack Fielding, Oliver Hayes, and Alex Simon.

Along the way, this project was supported by awards from the Arts and Humanities Research Council and by generous study-leave provision and a publication grant from the University of Warwick. Finally, I'm grateful beyond words to Cornelia Starks, Angela Ritter, Sir Andrew and Lady Christabel Watson, and Paula Byrne; to Cheryl Fenwick; and to Rosie and Bill Gough (for taming the little orchard: my best thinking place). My greatest debt is to my daughters: Rowan did the smart thing and set out for Africa; Bryony, generously, came home between degrees and spent three months as in-house editor chasing my references. (I thank you for your sharp eyes, your indefatigable attention to detail, and your laughter. But now, 'chick ... / Be free'.) My daughters are my life's experts on child's play, that business Erasmus called 'serio ludere'. And on the pleasures of 'Do it again! Do it again!' This book is theirs.

Chapter 1

'Behold the Child' or Parts for Children

Good luck, an't be thy will! What have we here? Mercy on's, a barne! A very pretty barne. A boy or a child, I wonder?
The Winter's Tale (3.3.67–9)

Children, as Peter Laslett has observed, were everywhere.
Keith Wrightson, *English Society 1580–1680*, 1982

Some people observed children very closely.
Keith Thomas, 'Children in Early Modern England', 1989

A city progress

Beginning with a desire to glimpse those early modern English children whom Laslett knows 'were everywhere', I start not with material traces, family portraits of the elite or funerary monuments, or woodcuts depicting the Elizabethan classroom or children's games, but with what Clifford Geertz would call an 'acted document', a performance staged on the streets of London, indeed, the 'original' Elizabethan public performance, a performance recorded by Richard Mulcaster and incorporated into Raphael Holinshed's monumental *Chronicles*.[1]

On Saturday, 14 January 1559, Elizabeth I, proclaimed Queen of England two months earlier at the death of her sister Mary, left the Tower where she'd spent the night to begin her progress through the City of London to Westminster, a civic display, showing the monarch to the people in advance of her coronation the following day.[2] She was 'richly furnished' and 'most honorably accompanied' and, entering the City, 'she was of the people receiued marueylous entierly' with 'prayers, wishes, welcomminges, cryes, tender words, and all other signes' that 'argue a wonderful earnest loue of most obedient subiectes towarde theyr soueraigne'. For her part, she showed 'her most gracious loue', not just 'toward the people in generall', but also 'priuately', to 'the baser person-ages', stopping to hear their words and to accept their humble gifts when they 'offred her grace … flowres'. At the end of the day, the branch of rosemary an old woman had handed her still remained (it was said) in her chariot. It was as if, wrote Richard Mulcaster, the City had been trans-formed into a vast theatre, and the citizens into spectators on this royal performance. London that day was 'a stage, wherin was shewed the wonderfull spectacle, of a noble hearted princesse toward her most louing people, & the peoples exceding comfort in beholding so worthy a soueraigne.'

But if Elizabeth played a 'wonderfull spectacle' to the City, the City played its own spectacles back to the queen. Five times along the route her progress was halted by performance. Near Fenchurch 'was erected a scaf-fold richly furnished, whereon stode a noyse of instrumentes, and a chylde in costly apparell' who was 'appoynted to welcome the queenes maiestie in the hole cities behalfe'. Elizabeth ordered her chariot 'stayde' and the noise 'appeased' so that the child's oration 'in Englishe meter' could be heard. Further on, at Gracechurch Street, a massive stage had been raised: battlements containing three arches, above them, smaller stages in degrees, and installed in these spaces, a living 'show' of the queen's right to the throne she claimed from her grandfather. At the lowest level, Henry Tudor (heir to the house of Lancaster) sat alongside Elizabeth York, a red rose springing from his arch, a white rose from hers, twining upwards into a single branch enclosing, on the platform above, Henry VIII and Anne Boleyn, and hence upwards to 'one representyng' their daughter Elizabeth, 'now our most dradde soueraigne Ladie, crowned and apparrelled' as herself. All of these 'personages' were played by children – and it was a child who 'declared' to the queen the 'hole meaning' of the pageant, Elizabeth not only ordering silence from the murmuring crowd so that she could hear the child's oration but 'caus[ing] her chariot to be remoued back' so that 'she could see' the children in the recesses set 'farthest in'. At the conduit at Cornhill, she encountered herself again: 'a chylde representing her maiesties person', 'placed in a seate of gouernement' supported by 'certayne vertues' – Pure Religion, Love of Subjects, Wisdom, Justice – who suppressed 'their contrarie vyces vnder their feete'. Again, a 'chylde' was placed to 'interprete and applye' the *tableau vivant*, and the queen again ordered her chariot 'drawen nyghe' so that she 'myght heare the chylds oration'. Moving on to Soper Lane she saw 'a pageant' presenting, this time, 'eight children' 'appointed & apparrelled' to represent the 'eight beatitudes'. At the Little Conduit in

Cheapside, a child appeared 'all cladde in whyte silke'; 'hir name' – '*Veritas*', 'Trueth' – was 'written on her brest', and '*Temporis filia*, the daughter of Tyme' was set in a cartouche above her head. This child named 'Trueth' handed the queen a 'booke … vpon the which was written *verbum veritatis*, the word of truth'. It was the Bible, in English.[3]

All of these pageants – including the last, a 'show' of Deborah governing Israel – were 'interpreted' by children. At every venue, children delivered orations in English and Latin. So, too, at 'Paules scole' and 'S. Dunstones church' where the 'children of thospitall' were 'appointed to stand with their gouernours'. Seeing the hospitallers put the queen in mind of what, she signalled, she must, 'in the middest of my royaltie', 'nedes remembre': the poor. Finally then, at Temple Bar, she encountered 'a noyse of singing children' and 'one child richely attyred as a Poet' who gave 'the queens maiestie her fare well in the name of the hole citie', Elizabeth answering, 'Amen' as she exited.

Passing through London, everywhere she looked, Elizabeth saw children, her populous city made into a visual performance text crowded with her 'minor subjects'. Momentarily, indeed, she was recalled to her own childhood – when she overheard someone in the crowd call out, 'Remember old king Henry theyght'. As Mulcaster recorded, at 'the very remembraunce of her fathers name' she acted the part of a 'naturall' child – and 'smiled'.

How very different had been her sister's coronation entry, five years earlier. Then, the pageants were made not by Mary's loving subjects, certainly not by children, but by foreigners, the City overrun by strangers, 'the Genowaies', 'the Easterlings', 'the Florentins' – and a Dutchman 'that stood on the weathercocke of Paules steeple'.[4] By contrast, it was noted, Elizabeth's London 'without anie forreyne persone, of it selfe beawtifyed it selfe'. But why, overwhelming this civic performance text, the children?

No doubt political tact played a part. A child playing the queen to the queen's face, 'boy' to her 'greatness', could hardly be taken for anything more than 'cipher' to her 'great accompt', no contest. But more explicitly, perhaps the City's meaning was 'interpreted' three days later, at the opening of Parliament. The 'common house' entered a motion for 'accesse vnto hir graces presence' to 'declare vnto hir matter of great importance' to 'hir … realme'. The 'matter'? 'To mooue hir grace to marriage' so that, said the speaker, 'we might injoie … the roiall issue of hir bodie to reigne ouer vs.' No rhetorical beating about the bush, then. The City, the Commons wanted children, royal issue, to secure the succession of a reign not yet three months old. Those children in the coronation pageants: if they weren't aphrodisiac (exactly) then perhaps they were aides memoire.[5]

From their point of view, the Commons and City were right to look anxiously for children. Simply, England had suffered turbulent times because the Tudors, as breeders, had been disastrous. Elizabeth's little brother, Edward VI, a child 'untimely ripp'd' from his dying mother's womb, had inherited as a nine-year-old in 1547, reigned for only six years, died issueless (with appalling consequences for England's Protestant Reformation), and left behind a succession crisis, the nine-day 'reign' of Lady Jane Grey that ended with multiple executions.[6] Elizabeth's older sister, Mary, was thirty-seven and unmarried when she was proclaimed queen – and immediately set about restoring Catholicism to England, a project that would depend ultimately on dynastic continuity, on children. And it looked as if her plans would thrive. Within weeks of her marriage to Philip of Spain in July 1553 it was announced that the queen was 'quicke with child'. Public prayers were ordered to acknowledge the 'good hope of certeine succession in the crowne ... giuen vnto vs'; there was 'busie preparation and much adoo', 'especiallie among such as seemed in England to carrie Spanish hearts in English bodies'. 'Midwiues, rockers, nurses, with the cradle and all' were organised for the 'yoong maister' whose birth was confidently announced across England and Europe with bells and bonfires the following June, one clergyman in London even describing in detail the person of the newborn – but for all that, the child refused to come.[7] Phantom pregnancy followed phantom pregnancy: 'neuer worse successe had anie woman, than had she in hir childbirth'.[8] Mary died of complications arising from dysmenorrhoea in 1558. Again, childlessness instanced radical regime change: Catholic restoration as crown policy died with Mary.[9]

Elizabeth herself was not exempt from this history. It was partly her father's inability to produce a (legitimate) male heir that prompted the divorce crisis of 1532. Elizabeth's birth the following year deprived sixteen-year-old Mary not just of succession but lavish paternal favour. (As a child, Mary's household had been allocated 18 per cent of the total outlay of the whole royal household.) These were reversals Elizabeth perhaps pondered later, growing up, when paternal favour was, in her turn, withdrawn: when she was declared illegitimate, the child of adultery (indeed, according to some, the child of incest); her mother executed for slandering not just the succession but her child by 'offend[ing] in incontinency'.[10] Progressing royally through London in January 1559, Elizabeth may have reflected ironically on the whirligig of Time coming full circle. She had been here before: Anne Boleyn had been nearly six months pregnant with Elizabeth when she'd followed the same route toward her coronation in May 1533.

Setting children so conspicuously before the new queen's eyes, the City was alluding to, recasting this history, using children to elicit the hopes and fears of the nation, to figure real political arrangements allegorically and to voice messages her adult subjects wanted heard in public, the children carrying a burden of representation that evoked adult fantasy, adult memory – and served to focus cultural anxieties. The City (as explanatory 'sentences' attached to each of the pageants informed spectators) wanted 'quietnes', 'unitie', 'all dissention displaced'; it wanted 'the seate of gouernaunce' upheld 'by vertue' and the queen to 'continue in her goodnesse as she had entered', both distributing and receiving blessings; it wanted her to remember 'the state of the common weale', to hold fast to 'Truth', and to reign as the new Deborah. It saw Elizabeth as the 'heire to agreement', hearing in her name a memory of the grandmother who, by marriage, 'ioyned those houses' that 'had ben th'occasyon' of 'ciuil warre within thys realm', civil wars that were only seventy years in the nation's past. The City was framing an entire ideological and aspirational programme of relationship between the monarchy and the people, representing it in 'speaking pictures', in dumb shows, and 'opening' it out to understanding in written texts on illustrative tablets and in spoken texts, orations. Presenting the City's policy, the pageant children were its conduits, messengers exempt from the message, speaking 'wiser' than they could possibly have been 'ware', who nevertheless 'stood in' for that policy, embodied it.

But what of the children themselves? Who were they? Who trained them? The young Latin orators: were they grammar school boys from Paul's or Christ's Hospital? What about the choristers? Or the children who played the queen? Were they girls? Or cross-dressed boys? On holiday? On duty? Fearless? Or rigid with terror? Were they miniature versions of those 'great clerks' Shakespeare's Theseus describes who, 'purposèd' to greet greatness 'with premeditated welcomes', 'in their fears' 'dumbly ... broke off', too frightened to speak (*A Midsummer Night's Dream*, 5.1. 93–4, 97–8)? I can answer none of these questions, for the children's history is, like Cesario's (fictional) sister's in *Twelfth Night*, 'a blank' (2.4.110).[11] Central to the day's activity and to its record, the children were somehow both at the centre of and marginal to Mulcaster's account of Elizabeth's 'passage', which was not written to record childish selves or even political agendas but the queen's majesty, the star of the day. Nevertheless, Mulcaster portrays Elizabeth looking intently and listening hard: 'notyng and obseruing' with a 'perpetuall attentiuenes in her face' as, speech after speech, 'the childes wordes touched' 'her person'. For its part, the City, promoting the kingdom's 'minor subjects' to speak for it, was privileging the future. Inscribed within the knowingly adult pageant-allegories was a deep sense of childhood's fragility in the face of adult waywardness and wasteful destructiveness. But also on show was childhood's awesome power: where would England have been on that Saturday in January had Mary's 'yoong maister' arrived when expected – or Mary's little sister died years earlier in the Tower? Again, I can offer no answers. Reviewing Elizabeth's coronation entry, I can only echo Peter Laslett – 'children were everywhere' – and apply Keith Thomas's comment to the day's chief spectator: 'Some people' in Elizabethan England 'observed children very closely.' And they observed them on stages, in performance.

A progress in the suburbs

To balance Mulcaster's elite 'Passage', I offer an extract from another 'acted document' – this one an altogether grubbier account of an Elizabethan watching children.

In the warm October of 1593 Will Shakespeare finally broke through his depressive bout of writer's block. He'd spent September in a garret around the back of Henslowe's Rose on the Bankside practising his signature. He had nothing else to do. The words weren't coming. The playhouse was closed, the players on tour. Now, though, Ned Alleyn and the Admiral's Men were back in town. Will, auditioning new actors, had glimpsed a young man right for the part that was suddenly on fire in his writerly brain – Romeo – and he was dashing off speech after speech for characters called 'Samson' and 'Gregory'. But his Romeo had vanished – and Will had to find him. So, ducking out of rehearsals, he began a swift scour of the Bankside, a kind of downmarket 'progress' on the 'wrong' side of the river through throngs as heaving as the crowds that had followed Elizabeth through the City thirty-five years earlier – but along streets altogether nastier. He didn't find his Romeo. Instead, he stopped to observe – very closely – a child. A child he'd seen on stage.

This 'acted document' isn't in Holinshed – or any other 'true' history.[12] It's in John Madden's 1998 film *Shakespeare in Love*, and I quote it in the spirit of Richard Wheeler's sane observations on the relationship between biography and interpretation, that 'Notions of the author', including 'some implicit assumptions about the author as a field of meaning', 'enter into all interpretation' of Shakespeare, underwrite all our 'statements about the plays'.[13] For the reverse is surely also true: if, as Simon During has found, 'transactions between texts and lives' constitute 'proper knowledge', we should be able to read those transactions in either direction.[14] Lacking 'true'-life writing about the 29-year-old Will Shakespeare in the autumn of 1593, *Shakespeare in Love*'s writers, Tom Stoppard and Marc Norman, recuperate that missing life from the playwriting. So they have Will, looking for Romeo, do what the plays tell them he *would* do: stop to talk to a kid. Who's sulking. Who's just auditioned on the Rose stage for the lead in Will's new play, *Romeo and Ethel, The Pirate's Daughter* – and, for his pains, been kicked out of the playhouse with the playwright's boot in his backside. Who's consoling himself, a feral street urchin in grimy hose sitting in the dirt, with other entertainment: feeding live mice to an alley cat. Who tells the grown-up (who's staring at the child with appalled fascination) that he 'was in a play once', *Titus Andronicus* – and loved it: 'plenty of blood', 'and the daughter mutilated with knives'. And tells him his name: 'John Webster'. (Underwriting this exchange is the notion that childhood, too, and individual children, constitute a 'field of meaning'.) Inventing this episode, filling in missing biography with surrogate fiction (with a nod, to those in the know, at another writerly 'real' life), Stoppard and Norman are, I want to suggest, nevertheless telling spectators something true: Shakespeare the playwright was one of Keith Thomas's early modern 'people' who 'observed children very closely'. And he put those observations on stage.

Before Shakespeare left Stratford for London and the theatre, he had a life crowded with children: a wife and three babies by the time he was twenty, still a minor, in the house on Henley Street that they shared with Will's parents and *more* children: his little sister Joan, sixteen, his brothers Richard, twelve, and Edmund, five. William was the eldest in the family, and if his youth was curtailed, as it must have been, by marriage, his childhood, before that, was just as probably prematurely ended by his father's fall from municipal respectability, a humiliating slide into debt. He'd almost certainly been a grammar school boy at 'the Kynges Newe Scole' (as it was named in its 1553 charter) in Stratford, but didn't go up to university as might have been expected, and may have been withdrawn from school early, aged no more than twelve or thirteen, to begin work in his father's glove-making business.

Katherine Duncan-Jones is surely right to see this childhood remembered later, in London, in the playwriting. For one thing, Duncan-Jones speculates, the boy's occupation in a trade that handled butchered animal skins provided raw material for some of the young playwright's most felt imagery in his earliest work, the three *Henry VI* plays.[15] But I want to go further, to notice how, from the first, childhood was remembered in those plays in more than imagery: it was remembered narratively, thematically, theatrically. This playwright trained his eye on children. And, from the first, he wrote extraordinary parts for them, the *Henry VI* plays offering first drafts of child roles he would rewrite, reshape for the rest of his career, an anthology of parts for children that think through what he would later call 'childness' – and through the body of the child.[16]

First calls for children

Henry VI is all about a child: a tragic meditation on wasted childhood played out across three plays and seventy-nine scenes, a tragedy framed by episodes where history 'means' through children. *Part 1* begins with a baby, kept off stage, significantly 'missing' at this traumatic moment of regime change, but cited over and over: the nine-month-old Lancastrian Henry, child of the warrior-king Henry V whose funeral the opening scene performs, now himself England's king. *Part 3* ends with a baby: the newborn Edward, son of the newly-installed (rebel king?) Edward IV, presented on stage in his swaddling clouts, heir to the house of York and infant hope of the upstart regime.[17] As the trilogy's opening scene shows, the orphan Henry has too much family for his subsequent good: uncles, legitimate and bastard, wrangling, even before the boy's father is in his grave, about his future custody; silent 'cousins' who will offer their services as hired gunslingers in the future civil wars; and perhaps most crushingly, that absent but persistent father whose reputation won't go away but hangs over the child's future like a blazing comet – beacon and curse.[18] But then, too, in the trilogy's final scene baby Edward York, surrounded by doting parents and an attentive court, has too much family: his twisted uncle Dickie, hunchback Duke of Gloucester and black joker in the family pack, is the last to step forward to plant a 'loving kiss' on the infant – whose murder he's already planning (*Part 3*, 5.7.32).[19]

The point about all this kin is that adults in the *Henry VI* plays *make* the child. Present or absent, children are narrated, 'told', fashioned in language by adults. They're objects of adult representation, (royal) pawns in adult power games who carry the burden of adult expectation, not unlike those royal stand-ins gracing Elizabeth's coronation progress who evoked adult fantasy, adult memory and cultural anxiety. Children are vulnerable to strategic refashioning. Thus, Henry is an 'effeminate prince', a 'schoolboy you may overawe' (*Part 1*, 1.1.35–6) because that construction serves Humphrey, Duke of Gloucester's attack on the Bishop of Winchester. And baby Edward, rocked in his daddy's arms, is invented as the mystified object of Yorkist enterprise because a legitimating fiction is what his father's desiring imagining needs him to be. 'For thee' we did it, York claims in a fantastic instant rewrite of 'history':

> Young Ned, for thee thine uncles and myself
> Have in our armours watched the winter's night –
> Went all afoot in summer's scalding heat –
> That thou might'st repossess the crown in peace.
>
> *Part 3*, 5.7.16–19

But if adults make children in these plays, children appear also to make themselves. The dramatic fiction, the immediacy and *presentness* of the child in front of spectators on Shakespeare's stage, gives children space to speak, to act for themselves, to simulate agency. And that fiction gives spectators four hundred years later a *kind of* look at early modern childhood, childhood that is otherwise largely absent from the documentary record.[20] I am put in mind here of the teasing epistemological contract between stage and spectator that the Chorus in *Henry V* tells us underwrites all theatre experience on Shakespeare's stage, that we 'mind [...] true things' 'by what their mock'ries be' (4.0.53): looking at theatrical fakery we may get somewhere close to historical actuality. Watching the performance of childhood as Shakespeare locates it in Rome, Scotland, Bohemia, may give us our best sighting of the early modern child. That said, simply the number of parts Shakespeare wrote for children privileges the child's point of view in the worlds he writes.

In *Henry VI* Shakespeare's extraordinary achievement is to locate child-consciousness at the very centre of the trilogy in the role of the child-king Henry. Compressing fifty years into fifteen acts, the plays show spectators the boy growing up yet refusing to become adult – where 'adult' means acting like Winchester or York, nakedly self-interested, scrambling for power in the bear pit the Plantagenets have made of politics. A baby in the opening speeches, but already, also, a schoolboy, when Henry makes his first, long-withheld entrance into *Part 1* acting as a referee between factious uncles (a role he played 'for real' in history, aged twelve), he speaks with childlike earnestness as if quoting *sententiae* conned from a grammar school textbook, his Cato or Cicero:

> Believe me, lords, my tender years can tell
> Civil dissension is a viperous worm
> That gnaws the bowels of the commonwealth.
>
> *Part 1*, 3.1.71–3

In 4.1, he's crowned King of France in Paris (historically, aged ten), and in that same scene learns of his uncle Burgundy's revolt with much more equanimity than the real fourteen-year-old Henry did – who wept bitterly. At the end of *Part 1* he's the twenty-three-year-old, betrothed to Margaret of Anjou; in *Part 2* he's in his late twenties (suffering the loss of his uncle, the Lord Protector) and thirties (the Cade rebellion; defeat by York in 1455); *Part 3* telescopes the final twenty years of Henry's life: deposed, exiled, captured, imprisoned in the Tower, restored, deposed again, returned to the Tower, finally murdered. His own son Edward (born 1453) turns up part-way through *Part 3* to be knighted (historically, an eight-year-old), then, three acts later, murdered by the York brothers at Tewkesbury (historically, eighteen years old).

Throughout, Henry's breathtaking (to some, infuriating) oddity is to retain the guileless simplicity of a child ('What? Doth my Uncle Burgundy revolt? ... Why then Lord Talbot there shall talk with him' (*Part 1*, 4.1.64, 68)) and to recoil from 'adult' valuations and 'adult' projects (as when he answers Clifford, who's urging him to promote 'this goodly boy', Prince Edward, as battle standard for the Lancastrian cause: 'tell me, didst thou never hear / That things ill got had ever bad success?' (*Part 3*, 2.2.34, 45–6)). Henry's enemies think him stunted, 'silly', 'childish', 'bookish', infantilised by his domineering uncles or his virago wife ('She'll ... dandle thee like a baby' (*Part 2*, 1.1.222, 242, 256; 1.3.140)). But where they, grown-ups, have knotted minds and subtle metaphors to go with them ('My brain, more busy than the labouring spider, / Weaves tedious snares to trap mine enemies,' says York (*Part 2*, 3.1.339–40)), Henry's speech is transparent. His metaphors issue from a child's memory, offer a child's clear-sighted perspective on the 'madness' that 'rules in brainsick men', that makes adulthood a state of fevered insanity (*Part 1*, 4.1.111).

In Henry, it's as though the original condition of his childhood is constantly remembered, present, and lived through: 'When I was crowned, I was but nine months old' (*Part 3*, 1.1.112); 'I was anointed king at nine months old' (*Part 3*, 3.1.76); 'No sooner was I crept out of my cradle / But I was made a king at nine months old' (*Part 2*, 4.9.3–4). When he articulates pain, he recalls childhood. Bereft of his uncle-Protector in *Part 2*, he stunningly reverses parent–child roles and fixes animal instinct adhesively to human grief to imagine Gloucester a calf hauled off to the 'bloody slaughter-house', bound by 'the butcher' who 'beats it when it strains'; himself, 'the dam', the cow who 'runs lowing up and down / Looking the way her harmless young one went', wailing 'her darling's loss' (3.1.210–12, 214–16). When he yearns for alternatives to history, when he yearns for another way of telling time than summing the death toll, he imagines the child-like simplicity of the shepherd's life, 'blowing of his nails', 'sit[ting] upon a hill', 'carv[ing] out dials quaintly ... to see the minutes how they run' (*Part 3*, 2.5.3, 23–5). He longs nostalgically for a childhood denied him – a childhood his own son, pushed by the mother, seems intent on daffing aside to get on with being a grown-up: 'Was never subject longed to be a king,' he wonders, 'As I do long and wish to be a subject?' (*Part 2*, 4.9.5–6). The waste of childhood – the children of England, boys and men – is borne in on him as he sits on a molehill watching the battle of Towton (*Part 3*, 2.5). From one door enters 'a Sonne that hath kill'd his Father', from the other, 'a Father that hath kill'd his Sonne' (Folio S.D., TLN 1217), and it's as though, now, all the deaths of all his subjects killed in this war whose insane emblem is *roses* return to haunt him. Like that son-killing father on stage beside him who makes himself his dead child's memorial – 'These arms of mine shall be thy winding-sheet; / My heart, sweet boy, shall be thy sepulchre' (114–15) – Henry later figures himself as his slain son's living tomb. When hunchback Richard comes to the Tower to assassinate the redundant king, it's his murdered child, his 'Icarus', his 'one sweet bird' whom Henry remembers, needs to talk about (5.6.21,15). Henry dies calling up prophetically a nightmare fantasy of slaughtered infants, England's future wasted by a murderous Richard set loose to prey, and with his final breath recalls Richard's childhood, replays that monster baby's nightmare birth as source story for apocalypse:

> The owl shrieked ...
> The night-crow cried ...
> Dogs howled ...
> Thy mother felt more than a mother's pain
> And yet brought forth less than a mother's hope,
> To wit, an indigested and deformèd lump ...
> Teeth hadst thou in thy head when thou wast born
> To signify thou cam'st to bite the world;
> And if the rest be true, which I have heard,
> Thou cam'st –
>
> *Part 3*, 5.6.44–56

But Richard wants to hear no more about his miraculous birth. He stabs, and stabs again – then heads off to court to greet his brother's newborn son.

Between baby Henry at the beginning and baby Edward at the end, the trilogy produces prototypes of the children Shakespeare will continually rewrite. There's the part of the schoolboy, figured in 'bookish' Henry and his counterpart, York's youngest son, Rutland. For little Rutland, his books – and the 'pupil age' they trope – are no defence when Clifford (a first draft of Laertes shrilling for revenge) stumbles upon the twelve-year-old in *Part 3* guarded only by his tutor. Helpless, hapless Rutland – 'the brat' whose crime is that his 'father slew my father' – weeps, pleads for his life: 'Be thou revenged on men, and let me live,' he implores (1.3.4, 5, 20). A man gets no credit killing a child. 'I am too mean a subject for thy wrath,' Rutland protests (1.3.19, and the audience hears puns on 'mean' and 'subject'). But Clifford stabs him just the same.

This Rutland predicts a line of schoolboys on Shakespeare's stage, children who both embody and parody Tudor confidence in education, the humanist belief that the 'study of *bonae literae*' was 'the means to engender wisdom and virtue and to eradicate greed and indolence … injustice and social disorder', and the Protestant belief that education (at its most fundamental) was an attempt at repairing in children the fall of mankind's first parents, Adam and Eve. The schoolboy brings onstage with him this original history – and a sense of what claims the child is entitled subsequently to make on the parental relationship. Providing for a child's education, it was understood, was the first duty of a parent; the tutor was a proxy parent.[21] So Desiderius Erasmus in *The ciuilitie of childehode* (published in English in 1560) instructs the child to treat his 'scolemaster' *in loco parentis*. 'By all meanes cause hym to beare thee fatherly affeccion' and 'beare vnto him the affection of a sone': 'For we owe asmuch honour vnto those that hath taught vs the maner of well lyuing, as to those that haue geuen vs the begynnyng of life.'[22] So Orlando in *As You Like It*, recalling a childhood betrayed, complains to a latter-day Adam that his elder brother has failed the conditions of their father's will, keeping him 'rustically at home', not 'at school'. 'His horses are bred better', Orlando bitterly protests, for they're not just fed but 'taught their manège', while Orlando is kept ignorant – and as a consequence, brutish. By withholding his 'education' his brother '[under]mines' his 'gentility' (1.1.6–7, 5, 10–11, 19).

Behind the original schoolboy Rutland comes Titus Andronicus's grandson, the schoolboy Lucius, carrying his Ovid; Mistress Page's William declining Latin pronouns in *The Merry Wives of Windsor* and Parson Evans's school of fairy 'oofs'; Mote, the 'well-educated infant' in *Love's Labour's Lost* (1.2.90); and the once-child pupils whom Prospero tutored into language and self-meaning, Miranda and Caliban. All of these schoolchildren demonstrate the complicated power dynamic between teacher and scholar, adult and child, and they show that what constitutes 'the maner of well lyuing' is disputed territory. If it is the adult's theoretical role to impose, it is the child's *actual* role to evade, to twist out from under tutorial control, to sabotage, and frequently to show the infant wiser than the man. The silent answer to Prospero's rhetorical question to Miranda, 'My foot my tutor?' (*The Tempest*, 1.2.473) is, quite simply, 'yes'. There's no guarantee that the schoolboy will be 'repaired' by education. 'You taught me language,' says Caliban, 'and my profit on't / Is I know how to curse' (1.2.366–7). (But then, perhaps there's learning a parent has to do too, to learn to 'Acknowledge' what he's bred: to recognise, if it *is* a 'thing of darkness', that this 'thing' is 'mine' (5.1.278–9).)

Then there's the child warrior, young John Talbot (the trilogy's original 'Icarus'), a 'maiden youth' (or, as the French disdainfully make him, a 'young whelp' brandishing a 'puny sword') who, summoned into France to be 'tutor[ed]' by his father 'in stratagems of war', arrives at the front in time to achieve manhood – and die (*Part 1*, 4.6.55; 4.7.38, 35, 36; 4.5.2). Talbot's 'boy' John is prototype for King Henry's 'boy' Edward – the audacious eight-year-old prince who says he will 'return with victory from the field' (*Part 3*, 1.1.263). And both of them are models for the boy soldiers in later plays: Banquo's Fleance, Old Siward's son, Brutus's squire, Coriolanus's son Martius ('I'll run away till I am bigger, but then I'll fight' (5.3.129)), and Falstaff's 'giant' page (1.2.1), a gift from Hal (and his substitute, a sign that the prince has outgrown his corpulent tutor). In *2 Henry IV* the midget page, an 'agate' (1.2.16), an 'ape' (2.2.65), traipses behind the gross fat knight from London to Gloucestershire to the wars and back again – onstage in almost every Falstaff scene but mostly mute, a sight gag or visual joke. In *Henry V* he turns up as a sidekick to (dead) Falstaff's post-mortem hangers-on, Pistol, Bardolph, Nym. A child, but more man than they, the Boy in *Henry V* shrewdly interrogates those three 'white-livered', 'red-faced' 'swashers'. Their French 'campaign', a parody of Henry's, is not manly conquest but mindless parasitical pilfering. They 'stole a lute case,' says the Boy. And 'a fire shovel' (3.2.33, 30, 43–4, 46). This Boy, though, never gets a chance to fight, to become, symbolically, man – he's a servant, merely one who 'must stay with the lackeys with the luggage of our camp' (4.4.70–1). And it's with the lackeys and luggage that the Boy is killed, literally wasted – when the camp is overrun by fleeing Frenchmen making ignominious spoil of the children to hurt in the back the foe they cannot beat face to face (4.7). If Talbot's son poignantly but sentimentally confirms what *1 Henry VI* is simultaneously registering as redundant, the myth of chivalric male heroism, Falstaff's Boy in *Henry V*, a disappointed idealist in whom yet traces of the ideal survive, unpacks the myth, exposes the absurdities of chivalric posturing. He is a composite of adult expectation, casual exploitation, devastating betrayal. But he's also an 'acted document'. Shakespeare gives him soliloquy, speech straight to the audience that puts him alone on stage, independent of adult interference, that expresses interiority, the 'authentic' voice of a child self.

The royal heir, the twisted child, the child of destiny, the hopeful babe. Spectators will see all these children from *Henry VI* again: Arthur in *King John*, the Princes in *Richard III*, Mamillius in *The Winter's Tale*; Caliban in *The Tempest*; the history-healing babies – Perdita, Marina, Elizabeth – brought on first as babes in arms in *The Winter's Tale*, *Pericles*, *Henry VIII*; mythical, iconic children drawn in to the play's present by allusion: Icarus, Ascanius, Herod's innocents, the boy Cupid. And here's another one they'll see again: the murdered child.

Child-killing in Shakespeare's imagination figures, from the first, as the unspeakable atrocity. Looking at it, adult voices choke. Surveying the camp strewn with slaughtered baggage boys, like so many scattered, ripped-up sacks, Henry V will say, 'I was not angry since I came to France / Until this instant' (4.7.53–4). Turning to see Lear approaching, cradling the dead body of his youngest child, Kent will see apocalypse, 'Is this the promised end?', and Edgar will echo him, 'Or image of that horror?' (5.3.238, 239). Macduff will be reduced to monosyllables: 'Did you say all? … All?' (4.3.218). In *3 Henry VI* Shakespeare writes the original scene of child-killing – not once, but twice. Rutland's death is grotesque – something like black comedy intensifying its savagery. 'How now,' mocks Clifford of the cowering child, 'is he dead already? Or is it fear / That makes him close his eyes? I'll open them' (*Part 3*, 1.3.10–11). Thus, little Rutland is forced to look his tormentor in the eye when, crying 'pity me!' and kneeling, he takes Clifford's killing blow (1.3.36). And spectators are required to look, too. But this killing isn't finished with the child's death. It goes on – into the next scene where Rutland's father, York, is taken captive and forced by Queen Margaret to 'stand upon this molehill here', a dizzying elevation to mock his dizzying ambitions to wear England's crown. Where, she taunts him, 'are your mess of sons to back you now?': 'wanton Edward'; 'lusty George'; 'that valiant crookback prodigy / Dickie your boy'? And then, silken in her cruelty: 'with the rest, where is your darling, Rutland?' (1.4.67, 73–6, 78). Margaret answers her own question. 'Look, York' – and brings into view a 'napkin' 'stained' with the child's blood, offering it to the father – if he weeps – 'to dry thy cheeks withal' (79, 83). York's response is appalled incredulity:

O tiger's heart wrapped in a woman's hide,
How couldst thou drain the life-blood of the child
To bid the father wipe his eyes withal …?
That face of his the hungry cannibals
Would not have touched, would not have stained with blood;
But you …

                                                    1.4.137–9; 152–4

Still the killing of Rutland isn't finished, not even with his father's death. Four acts later, it replays, intensified, with a new child-victim, and Margaret is brought to that same stunned incomprehension that York gave words to. The Lancastrian army routed, herself taken captive, Margaret, the mother, is forced to look on as the 'boy', the 'lad', the 'child', her own 'sweet Ned' is butchered by the grinning York brothers (5.5.51, 32, 56, 51). She's no innocent to atrocity. Spectators saw Margaret cross the threshold into the unspeakable long before when, the men already having reduced the Parliament to a shambles, she went that step further, to turn England's protected spaces, its nurseries, its school-rooms into abattoirs, by that act of soaking her linen in Rutland's blood. But even prepared by history, she still can't comprehend boy-killing when it happens in front of her eyes. It's unthinkable: 'men ne'er spend their fury on a child' (5.5.57). So how could these men do it? Her answer plumbs the black hole of her incomprehension – a line audiences will hear again years later, only a little changed, from Macduff: 'You have no children, butchers' (5.5.63). Margaret's huge demented grief, stumbling from corpse to killers and back again –

O Ned, sweet Ned, speak to thy mother, boy!
Can'st thou not speak? O traitors! Murderers! …
What's worse than murderer that I may name it?
No, no, my heart will burst and if I speak –
And I will speak that so my heart may burst.
Butchers and villains, bloody cannibals,
How sweet a plant have you untimely cropped!

                                                    5.5.51–2, 58–62

– recalls York's:

Wouldst have me weep? Why, now thou hast thy will …
These tears are my sweet Rutland's obsequies
And every drop cries vengeance for his death …

See, ruthless queen, a hapless father's tears.
This cloth thou dipp'd'st in blood of my sweet boy,
And I with tears do wash the blood away.
Keep thou the napkin and go boast of this;
And if thou tell'st the heavy story right,
Upon my soul, the hearers will shed tears.

1.4.144, 147–8, 156–61

(And both anticipate Constance in *King John* whose premonitions of her child's death turn her to mourning three scenes before he dies: 'Grief fills the room up of my absent child, / ... Stuffs out his vacant garments with his form' (3.4.93, 97).) Grief for dead children: in Shakespeare, this is big grief. Children are 'sweet', and their loss, written on the ravaged bodies of parents, memorialised in the strained utterances of mothers and fathers, is heart-breaking. (We think of the veteran soldier Sicilius Leonatus, who, learning that his sons were slain in war, 'old and fond of issue, took such sorrow / That he quit being' (*Cymbeline*, 1.1.37–8). We think too of Shakespeare himself, learning of the death of his only son, a boy called Hamnet, in 1596.[23])

Theatre writing in scenes like these made young Will Shakespeare's name in London. If the 'harey the vj' entered in Philip Henslowe's company accounts for Lord Strange's Men as a 'ne[w]' play on 3 March 1592 is Shakespeare's *3 Henry VI*, the cracking sum Henslowe took as his share of the day's box office – £3 16s 8d – indicates a substantial success for the new playwright.[24] And the play remained spectacularly popular: not only was it played fourteen *more* times across that four-month season (against five performances of *Friar Bacon and Friar Bungay*, ten of *The Jew of Malta*, and fourteen of *The Spanish Tragedy* – all proven crowd-pullers, the repertoire's anchors – and seven performances of *Titus and Vespacian*, but only one of *The Tanner of Denmark* – the season's other 'ne' plays), it took, on many of its dates, the kind of receipts expected of premieres.[25] Spectators, it appears, remembered scenes from this play, and talked about them – like the satirical writer of the 1592 *Groats-worth of witte* (supposedly Robert Greene on his deathbed, but perhaps Thomas Nashe, using his friend's corpse as cover, or maybe even Henry Chettle).[26] The satirist clearly expected his readers to remember the child Rutland, his killing, and the blood-soaked napkin in *Henry VI* when he parodied York's line to attack Shakespeare, calling him the 'upstart Crow' whose 'Tiger's heart' was 'wrapped in a Player's hide'. That Shakespeare, writing the tiger-hearted Margaret, was writing a kind of part that no one had seen on the Elizabethan stage is certain. Writing Rutland, Edward, John Talbot, and

Henry he was writing something equally extraordinary – and laying down a marker for his own future effort: complex parts for children, challenging roles for boy players playing parts for boys.

Performing childhood

Near the end of *3 Henry VI* comes an almost surreal moment of political farce. Warwick has 'revolted' back to Lancaster, bringing with him his son-in-law, Clarence, the middle York brother, and they have delivered Henry from the Tower, restoring his crown. But Henry has had enough of rule: he'll wear the crown, but 'lead a private life'. He wants to 'resign my government' to Warwick, who's 'fortunate in all [his] deeds' (4.6.42, 24–5). Warwick, however, demurs. He thinks Clarence should rule. Up pipes Clarence: 'No, Warwick, thou art worthy of the sway' (4.6.32). It's ludicrous: the same men who've been snarling over the crown like dogs over a bone now, coy as maidens, back off, all dainty propriety. Wearily – is there any hope for peace in England? – Henry patches up this latest faction of disingenuous power-refusniks: 'I make you *both* Protectors of this land' (my italics, 41). But then he turns and sees a child, and the scene shifts from the farcical to the messianic. 'What youth is that,' he asks Somerset, 'Of whom you seem to have so tender care?' It is 'young Henry, Earl of Richmond'. The king summons the child: 'Come thither, England's hope' (65–8). And he 'Layes his Hand on his Head' (Folio S.D., TLN 2453). As he does so, King Henry speaks a prophecy:

> If secret powers
> Suggest but truth to my divining thoughts,
> This pretty lad will prove our country's bliss.

He blazons the child's body:

> His looks are full of peaceful majesty,
> His head by nature framed to wear a crown,
> His hand to wield a sceptre, and himself
> Likely in time to bless a regal throne.

And he instructs his factious loyalists to unite in this child:

> Make much of him, my lords, for this is he
> Must help you more than you are hurt by me.

4.6.68–76

The child is Henry Tudor, the future Henry VII whose accession in 1485 will end the Wars of the Roses: the son of Edmund (but raised by his uncle Jasper, Earl of Pembroke, in Wales), grandson of Owen Tudor and Catherine of Valois, Henry V's queen and Henry VI's mother. The king is the child's great uncle. And the child in the scene is twelve years old.[27] At the end of Act 4, then, even as 'a Post' enters with news that the Yorkists have freed usurping Edward, that York has re-armed and mobilised, devastating news that spells the final end of Lancaster, the child Richmond, 'England's hope', promises a happy, if deferred, end to civil war. And when, several scenes later, he's brought into view, spectators will know that the 'final' baby the Yorkists propose at the end of *Part 3* as 'England's hope' is only a placeholder, that ironically he's saddled with a disputed title. Baby York is proleptically trumped by this 'pretty lad' of Lancaster.

In this scene of almost hieratic laying on of hands, a proxy coronation, Richmond stands silent. An iconic figure, a child endowed with adult expectation and elaborated with adult interpretation, he is a sign that means through the adult. (At the same time, however, Shakespeare directs significant two-way traffic here, for it's the child who reciprocally constitutes meaning in the adult: it's because Henry recognises the child and correctly names Richmond 'England's hope' that spectators see Henry as a true prophet, an authentic holy king.) As for Richmond himself, what he offers the scene is the physical fact of his childness, a performative body – a body that is all play – making theatrical meaning in excess of thematic meaning. Partly this excess is a matter of scale, partly a matter of silence. In terms provided by Shakespeare's *Sonnet 3* (one of the so-called 'procreation' sonnets that, in the opening lines, urges the youth whom they address to 'Look in thy glass, and tell the face thou viewest / Now is the time that face should form another'), a child is both a mirror and a window. That is, he reflects the family forms around him; reflects *on* the family's forms; offers a perspective onto the family's future; offers a way of thinking about the past. So, says the poet, 'through windows of thine age' the youth will 'see' again 'thy golden time'. Richmond in 4.6 is that window and mirror, a small watcher watching an adult world where roles are unravelling before his eyes: a king who doesn't want to be king; allies who bandy the imagery of peace yet remain factious; subjects who want to rule. Mutely, he registers what's at stake in all this. Richmond *is* the future. And the future, says the little body brought centre stage, is fragile, *just a boy* – weak, vulnerable, an easy target. (So Somerset, at the end of the scene, sends him off to what he hopes will be safety in exile.) But embodied in the paradoxical apparatus of infancy, the future is also portentous, prodigious: a seed in time, insistent, what *will* come, not to be denied, waiting, apparent.

Stray children, fugitive performances

In this survey of parts for children first imagined in *Henry VI* then rewritten, refashioned over the course of the playwright's career, I want to see Richmond, child of destiny, prefiguring two more roles that stick, that resonate in Shakespeare's creative consciousness: the foster child and the off-stage child – the child who belongs to Shakespeare's text but who doesn't appear on his stage. The first figures both what is lost and what is found, coupling death to kind nurture, even miraculous preservation; the second remembers absence, and a world elsewhere. These are figures who return – in imagination, and in person.

Foster children (from the Old English word for 'food'[28]), like children generally, 'were everywhere' in early modern England, fostering the way the culture dealt with its staggering mortality rates. In the plague year 1603, for example, one in ten Londoners died; throughout Elizabeth's reign, nearly 50 per cent of middle- and upper-class women died before reaching their fiftieth birthday, more than half of them from complications of pregnancy. We read in the letters of John Chamberlain (from the 1590s to the 1620s) the constant attention to the family business of settling marriages – not just first, but second and third marriages – and the concern to provide for the children of those marriages. Fostering structured that provision, compensated for material insecurity, but also provided cultural training. A child might be sent after a parent's death to a guardian to be reared or entrusted to a relation to be educated (or a political loyalist to be groomed); taken, if they were children of the elite, into the protection (nominally) of the Court of Wards; or put in household service to prepare for responsibility and usefulness and to learn social manners and behaviour.[29] Henry Richmond was one such child. Born posthumously, three months after his father's death from plague in 1457, he was seized by Edward IV in 1462 and made ward to a York loyalist. Eight years later when Lancaster regained power, Richmond, too, was restored, returned to his family, assigned for the rest of his minority to his Tudor uncle, Jasper.

The movement of aristocratic, even royal, children from household to household was a customary form of English family life. In 1538 Henry VIII confided to William Sidney the care of his son, the (motherless) infant prince Edward – who died in 1553, nine months short of his sixteenth birthday, in the arms of Henry Sidney, his foster brother and

closest companion throughout his short life. Near death in 1576, Walter
Devereux, Earl of Essex, bequeathed his eldest son, the eleven-year-old
Robert, to William Cecil, Lord Burghley, wishing him 'to bind' 'my
Sonne *Hereford*' 'with perpetual Frendship to you and to your House' and
desiring 'his Education to be in your Household' 'to the End that … he
might also reverence your Lordship for your Wisdome and Gravity, and
lay up your Counsells and Advises in the Treasury of his Hart'.[30] Essex's
other children were entrusted to Katherine, wife of Henry Hastings, the
Earl of Huntingdon, who, herself childless, seems to have made a lifelong
career of foster-mothering. The Devereuxs grew up alongside Sidney
children (Thomas, youngest brother to Philip) and Russell children
(Edward, heir to the earldom of Bedford). But they grew up also alongside
children like Margaret Dakins – untitled, but set to inherit a staggering
fortune. (She was eventually married in turn to two of her foster brothers,
Walter Devereux, then Thomas Sidney, younger sons of cash-strapped
households.[31])

In Tudor England, elite fostering, the circulation of children from
household to household, provided (in Patricia Fumerton's term) 'a generative cultural function': a network of relationship, affection, obligation,
minor dependency and economic profitability; a system of service and
civilisation, of patronage and domestic provision (read: marriage).[32] The
kind of civilising education children were expected to receive in households like the Huntingdons' was detailed in, for example, Erasmus's *The
ciuilitie of childehode*, which included chapters on 'The orderynge of the
eyes', 'A ioyfull and mery forehed', 'A clene Nose', 'At the Table and
howe a childe oughte to use and behaue hymselfe', 'To make cleane the
shell of an egge', 'Modestie in speakynge and laughyng', 'Not to report
the thynge that hath bene freely spoken at the Table', 'To be lyke thy
parentes in good maners and honestye'.[33]

But the 'generative function' of fostering wasn't confined to the elite. It
extended to every station in society. It was an idea embedded in the
deepest cultural, popular and religious memory: Moses and Jesus were
foster children; so was Oedipus, and Romulus and Remus, and Arthur
(reared by Merlin). Margaret Dakins (now, in her third marriage, Lady
Hoby) took in numbers of 'common' children: Averill Aske, Heather
Halles, Elizabeth Hunter, keeping Averill (and her modest yeoman's
inheritance) in trust until she married. In March 1603 Lady Hoby wrote
in her *Diary* that 'my Cossine Gates brought his daughter Iane, being of
the age of 13 yeares auld, to me, who, as he saied, he freely gaue me'; the
following month, 'I entertained my Cossine Dakins wiues daughter to
serue me'.[34] Much further down the social scale, Philip Henslowe,

entrepreneur and landlord of the Rose playhouse, adopted his brother's three minor children, paying for their schooling, putting them to trades, setting them up in business.[35]

With this kind of fostering we see family provision shading into that other, ubiquitous form of early modern child care (where 'fostering' even becomes synonymous with it), the apprenticeship. We note Lady Hoby's comment, that her cousin's daughter was 'to serue me', and we are reminded by Philippe Ariès that apprenticeship constituted 'a much wider meaning' of social relationship in early modern Europe 'than it took on later'. Children of 'all classes of society' were 'not kept at home: they were sent to another house, with or without a contract, to live there and start their life there, or to learn the good manners of a knight, or a trade, or even to go to school and learn Latin.' 'All education', whether the child was learning bricklaying or Ovid or the courtesy of waiting at table, 'was carried out by means of apprenticeship'. The child, at every level, was learning service, and the master – and mistress – stood *in loco parentis*, the apprentice, in effect, a foster child.[36] Once this connection is made, we can locate the foster child inside the playhouse for which Shakespeare was writing, for example, in the household of Edward Alleyn: a child called 'Pig'.

Like the Hobys, Edward and Joan Alleyn had no children. He was the famous tragedian and lead actor first with Lord Strange's Men then the Admiral's Men; she was the stepdaughter of Philip Henslowe who built the playhouse where Alleyn's companies were in residence from 1592. Alleyn's boy apprentice was one John Pig, and they seem to have treated him with the same affectionate care Margaret Hoby showed to Averill, like an adopted child. And perhaps out of the same instincts. By statute – the 1563 Statute of Artificers – apprentices were required to serve a minimum of seven years in the households of their masters, bound until they reached the legal age of twenty-four. But youngsters might enter service much earlier, and serve a much longer apprenticeship, from the age of seven or eight. That is, they might live their entire childhoods under an adopted roof.[37]

Pig (also spelled 'pyk', 'pigge', 'pyg' or 'pygge') first turns up among Henslowe's playhouse records in a spoof letter. It's undated, but probably written some time between July and October 1593 when the Rose closed on account of plague, Strange's Men were on tour, travelling first south-west to Bath and Bristol then as far north as York (and when, in *Shakespeare in Love*, Will is kicking his heels in London). Pig's letter is addressed simply 'mysteris', and goes:

Yo[u]r honest ancyent and Loving servant pige hath his humbell commenda[tion] to you and to my goode master hinsley & mystiris and to my m[aster's] sister bess for all her harde delyng w[ith] me I send her harty Comenda[tions] hoping to be behowlding to her agayne for the opinyng of the coberde: and to my neyghbore doll for calynge me vp in a morning and to my wyf sara for making clean my showes & to that ould Jentillman mounsir pearle [that] ever fought w[ith] me for the blok in the chemeney corner & though you all Look for the redy retorne of my proper person yett I swear to you by the fayth of a fustyan kinge never to retorne till fortune vs bryng w[ith] a Joyfull metyng to lovly London I sesse yo[ur] petty prety pratlyng parlyng pyg

By me John pyk

Then, written in the left-hand margin:

Mystiris I praye yo[u] kepe this that my mayster may se it for I gott on to wright it m[aste]r duotone & my m[aste]r knows nott of it.[38]

It's clearly a joke, since the letter is in Edward Alleyn's handwriting (not Thomas Downton's). But the signature may be autograph. If it is, if Pig and Alleyn cooked up the letter together to send home to 'mysteris Alline on the banck syd', this piece of writing may be the nearest we will ever come to the real boy ('petty prety pratlyng parlyng') who could have played the fictional Richmond or Rutland – and the nearest we can come to his 'real' thoughts, inscribed (somewhat destabilising the narrative, it has to be said) under the 'fayth of a fustyan kinge'.[39] We get a brief look into this child's domestic life, managed by women: roused from bed of a morning, clean shoes set out, food distributed from that closed and probably locked 'coberde'; a lad perhaps knocked into shape with some clips around the ear ('harde delyng'), jockeying with the household cat ('mounsir pearle', as I take it) for the warmest place in the chimney breast. And perhaps we catch something of the tone of the child's life among adults – an easiness, a jocularity, a life connected and related, observing hierarchy ('mysteris', 'master'), but if a 'servant', not servile.

Elsewhere in Henslowe's *Diary* and records we get further brief glimpses of the boy – now four years older – at work with the Admiral's Men at the Rose. In December 1597 the company is ordering 'a payer of yeare [that is, hair] sleavse of the bodeyes of pyges gowne', a 'womones gowne to play allece perce'. In costume inventories made in March 1598 several worn items for Pig are listed: 'j red sewt of cloth for pyge, layed with whitt lace'; 'Pyges damask gowne'; 'j harcoller [hair-colour] tafitie sewte of pygges'; 'j white tafitie sewte of pygges'; 'j littell gacket for Pygge'. Clearly, changing from 'sewt' to 'gowne', Pig is playing parts both for boys and women – and perhaps the lead in *Alice Pierce*.[40] In March 1598 he witnesses a loan from Henslowe to 'John haslette valter', and signs his name.[41] In these years, he's named in three stage plots: to *Frederick and Basilea* (1597), *The Battle of Alcazar* (1598 or thereabouts), and *Troilus and Cressida* (1599: Dekker and Chettle's play, not Shakespeare's),[42] plots that show how busy a boy's professional life could be and how crowded the stage with parts for boys – playing men *and* women.[43] In Pig, we see the beginnings of actor training located in the apprentice's fostering.

If, as I'm speculating, Pig, the boy player who toured with Strange's Men in the summer of 1593, gets us somewhere close to Shakespeare's Richmond, the child of destiny who appeared on the Rose stage in the winter of 1592, perhaps Pig the 'real' apprentice similarly evokes the fictional foster child who turns up so regularly in Shakespeare's scenarios, offers (as a kind of placeholder) a named site where cultural norms, playhouse practice, and Shakespeare's narratives get enacted. In *All's Well That Ends Well* the dying physician Gérard de Narbonne, like the dying Earl of Essex bequeathing his son to Lord Burghley in 'real' history, bequeaths his daughter Helena to the Countess Rousillon (whose husband in turn dying gives their minor son, Bertram, in ward to the King). Orlando and Rosalind are both foster children, the one left to his brother's grudging care, the other to her uncle's. ('It was your pleasure, and your own remorse,' protests Celia, that 'stayed' Rosalind in the court after her father's banishment: 'I was too young that time to value her'(*As You Like It*, 1.3.69, 66, 70).) As Lavinia frantically hopes for the miracle of pity from Tamora even as her sons are untrussing for rape – 'Some say that ravens foster forlorn children' (*Titus Andronicus*, 2.3.153) – so Macduff's little boy, told he's fatherless, adopts himself, like the proverbial sparrow, to do 'As birds do' (*Macbeth*, 4.2.32). In *The Winter's Tale* the Old Shepherd picks up baby Perdita, left exposed on the coast of Bohemia, and raises her as his own; Pericles hands over Marina, his 'Poor inch of nature' (Scene 11, 34), born at sea in a storm, the death (apparently) of her mother, to Cleon and Dionyza to foster, 'To give her princely training, that she may be / Mannered as she is born' (Scene 13, 16–17). King Cymbeline, his own two sons cradle-snatched, 'takes the babe', born 'Posthumus', son of his loyal general Leonatus, and fosters him, 'Breeds him', 'makes him of his bedchamber', offers him 'all the learnings that his time / Could make him the receiver of' (1.1.40, 41, 42–4). Meanwhile, in Wales, the kidnapper, Belarius, rears Cymbeline's stolen boys,

'Instructs' them 'how t'adore the heavens', hunt, keep house in a cave – and shun the 'poison which attends / In place of greater state' (3.3.3, 77–8). In *The Tempest* Prospero raises the child of Sycorax, and like the Countess Rousillon considering Helena, Pericles Mariana, and Orlando himself, Prospero sees in Caliban the twin motives that shape all children (on Shakespeare's stage) into adults, their 'nature' struggling with their 'nurture' for control. Children inherit their 'dispositions', but they're endowed with education, 'princely training', 'learnings'. The question is whether 'nurture' in Caliban, the child said to be 'born' a 'devil', will 'stick' on 'nature'. Will 'pains, / Humanely taken' 'inoculate' the 'old stock' (*Tempest*, 4.1.188–90, *Hamlet*, 3.1.120)? A child's 'gentility' may be '[under]mined' by a deprived education – or confirmed by his training, yielding him 'mannered' as he is 'born'. Equally, though, as the children lost to Leontes, Cymbeline, and Pericles optimistically demonstrate, in the truly noble, no amount of 'beastly' training can 'hide the sparks of nature' (*Cymbeline*, 3.3.40, 79).

In early modern English culture, fostering, exchanging children, aimed in its elite form to mimic and instantiate the culture's largest aspirations: to locate the court as the centre of aristocratic child-gift circles (as, that is, the centre of English culture); to establish this form of gift-giving, this form of human society, as a substitute for war, human alliance knitting families so seamlessly that faction disappears into social fabric and war becomes redundant; and to 'elevate generosity into what may be called a *spiritual* fact'. 'Freely giving children', writes Fumerton, the English aristocracy 'generated social bonds that communicated a mystical force seeming to sustain life in the face of death'.[44] But if that's how fostering was meant to work in real life, it's hardly how it works on Shakespeare's stage: instead of alliance, the foster child (from Rosalind to Posthumus, Bertram to Marina and Perdita) constantly produces uproar – a specific case of which I want to look at shortly.

Last, then, is the child Shakespeare writes – but doesn't bring on stage: in *Antony and Cleopatra* the lovers' bastard brood ('all the unlawful issue that their lust … hath made between them' (3.6.7–8)); in *The Winter's Tale*, Antigonus's three little girls; in *Titus Andronicus*, the baby that Aaron the Moor knows was born 'yesternight' to 'one Muliteus my countryman' (4.2.152, 151). (There are more: the children of Harfleur, Corioli, Rome, civil war-torn England, children threatened with slaughter, tossed – remembering Herod's infant genocide – on the blood-dulled soldier's pike.) The off-stage child, as I'm calling him, so intensely present in the immediate 'nowness' of his absence, so momentarily evoked and rendered live in the story, is recruited in these instances to adult political work. Adults mean by them. Octavius Caesar, apoplectic at the latest gossip from Alexandria, reports Antony's newest insolence. He hasn't just staged his own enthronement, and Cleopatra's, giving her, pranked up 'In th'habiliments of the goddess Isis', the 'stablishment of Egypt'. He's put the children on display, 'in the public eye', in the 'common show-place' of the city, proclaiming them 'the kings of kings' and handing titles, kingdoms, crowns, the fabulous empire of the east like gold-wrapped sweets into their infant hands. To 'boggler' Cleopatra's lawless 'race', that is, has been given Octavius Caesar's property, his imperial inheritance (*Antony and Cleopatra*, 3.6.17, 9, 11–13; 3.13.111, 107). These children he later holds hostage for their mother's life, fuelled, it seems, by not a little sibling rivalry, detesting the very idea of 'Cesarion, whom they call my father's son' (3.6.6). He intends to lead them in triumph in Rome, and informs the queen that if she takes 'Antony's course', kills herself, she puts her 'children / To that destruction which I'll guard them from' (5.2.126, 127–8). How blandly euphemistic is his rhetoric, the rhetoric of a (child-less) civil servant, nicely balancing threat with promise.

Antigonus summons his daughters for equivalent political work. He offers them to the mind-blown Leontes as human wagers, stake down upon the queen's virtue. Antigonus knows Hermione is true and that the baby she's carrying is the king's. Indeed, if *she's* 'honour-flawed', he protests, no woman in the world can possibly be imagined chaste – and he'll take preventive measures to amputate iniquity in his own family:

> I have three daughters: the eldest is eleven;
> The second and the third nine and some five;
> If this prove true, they'll pay for't. By mine honour,
> I'll geld 'em all. Fourteen they shall not see,
> To bring false generations.
>
> 2.1.146–50

For Aaron in *Titus* there's no contradiction between his own sudden fierce possessive paternity and the casual commodification of children he imagines in others. 'Nor great Alcides, nor the god of war,' he protests, 'Shall seize this prey', this 'Sweet blowze', this 'beauteous blossom', this newborn baby, 'out of his father's hands' (4.2.94–5, 72). But 'Muliteus my countryman' might sell his child to fill the Empress's embarrassingly vacant cradle. 'Go pack with him,' Aaron advises, 'and give the mother gold, / And tell them … how by this their child shall be advanced': Saturninus, the witless cuckold, will act the unwitting foster father, will 'dandle' the changeling 'for his own' (4.2.151, 154–56, 160).

Subsequent children

Counters, as I'm seeing them, in various games of human shuffleboard, Shakespeare's off-stage children are figures that bridge the two halves of my project in this book, that move me from his texts and theatre to ours, to enable me to think about the work children are doing on Shakespeare's stage today, and to notice that these days Shakespeare's absent children exhibit a tendency to exceed their texts, to tease subsequent actors, directors, audiences into further imaginative thought, and themselves into representation. They offer sites to multiply the child parts Shakespeare wrote. That is, they come onstage. They get themselves enacted. They turn audiences into Orsinos, listening to Cesario's story in *Twelfth Night* of that elusive 'daughter [...] of my father's house' (2.4.120). They make us want to know more, to fill in the 'blank' history: 'But died thy sister of her love, my boy?' (119). What happens to the Moorish babe born 'yesternight'? To Antigonus's bairns once their father fails to return from that awful voyage that ends for him when he's eaten by a bear? To Cleopatra's children? (Plutarch reports that Cesarion was betrayed to Octavius by his schoolmaster while his siblings were conveyed to Rome, raised by Antony's Octavia. How did they fare in imperial Rome, those dark children of Nilus, of the strange crocodile and the gypsy bacchanal?) To offer some answers, if only obliquely, I want to remember two recent productions that foreground our current cultural preoccupation with children, our need to look at children and to circulate our ideas of children through Shakespeare, productions that introduced Shakespeare's off-stage children into the performance, putting those children at the centre of the story they had to tell.

In 2005 at the RSC the director, Gregory Doran, brought the Indian boy onstage in *A Midsummer Night's Dream*, and in doing so, figured the fairy plot as a story of a family at war.[45] The boy is the cause – cited in 2.1 – of the uproar in the fairy kingdom. Oberon wants 'the little changeling boy / To be [his] henchman', 'Knight of his train, to trace the forests wild' (2.1.120–1, 25). Titania refuses to hand him over. 'Set your heart at rest,' she roars. There'll be no negotiations: 'The fairy land buys not the child of me.' Why? Because:

> His mother was a vot'ress of my order,
> And in the spicèd Indian air by night
> Full often hath she gossiped by my side,
> And sat with me on Neptune's yellow sands,
> Marking th'embarkèd traders on the flood,

When we have laughed to see the sails conceive
And grow big-bellied with the wanton wind,
Which she with pretty and with swimming gait
Following, her womb then rich with my young squire,
Would imitate, and sail upon the land
To fetch me trifles, and return again
As from a voyage, rich with merchandise.
But she, being mortal, of that boy did die;
And for her sake do I rear up her boy;
And for her sake I will not part with him.

                                                    2.1.122–37

This gorgeous, but Amazonian, story is all about women: women's devotion, women's work, women's remembering. It's about gossip and service; women's bodies. It's about the trifling – and about the 'merchandise' that's beyond price, the crammed belly, the 'little room', stuffed with 'infinite riches'.[46] Artfully, it talks about the natural. But bluntly it's also about a woman dying in child-birth, and a foster-mother adopting her baby, rearing the orphan 'for her sake'; 'for her sake' refusing to part with him. And what of the child himself? About memory and loss, the story makes the child an object, a *memento mori*, a fetish. It prizes the boy, but takes him captive: his future, in the court of the Fairy Queen, is arrested development, to be kept in petticoats, never breeched, never permitted the hunter's weapons; fostered, but somehow a lost boy, not allowed to grow up. Fostering, then, as Titania practises it may be affective, even 'mystical', but hardly 'generative'. And it's no antidote for war – rather, a provocation.

There is, however, another back-story to this child. It makes him still an object, but of another order. According to Puck, the kid, Titania's 'attendant', is a changeling, kidnapped: 'A lovely boy stol'n from an Indian king' (2.1.22). No orphan, then, but male property – filched. Bringing the Indian boy onstage, Doran's *Dream* brought this dispute onstage: was he to be mothered – or fathered? In this dream-space where Titania remembered the 'vot'ress', Oberon proxied the 'Indian king', and the two wrangled like divorced parents in a custody battle, the question was: whose rights to the child had the higher claim? Whose vision of the child's future?

To look at, Doran's *Dream* in the fairy scenes was equal parts Arthur Rackham and *Stig of the Dump*. A backcloth of dark purple sky twinkled with stars but turned into a nursery illustration by Cicely Barker when, backlit, projected upon it appeared the giant silhouettes of a pair of dragonfly-winged Edwardian flower fairies. Framing this pretty picture, disconcerting the eye: a seeming *intaglio* – that eventually came into focus as a tangle of urban junk, trashed bicycles, bedsprings, prams, broken ladders, bent watering cans. Fairyland was built on a tip. Titania (Amanda Harris) and Oberon (Joe Dixon) were by Klimt-after-Ovid: spectacular, fine-boned, glittering, and caught as if half-way through a metamorphosis, he stripped to the belly, becoming a lion; she in gauze slashed to the thigh, almost a gazelle. The attendant fairies were punks in cycling shorts, bovver boots, elbow gloves, striped stockings and tulle – who remembered Fuseli as they manipulated grotesque plastic winged baby-doll versions of themselves, the toys' heads as ugly as anything lurking around the canvas edges of Fuseli's 'Titania Awakes' (1794). There was breathtaking beauty here – but also dark Rackham-esque menace, a landscape not of 'namby-pamby nymphs' but 'sprung from seed found in the fancies of Dürer'.[47]

The Indian boy was pot-bellied, big-eyed, a toddler, naked, racially marked, not black (like Rackham's[48]) but brown. And he was a puppet. So *literally* an object. His articulated body was manipulated by fairies moving

Plate 3 Titania (Amanda Harris) and her fairies at play with the Indian Boy as Puck (Jonathan Slinger), and Oberon (Joe Dixon), far right background, plot kidnap in Gregory Doran's 2005 *A Midsummer Night's Dream*. (*Source*: Stewart Hemley photograph © Royal Shakespeare Company.)

each of his limbs so that gestures were detailed, reactions oddly life-like: when his 'parents' started bickering, he plonked his baby bottom down and let out a caterwauling. But this child, perforce, was always surrounded by a gang of adults.[49] Spectators saw him as an oddity (like all children?). Beloved (Titania scooped him and cuddled him; sent him to play while she napped in the bower). But also a pawn. In a sequence Dr Caligari might have invented, the sentinel fairy who stood on duty while Titania slept was coshed over the head and dragged off as the monstrous misshapen silhouette of Oberon appeared, filling the whole cyclorama, looming over his queen as he pinched the love juice in her eyes. Simultaneously, Puck snatched the kid, kidnapping the kidnapped, then sat with him, a big delinquent 'brother', cheekily instructing the little boy to wave at spectators – goodbye! goodbye! – as horror-film music filled the theatre – and the stage went to blackout.

That scene of abduction before the interval chilled the blood of any spectator who saw in it a distant replay of a national nightmare, another scene, twelve years past but also somehow only yesterday, of a little boy led by a bigger boy through a shopping precinct in Liverpool.[50] Even if Doran's *Dream* ended with joy – and it did: the final fairy tableau saw the king and queen reconciled, 'father' and 'mother' holding their child *together* – it didn't erase the dark memories it evoked, the dream of idyllic childhood ruined. How to explain the nightmare of what happened? Search childhood – in Liverpool *and* Athens.

Here, Doran gave spectators the story of a kid so wanted by jealous parents that he was causing a war – but he produced another story in parallel of a child neglected, a child ignored: Puck. As Jonathan Slinger played him, Puck was an over-grown, over-weight kid in a grubby string vest; a blubber-lipped slob with a red Tin-Tin quiff that looked like it had been aerosoled in place. Promising dully to 'put a girdle round about the earth / In forty minutes' (2.1.175–6), he slouched off flat-footed. Seconds later, a star shot across the sky. But then came the crash. This Puck's truculence was born of despair: he sat, cross-legged at Oberon's feet, listening to his 'father' tell his desire for *another child*, staring straight out into the void of his un-lovedness. A lost boy. An Ariel in the making ('Do you love me, master? No?' (4.1.48)) whose longing wasn't even noticed. Of course this sulky kid was prepared to see the baby brat hurt! Putting the Indian boy on stage, Greg Doran traced, in the visual interstices of the bigger picture, a story of sibling rivalry, a 'new' story of Puck and Oberon, of bad parenting and the avoidance of love. For every child doted upon another, said this *Dream*, is cast carelessly aside.

A year later, Kneehigh Theatre Company's adaptation of *Cymbeline* (2006) also thought about lost boys, hurt, and remembering; about warring families, dysfunctional parents, sibling rivalry, rough fostering.[51] It told a story of coming home. But it began as a story of absent children.

In a post-modern, post-urban dystopian Britain, King Cymbeline lived behind a barricade, a perimeter fence of industrial-weight steel mesh. In half-light, furtive figures in parkas, hiding their faces, checking their backs, a hit squad (it seemed) of the socially excluded, graffitists, approached the fence. One hung up a teddy bear on the mesh by his ear with clothes pegs; another, a bunch of flowers; a pair of baby booties; more and more flowers; a piece of cot quilt; and then crumpled photo-copies of old black-and-white photographs, enlarged to life-size, the origi-nals perhaps cut from a newspaper or police forensic report, the bodies of two babies, face down, asleep – or maybe dead; last of all, a cardboard box, ripped open, flattened, bulldog clipped to the top of the mesh, a headline, a single word, aerosoled in red, letter by letter, 'M, B, R, E, E, M, R, E': REMEMBER. The gang stood; looked; instantly dispersed. Leaving spectators to realise that what they were looking at was a shrine to Britain's lost boys: Cymbeline's sons, the absent children who exist for the nation only as memories, as citations; who never appear, *can* never appear in Shakespeare's play because those babies were kidnapped from their nursery twenty years earlier. Just then, Cymbeline (Mike Shepherd) appeared, a bullet-headed Herod in pyjamas, roared, began ripping down the street-art tribute, as 'Queen Beverly' (Emma Rice), formerly his nurse, now his wife, emerged, syringe in hand, injected him, and led him off. Cymbeline's business, clearly, was the need to forget.

Kneehigh's contemporary rewrite of Shakespeare's original was both respectful of the play's deep structures and irreverent of its surface trans-actions. Quirky, anarchic (even occasionally raunchy) physical theatre, this *Cymbeline* exploded Shakespeare's text to put in its place a perfor-mance that worked, profoundly, as a poetic intertext – like Auden's *The Sea and the Mirror* in conversation with *The Tempest*. Posthumus (Carl Grose) arrived in Italy clutching a phrase book and a typewriter; the 'manacle of love' he left behind was a clunky wristwatch: so Imogen (Hayley Carmichael, wonderfully, dopily, a kid in school shoes and bunches) could count the hours, the minutes, the seconds of their separa-tion (and we, how quickly Posthumus fell for Iachimo's lies); the 'messen-ger' was a radio-controlled toy car; Caesar, a face wheeled in on a mobile political hoarding; Cymbeline, drugged, pruned bonsai in slippers and a string vest; his dominatrix 'Beverly' sang the blues; 'Wales' was a card-board city for the homeless; the wars were played on a floor map, the

Plate 4 King Cymbeline (Mike Shepherd) rips down the street people's memorial to his lost boys in Kneehigh's 2006 *Cymbeline*. (*Source*: Steve Tanner photograph © Steve Tanner and Kneehigh.)

armies pushed around like counters in shove ha'penny. When she received the first letter – 'Meet me in Milford Haven' – Imogen was ecstatic, Pisanio (Kirsty Woodward) baffled – 'Where's Milford Haven?' – until Imogen, spinning the globe she kept in her bedroom, squawked 'It's in WALES!' with a rapture that put Wales somewhere on the moon. The second letter, the one ordering her death, left Imogen dumbfounded. She read aloud, '"Dear Pisanio, Thy mistress hath played the trumpet in my bed"'; stopped; bewildered, 'But I can't play the trumpet.' Pisanio screamed 'STRUMPET!' – and spectators remembered the battered typewriter.[52]

For all its visual inventiveness, the almost child-like gags and laughter, this *Cymbeline* was anchored to loss. And it put a particular experience of bereavement at its centre. What happens, it asked, when a nation loses its children? (The photographs clothes-pegged to the perimeter fence had to put spectators in mind of other images of infant 'desaparecidos' around the world: the children of Darfur, of Haiti, of Rwanda, of Argentina – twenty, thirty years back, but still remembered in the photographs the mothers of the Plaza de Mayo carry as they march. And of contemporary Britain: posters in train stations, images on web-sites. 'Have you seen this missing child?' In the UK, 77,000 of them *every year*.[53]) What happens when a family loses its children? Kneehigh's King Cymbeline confessed to a daughter he couldn't talk to in a speech she couldn't hear: 'I am like I am with you / Because to lose you too / Would be the death of me / My daughter, my love.' He was a man who 'mourned his wife', the mother of the stolen boys: 'The waiting' was 'what killed her': she 'died from all that hope'. He mourned 'his two vanished sons'. But he 'did not know how to take his daughter's / tiny hand at the funeral'. So now all that remained to her, bereft of mother, and brothers ('I wish whoever had taken you / Had had enough hands / To have taken me too'), was the absence, the empti-ness of 'You. My father'.

And what happens to the children themselves?

In *Cymbeline* the lost children, gone, return. Lost to their parents, they, of course, have been other men's 'findings' (as the Young Shepherd in *The Winter's Tale* will have it (3.3.124)): Posthumus adopted by Cymbeline, Arviragus and Guiderius by Belarius, Imogen as Fidele by a family she finds in the wilderness. For all of them, the adoptive interlude is genera-tive, formative, educative, and mystical, a triumph of the 'invisible instinct' that has 'frame[d] them': miraculously, that which 'wildly grows in them' 'yields a crop / As if it had been sowed' (4.2.181, 182). Their returnings are a wonder, and play out a deep longing which our culture, from the Greeks, calls 'nostalgia', the longing for a place called 'home'. At the end of Kneehigh's *Cymbeline* all the children made it home. In the final scene, metal-frame beds were pushed on, the 'nursery' reassembled, the memory of that night erased, when sleeping babies were snatched, cradles emptied. Now, two by two, the children climbed into bed, tucked up by 'daddy' Cymbeline, sung asleep with a full-company lullaby: 'Heaven knows / The past is deep / But I'll be watching as you sleep ... / Let go. / Let go / ... I'll catch you tomorrow.' Behind them dropped a quilted banner – reminiscent of that piece of cot quilt pegged to the fence. Home.

Like Greg Doran's *Dream*, however, this *Cymbeline* in the end refused to duck the hard questions it raised. In Shakespeare's play, when Jupiter appears to sleeping Posthumus he leaves behind a book, inscribed with a riddle, which, deciphered in the final lines of the play, tells Posthumus's history – and Britain's future. In Kneehigh's *Cymbeline*, Jupiter left a box. Opened, it was found full of photographs – of children. Of themselves. They stared, dazed. They held them up – to each other, to spectators. The discovery was both sweet and sad. Arviragus, Guiderius, Imogen, Posthumus: they were 'found objects', adults. But what of their child selves? What of their childhoods whose only evidence remained in the dog-eared photographs, records of disappearance? Those children were lost. Their beginnings, lost. We would never see those children again.

And yet, and yet ... amazingly, the photographs showed that somehow those children survived, persisted. In Kneehigh's programme, the usual actor mug-shots were absent; in their place, photographs of the company as children. Emma Rice at the seaside among sandcastles. Kirsty Woodward missing her front tooth. Mike Shepherd pedalling his 'Lightning' go-cart. The kids: they weren't 'lost'! We could see them – outlines, traces – in the adults we'd been watching 'play'. In that recognition, *our* recognition, the loop was completed. Like the original photographs offered in this production as a trope of memory, performance, too, spectators realised, is a way of remembering; and play, particularly Shakespeare's play, offers our culture not just a way of watching children, 'observing children very closely'. It offers us a way of remembering, watching ourselves.

Cymbeline, King of (Roman) Britain on stage in 2006, returns me to Elizabeth, Queen of England en route to her coronation in 1559, and in the return, makes something clear. Whatever moment in history I'm looking at, I see cultural anxieties, insecurities about children that are addressed only through performance. But I see also anxieties, insecurities about ourselves that are addressed only through the child. In Shakespeare – on his stage, on ours – these issues are urgent; but so too are other issues: delight, pleasure, anarchy, and play. In Shakespeare, the child is precious: the threat to the child awful, the loss of a child, heartbreaking. But the strength of the child is awesome, and his ability to wreak his revenge on adults – like the 'ape' on Falstaff – is stunning. We remember that Mote, in the interlude of the Nine Worthies in *Love's Labour's Lost*, plays Hercules. That's instructive. The physical presence of the performer insists that there's more power in the part than the playtext would suggest. Mote-as-Hercules tells us something: that the child in Shakespeare is not only what adults project onto him. It's what the actor in the part projects into the cultural space of performance. In the chapters that follow, I have Mote in mind.

Chapter 2

The Alphabet of Memory in *Titus Andronicus*

Renaissance man is rhetorical man, whose repertoire of formal linguistic structures and accompanying physical gestures is a way of ordering the chaos of experience.

Jonathan Bate, *Shakespeare and Ovid*, 1993

TITUS: Lucius, what book is that she tosseth so?
BOY: Grandsire, 'tis Ovid's *Metamorphosis*;
          My mother gave it me.
MARCUS: For love of her that's gone,
          Perhaps she culled it from among the rest.

Titus Andronicus 4.1.41–4

The arc of the story is the child's; the story's brought to life by the boy's vision.

Julie Taymor, *Titus* DVD Commentary, 1999

'Learn of us'

Thirty lines from the end, *Titus Andronicus* produces a disconcerting moment of revisionist history. Six bodies are dead on stage, four freshly killed, two spewed-up across a dinner table, broken meat from a half-consumed pie. Reeling back from this sudden slaughter, the 'sad-faced men … of Rome' who are its witness stand aghast at the extravagant atrocity. 'Severed' by these 'uproars', they are like 'a flight of fowl / Scattered by winds' – or 'scattered corn' that Marcus says he would 'knit again / … into one mutual sheaf' (5.3.66–70).[1] The labour Marcus sets himself in this metaphor is Sisyphean: Rome's battered, scattered people are a field flailed by a storm; he is a latter-day Semele sorting seeds. To fix Rome he'll have to restore each grain of wheat to its husk, then attach each husk to its head, then gather up all the storm-tossed ears into 'one mutual sheaf'. To 'knit' corn, though, may strike the play's spectators as no more or less an effort of impossibility than the parallel knitting project Marcus proposes: to heal the metaphoric body politic by teaching Rome 'how to knit again / … These broken limbs … into one body' – this, in a Rome that already knows too much about actual bodies broken, severed, mutilated, amputated, dismembered (5.3.69–71).

Turning to Marcus, a Roman Lord demands that he 'Speak', that he tells 'The story' that attends this appalling spectacle (a story that he imagines will echo an older tale of a civilisation in ruins, told by Aeneas discoursing 'To lovesick Dido's sad-attending ear' the 'story of that baleful burning night / When subtle Greeks surprised King Priam's Troy' (5.3.79–83)). But Marcus declines. 'Floods of tears will drown my oratory,' he says, and 'break my utterance' just when 'it should move ye to attend me most' (5.3.89–91). That is, as 'rhetorical man' he will fail. He won't be able to order 'the chaos of experience' with 'linguistic structures' and 'physical gestures'. In default, Marcus nominates a stand-in, Lucius, Titus's sole surviving son: 'Let him tell the tale' (5.3.93). Beginning, significantly enough, with Chiron and Demetrius – adopted sons of Rome – Lucius catalogues horrors: murder, rape, perverted justice, monstrous ransom, banishment, unholy alliance with Rome's enemies. It makes a sorry story. But when this public business of narration is done, when the crimes are exposed and the 'civil wound' is searched to the quick (5.3.86), the city gives a sign that mending – perhaps – can begin. With 'common voice', Rome names Lucius emperor (5.3.139). Only then does Lucius require private space, asking Rome's 'gentle people' to 'Stand all aloof' while the last of the Andronici, the only adult survivors, a chorus of two, 'shed obsequious tears' upon Titus's 'bloodstained face'. The son first, then the brother, weeps 'sorrowful drops' and prints a 'warm kiss' on the old warrior's 'pale cold lips', performing 'mutual closure' in these 'last true duties' (5.3.148–54, 134).

Closure in these last rites, however, is denied – or better said, delayed. For now the scene takes a turn it hasn't prepared for. Lucius speaks. 'Come hither, boy' (5.3.159).

The child who steps forward is a complete surprise. First appearing in the play only lately – in the Quarto he doesn't come on until 4.1 – and last seen in 4.3, the boy, Young Lucius, hasn't been noticed so far in 5.3. No stage direction in either Quarto or Folio marks his entrance or puts him on stage here.[2] Summoned out of the blue by his father at line 159, suddenly 'there', a material body that the stage must reckon with, the boy forces a radical reassessment of the scene. He requires readers – including actors, directors, and editors – to retrace their steps in 5.3, to reframe how we look at this *as a scene of child-looking*, its atrocity a spectacle the child watches, witnesses, or maybe performs. Precisely when does the child enter? With whom? How much does he see? What is he doing across those first 159 lines as the scene achieves its terrible climax: as, that is, the child's exiled father returns home, Rome's royals arrive for dinner, the 'table [is] brought in', his grandfather 'Enter[s] … like a cook' (SD 5.3.25), serves humble 'pie' (5.3.59), snaps his aunt Lavinia's neck (or otherwise kills her), reveals the house recipe for boy-bake, stabs the empress who has cannibalised her children and in turn is killed by the emperor his father kills? What is he doing as, subsequently, his uncle Marcus gives the nerviest speech of his political career – no wonder the strain shows in its metaphors – to persuade 'our Rome' (5.3.86) that it's not another Troy, that it hasn't been taken over in a Gothic coup led by Lucius Andronicus, a man who, to all eyes, including his son's, must look like a turn-coat? And perhaps the most pertinent questions of all: why does Shakespeare put the child in the scene? What theatrical work does the boy perform?

To begin answering these questions I need to return to the oddity I cited earlier, the 'new history' that enters the narrative with the child's entrance. Lucius is a schoolboy, and his exchange with his father over his grandfather's corpse, which reads like a mock examination that tests the child not just on rhetorical figures of rudimentary grammar and logical argument but on adult knowledge, gathers up in a final display the play's persistent interest in the performance of rhetoric. 'Come hither, boy,' bids Lucius, 'come, come and learn of us' (5.3.159).[3] What is the child to learn? 'To melt in showers' (5.3.160) – that is, to weep; indeed, to weep until the boy's flesh dissolves and his solid body changes into water, into rain. In rhetorical terms, metamorphosis is the object of the exercise. Gazing at dead Titus, the adult Lucius offers his son a precept or major principle – as if culled from Culmannus's early modern grammar school text, *Sententiae pueriles*: 'Thy grandsire loved thee well' (5.3.160). And he uses this principle to organise his speech, proceeding through amplification to demonstration and instruction, retrieving from the boy's prememory this history:

> Many a time he danced thee on his knee,
> Sung thee asleep, his loving breast thy pillow;
> Many a story hath he told to thee,
> And bid thee bear his pretty tales in mind
> And talk of them when he was dead and gone.

5.3.161–5

Marcus interrupts with an *exclamatio*. A cue for emotion, this interruption is also a prompt to action:

> How many thousand times hath these poor lips,
> When they were living, warmed themselves on thine!
> O now, sweet boy, give them their latest kiss:
> Bid him farewell, commit him to the grave;
> Do them that kindness and take leave of them.
>
> 5.3.166–70

The art of this rhetoric is persuasive. An apt scholar, the child translates his elders' learning into his own expression. He applies his lips to his grandfather's, kissing him farewell, and he applies his speech to the act of mourning. But almost immediately, utterance fails, literally choked:

> O grandsire, grandsire, e'en with all my heart
> Would I were dead, so you did live again,
> O Lord, I cannot speak to him for weeping,
> My tears will choke me if I ope my mouth.
>
> 5.3.171–4

Clearly, Lucius's speech to his son works as an exercise in rhetoric, and we're reminded by George Hunter that rhetoric – 'a science (or art or *techne*) of persuasion, an art, that is, of public activity' – is 'a science of *doing* rather than knowing, a means of power over others.' The object of rhetoric is 'victory', scoring points, winning, not achieving knowledge or 'understanding'.[4] Lucius secures parental authority, 'wins' his objective, when he persuades the child to give the pale-lipped corpse a kiss.

Strangely *unclear*, however, is the status of this persuasive reminiscence as 'real' history. Spectators may have trouble locating trace memories of a maternal Titus – a Titus who 'danced' baby Lucius on his knee, sang him asleep and hugged him to his breast – anywhere in Titus's 'real' past, the past established in the play's opening scene where the story Marcus told was of a general who had spent the past decade mobilised in continuous wars against the Goths, interrupting his 'terror' (1.1.29) to return 'bleeding to Rome' only on the five occasions when he carried home 'his valiant sons / In coffins from the field' to bury them (1.1.29, 34–5); the kind of 'real' past that produces the sort of Titus whom Kenneth Tynan saw on stage in Stratford-upon-Avon at the Shakespeare Memorial Theatre in 1955. Laurence Olivier was no baby-dandling nurse, not even 'a beaming hero', wrote Tynan, but 'a battered veteran, stubborn and shambling, long past caring about the people's cheers'; a man toughened by his trade, a 'hundred campaigns' having 'tanned his heart to leather'.[5]

Pondering these discrepant 'histories', I want to pursue two ideas suggested by Lucius's speech over dead Titus, and a third idea prompted by the theatre of the scene: first, that the duty of the child is to remember in story, to translate the past into the future by bearing 'in mind' and reciting 'pretty tales' that keep the dead alive in 'talk' when they are 'gone'. Second, that the function of story is not just didactic but affective, to instruct and to move, teaching both the teller and the told 'to melt', to change, to become, as *King Lear* has it, 'pregnant to good pity' (4.5.222). In some profoundly Ovidian way – and Ovid produces the core source texts for *Titus* – story operates a metamorphosis upon its listeners. It translates hardened men into weeping women, a translation *Titus Andronicus* habitually figures as feminised. And it's not just tears that turn leather-hearted men into women; it's story that does it. For in *Titus*, significantly enough, the stories that brokenly circulate, that keep coming round on a treadmill of pain, that men keep repeating, are stories of women. Finally, positioning the boy Lucius as a spectator, 5.3 positions him to 'look like a child' – a phrase, as I always intend it, that works punningly (and half the time, ungrammatically). It means 'to look with a child's eyes', to see as a child sees, but also 'to be physically a child', to be child-sized, childlike. Situating Lucius to 'look like a child', 5.3 sets an important precedent for Shakespeare's dramaturgy. Here in *Titus Andronicus*, early in his career, Shakespeare invents a theatrical trope he will use time and time again at moments of generic crisis, moments when the story he is telling hits a fork in the narrative road where it must either lurch into tragedy or veer giddily into comedy: he puts a child on stage, a child who looks and is looked at; a child whose look focuses with a terrible clarity what's at stake in the scene. In *Titus Andronicus* the child's gaze is generational and dynastic, and therefore (arguably) recuperative. But for all that, it frames potential futures that, as it happens, may ultimately offer neither consolation nor resolution nor consensus but more questions, not least because at the end, it's not just one child but *two children* who are left in the scene gazing (curiously? blankly? defiantly? uncomprehendingly?) at their elders: Lucius's boy, Aaron's baby. As these children gaze on, spectators are told to 'Behold the child' (5.3.118). Is the future we 'behold' in these children 'black' or 'white'? 'Civilised' or 'barbarian'? 'Bastard' or 'legitimate'? Or does looking like a child at the end of this play make nonsense of such categories? Is the look rather metamorphic, an agent of change? To explore these questions I will turn to Julie Taymor's film *Titus* (1999) to argue that looking like a child offers a 'saving' perspective, a perspective that translates Titus's tragedy into something that looks like comedy. To 'remember in story', to 'melt in showers', to 'look like a child': this is the work Shakespeare requires of the child in *Titus Andronicus*.

Becoming 'stories everyone will tell'

Remembering is one thing; hearing, another. What stories does Rome tell her children? Are Rome's stories fit for children's ears? And how, offering precedents, do old stories prompt the children who are the future to new business? Knowing the answers to these questions is crucial, for by the time the boy Lucius enters the Quarto *Titus* at 4.1, spectators are well aware that storytelling is how adult culture conducts itself in Titus's Rome. *Titus Andronicus* is a story that tells itself by telling stories.

Romans and Goths alike recruit stories from the past, bundling them into the present like hostages or oracles to speak against the current event. In 5.3, the Roman Lord needs a story. He summons Dido. Remembering the story 'of that baleful burning night' long ago 'When subtle Greeks surprised King Priam's Troy', and remembering the story of the retelling of that story to Dido's 'sad-attending ear' (5.3.82–3, 81), the Roman Lord sizes up his own story, the tragedy that has laid waste to his city, by glossing it against Troy's. Only the memory of Troy's streets running with blood, of Priam, clutching the god-stone, slaughtered, Hecuba wild with grief, the city betrayed, and like that city, another city and its queen, Carthage, later, too, betrayed; only a tragedy of this magnitude can offer terms for making sense of the baleful scene of carnage spread out, now, before Rome's eyes. Setting Priam's Troy against Titus's Rome, the Roman Lord understands their equivalence, the way they are the same: 'our Troy, our Rome' (5.3.86).

The play declares its interest in story from the outset. The opening is a sequence of three episodes that offer models of storytelling: the sons' electioneering, the father's triumphant return, the mother's plea for her son's life. First, Rome hears competing recitals of the self – literally, self promotions – from the sons of dead Caesar, Saturninus and Bassianus, delivered as campaign speeches to win Rome's votes. But they're shallow, callow stories. They lack depth-of-field, and immediately they're trumped by a better story, an epic story, reported of Titus, who, campaigning in deeds, not words, has finally 'yoked' the 'barbarous Goths', a 'nation strong, trained up in arms' (1.1.28, 30). Now 'accited home / From weary wars' (1.1.27–8), Titus Andronicus, as Marcus announces, is elected emperor on the strength of his *vita*:

> Know that the people of Rome
> ... have by common voice
> In election for the Roman empery
> Chosen Andronicus, surnamed Pius
> For many good and great deserts to Rome.
> A nobler man, a braver warrior,
> Lives not this day within the city walls ....
> Ten years are spent since first he undertook
> This cause of Rome and chastised with arms
> Our enemies' pride; five times he hath returned
> Bleeding to Rome, bearing his valiant sons
> In coffins from the field.
>
> 1.1.20–35

Not insignificantly, story works here not just by remembering deeds but by discovering a backstory, a precedent to Titus's personal history coded in his honorific. Titus is 'Surnamed Pius', and that surname affiliates him with Virgil's 'Pius Aeneas', founder of Rome, an affiliation that releases into Titus's present a flood of testimony from antiquity. As the scene continues, more backstory emerges: Titus has a daughter named Lavinia, namesake of Aeneas's Latin bride in Virgil, the 'mother' of Rome. His eldest son is Lucius, recalling Lucius Junius Brutus, the republican hero who, outraged by the rape of his kinswoman, Lucretia, threw the Tarquin tyrants out of Rome. Precedents like these inform the Andronici dynastically and tie their stories to Rome's heroic origins.[6] But as a function of memory, precedent does something more. It suggests that the story being told is merely the latest in a series, the surface of a palimpsest that produces human biography as a continuous rewriting and imperfect erasing of what went before, human remains layering stratum upon stratum the sediment of memory's report, no one uncontaminated by the past, which drains freely into the present: ancestors are conduits; children, cisterns that may be clear or contaminated. Crucially, then, the present must observe the seepage and manage the flow. Good storytellers understand this; bad ones don't.

When Titus enters at 1.1.173 and begins telling his own story, residual histories surface – some consciously called up, but others apparently arriving unbidden. The question is how knowingly Titus manages these stories – and to what effect. At line 82 he deploys precedent consciously. Wearing the victor's wreath, flanked by captive Goths on one side, his family's 'poor remains, alive and dead' (1.1.84) on the other, preparing to bury the latest tranche of Andronici boys killed in Rome's defence,

Roman Titus suddenly, passingly, remembers Troy – and another father of 'valiant sons'. The 'five-and-twenty' Titus counts his own are, he says, just 'Half of the number that King Priam had' (1.1.82–3). As he's speaking, however, Titus is simultaneously citing another precedent. Not uttered. Written on his body. He has returned to Rome, he says, 'bound with laurel boughs' (1.1.77) – the victor's wreath. That marks him as Apollo's proxy, for the laurel is exclusively Apollo's sign, adopted his sacred emblem in Book I of Ovid's *Metamorphoses* where (in Golding's Elizabethan translation) the god promotes the laurel's 'boughes and braunches lythe' to special dignity, to a unique memorial future:

> Thou shalt adorne my golden lockes [he tells the laurel], and eke
> my pleasant Harpe,
> Thou shalt adorne my Quyver full of shaftes and arrowes sharpe.[7]

In perpetuity, the laurel will crown those whose acts are dedicated to Apollo's patronage:

> Thou shalt adorne the valiant knyghts and royall Emperours:
> When for their noble feates of armes like mightie conquerours,
> Triumphantly with stately pompe up to the Capitoll,
> They shall ascende with solemne traine that doe their deedes
> extoll.
>
> Book I, 687–90

Titus fits this projection to the letter. But what about the history it inscribes? We remember what every Roman (and Elizabethan) schoolboy knows, versed in Ovid: that Apollo is only doing all this as an act of memorial remorse. For the laurel was once a girl, Daphne. Who changed into the tree to escape Apollo – and rape. Wearing 'daphne', does Titus remember the metamorphosis remembered in the 'victory' wreath – and the original outrage it tropes?[8] Just how much of the old story makes it into the newest redaction? Do such precedents signal the Andronici as heirs not only to Aeneas and Lucius Junius Brutus but to Daphne and Lucrece, a history stained with stories of rape?

If the ambiguous laurel cannot, finally, be deciphered, the earlier citation of King Priam remains equally problematic and curiously flat. Is it contrastive or comparative – does Priam (with his *fifty* sons) figure Titus half the man or as much the father as Priam, yielding, like him, all his sons to 'our Troy, our Rome'? Or is the citation ironic? Burying yet more sons, has Rome learned nothing from Troy? For now, Titus uses story like a poor rhetorician, more occupied with the *verba* of his citations than the *res* – merely the words, not the matter – while his allusions (from Latin, *alludo*, 'to play with') bring into play secondary sources or backstories that serve only to baffle the present.[9] The process of the play will teach Titus a thing or two. Like Lear learning to 'See better' (1.1.156), Titus will learn to 'play with' better. In the play's opening scene, however, the obvious contrast is with Tamora.

Lucius has demanded 'the proudest prisoner of the Goths', Tamora's first-born son, for sacrifice *Ad manes fratrum*

> Before this earthly prison of their bones,
> That so the shadows be not unappeased,
> Nor we disturbed with prodigies on earth.
>
> 1.1.99, 101–4

Tamora fiercely resists: 'must my sons be slaughtered in the streets,' she demands, 'For valiant doings in their country's cause?' (1.1.115–16). She invokes an immediate precedent, Lucius's brothers, those same 'shadows' of the Andronici dead that, hanging around for post-mortem appeasement (according to Lucius), yet 'hover on the dreadful shore of Styx' (1.1.91). But, urges Tamora, it's precisely their life story that warrants her sons' actions and their example that urges mercy. Sons on both sides are more alike than different: 'our Roman, our Goth'. For if, argues Tamora,

> to fight for king and commonweal
> Were piety in thine, it is in these.
>
> 1.1.117–18

Then Tamora warns: 'Andronicus, stain not thy tomb with blood' (119). It's good advice. Authorised by precedent. The story she undoubtedly has in mind takes memory back – again – to Troy. To another tomb – Achilles's – and to another 'unappeased' shadow – his – that disturbs the living with 'prodigies on earth'. In the story that Golding's Ovid tells in Book XIII, dead Achilles, 'rysing gastly from the ground' (529), accuses Agamemnon of forgetting. The war is over; the Greeks have won; burnt-out Troy lies smouldering; the child Astyanax, Priam's grandson and heir, is dead, thrown from the last tower still standing over Ilium; Hecuba, found 'amid / The tumbes in which her sonnes were layd' (509–10), has only time to seize 'a crum of Hectors dust' before she is dragged to the ships where the Greeks have hoisted sails for home. But – it must be some god's doing – the fleet is storm-beaten onto the coast of Thrace. There, Achilles's 'cruell ghost' threatens them. He wants to be remembered with 'dew honour', not forgotten, not 'buryed in the dust' outside Troy (534, 533). So he orders a blood sacrifice: 'Let Polyxene ... bee slayne upon my grave' (535), a sacrifice Golding's Ovid calls 'cursed' (540) (and Seneca's Agamemnon in *The Trojan Women* considers mad: 'Where is such custom known?' he asks. 'Where is man's life / Poured out in payment to the human dead?'[10]). In Ovid Polyxene dies fearless – only pausing to observe with devastating understatement (given the immediate futures Ulysses, Agamemnon and the others have in front of them) that with 'such a sacrifyse no God yee can delyght' (552). As the blood of one daughter oiled the Greeks' entrance into this war, the blood of another lubricates their exit. No good comes from either. The precedent is clear.[11] And so is its message: 'stain not thy tomb with blood'.

But Titus won't hear it. So as Tamora's eyes turn to see Alarbus metamorphosed – his body already lopped and fed to 'the sacrificing fire', rising in 'smoke like incense' to 'perfume the sky' (1.1.47–8) – her second son, Demetrius, proposes another precedent to gloss the event. It's a precedent that translates Tamora from wailing queen to tiger:

> The self-same gods that armed the queen of Troy
> With opportunity of sharp revenge
> Upon the Thracian tyrant in his tent
> May favour Tamora, the queen of Goths ...
> To quit the bloody wrongs upon her foes.
>
> 1.1.139–44

Here, in Demetrius's citation, is more Troy, more Hecuba, more slaughter in the household of King Priam. And more story that every schoolboy knows. In this latest reference to Ovid, the story has reached the point where Achilles's death wish has been fulfilled: Polyxene has been sacrificed, and Hecuba is kneeling on the shore, washing her daughter's body in the shallows. Like flotsam on the waves another corpse rolls up. A small body. A child's. Its throat slashed. Which of the gods can be delighted by this 'sacrifice'? The child is Polydore, Hecuba's last, her youngest son, sent in infancy as a 'nurcechyld' to the King of Thrace to 'bee out of daunger from the warres' (519), now strangely returned to his mother, murdered by the foster father. (Seeing what was in store for Troy, practical Polymnestor decided to cut his losses.) Recognising Polydore, Hecuba's women 'shreeked out'. But Hecuba herself 'was dumb for sorrow' (645):

> The anguish of her hart forclosde as well her speech as eeke
> Her teares devowring them within. Shee stood astonyed leeke
> As if she had beene stone …
> Shee looked on the face of him that lay before her killd.
> Sumtymes his woundes, (his woundes I say) shee specially behilld.
> And therwithall shee armd her selfe and furnisht her with ire:
> Wherethrough as soone as that her hart was fully set on fyre,
> As though shee still had beene a Queene, to vengeance shee her bent
> Enforcing all her witts to fynd some kynd of ponnishment.
>
> Book XIII, 646–55

Polydore's wounds (his wounds told *twice*) teach Hecuba revenge. The queen contrives a meeting with Polymnestor, and when the bald-faced murderer swears 'With flattring and deceytfull toong' (666) to continue her (dead) child's protector, she leaps at him. As Golding's Ovid tells it, Hecuba

> Did in the traytors face bestowe her nayles, and scratched out
> His eyes, her anger gave her hart and made her strong and stout.
> Shee thrust her fingars in as farre as could bee, and did bore
> Not now his eyes (for why his eyes were pulled out before)
> But bothe the places of the eyes berayd with wicked blood.
>
> Book XIII, 673–7

Hecuba's story, then, offers Tamora a pair of precedents: the grieving mother 'astonyed' in her sorrow; the Fury, 'all her witts' applied 'to … ponnishment', boring savage 'fingars' into empty, bleeding eye sockets. Both stories teach Tamora to change, but not 'to melt'. And they teach her to imitate not just the *verba* of the story but the *res*.

The three episodes of storytelling that open *Titus Andronicus* – the sons', the father's, the mother's: curtain-raisers to the play's larger storytelling project – suggest some ways of theorising the play's impulse to 'storicise'. To tell a story is to fashion a self – indeed, in *Titus Andronicus*, it is the chief way to fashion a self. And to recruit others stories to that business is to inform the self with other selves. In story, the past is reanimated to supply examples as living instructions to the present for action in the future: 'What's past is prologue' (*The Tempest*, 2.1.258). Memory, then, is crucial to storytelling because memory carries the traffic between past and present, between example and imitation. The patron of story is Memory – who, it should be remembered, is also the Mother of the Muses. And Memory mobilises story as the agent of cultural renovation: stories *of* change *effect* change.[12]

Formally, stories organise experience (or better said, *reorganise* it) into something the storyteller wants told. They give shape to the formlessness of events, most basically by marking beginnings and endings (even as they problematise the very notion of beginning and ending). Extracted, limited, shaped, packaged as *exempla*, stories are turned to discursive application: instructive or consoling, heuristic or hortatory, warning, advising, interpreting, analysing, inciting, motivating. Stories offer cultures a way of making sense of themselves, or of telling lies about themselves, or even of avoiding themselves. They're a kind of talking cure for cultural anxiety or perplexity that provide a 'space between' for the duration of the telling, a 'pass time' for cultural recuperation and regrouping before re-entry into 'real' history. Thus Dido sits listening to Troy's story; and Titus at the end of 3.2 exits with Lavinia to her 'closet' to 'read … / Sad stories chanced in the times of old' (3.2.83–4). Of course, the application of story is only ever approximate. Some details from the source won't fit. There will be too much story – or not enough. Stories, then, will always say more than they mean – or less. Only ever allusive, their very allusiveness is constitutive of the work story does, for allusion is a way of bringing discrepancy into play, and marking difference is as significantly the function of story as identifying similarity, not least because stories, it turns out, are the way adults talk to the young.

In *Titus Andronicus* (as in *Metamorphoses* or the *Aeneid*) individuals telling their life stories simultaneously tell stories of national formation and the configuration of national identity – what historians call 'social memory'. Rome's story is Aeneas's story; Troy's is Hecuba's; Titus's Rome is his story read against Aeneas's, handed down from one Lucius to the next. But if stories 'tell' a nation and 'belong' to a culture, nevertheless, no culture has a monopoly on the stories that are told. Being portable, travelling from mouth to mouth or from book to book, stories can be translated, hijacked, refashioned, appropriated to tell other national stories or to undo 'the' national story, 'telling' the nation to be a site of struggle or difference. And in this process, forgetting (what Peter Burke calls 'social amnesia') is as important as remembering.[13] Thus, Trojan Hecuba, like Trojan Aeneas, tells a Trojan story. Then that story is adopted as Roman, absorbed into the new myth of nation. That is, it becomes material to authenticate the *translatio imperii*, to document the transmission of civilisation, the inheritance from the burnt-out culture of the East to the phoenix rising out of Troy's ashes in the West, 'our Troy, our Rome'. But in *Titus*, Hecuba's story is 'captured' by the enemy and barbarised (or is the barbarian 'civilised' in the capture?). Hecuba, the captive queen, the grieving mother, the Fury (a bit of the story that amnesiac Rome seems inclined to forget) serves as Tamora's paradigm and, stunningly, legitimates her revenge, 'our Trojan, our Goth'.

Clearly, story sustains a relationship with time. But what is its relationship with truth? The story of Titus nursing baby Lucius: is it *true*? This turns out to be the wrong question. For Shakespeare and his contemporaries, the 'truth' status of the story matters little; what matters is that stories *work*. Stories get things done. Stories are performatives. For this reason Erasmus in *De Copia* – a text every Elizabethan schoolboy knew – advises the orator – whose object, always, is persuasion – that he should be equipped with a rich store of examples both old and new: and he ought not merely to know those which are recorded in history or transmitted by oral tradition or occur from day to day, but should not neglect even those fictitious examples invented by the great poets. For while the former have the authority of evidence or even of legal decisions, the latter also either have the warrant of antiquity or are regarded as having been invented by great men to serve as lessons to the world.[14]

As this argument goes, fables, Jonathan Bate comments, 'have all the rhetorical power of histories.'[15] More than that, the stories of history, the stories of gossip (Erasmus's 'oral tradition'), the stories of daily experience, and the stories invented by the poets (which employ history, gossip, experience, and fabulous invention) all possess equal authority as 'examples'. When fable works like history, when fable 'lies like truth', the rhetorical paradigm is operating that will license Iago – and damn Macbeth. Stories, then, are potentially dangerous. They can mystify; they can lie – and get results. So Tamora in 2.2 will invent a luridly preposterous story about her doings in the forest, not, as she contrives it, an assignation with Aaron but ''ticed ... hither' by Bassianus and Lavinia to her own assassination. 'They showed me this abhorred pit,' she tells the sons who have shown up in the nick of time to 'save' her. 'They told me ...,' she goes on; 'they told me ...'; 'they called me foul adulteress ...' This story's sensational *copia* persuades action: 'Revenge it as you love your mother's life,' she urges (2.2.92, 98, 99, 106, 109, 111). And the boys do.

Almost at the end of his life Titus Andronicus, seeking instruction from the past, cites a final story from antiquity and asks his dinner guest to interpret it:

> My lord the emperor, resolve me this:
> Was it well done of rash Virginius
> To slay his daughter with his own right hand,
> Because she was enforced, stained and deflowered?

5.3.35–8

The audience is a lot smarter than Saturninus at this moment. The story they hear ironically discloses its correct interpretation. 'Rash' and 'right hand' are giveaways, for Titus *is* neither, *has* neither.[16] Anyway, Saturninus produces his 'reason' and Titus responds,

> A reason mighty, strong, and effectual;
> A pattern, precedent, and lively warrant
> For me, most wretched, to perform the like.

5.3.42–4

He kills his daughter, and with his daughter, her shame and his sorrow. But in making the story of Virginius 'A pattern, precedent, and lively warrant', Titus demonstrates just how far he has travelled from his unconsidered citation of history in the opening scene. Now he understands how story works. A 'pattern' (deriving from Middle English and French, 'patron') is 'the original proposed to imitation; the archetype; also 'anything fashioned ... to serve as a model', a 'design, plan or outline'.[17] A 'precedent' is 'a forerunner', an 'example ... for subsequent cases' 'worthy to be followed or copied' and one that justifies 'some similar act'.[18] And a 'warrant may be either a person or a document': someone who 'protects or authorizes', 'an authoritative witness', 'one whose command justifies an action'; but also 'a conclusive proof', a 'justifying reason or ground for an action', a writ of execution.[19] All of these senses of meaning play across each other in Titus's citation of Virginius's story, all of them nuancing the story and slightly shifting its application. Perhaps most teasing is that word 'lively', playing oxymoronically against the sense of death in 'warrant'. It may mean 'striking'.[20] But for Shakespeare's contemporaries the clearest echo was likely to have been the Book of Common Prayer, which, in that great prayer 'for the whole State of Christes Churche militant here in earth', asks that 'grace' be given clergy 'that they maye ... set foorth' God's 'true and lyuelye woorde'.[21] Scripture is understood to be 'alive', 'life-giving', 'living'. Stories, then, potentially present not just striking examples, but living examples. And the hard application of such 'lively-ness' is to understand the terrible paradox of Lavinia's (like Lucrece's) death: dead, she is alive. Dead, she lives in story. Dead, she preserves the future story of Rome.

Where is the boy Lucius in all this? Is he on stage at 5.3.45 to hear his grandfather cite Virginius and then to translate into action the 'precedent' quoted in the 'pattern' which provides the 'lively warrant' for his aunt's execution, 'Die, die, Lavinia'? If so, if he's listening, he hears his grandfather becoming story, for in this newest telling of the ancient tale,

Titus inserts himself into the narrative: he makes himself Virginius. If, in addition, young Lucius is also *watching*, he *sees* Titus becoming story. Sprawled across the bloody banquet table still looking 'like a cook' in that bizarre 'attire' that renders his hospitality a black joke and the image comically grotesque, Titus performs in a spectacle that translates him into death, into 'history', and into material for other storytellers – who immediately pick up the scattered pieces and begin to 'knit again' another story, another 'pattern, precedent and lively warrant'. So Lucius calls to his son: 'Come hither, boy'. And starts: 'Thy grandfather loved thee well.' Every act of narrative culminates, finally, in an act of nomination and thus in a scene of recognition that prompts the next cycle of story.[22]

We tell stories; but we also become stories. Indeed, as Hecuba at the end of Euripides' retelling of her story understands, the point of human life, of the suffering that constitutes human life, is to become 'stories everyone will tell'.[23] Talking with the dead, talking for the dead, in storytelling we understand ourselves to be, proleptically, the dead talking. No wonder, then, that we impose upon the child the duty 'to remember in story'.

Dido's ear, Philomela's tongue

In Rome, the stories adults circulate among themselves – whether as 'real' history or cultural shorthand or legitimating fiction – they teach their children. There's no hedging their 'adult content', no expurgation. Ovid's vast and turbulent sea of stories, *Metamorphoses* (the core text Shakespeare raids for *Titus Andronicus*), is schoolboy literature. So are *Heroïdes* and *Fasti*, Virgil's *Aeneid* and Livy's *History of Rome*. (Shakespeare raids these, too, his borrowing in *Titus* 'deep, not wide.'[24]) Would we predict, though, that the stories that obsess *Titus*, that this male-driven, testosterone-fuelled play tells over and over, would be stories about women – Dido, Hecuba, Lucrece, Philomela? Stories of sex, betrayal, outrage, violence and revenge, these are stories that the schoolboy in *Titus Andronicus* memorises; stories that the play's grown men remember. They offer patterns, precedents, and lively warrants for male action; but more extravagantly, they work an Ovidian metamorphosis in *Titus*. They change men into women, boys into weeping Didos.

The four stories are connected by rape.[25] The bitter history Hecuba thinks she is finishing in Book XIII of the *Metamorphoses* began with her son Paris's rape of 'sweet' Helen more than half a lifetime earlier, and the aftershocks of that rape are going to be felt long after Hecuba's death, in Dido's Carthage, when those who survive the madness in Troy wash up on her shore. In the *Aeneid*, Helen's rape is remembered in the gifts that

Aeneas, the refugee and suppliant, gives the Queen of Carthage (in Thomas Phaer's Elizabethan translation): 'A royall pall, that all with gold and stones was ouerset, / And eke a robe with borders riche' ('The first booke', 623–4). For these were 'sometyme ... the wede / Of Helene bryght, whan Paris her from Greece to Troy dyd lede' (664–5). When Dido puts them on, they fashion her a new Helen – and reanimate memories of yet another rape, the 'original' violation: for before they travelled to Troy, the robe and veil, 'a wondrous worke', had been a 'gift' to Helen: 'Her mother Ledas gift it was' (625).[26]

As Virgil tells it in the *Aeneid*, then, Rome's ancient history began with that original abuse, the raped Helen (herself the child of rape) serving as a precedent warranting Aeneas' subsequent 'rape' of Lavinia, a woman already betrothed to Turnus when the Trojan arrived in Latium and claimed her as his bride of destiny. But the precedent also patterns out, centuries later, the rape of Lucrece, the outrage that marks the beginning of the modern history of Rome, when, in revulsion, the Tarquins are expelled and the Republic instituted. And both of these rapes are remembered in *Titus*: Lavinia is 'raped', as Saturinius has it at 1.1.409, by the man to whom she is betrothed, and raped again and again by another set of brothers, Chiron and Demetrius, Goths naturalised to Rome, who cite her as a second Lucrece.

Parallels and cross-references connect the four women's stories in a web of intertextuality. In Hecuba's story, a king of Thrace is entrusted foster parent to a child; in Philomela's story, another Thracian king is given the same trust, charged to 'love / ... hir' 'as a Father'(*Metamorphoses* Book VI, 637–8). But Tereus, no loving 'Father', rather a fantasist of sexual violence, is already hot for Philomela,

> As if a man should chaunce to set a gulfe of corne on fire,
> Or burne a stacke of hay,

imagery from Ovid via Golding that Demetrius in *Titus Andronicus* perhaps remembers, quipping, pragmatically, on the husbandry of raping Lavinia: 'First thrash the corn, then after burn the straw' (2.2.123). Supposed to be escorting Philomela to her sister Progne, Tereus instead conveys her to 'woods forgrowen' and rapes her (664) – the story told with brutal economy: 'so by force because she was a Maide / And all alone he vanquisht hir' (667–8). Philomela's first response is silence, but afterwards 'mazednese', rage. She threatens to 'bewray' Tereus, to 'blase' her wrongs: 'my voice the verie woods shall fill', like (she says) Orpheus, and 'make the stones to understand'. So Tereus silences the 'bewraying' voice.

'With a paire of pinsons' – pincers – he catches 'hir by the tung / And with his sword did cut it off' (709–10). In the bizarre sequel, the amputated tongue won't stop talking:

> The stumpe whereon it hung
> Did patter still. The tip fell downe and quivering on the ground
> As though that it had murmured it made a certaine sound.
>
> Book VI, 710–12

The grotesquely labouring tongue tropes the urgency to communicate, and voiceless Philomela finds a way. She applies a new 'techne'. She sets up a loom. What her tongue can't 'bewray', a new rhetoric of persuasion will:

> A warpe of white upon a frame of Thracia she did pin,
> And weaved purple letters in betweene it, which bewraide
> The wicked deede of Tereus.
>
> Book VI, 736–8

When the text-in-cloth is delivered, unfolded, and 'hir wretched fortune' read, Progne's reaction is silence: 'sorrow tide hir tongue'; 'weepe she could not' (742, 744 746). But her thoughts are racing: 'Ryght and wrong she reckeneth to confound, / And on revengement of the deed hir heart doth wholly ground' (746–7). Taking the feast of Dionysus as a pretext, Progne and her women dress as Bacchants and arm themselves with 'all the frenticke furniture' the festival requires (753). Thus 'gaddes terrible Progne', and when the 'sting of sorrow' maddens her, she feigns Dionysian ecstasy, a cover story that conceals Philomela, too, when she is found, freed, veiled in 'Bacchus mad attire' and taken home (756, 757, 767). 'Fully bent all mischiefe for to trie', Progne chafes, plots:

> This pallace will I eyther set on fire, and in the same
> Bestow the cursed Tereus the worker of our shame:
> Or pull away his tongue: or put out both his eyes: or cut
> Away those members which have thee to such dishonor put:
> Or with a thousand woundes expulse that sinfull soule of his.
> The thing that I doe purpose on is great, what ere it is,
> I know not what it may be yet.
>
> Book VI, 779–85

Just then, comes 'Itys in', her son – the double of his father. Seeing Tereus in the child instantly teaches 'hir what to doe.' As 'A Tyger' takes 'a little Calfe', Progne seizes Itys, kills him, chops him in 'gobbits', roasts him, and when the child is ready, invites her spouse to a private dinner where he swallows 'the selfsame flesh that of his bowels bred' (786, 806, 825). Full of meat, Tereus jovially bids 'Fetch Itys hither', then sits uncomprehending at Progne's reply: 'The thing thou askest for, thou hast within' (826, 829). Tereus's dumb doubt ends when, appearing suddenly, Philomela throws 'the bloudy head / Of Itys in his fathers face' (833–4). The 'tyrant with a hideous noyse away the table shoves', curses, tries 'with yawning mouth' to 'perbrake up his meate againe', weeps (837, 838, 839). Then, with 'naked sword and furious heart', he goes after Pandion's daughters (842). But they've flown, metamorphosed to birds.

Remembering Philomela in Ovid in such detail is instructive, for Shakespeare lifts her straight from the source into *Titus Andronicus* – lifting he conducts audaciously, introducing Ovid into performance in 4.1 when, literally holding the story in his hands, Titus's grandson Lucius brings a copy of *Metamorphoses* onto the stage. At that moment, what spectators see puts the story (of wrecked childhood) and the child (who doesn't yet know that Philomela's story, that Itys's story are the stories of his family) into terrible intimacy.

Equally, reciting Philomela is a way of remembering the other women's stories circulated in multiple tellings (both anciently and currently, in Ovid, in *Titus*), stories that childhood, too, inherits. Like Progne, Hecuba faces outrage with silence, 'astonyed'; like 'terrible' Progne, she goes mad. Indeed, in *Titus*, terrified little Lucius assumes it's Hecuba's story that he should read as the parallel text to his aunt Lavinia's 'frenzy':

> For I have heard my grandsire say full oft
> Extremity of griefs would make men mad,
> And I have read that Hecuba of Troy
> Ran mad for sorrow.
>
> 4.1.18–21

In her 'frantike … ramping rage' Virgil's Dido, like Ovid's Progne, is 'like a gide of Bacchus rout / Whan … thei run by night, / In freke of Bacchus feast' ('The fourth booke', 323–4, 325–7). She sees Aeneas as a violator of guest-right – one of Tereus's crimes. Like Progne, she forms a plan of criminal insanity, her 'mynde on madnes bent' (551).

All four stories cite the violation of women in the work of weaving. Women's work, 'home' work, weaving is the work of women's hands and households, but also, materialised in cloth, a space for storytelling.[27] Philomela weaves rape into her 'clout'; Hecuba, imagining captivity, sits herself at a loom, sees herself as the object of the story, once a queen, now 'a gift', 'Presented to Penelope' – the famous spinster – who,

> shewing mee
> In spinning my appoynted taske, shall say: This same is shee
> That was sumtyme king Priams wyfe, this was the famous moother
> Of Hector.

Book XIII, 615–17

Lucrece's 'incomparable chastity' is proven beyond dispute when (in Shakespeare's 1594 *The Rape of Lucrece*), surprised 'late in the night', she is found not revelling like other wives, but 'spinning amongst her maids' ('The Argument'); and Dido's claims upon Aeneas are figured in the clothes she gives him, woven by her own hands ('Quene *Didos* worke it was, her precioue gift of loue to hold, / Her self the web had wrought'), clothes that 'translate' him, naturalise him to Carthage: a 'roabe of Moorishe purple', a 'mantle' that 'from his shulders' hangs, '*Morisko* gise' ('The fourth booke', 283–4, 281, 282).

Most significantly, all four stories tell of huge acts of women's implacable vengeance. Lucrece exacts an oath of revenge from her menfolk before revealing Tarquin's crime and stabbing herself – a suicide that brings down the tyrant's government. Hecuba, 'forgetting quyght that shee / Was old, but not her princely hart', dupes Polymnestor into incriminating himself – then squeezes his eyeballs to pulp (Book XIII, 659–60). Progne's preparations in the kitchen are as elaborate as Dido's in the courtyard: one woman wields pots and pans and roasting spits, the other orders in the innermost court of the palace a funeral pyre built, lays it out 'in mourning gise' with 'all the robes' she'd given Aeneas, 'His sword', and 'faier' on this 'bed' his 'picture newe', this proxy marriage couch (with its proxy spouse) watered with a potion made from 'wedes & herbes of mischief' gathered 'by lyght of mone' with 'hokes ful hard of brasse' ('The fourth booke', 557, 558, 565–6). The effort is extravagant – but so too is the ferocity of the revenge. Hecuba's fingers slide into Polymnestor's brain; Philomela tosses the child's bloody head into play like a football; Dido, like Progne, fantasises atrocity:

> Could I not him by force haue caught, & pece from pece have torne?
> Or spred his limmes in seas, and all his people slayne beforne?

661–2

And she imagines visiting Itys's fate upon Aeneas's child:

> Could I not of Askanius chopping made? and dresse for meate
> His fleshe? and than his father done therof hys fyll to eate?
>
>   663–4

Rape and revenge, insupportable grief, fury, madness, mutilation and cannibalism, weaving and storytelling, woman's wit tirelessly fashioning retribution exacted with animal ferocity: these are the scenarios which Shakespeare's source texts offer *Titus Andronicus* – and the material they present the little boy Lucius, the one who's there at the end, looking and listening, tasked with bearing 'in mind' the 'tales' he's learned and 'talk[ing] of them' in times to come, doing something with them.

For stories, once told, aren't finished. Functioning in *Titus Andronicus* as collective social memory, stories go on performing cultural work. Held in common, circulating as shared discourse (not least because they were learned in childhood), they suggest what happens next. In 1.1, Tamora's Demetrius knows the story of Hecuba's revenge; in 4.1, so does Titus's grandson. Tamora, Titus, and the Roman Lord all know Dido's story. Tamora remembers the erotic Dido making love to Aeneas in a cave when the hunt is rained off (an episode she wants replayed with Aaron in 2.2). Titus and the Roman Lord remember the 'sad-attending' Dido who listens to Troy's tragedy and bids Aeneas repeat 'the tale twice o'er' (3.2.27). Aaron thinks about Lucrece in 1.1; Lucius rethinks the story in 3.1: the Moor proposes rape; the Roman, revenge. Aaron calculates Chiron and Demetrius's hopeless chances of seducing Lavinia: 'Lucrece was not more chaste / Than this Lavinia' (1.1.608–9) – but the mere mention of Lucrece prompts the through-line of thought. If Lavinia is like Lucrece, chaste, then Lavinia, like Lucrece, may be raped. Later, for Titus's son Lucius, who reads Lavinia's rape as an act of tyranny, Lucrece offers a political precedent. He promises to requite his sister's wrongs by replaying his ancestor, making 'proud Saturnine … / Beg at the gates like Tarquin' (3.1.298–9). Titus, too, conflates the act of rape with the act of tyranny through Lucrece's story: in 4.1, before Lavinia reveals her abusers' names, Titus thinks 'Saturnine' was the 'Tarquin' who raped his daughter (4.1.63).

Most devastatingly, the Andronici are forced to read and reread, and reread over with agonised attention to the text, Ovid's tale of Philomela. Again, it's a story Tamora's boys know by heart, first cited in Demetrius's '*Sit fas aut nefas*' (1.1.632). The verbal glance is at Progne, daffing aside morality to get at Tereus: 'fasque ne fasque / confusura ruit'. (Golding translates, 'Ryght and wrong she reckeneth to confound' (Book VI, 746).) Tellingly, Demetrius removes the line to the top of the tale. He doesn't associate it with Progne's revenge but quotes it to license his replay of Tereus's rape (an act of 'bad' reading I will return to). The rape itself darkly replays Ovid. Like Tereus, Shakespeare's boy rapists respond to the prompts the woman gives them: like Philomela, Lavinia won't stop talking, won't accept in silence her metaphoric place in the apophthegm, 'First thrash the corn, then after burn the straw' (2.2.123). Where Philomela promises defiantly to 'blase' Tereus's crime, Lavinia starts by begging. She would 'entreat ... a word', 'entreat ... a woman's pity' (2.2.138, 147). 'O, let me teach thee,' she implores Tamora, to 'open thy deaf ears' to what 'womanhood denies my tongue to tell' (158, 160, 174). But all these appeals to speaking and hearing, ears and tongues, are utterances that Chiron, like Tereus, finally needs to silence: 'Nay then, I'll stop your mouth' (184).

Mimicking the rape of Philomela, mimicking the mutilation of Philomela, the outrage committed upon Lavinia exceeds the Ovidian original, it becomes clear, when, dragged off in 2.2, she returns in 2.3. She has no hands. The blackness of this 'academic' joke gradually dawns upon spectators: knowing their Ovid, Chiron and Demetrius know how Tereus's crime was exposed. So they cut off that possibility – sardonically alluding to it as they mock maimed Lavinia with taunts to 'tell', 'speak', 'write'; to 'bewray', like Philomela, 'thy meaning':

DEMETRIUS: So, now go tell and if thy tongue can speak,
Who 'twas that cut thy tongue and ravished thee.
CHIRON: Write down thy mind, bewray thy meaning so,
And if thy stumps will let thee, play the scribe.
DEMETRIUS: See how with signs and tokens she can scrawl.

2.3.1–5

Moments later, Marcus finds his mutilated niece. He's Hecuba, 'astonyed':

If I do dream, would all my wealth would wake me;
If I do wake, some planet strike me down.

2.3.13–15

Only when Lavinia opens her mouth to pour out blood, not words, does Marcus connect this outrage to its precedent: 'sure some Tereus ...' (2.3.26). Appalled awareness grows in him that imitation has bettered the instruction:

Fair Philomela, why she but lost her tongue,
And in a tedious sampler sewed her mind;
But, lovely niece, that mean is cut from thee.
A craftier Tereus, cousin, hast thou met,
And he hath cut those pretty fingers off,
That could have better sewed than Philomel.

2.3.38–43

This awful recognition of associated crimes, however, remains dormant, or perhaps strategically forgotten – as Anthony Dawson might have it[28] – in the play for another two acts while Tamora and Aaron pick off Titus's children one by one then arrange for him perversely to embody the savagery they're so conspicuously organising by lopping off his own hand. By the end of 3.1, how nearly Tamora has succeeded in her Act 1 resolution to 'raze their faction and their family' (1.1.456) is confirmed as the Andronici stage a hollow re-enactment of Act 1's triumphal entry, the family assembling now as wreckage: Lavinia mutilated; Titus handless; Marcus, the stoic, railing; Lucius exiled; his brothers executed, their decapitated heads dumped with their father's hand at the family's feet. The scene stages desolation – in lines that strike grief to the heart: Lavinia's kiss 'is comfortless / As frozen water to a starved snake' (3.1.251–2). Lucius wonders in monosyllables that life can endure so much:

Ah, that this sight should make so deep a wound
And yet detested life not shrink thereat!
That ever death should let life bear his name,
Where life hath no more interest but to breathe!

3.1.247–50

And yet the family's crisis, like a fever, is about to peak and break. At 3.1.265 Titus laughs – laughs because, he says, 'I have not another tear to shed' (3.1.267); and while the end of the scene sees a stage emptied to near vacancy – Lucius left alone speaking farewells to absent bodies before exiting to 'oblivion' (3.1.296) – Titus's 'Ha, ha, ha' has somehow turned the tide of woe that he embodied when he claimed 'I am the sea' (3.1.226).

Then, too, the processes of desolation, of emptying, are reversed theatrically. Act 4 Line 1 explodes onto the stage with mad action that signals purpose, objective, even the strange beginning of restoration. As the Quarto stage direction has it, '*Enter Lucius sonne and Lavinia running after him, and the Boy flies from her with his Bookes under his Arme.*' Then: '*Enter Titus and*

Marcus.' In the Quarto, this is the scene that brings the child on stage for the first time, a scene that juxtaposes the exit of one Lucius, to 'oblivion' (to, that is, 'forgetting') with the entrance of another Lucius, flying (but not just 'flying', also 'remembering'). Those '*Bookes under his Arme*' are charged theatrical signifiers. They say 'schoolboy' as evidently as the dog and the thornbush say 'moonshine' in *A Midsummer Night's Dream*. Routinely, as Anthony Dawson points out, theatre 'invests the objects it shows with more than they carry in themselves', but in this scene, what they 'carry in themselves' is precisely the objects' most potent investment – for these books are carrying the texts of memory that disclose what Lavinia can't.[29]

In the blackly comic scene that follows spectators watch a grotesque parody of a school exercise, opening up to Marcus and Titus (rather dense, over-aged pupils) the elementary Ovidian text that falls at their feet, Lavinia 'busily' shuffling the pages with her stumps until she finds the tale of Philomela – the story that is *her* story. Set up to enact male incomprehension, the scene urges the men to study the woman as the woman forces the woman's story upon their readership, the open book – the text – standing in place of Philomela's textile, recalling the moment in Ovid when Progne 'unfolded' the 'clout' and read her sister's 'wretched fortune' (741–2).[30] But it's not just the story, or Lavinia's violent insistence that the men read it, that this moment codes female. It's also the *act of reading* itself. Bewildered by Lavinia, Titus asks his grandson, who first thought that, like 'Hecuba of Troy', his aunt 'Ran mad for sorrow' (4.1.20–1), 'Lucius, what book is that she tosseth so?' The boy replies, ''Tis Ovid's *Metamorphosis*; / My mother gave it me' and Marcus adds, 'For love of her that's gone, / Perhaps she culled it from among the rest' (4.1.41–4). A gift from his mother, a token remembering his mother and connecting her to the present in a network of love, the book – or more properly, the book's contents, the *reading* of the book – turns out to be a gift from his aunt. For Lavinia is the original Ovidian reader in *Titus*; Lavinia is the one who taught the boy to read Ovid's 'sweet poetry'. And her reading connects literacy – the written record of story – with a female line of exemplary, *storied* women like the mother of the Gracchi whom Marcus now cites as a precedent, pattern and warrant in his attempt to calm the boy's terror:

> Ah, boy, Cornelia never with more care
> Read to her sons than she [Lavinia] hath read to thee
> Sweet poetry and Tully's *Orator*.
>
> 4.1.12–14

(What kind of coincidence is it in *Titus* that another careful nurse to male infancy, the midwife who presides at Tamora's monstrous lying in, is also called Cornelia?)

Reading Ovid over Lavinia's bowed head, the men finally have to hand the parallel text that informs her 'martyred signs' (3.2.36), that puts legible coordinates on her 'map of woe' (3.2.12) and that translates 'dumb action' (3.2.40), pain, into forensic evidence of crime, a process that further translates passive suffering into active retribution – a change sensationally evidenced in Ovid where the story that begins with Philomela's rape ends with Progne's revenge. Titus in 3.2 imagined that he could 'wrest an alphabet' from Lavinia's 'speechless' signs and 'by still practice learn to know [her] meaning' (3.2.44, 39, 45). In 4.1 he learns how inadequate the body-text of dumbshow is, how much more meaning can be delivered using another kind of text, one written using the alphabet of memory. And just as violations committed upon the body of Philomela are translated by the body into something new (so that the victim of outrage becomes the agent of outrage's revelation), so violations committed upon Lavinia are similarly translated. Among the stunning metamorphoses the story effects is the Ovidian transformation of Titus himself. For if, by precedent and pattern, Lavinia is Philomela, Titus becomes Progne.

Like Progne unfolding the 'clout' in Ovid, it is given to Titus to read out 'the processe whole' of Lavinia's 'wretched fortune' (Book VI, 741, 742), to voice the three words written in sand: '*Stuprum – Chiron – Demetrius*' (4.1.78). The Stoic instantly lapsed, Marcus shrills for action, wants to 'prosecute ... / Mortal revenge upon these traitorous Goths' (4.1.92–3). Titus, by contrast, goes curiously slack, even conventionally 'feminine'. His immediate reaction is to remember Phaedra in Seneca's *Hippolytus*, '*Magni dominator poli, / Tam lentus audis scelera, tam lentus vides?*' (4.1.81–82)[31] and then blandly to daff aside Marcus's call for blood: 'You are a young huntsman, Marcus. Let alone' (4.1.101). So what will Titus do? Like Philomela, he will translate violation into something new. Something that will last. Be remembered. He 'will go get a leaf of brass / And with a gad of steel will write these words.' And then what? 'Lay it by' (4.1.102–4).

That is, like Progne, he will seem to do nothing. But like his Ovidian precedents, he will think laterally, like the women who are his patterns, like the Sibyl he invokes, adopting himself female (yet again) in a guise that offers a model of prophetic utterance and ties it oxymoronically to stymied communication – for the Sibyl's messages-of-truth, written on leaves, were notorious for blowing away before the suppliant had a chance to read them. Both Marcus and the boy Lucius are mystified by such womanishness. The child is ready to hunt the rapists to 'Their mother's bedchamber' (4.1.108). Unconscious of any irony, Marcus approves the child's 'manly' will to suicidal violence. But Titus proposes instead a womanish manoeuvre, a performance that uses the apparatus of manliness parodically. 'Come, go with me into mine armoury,' he tells the boy. 'I'll fit thee' – that is, 'equip' but not 'arm thee' – with 'Presents' to 'the empress' sons' (4.1.13–15). *Presents*? What little Lucius doesn't yet realise is that the weapons womanishly masquerading as gifts are a subterfuge as delicious as Progne's hospitality masking the 'foyld' chamber. And reading the gifts, Chiron and Demetrius will be as dim-witted as Tereus swallowing what 'his bowels bred'.

Turning now to business, Titus, father of twenty-five sons, takes on women's work with a vengeance. He has run the gamut of female responses patterned in Hecuba and the rest and exhausted them. In 5.2, with Tamora's boys in his grip, translated from pledges to victims, he finally demonstrates that his reading of Ovid comprehends not just *verba* but *res*; and where Chiron and Demetrius improved upon Tereus's instruction to rape, so Titus betters Progne's instruction to revenge. He forces them to simulate Lavinia's case. Bound, they have no hands. Gagged, they have no tongues. And in a replay of their brutal game of anticipation ('First thrash … then after burn …') Titus requires them not only to relive the crime they committed upon Lavinia but to imagine the crime he intends them to commit post-mortem upon their mother when, consumed, they will spoil her in a monstrous act of pollution:

> Hark, wretches, how I mean to martyr you:
> This one hand yet is left to cut your throats,
> Whiles that Lavinia 'tween her stumps doth hold
> The basin that receives your guilty blood.
> You know your mother means to feast with me,
> And calls herself Revenge and thinks me mad.
> Hark, villains, I will grind your bones to dust,
> And with your blood and it I'll make a paste,
> And of the paste a coffin I will rear,
> And make two pasties of your shameful heads,
> And bid that strumpet, your unhallowed dam,
> Like to the earth swallow her own increase.
> This is the feast that I have bid her to,
> And this the banquet she shall surfeit on:
> For worse than Philomel you used my daughter,
> And worse than Progne I will be revenged.

5.2.180–95

When Titus takes his knowledge from women, the violence he elaborates is extravagant. And the satisfactions it delivers to spectators in the theatre are primal.[32]

Learning Thisby's part

Learning to remember, learning to weep – the duties imposed by the father at the end of *Titus Andronicus*: for young Lucius, this is the stuff experience teaches. He watches his family's history, and he chokes on tears. But it's also the stuff his books teach, stuff he learns from reading. What happened to Hecuba in Troy, Philomela in Thrace, Dido in Carthage: these were earlier tellings of the Andronici in Rome. Titus 'authors' young Lucius. So does Ovid.

But learning to melt, if it's a cultural imperative that belongs 'authentically' to the time of the play (perhaps set in the fifth century AD; fictional Titus is a contemporary of Augustine of Hippo), belongs more immediately, more recognisably to the time of Shakespeare's audience. Such learning is one of the chief objects of humanist education, the kind of education Shakespeare received at 'The Kynges Newe Schole' in Stratford upon Avon – the 'grammar' – where, from the age of seven or so, he began reading the same books, shouldering the same cultural cargo, that young Lucius carries in *Titus Andronicus*. Shakespeare's literate spectators would have known those books. For the joke is that while Lucius's Latin *texts* are classical, his Latin *books* are Elizabethan. As theatre properties, as material objects, these books perform a stunning double take: they operate as anachronism – or better said, in a place where time folds over itself, where the past 'remembers' the future, warping to bring two presents simultaneously into view. (And not for the only time in *Titus*: there's a (post-Reformation) 'ruinous monastery' (5.1.21) in the play, and a Clown with a basket of pigeons who's really an Elizabethan Londoner time-travelled to the late empire.[33]) Lucius's Ovid and the other authors he's hugging – among them, Cicero – are classical texts. But they're presented on stage (bound into folios, or perhaps into schoolroom sized quartos) as Elizabethan books (and if Elizabethan books, then *printed* books). In the play, they're cited by their familiar Elizabethan schoolroom names (*De Oratore*, for Marcus, is 'Tully's *Orator*'), and some of these books clearly are not original texts at all but Elizabethan editions, schoolroom anthologies. (William Lily's *Grammar* must be one in the pile: the line of Horace that Chiron remembers at 4.2.23, having 'read it in the grammar long ago', comes from Lily.) As schools texts, Ovid and the rest are Elizabethan primers. (Indeed, their status as Roman 'Dick and Jane' is what first puzzles Titus. Why is Lavinia trying to grab them off Lucius? She is 'deeper read and better skilled' and could 'take choice of all my library' to 'beguile' her 'sorrow' (4.1.33–5).) Common culture, learned 'in the grammar', these books speak the *lingua franca* that connects all the literate players in *Titus*'s tragedy, young and old, 'barbarian' and 'civilised', Roman and Goth, man and woman. Lavinia has read them. So have Tamora's boys. And Aaron. But most significantly of all, when they land on the stage, Lucius's books bring with them not (or not only) a (fictional) fifth-century Roman attitude to the schoolboy and his reading, but a (topical) sixteenth-century Elizabethan understanding of what education is meant to achieve. Writing this play, Shakespeare is generalising his own experience, the 'reserved' experience of that part of the population – only boys – who attended grammar schools. Watching this play, every spectator in the theatre gets exposure to that school programme: to its agenda, its aims, its successes – or not.

One effect of Lucius's sensational anachronism – his (Elizabethan) Ovid, (Elizabethan) Cicero, (Elizabethan) Horace – would seem to be to insist that spectators read the past, the 'history of Titus', through contemporary cultural valuations, to apply difference as interpretation. Bringing on stage the Elizabethan grammar school syllabus, Lucius's books make spectators see *Titus* through the apparatus of humanist teaching.[34] They access and put into play not only what's implicit in the school syllabus, those core texts, but further, an Elizabethan theory of education and an Elizabethan model of pedagogic practice, both of which offer formal and theoretical structures for making sense of the knowledge *Titus Andronicus* delivers. Tied to the grammar school's primary, utilitarian objective – they taught Latin the way today's schools teach Information Technology – was idealist ideology, the humanist aspiration that, by learning Latin, boys would acquire texts that would inform them in the best practices of being human.[35] All of the reading, writing and speaking exercises boys did were aimed at this ideal.

Thanks to T.W. Baldwin, Walter Ong and others, we know a great deal about the 'limited but intense' school curriculum the 'Elizabethan' Lucius would have followed.[36] We know boys learned Latin by rote, beginning, aged seven, at the traditional rate of two words a day, moving on, aged ten, to memorising a book of *Metamorphoses* a year. We know they used Lily's *Grammar* for composition, and 'Cato's Distichs' for translation (laid out, as the title implies, in couplets set up as binaries). We see that, once learned, distich thinking installed rhetorical habits of mind that lasted a lifetime – in a Polonius or a Chiron, and certainly in a Shakespeare. We know that boys perfected their grammar with exercises in double translation: from Latin into English then back into Latin, the object being to match the pupil's efforts against the author's and to impress the original in his memory so that the precedent served as the internalised pattern for imitation. In this pedagogic scheme, memorisation was the method, and imitation (not invention) was the object.[37]

Moving on to the upper school, boys began reading the Latin poets in full texts, not extracts, and foremost among them, Ovid, not just *Metamorphoses*, but *Fasti, De Tristibus*, and *Epistolae Heroidum* (and more exceptionally, *Ars Amatoria, The Art of Love*). They learned versification, practised composition by writing epistles, orations, and themes, memorised tropes and figures, and turned writing into speaking, learning to pronounce 'naturally and sweetly without vaine affectation' – for speaking Latin was as important to the Elizabethan syllabus as reading and writing Latin.[38] Setting Titus's grandson in this school, we can see that he's versed in 'Tully's *Orator*' and well forward with his Ovid: he knows Philomela's story from *Metamorphoses* Book VI and has read Hecuba's in Book XIII. Clearly the grammar school regime, depending on memory, on learning proverbs, dialogues, even whole texts by heart, has equipped him to 'remember in story'.

But there's another part of the syllabus that interests me as I think about Lucius's prep in *Titus Andronicus*. It's the *ethopoeia* (literally, 'character making' or 'impersonation'). If, in composition exercises, boys followed 'recipes' found in various instruction manuals and learned, by imitation, to write in a range of genres (fable, proof, commonplace, praise, comparison, description) which required them to submit themselves, in writing, to the formal requirements of the genre, to 'become' the speaker of the piece, in the *ethopoeia* or 'speech for a character', they were set an extreme version of this assignment. For *ethopoeia* regularly required them to impersonate women, to role-play femininity, to explore 'being human' by becoming Other. And the point of 'becoming women' was to exercise (literally, in rhetorical terms) emotion.[39] In other words, then, the grammar school curriculum that comes discursively into play in *Titus Andronicus* when 'Elizabethan' Lucius drops his books was designed to teach boy-children precisely the lessons *Titus* wants learned, 'to remember in story' and 'to melt in tears'. And the way it taught them was by setting them the exercise Quince sets Flute in *A Midsummer Night's Dream*, to become woman, to learn Thisby's part. As it happens, it's Ovid who gives Lucius (and Flute) abundant material to play with – and just the right kind of material, an alphabet inscribed in the memory.

The early modern classroom inherited *ethopoeia* from both medieval and classical rhetorical pedagogy. It required students to use texts they already had to hand to evoke, according to set rhetorical conventions (repetition, variation, figuration), the feelings of a specific character in a specific situation, usually states of high emotion, anxiety or agitation. Marjorie Curry Woods, in important work on medieval schooling, tells us that these 'impersonation' exercises 'encouraged students to examine the psychological as well as the technical aspects of rhetorical techniques', and given that grammar school education was almost exclusively male, what's striking is that the *ethopoeia* routinely found its material in stories that focused on women's feelings.[40]

In 'one of the earliest recorded mentions of such an exercise', writes Woods, Augustine in *Confessions* I.17 remembers himself a schoolboy tasked with writing a composition in imitation of Juno's speech near the beginning of the opening book of the *Aeneid* where she, who has pledged herself to the utter ruin of Troy, expresses her rage and bitterness that she's being foiled. The immediate point of the exercise, as Augustine remembered, was to find 'the best words to suit the meaning and ... feelings of sorrow and anger appropriate to the majesty of the character he impersonated'.[41] But the larger educative point, writes Peter Brown of the (unfortunately lost) composition, was that it 'would have taught Augustine to express himself. He was encouraged to weep, and to make others weep.'[42] The affective aim of this exercise evidently impressed itself profoundly upon the child, for while, in middle age, Augustine-the-bishop, casting back to Juno, disdained her ('What has that to do with me! Surely all this is so much smoke and wind'), he admitted twenty years later that the *Aeneid*'s 'smoke and wind' still filled his head. An old man in his sixties, he remembered Virgil, 'the great poet' 'we once read as boys'. Such poets, 'Absorbed at the earliest occasion', memorised in childhood, turned out to be unforgettable – even to one headed for canonisation. Across the *Confessions* Augustine returns three times to 'infelix Dido', to identify with her pain at betrayal and to bewail her death.[43] For the boy Augustine, the *ethopoeia* provided the rhetorical space to learn to 'melt in tears'.

And that was exactly its function in the early modern classroom. Boys 'became' women to role-play 'feelings', to find 'the best words to suit the meaning'. They impersonated Hecuba speaking after Troy has fallen; Niobe, seeing her children lying dead; Thetis, gazing at dead Achilles; Medea, railing against false Jason. All of these were 'real' exercises set in Aphthonius's standard textbook, *Progymnasmata*. 'Infelix Dido' was the most frequently recited subject of *ethopoeia* in the medieval and early modern schoolroom, and Niobe was so firmly fixed as 'adolescent' material that she could be satirically dismissed by those (like Pico della Mirandola) seeking 'adult' intellectual fame.[44]

In the Elizabethan schoolroom the *Metamorphoses* offered boys a vast range of charged emotional speeches to impersonate, and Shakespeare's grown men – Hamlet, Mercutio, Lucentio, Lorenzo, Mark Antony, the bearded witches of *Macbeth*, the would-be actors, Quince, Bottom and Co., the serving men duping Sly, and of course the Andronici – remember Ovid's women. But more than remembering, by rhetorical repetition, by *ethopoeia*, Shakespeare's grown men re-cite the playwright's grammar school childhood, verbally cross-dressing, 'becoming women'. Lear incoherently threatening revenge upon his daughters, 'I will do such things – / What they are, yet I know not; but they shall be / The terrors of the earth' (2.4.275–7) echoes Progne. Prospero, summoning his powers – 'Ye elves of hills, brooks, standing lakes and groves' (5.1.33) – ventriloquises Medea in *Metamorphoses* Book VII (265–6). And Flute, elbowing Bottom out of the way, finally *is* Thisby. Her part in *Metamorphoses* Book IV,

> Alas what chaunce, my Pyramus, hath parted thee and mee?
> Make aunswere O my Pyramus: it is thy Thisb', even shee
> Whome thou doste love most heartely, that speaketh unto thee.
> Give eare and rayse thy heavie heade'
>
> (172–5)

is translated to the 'more condoling' version scripted by Quince:

> Asleep, my love?
> What, dead, my dove?
> O Pyramus, arise.
> Speak, speak. Quite dumb?
> Dead, dead? A tomb
> Must cover thy sweet eyes.
>
> 5.1.319–24

But I want to argue that another Ovidian text studied 'in the grammar' served Shakespeare's men equally well for women's matter, the *Epistolae Heroidum* or *Heroïdes* – and at a guess, I'd make this one of the books Lucius carries on stage in *Titus Andronicus*. Cast as letters written by illustrious women – Penelope, Phaedra, Dido, Medea, Helen (in all, twenty-one of them) – to their absent husbands or the lovers who've abandoned them, the *Heroïdes* are essentially soliloquies: passionate, grief-stricken, rage-filled, threatening, lyrical, cajoling, sexy, dangerous, uninterrupted voicings of the woman. Shakespeare knew them, it seems, the way Augustine knew Dido. Lucentio seducing Bianca under cover of schooling her in *The Taming of the Shrew* starts with the opening lines of the opening letter in the *Heroïdes*, Penelope's to Ulysses, '*Hic ibat Simois, hic est Sigeia tellus, / Hic steterat Priami regia celsa senis*' (3.1.28–9). Cleopatra waspishly taunting Antony 'What says the married woman – you may go? / Would she had never given you leave to come' (1.3.20–1) remembers Dido to Aeneas in the seventh Epistle, 'Sed iubet ire deus, uellem uetuisset adire' (which George Turberville translates: 'But God doth force thee flee, / would God had kept away / Such guilefull guests, and Troians / had in Carthage made no stay'[45]). Lorenzo stargazing with Jessica in *The Merchant of Venice* remembering 'Dido with a willow in her hand / Upon the wild sea banks' (5.1.10–11) is actually recalling Ariadne in *Heroïdes* X (a scene I'll return to).

Schoolboys like William Shakespeare and *Titus*'s 'Elizabethan' Lucius would have used *Heroïdes* for composition exercises – letter writing in the style of, let's say, Oenone or Hermione.[46] But they also used them for oration, that is, speaking practice, memorising a letter as they memorised a section of *Metamorphoses* – Thisby's part, for instance – then performing that 'part' in 'play'. Pedagogically, play was close to the hearts of Elizabethan educational theorists. (Roger Ascham in *The Scholemaster* wanted the schoolroom to be a 'ludus literarius', a view John Brinsley echoed, titling his 1612 book on education *Ludus Literarius or The Grammar Schoole*.) Play was built into the syllabus. Looking at the grammar texts, dialogues and proverbs boys were set, 'it soon becomes clear', writes Peter Mack, 'that the potentially tedious learning by heart and drilling' was 'enlivened by a spirit of play'. Erasmus's list of greetings in *Opera omnia*, for example, starts with conventional stuff, but soon moves 'into the inventive, the insulting and the absurd'. Thus pupils learned 'that language-learning was an opportunity for linguistic play and competitive ingenuity'.[47]

Learning became play when progressive and humane practices were instituted – something like Tranio's reformed academic regime in *Shrew* where 'Aristotle's checks' are to be relaxed, sweetened, by 'music and poesy', and above all, by honey-tongued Ovid (1.1.32, 36). Brinsley was clear on the usefulness of rote learning: it 'furnished' vacant minds and taught students tropes of expression. By 'perfect learning, & oft repeating … in their first Authors' – 'their *Sententiae*, Cato, Esops fables'[48] – students made 'not onely the matter of their Learned Authour their owne, but also his phrase'; 'so furnished', 'any man wil take delight to heare them.'[49] Moreover, a boy who memorised his authors word for word 'without book' made 'the very phrase and matter of their Author' 'their owne to vse perpetually' by literally incorporating those texts into the fabric of his being, 'imprinting the originals in his hart'.[50]

But learning Latin was not complete until a child could speak Latin. First came correct pronunciation; after that, decorum of speaking, turning memorised texts into 'live' speech. Students must 'pronounce euery matter according to the nature of it', especially, Brinsley insisted, 'where persons or other things are fained to speake'. They should 'vtter euery dialogue liuely, as if they themselues were the persons which did speake in that dialogue, & so in euery other speech, to imagine themselues to haue occasion to vtter the very same things'[51] – role play functioning here as an early modern version of method acting.

'Imprinting the originals in his hart' and 'saying [speeches] without booke' 'as if' he were the very person 'which did speake' moved the Elizabethan schoolboy from classroom composition to performance, from literary imitation to 'lively' impersonation, from learning Thisby's part to playing it. 'As if' made him a player, and *Heroïdes* aided the transformation by furnishing him with 'woman becoming' texts to play the part that 'encouraged him to weep, and to make others weep'.

Operating as saturated signs of this Elizabethan business, the books young Lucius carries on stage in 4.3 trope his metamorphosis from schoolboy to 'weeping Dido' as they trope Titus's from patriarch to Progne. But in *Titus Andronicus* Shakespeare does not unpack this business, rather leaving it to spectators to make connections between the boy, his books, and the imperative to 'learn' the 'woman's part'.

Elsewhere, however, in *The Two Gentlemen of Verona*, Shakespeare puts these things squarely in view by *staging* the complicated exchange *Titus* alludes to. Dressing as a boy to follow her love to the court, Julia learns when she gets there that Proteus has discarded her – from Proteus himself, who doesn't see through her disguise as 'Sebastian'. Worse, humiliatingly, Proteus engages 'Sebastian' as messenger boy to Silvia – who isn't interested in Proteus but only in the lover she knows Proteus has abandoned. Silvia quizzes 'Sebastian' about Julia: 'Is she not passing fair?' 'How tall was she?' (4.4.145, 154). The (double) cross-dressed 'boy' Sebastian/Julia replies:

> About my stature; for at Pentecost
> When all our pageants of delight were played,
> Our youth got me to play the woman's part,
> And I was trimmed in Madam Julia's gown,
> Which servéd me as fit, by all men's judgements,
> As if the garment had been made for me;
> Therefore I know she is about my height.

> And at that time I made her weep agood,
> For I did play a lamentable part.
> Madam, 'twas Ariadne, passioning
> For Theseus' perjury and unjust flight;
> Which I so lively acted with my tears
> That my poor mistress, movèd therewithal,
> Wept bitterly; and would I might be dead
> If I in thought felt not her very sorrow.
>
> 4.4.155–69

This textbook reply could have been lifted from Lily's *Grammar*. It's a perfect rhetorical set piece. The first three words answer Silvia's question; the next five-and-a-half lines rhetorically amplify the answer with illustration; the seventh line repeats the opening statement as a 'proof'. And the next seven lines figure as 'copia', further amplification introduced by that stunning *non sequitur* 'For' at line 163.

But for my purposes, what's more important is how the speech works theatrically to demonstrate by bringing them together the processes of impersonation and play that I have been observing. Two stories are told in this speech: in the first seven lines, in what sounds like an everyday story of early modern performance practice (exactly what the boy player performing Julia on Shakespeare's stage would have been doing), a 'boy' tells of dressing 'to play the woman's part', borrowing 'real' clothes to perform in the Pentecost pageants, a gown that 'servèd me as fit … / As if the garment had been made for me'. But this 'true' story of theatrical faking is itself a fake, an alibi or double bluff to cover cross-dressed Julia's faking it as a boy. In the second half, the speech moves beyond performance practice to the affect of performance, telling a story of 'becoming' the woman that Julia 'really' is under her disguise, but telling a story, too, of a boy player 'becoming' a woman, 'becoming' the role by 'passioning' the 'woman's part' – precisely, that is, the job of the actual cross-dressed Elizabethan boy player who is playing Julia. And what woman's part is it? Ariadne in *Heroïdes* X – a desperately 'lamentable part', the part of a woman betrayed, deserted, left for another.

In that story, woken from sleep to find Theseus gone, Ariadne (in George Turberville's translation) stands on the clifftops of Naxos calling after his fast-disappearing sails, 'Why? wither fleest?', and desperately signalling herself bereft:

> Upon a pole I hoong
> a flittering kerchffe white:

That might revoke to minde, that thou
hadst mee forgotten quite.

81–4

Soliloquising her sorrow, writing it all down in a letter (but how will the letter ever be delivered?), and savouring the bitter ironies of her situation, she imagines Theseus (who used Ariadne's insider knowledge on Crete to slay her 'brother monster' (155), the Minotaur) returning triumphant to Athens, while she, deserted on Naxos, will be savaged by monsters, 'shagheard Wolues' (166), 'ruthlesse Tygres' (172) – or worse than monsters, men. She foresees her miserable future, a death unmourned, like Tamora's in *Titus*: no 'mothers teares' (237), no 'friendly fist' (240) to 'close mine eyes' (239); her 'bones ungraude' (245), like Tamora's, left for spoil, for pitiless birds to pick. This is a part that ends in tears, with Ariadne imploring Theseus to imagine her: 'In thy minde survay, / Mee clinging to the beaten rocke' (269–70). She can hardly form the alphabet to inscribe her memories:

My carkas quakes as corne
enforst with Boreas might:
My trembling fist the letters marres
as I my lines doe wright.

277–80

Those same 'fainting fistes' (287) reach out to him 'through ouerwandring flood' (290) as tragic Ariadne ends her letter:

(Good Theseu) turne thy ship
with wrested winde retourne
Though ere thou come I die,
yet of the bones thou shalt be sure.

297–300

The 300 lines of *Heroïdes* X, as I take it, compose the 'lamentable part' which the boy player (of 'Sebastian's' supposed impersonation) performed in the 'Pentecost pageants' that are reported to Silvia. 'Imprinting the originals in his heart', he 'became' woman, acting the part 'so lively' that he wept real tears, tears that 'moved' 'my poor mistress', watching the pageant, to imitation. She 'wept bitterly' – such that 'Sebastian', in role, 'felt … her very sorrow.' In 'Sebastian's' speech, weeping for Ariadne takes on a double, triple, even quadruple charge.

Her plight performed (as Bottom might urge) asks tears in 'the true performing / Of it' (*A Midsummer Night's Dream*, 1.2.21–2): and so the boy player weeps 'for' Ariadne. But that 'passioning' draws tears from his spectator – 'my poor mistress' – that are reciprocated by the 'movèd' player inside the fiction. He (who should be weeping for Ariadne) becomes a spectator on his spectator – and weeps for *her*: his tears, then, make him *twice* the weeping woman. And the whole memory, by reanimating the scene and provoking fresh tears in 'Sebastian', covers the tears that Julia (under cover) is shedding for the heartbreaking situation she's in, while the scene itself acts as a demonstration of the school exercise young Lucius, 'Sebastian', Shakespeare, and thousands of other Elizabethan grammar school boys must have performed in their own version of the 'Pentecost pageants'.[52]

Teaching boys 'to melt in tears', to 'weep for Ariadne', the Elizabethan grammar school did not protect children from brutality and pain. There are no happy families in Ovid, as there are none in Shakespeare, and little Lucius knows his aunt Lavinia's story before it happens to her – from reading Philomela's. As boys encountered it in *Metamorphoses*, childhood was traumatised. The 'nurcechyld' Polydore has his throat cut, Itys is chopped into gobbets, and Phaeton is immolated as he recklessly, heartbreakingly, tries to prove who his father is. As boys practised it through *Metamorphoses* and *Heroïdes*, the 'speech for a character' taught them to construct a self by constructing a story. Ariadne gave them tools in a self construction kit: in her letter to Theseus she realises a theatre, recovering, in soliloquy, a scene, a stage, props, costumes, her performance. She produces 'play', and part of that 'play' is the presentation of the rhetorical apparatus for 'becoming' a woman. Becoming Ariadne, then, or learning Thisby's part, the schoolboy studies the grammar of emotion. It may be, as he passes into adult masculinity where reason regulates selfhood, that he must, like Augustine and Pico, repudiate the 'smoke and wind' of poetry, the 'puerile [literally, 'boyish'] questions' poetry proposes and the emotion that it codes as feminine.[53] Repudiation, however, will ultimately prove futile. For rhetoric learned by rote is written on his heart. The grown man will weep, and weeping, he will return both to boyhood and to the woman his boyhood played – like Lear, like Coriolanus, like Titus. In these terms, then, learning Thisby's part is not an alternative to adult masculinity; it's constitutive of it. Ovid, studied in 'the grammar', teaches not just the art of love but the craft of adulthood.

Looking like a child – or – *Titus:* The comedy

So far, I have been thinking about *Titus*'s Lucius almost exclusively in terms of rhetorical performances: the part played out in and around the text as it instructs him to 'remember in story' and 'melt in tears'. Now, turning to the third duty *Titus Andronicus* requires of the boy, the one implied by the others, the duty to look, to keep his eyes open and gaze unflinching, to witness, I make the move from text to performance. I want to read Julie Taymor's *Titus*, a film remarkable for the way it picks up Shakespeare's textual prompts in 5.3 and, while leaving most of 5.3 on the cutting room floor, translates those prompts into the film's visual idiom. In Shakespeare, the instructions to 'remember' and to 'melt' are textually specified. But nobody tells little Lucius to 'look'. Nobody has to. For looking is what the boy is doing in the scene, filling the gap of his silence with watching, all eyes. In Taymor, the filmmaker's inspiration is to lift this performance idea from the stage and establish it as the way her film looks: in Taymor, young Lucius's looking frames the story, which emerges as a story seen entirely through the child's eyes. But what does it actually mean in performance terms to 'look like a child'? Shakespeare's *Titus* script gives us little enough help, for in *Titus* the playwright leaves the 'look' of the part almost entirely unwritten. So to answer, I need to look elsewhere briefly first, at another child, Hermia, in another play, *A Midsummer Night's Dream*. Written about the same time as *Titus Andronicus*[54] and based, like *Titus*, on Ovid and *Metamorphoses*, *A Midsummer Night's Dream* is a play that makes looking both a privilege and a problem, simultaneously commanded and cursed, a test of what it means to be a child. Athenian Hermia gives us pertinent preliminary instruction for looking again at Rome and Lucius – looking at child-looking in performance, and *Titus* in Julie Taymor's film.

Looking at *A Midsummer Night's Dream* we see, to begin with, a crisis in looking arrangements. Twenty lines into the play when 'merriments' and sportive 'triumph' have been ordered up to distance the past, to forget the 'injuries' inflicted in the play's prehistory (when the 'triumph' was martial), Egeus comes crashing in upon Theseus's premarital tête-à-tête: 'Full of vexation … with complaint / Against my child, my daughter Hermia' (1.1.12, 19, 17, 22–3). Hermia is refusing to marry her father's choice. She has eyes only for Lysander. Retaliating, the child-changed father demands 'the ancient privilege of Athens', to 'dispose' of what is 'mine' 'either to this gentleman' – Demetrius – 'Or to her death, according to our law' (41–4). 'What say you, Hermia?' asks Theseus (46).

'I would my father looked but with my eyes,' she answers. But Theseus counters: 'Rather your eyes must with his judgment look' (46, 56, 57). That exchange, in a nutshell, formulates the impasse Shakespeare's most optically challenged (and challenging) play is going to explore, setting up a contest of looking strategies that *Dream* is never going to reconcile, only, finally, to finesse. The child Hermia wants her father to look like a child, with 'eyes' that metonymically figure desire, fancy, doting, the 'quick bright things' that dazzle and prevail upon sensible, impressionable youth. But the father looks different, with judgment: that is, in terms the OED (Oxford English Dictionary) gives us, with 'deliberation', 'discretion', the 'faculty of judging', connecting 'judgment' back to its primary site of meaning located in the judicial, in the law. Looked at like this, their stand-off is more than one of perspective. It's a stand-off of generic positions. Simply put, looking like Egeus, *A Midsummer Night's Dream* looks like tragedy; looking like the child, like comedy.

It is clear, in *Dream*, what the elders are objecting to: child-sight is giddy, as changeable as taffeta, as unsettled as a gadfly, antiauthoritarian, anarchic. But it's also forgiving, restorative (both reconstructive and medicinal), saving. Looking like a child is what the New Testament (a book – invoked when Bottom wakes in Act 4 – that's as much an anachronism in the Athens of Theseus as Lucius's printed grammars are in Titus's Rome) instructs us to achieve in order to understand grace and salvation, the new dispensation built on the ruins of the old, codified law. Culturally, looking like a child is liberating: breaking the rules means improvising, experimenting (in what Louis Montrose has called an 'anti-structural space'[55]) with alternative cultural possibilities that just might promote cultural change. It's here that looking like a child aligns itself with theatrical looking, for one of the triumphs of theatre is its capacity to play out scenarios that suggest cultural alternatives and innovation.

In *Dream*, though, Egeus never does come round to Hermia's way of seeing.[56] When, on the morning after the night before, the runaways are discovered asleep in the woods and wake (seeing 'double') to talk 'amazedly', finding their 'minds transfigur'd' (4.1.189, 145; 5.1.24), their rivalries transformed, their sick appetites restored to health, loathing turned to loving, in short, their world utterly changed, Egeus's world looks just the same. Still stuck in Act 1, he's still the *senex iratus*, still utterly rigid – and still saddling the play with a death wish, clamouring, 'the law, the law!' (4.1.154). Ironically, Egeus, like Bully Bottom rehearsing *Pyramus and Thisby*, seems to have no idea what kind of play he's in. Stranded inside an Ovidian narrative, but ignorant, evidently, of Ovid, he doesn't know how to read 'the plot'. He's unprovided with the key classical text that would inform him on the saving subject of transformation, the imperative 'change or die'. He's without a *Metamorphoses*.

That, of course, is where the Roman father has the edge over his Athenian counterpart. It seems clear to me that *Titus* and *Dream* are companion plays, Shakespeare as pseudo-Plutarch setting up Andronicus and Egeus as parallel lives and *Metamorphoses* as their parallel text. (Shadows of the other play tease their surfaces: *Titus* has the death of Pyramus in mind at 2.2.231; and the hunting scene in *Dream* that discovers changed children in the woods recalls the terrible precedent in *Titus*.) One difference is that Titus owns the better library. Spectators may think that he's slow on the uptake, that he should have thought about Philomela in Act 3. But when young Lucius's copy of the *Metamorphoses* finally falls violently open at his grandfather's feet in 4.1, its 'leaves' 'quote[d]' to him in the urgent actions of his daughter, Titus demonstrates that he knows his Ovid (4.1.50). He's willing to look different. Earlier, he refused to 'see! O see …!' what he'd done, killing his son, Mutius (1.1.346). But confronted with the appalling metamorphosis-by-mutilation inflicted upon Lavinia in 3.1, Titus 'Will … see it' (62), and he forces his son's look back when the grown-up Lucius (reduced to a child by the killing sight, his knees buckling) wants to turn away. 'Faint-hearted boy,' roars Titus, 'arise and look upon her' (66). To Lavinia Titus says, 'Had I but seen thy picture in this plight, / It would have madded me' (104–5). Then he asks, rhetorically as he thinks, because she cannot answer, 'What shall I do / Now I behold thy lively body so?' (105–6). What Titus does is what Lavinia, aided by little Lucius's schoolboy text and patterned by the boy's traumatised witness in 4.1, teaches him – to look like a child, to concentrate on seeing how Lavinia looks and, reading 'all her martyred signs', to 'wrest an alphabet' to decipher what she needs him to see (3.2.36, 44).

Bizarrely, Hermia's wish, 'I would my father look'd but with my eyes,' comes good in *Titus Andronicus* – and launches the black retributive comedy of the final act where Tamora's boys, those awful children Chiron and Demetrius, bound, gagged, able to communicate only with their eyes, become their looks, a grotesque refiguration of 'looking like a child', served up by Titus 'trimmed' to make their mother look at them with new eyes.

'Looking like a child' in my formulation is, as I said earlier, a *double entendre*, suggesting not just what the child looks like to spectators, his appearance, his presence on stage and what spectators make of it, but how he's looking, the act of his seeing, including how spectators look at him looking. The child Shakespeare puts on stage in *Titus* to trouble spectatorship is no isolated effect. Rather, Shakespeare, at the beginning of his playwriting career, was testing a theatre trope that he was going to reuse regularly across his work to rescale, recalculate, refocus, redirect adult investment in scenes marked as adult viewing. So, for example, in the closing sequence of the *Henry VI* trilogy, Edward IV will hold up a baby, his heir, to show that, after three plays and fifteen acts of slaughter, the Wars of the Roses are done – then he will invite his twisted brother Dickie to give the infant 'hope' a kiss (*3 Henry VI*, 5.7.46, 32). Banquo will stand in the dark, the moon down, praying the 'Merciful powers' to 'Restrain' in him 'the cursèd thoughts that nature / Gives way to in repose' (*Macbeth*, 2.1.7–9), the thoughts, that, acted, would make his life, like Macbeth's, tragic 'nothing'. Beside him will stand his boy, the child Fleance, holding his father's sword. Coriolanus, determined to burn Rome 'all into one coal' and to pack cards like a turncoat with the enemy to do so, faced with his child, will bless the boy's future (in a Rome the father has desolated?), praying that he will be the kind of soldier who will 'stick i'th'wars / Like a great sea-mark standing every flaw / And saving those that eye thee!' (*Coriolanus*, 5.3.73–5). Leontes, already feeling the killing 'infection of my brains', will scan Mamillius's 'welkin' face for the antidote, the medicine, the 'childness' that 'cures … / Thoughts' that 'thick [the] blood' (*The Winter's Tale*, 1.1.147, 138, 171–2). Cleopatra will draw attention to the strange nursling she suckles, which, consuming her, will save her life from tragedy as Caesar's spoil by turning her death into comic apotheosis: 'Peace, peace. / Dost thou not see my baby at my breast, / That sucks the nurse asleep?' (*Antony and Cleopatra*, 5.2.303–5).

Recent Shakespeare films show directors picking up Shakespeare's theatre cues, and elaborating them, inventing supplementary performance texts that, privileging children, invite the spectator to look like a child. For instance, there's the long tracking shot that follows Kenneth Branagh's *Henry V* (1989) as he strides across the blood-mudded battlefield of Agincourt carrying over his shoulder the body of the dead baggage boy, Falstaff's boy, '*Non Nobis*' building from a single voice to a wall of glorious sound that effectively hijacks the brutal image, thereby to incorporate child slaughter into the larger heroising project the film puts on offer. Or there's the opening sequence of Richard Loncraine's neo-Edwardian *Richard III* (1996) that, following on from the credits where the title is written in machine-gun fire, wipes out the brutal memory of war in happy images of the Yorks at play (this 'Edward' is David, his queen, Wallis, their reign the restoration-post-abdication that Hitler dreamed of). The camera catches the little princes, naked and delightedly shrieking, chased by a nanny holding out a towel – a sequence set up to rhyme visually with one later that puts the younger prince in tight close-up, playing, concentrating on the model train track running round the palace floor while behind him, voices off, the adults talk politics. Suddenly, a gigantic black jackboot comes down through the frame, stopping the train in its tracks. The camera cuts from the child's inquiring frown to the rancidly smiling brown-shirt murderer, Tyrell. Or from Baz Luhrmann's *Romeo + Juliet* (1996), there's the pullback from the close-up on Juliet's open, childlike face (almost a woman's, waiting for night, waiting for Romeo) to show her sitting on her bed in a room that belongs to a little girl, her shelves lined with dolls, what passes for a prie-dieu set in front of a teen-angel Madonna flanked with baby-pink cherubs. This is a sequence that rhymes strangely with the one just before it, the death of Mercutio, where again, the camera has pulled back from a beautiful, almost girlish face. But Mercutio's dying face is wrecked – and the pullback watches his dying watched by children. As a sandstorm kicks up and grit-devils swirl, desolating the beachscape, the film cuts to a little black girl watching from a beach caravan window. It cuts again to a pair of grubby Chicano children staring through the torn mesh of a chain-link perimeter fence, looking, powerlessly, like kindergartners watching the big kids trash the playground. Finally, there's the sequence from John Madden's *Shakespeare in Love* (1998) that has Will, on his way to his shrink to cure his writer's block, stop to talk with a kid who's torturing mice. Will's best play, says the boy, is *Titus Andronicus*. And this spoiled child is? John Webster.

What these earlier films take as passing reference Taymor's *Titus* makes its structuring vision, tapping in to an urgently contemporary, even millennial, concern with 'childness', with negotiating the emotive subject of the child in our culture, a negotiation conducted not just via representations in theatre and on film but in fine art, photography, the novel, the media, the internet.[57] Released in the US in 1999 and in Britain the following year, Taymor's *Titus* began its life on stage, as a production for Theatre for a New Audience in New York in 1994. The later film project, then, was a translation exercise that needed to discover a film language big enough, flexible enough, sophisticated enough to rewrite Shakespeare's dense poetic text in visual imagery. And Taymor found it: a highly self-conscious and co-optive language that revelled in meta-textual and meta-cinematic discourse, pulling in references left, right, and centre to other films, genres, styles, sometimes as homage, sometimes as self-conscious parody, quotation, imitation or unconscious 'remember-ing'.[58] Taymor's film cites children's (and adult's) literature (*Alice in Wonderland, The Hardy Boys, The Time Machine, A Clockwork Orange*) and other films (*The Silence of the Lambs*, *Mad Max*, Jarman's *Jubilee*, Fellini's *Satyricon* and *La Strada*). She quotes fashion statements (David Bowie's make-up, Brandon Lee's leather coat from *The Crow*). She borrows (consciously? coincidentally?) from Adrian Noble's filmed version of *A Midsummer Night's Dream* (1998) and raids both Jane Howell's 1985 BBC television *Titus Andronicus*[59] and Deborah Warner's 1987 Royal Shakespeare Company *Titus*. (This was the *Titus* that, played in close-up on the Swan stage, would have taught Taymor what the post-Tarantino generation understands very well about the genre T.S. Eliot called 'savage farce', that laughter isn't an embarrassment, an impropriety to be killed or gagged. Laughter in *Titus* belongs.[60])

In Taymor, John Brinsley's early modern *ludus literarius* is re-imagined for a post-literary world: the 'ludus' survives, but Ovid is out, Mattel in, and schoolbooks are nowhere in evidence, only kids' games. Taymor is interested in toys, in play, in the fantasy life of objects metamorphosing – and in the violence that toys trope. She manipulates ideas of space and time. Space is location, a 'real' fixed place; but it's also, as in child's play, a way of thinking about size and scale. Time is reckoned on a kid's clock (where, instead of figuring history and memory as it does for adults, time runs at unpredictable speeds, bulging, warping or lapsing in dream-time, reverie, fantasy, nightmare). Behind her camera, Taymor is interested in photography, in looking through *other* apertures to frame, limit and direct spectators' vision. (She shoots through open windows, through doors squeezed shut or flung wide, fissures in walls and pavements, eye holes in masks). She's visually fascinated by surfaces that work like lenses – rain drops running down a window, the domed glass of a specimen jar, water pooled in a puddle – and that, photographed, set up complicated looking economies. Most intriguingly (and ironically, given the fact that censors rated the film 'R' in the US and '18' in Britain, judging it inappropriate viewing for children) Taymor's *Titus* is seen almost entirely through the eyes of a child.[61]

The film's opening shot fixes on the face of a child looking straight to camera.[62] Only, to begin with, spectators don't know it. For the camera is too tight in close-up on the object that fills the frame for spectators to make sense of what they're looking at. Gradually, dissolving from a black screen to pin-pricks of light, the shot comes into focus as a pair of eyes, but disconcertingly, eyes not set in a face. They're looking out from holes torn jaggedly in what spectators can now see is a paper bag hood.

As the camera pulls back and we get our bearings we find ourselves in an American kitchen, circa 1959, at a table covered with toys and after-school food, and we see what we're looking at is a child who's wearing over his head the kind of brown bag mask that anybody of Taymor's vintage made for Halloween – a play mask that tropes masks military and theatrical, a mask, significantly, like the Greek mask of tragedy, that keeps its eyes open, unable to turn its gaze away from what appals. The lone masked 'man' at the kitchen table, it turns out, is watching another masked man – on TV: flickers of light from the screen he's watching bounce off the paper surface. As he raises a hotdog to his teeth through the torn mouth-hole, we hear noises off – 'Heigh-ho Silver!' – a cue to imagine the pictures on screen. The Lone Ranger, ushered by that tinny military bugle that always announces the 'good guy' in the Western, is spurring his white horse to the gallop, riding in with the cavalry to save the day – that most enduring trope of American history's nostalgic self-definition. But this 'toys' picnic' mobilises other models of masculine adventure and their killing technologies. It simultaneously both remembers an ancient world of violence and heroism and futuristically anticipates (in the post-Hiroshima Cold War era that the film is citing as its 'present') more terrifyingly apocalyptic ways to die: there's a platoonful of GI Joes on the table crowding out the cake, half-drunk glass of milk, mustard and ketchup bottles. There are World War II dinky toys and battery powered action men in motion. But there are also Roman gladiators and sci-fi robots.

In this adult-free zone we see the child's toys as more than playthings – as indeed the residues of adult absence. Toys, as Don Fleming reads them, function 'as a kind of cultural construction kit', equipping children to order the 'overheard' world of adults. They should be seen 'not as objects, or not only as objects' but as 'events' generating 'traffic – called "play"'.[63] But as David Cohen sees them – and politicises them – toys are 'the stunted hallmarks of a materialist culture' that condition children to accept the adult world.[64] Roland Barthes goes further. For him, toys '*literally* prefigure the world of adult functions', and this means that toys 'obviously cannot but prepare the child to accept' all those 'adult functions' 'by constituting for him, even before he can think about it, the alibi of a Nature which has at all times created soldiers, postmen, and Vespas.' Thus, toys groom children for adulthood in a world they have naturalised. As objects, writes Barthes, toys reveal 'the list of the things the adult does not find unusual: war, bureaucracy, ugliness, Martians.'[65]

Moreover, in Taymor's adult-free zone we see the continuity between consumption, violence, and play, and the tendency – almost a law of physics – for all of them, in performance, to exceed their texts, their rules, to go beyond the limits. So this space transforms before our eyes into a kitchen-sink-sized impromptu theatre of cruelty. The table becomes a battle zone, the kid in the mask, a monster, his child's play accelerating into frenzy. The Boy lops the head off a robot, slams his fighter plane nose down into the cake, trashes the table, smearing it with ketchup. Food becomes blood; bodies are dug into like Hostess Twinkies; culture gets symbolically dismembered as mayhem produces pleasure and jokey subject positions. The mechanical head on a wrecked toy crazily whizzes around 360°. This is play!

Suddenly, the Boy, twisting in pain, clutches his hands to his head as if trying to protect his ears inside the paper bag. His knees buckle. Leaping down from the chair he doubles up under the table – assuming the 'bomb drop' position that school children in the US in the 1950s were taught would save their lives in case of nuclear attack – as the kitchen window blows in under the force of a huge explosion. From smoke and falling debris, the camera cuts to the child being pulled out from hiding by a huge man. Burly, stubble-faced, he's a bizarre visual throwback to another age, in a grubby singlet, a prize fighter's belt over leather trousers and Godot boots, a World War I fighter pilot's leather bonnet on his head, the goggles up. The strongman yanks the paper mask off the Boy's head, then, cradling the sobbing child in his arms, carries him down the burning stairs (Taymor's take on Alice's rabbit hole), kicks open the front door – and steps into the past, a past absurdly animated by the Boy's own violent play. In a gigantic theatre of cruelty, a Roman coliseum, the Boy is lifted up like a trophy over the strongman's head, ancient ghosts roaring approval from the dark empty stone tiers. Once massive, controlling the toy world, the Boy is now miniaturised, the world's toy. Set on his feet, looking down, he's stunned to see one of his toys poking out of the wreckage. A gladiator. If it's a kind of psychic souvenir, retrieved from the mud and held wonderingly in his hands, it's also a monstrous prompt: there's a noise; the child's head swivels; the camera cuts; the gladiator *has come alive*, his mud-caked face like a mask. Behind him dozens of gladiators, exact replicas of each other, are marching toward the Boy like wind-up toys in clockwork precision, the antique world descending implacably upon him.

As this epic sequence proceeds – and it goes on for another three minutes – we see pairs of Roman chariots pulled by horses; warriors in authentic helmets and spears from Roman antiquity; but then, bizarrely, a squadron mounted on 1930s motorbikes followed by a company of primitive armoured personnel carriers that look like monstrous plated insects or the tinpot tanks that patrolled Dublin after the Easter Uprising in 1916. The war treasure is stuff from antiquity – gold breastplates, armour, masks, chokers, chains – but it's piled into a plexiglas coffer, which in turn is mounted on a motor-driven axle.

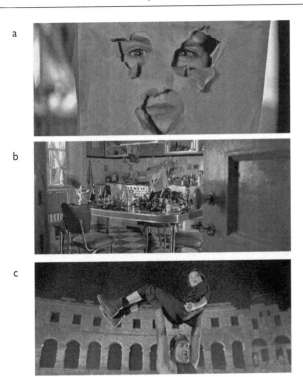

Plate 5 *Titus*, opening shots, directed by Julie Taymor. (*Source*: Clear Blue Sky
    Productions, 1999.)
    a Masked boy (Osheen Jones)   b Kitchen spread
    c Trophy child

Seeing as the child sees – and edits keep cutting back to the child
looking – we understand what he shortly discovers, that he's Titus's
grandson, Lucius, and that the past that has captured him involves not a
simple time shift between 'now' and 'then'. Rather, the past is 'then',
'now', and everything in between, a temporal palimpsest that displays
itself everywhere this film looks, showing the ancient world – its buildings,
its monuments, its statues, its civil habits and personal protocols, its style
and aesthetics – surviving in our own. This past is not 'a foreign country'
where they 'do things differently'[66]: the past is the ground we're standing
on. The primitive is the material constructing both modernism and postmodernism. With brilliant film aptitude, Taymor achieves on film using
post-modern pastiche what young Will Shakespeare achieves in his
playtext using early modern pastiche. Like Shakespeare collapsing 'the

Plate 6 *Titus*, opening shots, directed by Julie Taymor. (*Source*: Clear Blue Sky Productions, 1999.)

   d Childhood's souvenir   e Inspecting the toy
   f The toy comes alive

whole of Roman history, known to him from Plutarch and Livy, into a single action'[67] to make Troy, the Tarquins, Caesar and the Goths all simultaneously available to his story, Taymor pulls all time into the same frame. For example, in a later sequence, when she brings Rome's warring factions and their ideologies into confrontation, she puts Titus on horseback, the fascistic Saturninus in a black Mussolini car, and his 'straight', clean-cut brother in a white Thunderbird convertible, like Jack Kennedy's. As importantly, by transporting the modern child into the historic narrative (while keeping him always in twentieth-century T-shirt and trainers) Taymor mobilises for the purposes of the narrative contemporary analyses of its history. What is the relationship between culture and violence, she asks; between subject peoples and their conquerors, the colonised and the imperialist? When does cultural practice become oxymoronic, 'irreligious piety'? When does it become redundant, require us to seek new forms? What are we doing to the children? And what are the children doing to *us*?

It's only retrospectively that we'll really be able to decipher Taymor's opening sequence and to see the toys as more than transitional objects for ethical growth, as prostheses used, like theatre props, to 'simulate a rehearsal for real roles'.[68] We'll understand them as proleptic, cuing the film's worst – and best – moments, the child here literalising aesthetically, in play form, the violent actions that will be repeated over and over 'for real'. So the child's black, comic delight as he decapitates his robot prefigures Aaron's pleasure, presiding over Titus's joke dismemberment, and Chiron's glee, preparing for rape, straddling Lavinia's terror-frozen torso, slicing off the long row of buttons down the back of her dress. (Taymor's Rome, we'll see, is littered with body parts, hands, feet, arms fallen off monumental statuary.) As toys become life-sized playthings, so Lavinia is the 'doll' Tamora's ugly boys make their sport, transforming her from Grace Kelly to Struwwelpeter, her bloody stumps turned into macabre travesties of toys, stuck with dry sticks, a surreal prosthetics.[69]

Retrospectively, too, we'll appreciate the full implication of the biggest change Taymor makes to Shakespeare's opening, starting not with politics – the election of the emperor – but with play, the play of violence, violence as play – play politicised. It's the Clown who has rescued (kidnapped?) the Boy. He's Zampano, straight out of Fellini's *La Strada*, and the Boy is going to be meeting up with him again later in the story. So that unmasking in the exploded kitchen is significant.[70] The wordless look which the Boy and the Clown exchange face-to-face recognises and claims a continuity between their separate projects that it will take the rest of the film to decipher. Taymor sees the Clown as 'an interventionist in Shakespeare'.[71] When she aligns the look of this film with the look of the child, then immediately complicates that alignment by further attaching the Boy's elite look – he is, after all, a member of the patrician Andronici family – to the look of the low art, plebeian Clown, Taymor signals that the Boy, too, will be an interventionist. Further, 'low art' interventionism will recruit even Titus Andronicus to its practices: the carnivalised look of the bizarrely dressed strongman is the point of view that Titus will finally achieve as the Clown's double much later on.

Titus's triumphal re-entry into Rome initiates the Boy into the rituals of death and blood. Young Lucius helps his grandfather heat the instruments of sacrifice; observes his father return with the basin full of Alarbus's entrails; follows as the long row of empty combat boots, what remains of Titus's dead sons, is filled, libation-wise, with sand. He's initiated, too, into politics. Sitting alone on the steps of what any Italian viewer would instantly recognise as Mussolini's old government building, his so-called 'square coliseum' that will serve as Saturninus's headquarters, the Boy catches a stray newspaper blowing past, reads the headline, 'Death of Caesar', hears loudspeakers, and runs to join the political rally where the rival parties have converged like gangs of yobbish football supporters. Later he stands among the Andronici as Titus declines the election. Curious, active, keen, the kid has untroubled eyes. Until Titus kills his uncle Mutius. Then, for the first time, young Lucius turns away, can't look his grandfather in the face.

Earlier, I suggested that Lavinia, after the rape, is the child who teaches Titus to look – and that's certainly how Taymor directs Anthony Hopkins and Laura Fraser. Old knowledges wiped, traumatically illiterate, Hopkins's Titus is a grizzled child, poring over Lavinia like a hard primer, trying to work out its strange letters. But Taymor also aligns Lavinia's look with the look of young Lucius, almost morphing their faces into one another – as in the sequence she constructs from materials she finds in Shakespeare's 3.1, a sequence that dissolves from the family at the crossroads (weeping into a puddle that mirrors their grief as it catches their tears) to a face staring from a window through rain. Titus has been kneeling in the black stone-paved road, writing his sorrows, he says, in the dust, ignored by the parade of Romans and tribunes who pass him by, transporting his sons to execution for the murder of Bassianus. A long shot sees Titus prostrate, desolate, tiny against the black pavement where four roads converge. Finally looking up, past his son Lucius, Titus sees Marcus approaching the crossroad. He's carrying Lavinia in his arms. When her mutilation is revealed Titus says to the daughter whose face is smeared with blood, 'Let me kiss thy lips' (3.1.121). But she flees his love, his touch, retreating, as if ashamed, to kneel over a pool of rain in the road, looking at her wrecked self on the water's surface. Titus follows, kneels alongside her and looks, Marcus and Lucius coming in behind, the family huddling in sorrow.

The film cuts, sees their reflections in the puddle, and watches as raindrops, starting to fall, break up the image, dismembering it, blurring the vision like tears in the eyes. A dissolve gives a close-up on a face. It's seen through glass, through rain running down the window pane. Spectators think it's Lavinia – until we notice, pressed up against the glass, a hand. Then we recognise through the distorted optics the beautiful face as the Boy's. Appallingly, the moment this connection is made, suggesting that Lavinia's history will be experienced also through his eyes, another connection is made: a series of shots/reverse shots shows the Boy looking down at what he can't yet recognise, can't yet interpret, 'black' Aaron, under a black umbrella, arriving through the storm at Titus's door to find the master not at home, turning away, then looking up, seeing the child in the window, exchanging looks that follow the child's gaze as it turns to see Lavinia brought home by his grandfather, carried in his father's arms. Contaminating the Boy's look with Aaron's, making him unwittingly collude with the next step in the project – for Aaron has come seeking Titus's hand – makes this sequence almost the ugliest in Taymor's film.

After this, in a series of extraordinary moves, Taymor begins to use the look of the child to map an alternative visual education on Titus – and *Titus*. The Boy watches his grandfather utter 'sorrows deep … passions bottomless' (3.1.17–18), a 'deluge overflowed and drowned' (230), a heart-shocking speech that covers Titus's wait for what he's duped into thinking is going to be Quintus and Martius's release – redeemed by the hand Titus has willingly urged Aaron to chop off and present to the emperor as ransom (in this version, transported hygienically in a plastic ziplock food bag). The Boy hears something. The sound of his grandfather's mighty despair is penetrated, incongruously, by the sound of the circus. Running through the courtyard the Boy flings open the gates of the villa, sees careering wildly down the road in a fog of exhaust fumes a three-wheeled 'apé' – like Zampano's in *La Strada*, an on-the-skids Mussolini-vintage delivery vehicle, its battered corrugated iron box perched on the back axle. Out of the cab climbs the Clown, carrying a loudspeaker, which he bawls into, his Italian, guttural: 'roll up, roll up'. He moves disjointedly, like Charlie Chaplin on silent film played out of synch, to the sound of that bizarre music (that could be the soundtrack to Fellini's *8½*).

Recognising the Clown – the Clown! – from the kitchen rescue brings a smile to the kid's face. He keeps smiling as the showman's assistant – a red-haired girl, like Giulietta Masina's strangely old and infantile Gelsomina – sets out stools and dances an invitation to the punters. One by one they emerge from the villa – Titus, Marcus, Lavinia, Lucius. It's comic. It's absurd. It's 'popular'. And all the time that cartoon music is playing. Until the Clown takes up a position beside his vehicle and with a sudden heave throws up the metal shutter-siding to reveal an exhibition scene from a pre-war travelling freak show: in front of draped velvet bunting in glass display jars, the heads of Martius and Quintus stare wide-eyed alongside the neatly splayed hand of Titus Andronicus. So the Andronici are required to look at the sick joke made of their grief. The Clown's flat commiseration blares over the loudspeaker: 'Worthy Andronicus, ill art thou repaid / For that good hand thou sent'st the emperor' (3.1.235–6). But if this is a freak show that remembers 'pop goes the weasel' decapitations in the toys' party kitchen at the beginning of the film, it's also a sideshow that prompts the child to think laterally, that takes him to another place: a place, bizarrely, that offers an uncanny version of what he's just been looking at. So while the father Lucius exits to the Goths and one kind of (violent) repair, the child Lucius goes elsewhere.

The film cuts to a door whose glass panes are thick with sawdust, the long display windows on either side filled with a dusty jumble of heads and hands and wings. Dimly, over the Boy's shoulder, we see into a workshop, where a bearded man, shirtsleeves rolled up, sits at a battered bench among glue pots and mallets, rubbing sandpaper over wood.

The Boy pushes open the door and enters a strange, beautiful but disturbing room, halfway between a museum and a morgue, filled with Renaissance body parts – hanging torsos, bodiless heads, a St Sebastian without his arms; devout mannequins, their eyes cast heavenwards through haloes; wingless angels; plaster moulds for hands of all sizes posed in all manner of benevolent gestures strung out on a washing line; a work table full of legs and feet, booted, bare, that belong to disciples and penitents and pilgrims, neatly laid out. These delicate, maimed statues in for restoration belong to a Rome that's a far cry from Saturninus's monumental, narcissistic brutalism, a Christian Rome whose artists' material of choice is wood, not marble; a Rome that, indebted to a tree shaped into a crucifix, acknowledges salvation through suffering, makes sense of loss through redemption, and conquers death through resurrection, capturing life, miraculously, for a divine comedy. As the camera, its movements underscored by music that could be Monteverdi's, pans across a worktable laid out with row upon row of hands, the Boy, wondering, calculating, passes his own hand over them, stops, picks one up, holds it close to his face as if measuring it, weighing it. The film cuts; we see him, silhouetted against a bright sky, running into the dark doorway of the villa, carrying a box tied with string. Finding Lavinia, he puts the parcel on her lap, unties it, opens the lid, to show her, lying in wood shavings, a pair of delicate, open hands. This hauntingly poetic sequence that travels over body parts, redeeming damaged imagery from pain and gruesomeness and restoring mutilation to beauty, remembers the Clown, remembers the freak show heads in jars, remembers back to the film's beginning. But more than that, demonstrating a child's sideways understanding of what is possible, the scene looks like a child, seeing in the craftsman a restorer who puts angels back together, a creative artist whose dealings with the dismembered body make it not a horror but a wonder. Giving Lavinia the gift of restoration, giving her toy hands, Lucius makes her look like a child – but also like a work of art.

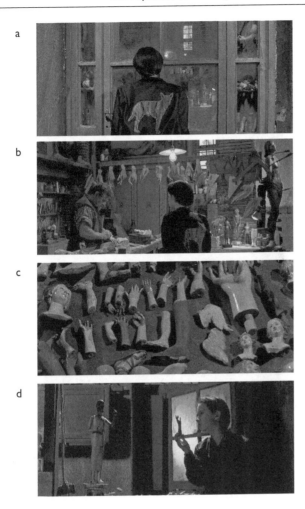

Plate 7 *Titus*, restoring Lavinia, directed by Julie Taymor. (*Source*: Clear Blue Sky Productions, 1999.)
a Boy in search of repair
  (Osheen Jones)   b The craftsman's studio
c Body parts for angels   d Selecting gracious prosthetics

In the scene that follows (Folio, 3.2), as the Andronici sit down to dinner, as Lavinia tries with comic awkwardness to make her hands work, and Titus, watching her fail, concentrates his looking on her, the Boy once again looks at objects sideways – and thereby achieves the saving

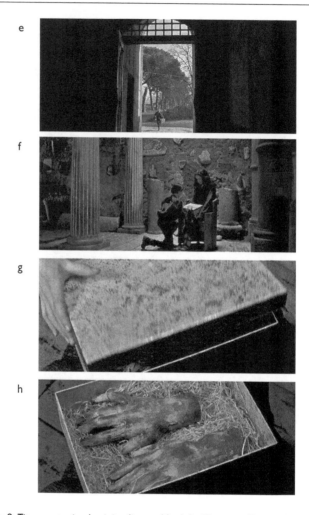

Plate 8 Titus, restoring Lavinia, directed by Julie Taymor. (*Source*: Clear Blue Sky
Productions, 1999.)

e Running home   f A gift for Lavinia (Laura Fraser)
g Hands on a box   h Boxed hands

perspective. In Shakespeare, 3.2 is the first of two banquets; in Taymor, we
read it as one of a series, all of them replaying the Boy's original kitchen
spread. At this meal, a sudden loud movement from the Boy meets with
Titus's rebuke: 'What dost thou strike at, Lucius, with thy knife?' 'At that
that I have killed, my lord – a fly,' an answer that unleashes Titus's rage:

'Out on thee, murderer. Thou kill'st my heart.' The child protests, 'Alas my lord, I have but killed a fly' – only enraging Titus more: '"But"? / How if that fly had a father and a mother?' (52–4, 59–61). Once again young Lucius has an answer, one that turns the scene around. For like Peter Brook on stage in 1955 (who gave Marcus's lines to young Lucius), Taymor has reassigned the fly killing. Making the speech the Boy's, she makes this scene a micro re-enactment of his earlier frenzy.[72] But more importantly for her purposes, Lucius, the twentieth-century kid, coming into speech *for the first time in this film* – no longer a mute – constructs speech as play. He turns this dispute with his grandfather into a game: the fly, the Boy tells him, 'was a black ill-favoured fly / *Like to* the empress' Moor' (3.2.67–8, my italics). So, framing killing 'as if', he teaches Titus to play. And Titus, instantly picking up the game – crying 'Oh, Oh, Oh!' (69), a gleeful co-conspirator – pulps the fly with hyperbolic fury '*as if it were* the Moor' (73, my italics). The effect for the whole family is a collapse into laughter, into childness – and for the old man, a release into the serious play to come. And play he does, for the rest of the play, taking over Tamora's revenge play, recasting her players in a new plot. In Shakespeare's playtext, Marcus, the original fly-killer, comments, 'Alas, poor man! Grief has so wrought on him / He takes false shadows for true substances' (80–1). In Taymor we see him rather learning from his grandson to look like a child and play, 'Minding true things by what their mock'ries be' (*Henry V*, 4.0.53). Here, the child transforms what adults look like.

For the rest of the film, young Lucius serves Titus as production assistant or 'best boy', carrying 'toy' weapons wrapped up in Latin tags to Chiron and Demetrius in their gothic games room underneath the palace; pulling a child's wagon through Rome's streets, knocking at doors, calling up a 'cosa nostra' that will come to Titus's aid; finally, dressed identically to Titus in a spotless white uniform, standing under-chef at the final dinner party where Titus 'plays the cook' and serves up boy-pie to Tamora – a scene that's bizarrely set up by a series of cuts, from the boys-as-presumptive-carcasses, hanging naked from their heels on meat hooks in the villa's nearly dark kitchen abattoir, Titus cutting their throats then, in head shot, calmly wiping the knife on his towelling dressing gown; to a close up on two, steaming lattice-topped pies cooling in a sunny rustic window, curtains flapping as the Sinatra-style crooner sings 'Vivere' – 'life!' – on the soundtrack; to the mid-shot entry of the guests into the formal gold dining room. Titus and the Boy, a bizarre apparition and a disconcerting double act, come on behind, through a red curtain yanked back, as if going on stage, Titus in his tall cook's hat performing with comic brio, dumping a slab of pie on Tamora's plate with a thud.

When they happen, young Lucius is inches away from the killings, the last, performed by his father, who shoves a long-handled serving spoon down Saturninus's throat, then pulls out his revolver and fires. A freeze stops the action dead – spit is caught mid-air. Then over the trapped frame the sound of the shot kicks the action back into motion and triggers a fast zoom back: we see the table and the carnage suddenly relocated. The domestic interior is set uncannily in long-shot in the vacant centre of the arena in the dark coliseum that was the original site of Titus's triumph. Only now the surrounding tiers of stone seats are full. Modern faces are looking on, the camera cutting between still images, superimposing spectators' faces onto spectacle. As Marcus steps to a microphone as if to a press conference to address the 'sad-faced men … of Rome / By uproars severed, as a flight of fowl / Scattered by winds', to try to teach them 'how to knit again / This scattered corn into one mutual sheaf, / These broken limbs again into one body' (5.3.66–71), the Clown is shaking out industrial-sized sheets of clear plastic, covering the bodies where they lie, securing the scene for the forensics squad – and laying a lens between us and the corpses that disturbs our focus on them. 'Now it is my turn to speak,' says Lucius. 'Behold the child' (118). The camera cuts, the Clown is holding up a boy like a trophy over his head – a shot that replays the opening of the film – only this time it's Aaron's baby, exposed to the view in a black metal cage. 'Give sentence on this execrable wretch,' a Tribune demands (176). The child? No. The film cuts to Aaron as he's set 'breast-deep in earth': 'There let him stand and rave and cry for food,' Lucius instructs. And threatens: 'If anyone relieves or pities him', for this 'offence he dies' (178, 180–1). Thus Lucius pronounces the end – an end that is about the end of pity:

> Some loving friends convey the emperor hence,
> And give him burial in his fathers' grave;
> My father and Lavinia shall forthwith
> Be closed in our household's monument;
> As for that ravenous tiger, Tamora,
> No funeral rite, nor man in mourning weed,
> Nor mournful bell shall ring her burial,
> But throw her forth to beasts and birds to prey:
> Her life was beastly and devoid of pity,
> And being dead, let birds on her take pity.
>
> 5.3.190–9

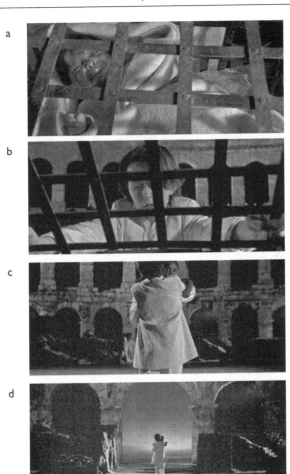

Plate 9 Titus, closing shots, directed by Julie Taymor. (*Source*: Clear Blue Sky Productions, 1999.)
a Aaron's baby
  (Bah Souleymane) caged   b The child freed
c Two boys exiting the
  killing field   d The baby looks back

Shakespeare's ending to *Titus Andronicus* concentrates on story, memory, and the obligations of survivors to *tell*. Aaron's so un-Iago-like contempt for silence (even as he's 'fastened in the earth' he's railing, 'Ah, why should wrath be mute and fury dumb?' (183)) is put against the assignment Lucius gives his son, to 'bear' Titus's 'tales in mind / And talk of them when he [is] dead' – even if 'tears … choke' his utterance (5.3.164–5, 174). Shakespeare, at the end, reprises Rome's rituals: election, funeral, mourning, taking us back around to the play's beginning, the play's own past, and placing the looking child at the centre of the scene.

But Taymor's film doesn't end on Shakespeare's final word.[73] She gives spectators more. Cutting young Lucius's lines remembering Titus, and his lines remembering his obligation to remember, Taymor severs the child from the past – but locates him on film to mark the present, to register the implications of the sentences his father, now emperor, has just pronounced. In a close-up on the adult Lucius's face, the film hangs on his last word, watches him drop his eyes after 'pity', passes into silence, then hears, off camera, an animal, or maybe an infant, crying. The film cuts to the sight of Aaron's baby in the cage. Hands reach into the frame, opening the bars; a close-up on young Lucius's face shows him gazing down at the infant, then registers him, through half-closed eyes, listening to a welter of sounds in his head, baby wailing layered upon wailing as if centuries of tears echoing down the ages tracked an aural history of mankind. The crying modulates into a cacophony of sound effects, birds and bells jangling tunelessly, a soundtrack to underscore the pitilessness his father just imagined for Tamora.[74] Acoustically, it's as if the Boy is conducting in his head a counter-textual version of all those memorial rites his father's pitiless future wants denied. And it's this pitiless future the child walks away from. Lifting Aaron's baby out of the cage and holding him against his chest, he turns his back on the camera, on Rome, on us, and starts his long, slow-motion exit from the coliseum killing field, a shot that symmetrically matches the film's opening but reverses it, watching for nearly three minutes as the Boy crosses the arena and passes through a broken archway into the open where, as dawn sun breaks over the horizon, the frame freezes.

In Shakespeare's *Titus*, as Bate observes, 'retribution is a matter of human, not divine will'; 'This is a world in which people make their own laws'.[75] What sort of laws, then, will people make at this ending? Does pain improve us? Do we suffer into knowledge, grow 'pregnant to good pity' (*King Lear*, 4.5.222)? The two Luciuses are finally instructive. The child who has explored the uses of play knows on his nerve endings what the modern psychologist has also discovered, that play 'is a systemic mode of meta-communication', and that 'as a meta-communicative channel, play has a higher survival value than does ritual'[76] – particularly ritual violence. Taymor at the end scans the face of young Lucius as intently as Leontes in *The Winter's Tale* searches Mamillius's for the 'childness' that 'cures' (1.1.170). Making us 'look like a child' she offers us – along with Titus – an alternative visual education, teaching us to 'listen visually' and transforming – metamorphically – her framing device into her film's mode of production. Requiring her spectators to look at the story through the eyes of the child, she translates *Titus* into something *like* comedy, and leaves us with a comedy that, like Shakespeare's, disturbs our looking: for it is finally not the look of the child that we're left with; it's the look of Aaron's baby looking back.

Titus Andronicus – or – A Clockwork Orange

At the end of Taymor's film, my mind travels back across the stories *Titus* tells, across the books that prop those stories up, and I wonder about the strategy, the responsibility of 'making' children out of narrative 'makings'. The image of those two little boys, locked like brothers in each other's arms, stepping into the dawn of a new world empty of adults and their 'functions' is not amnesiac. It can't blot out memories of what they've left behind, a wasteland strewn with dead brothers, lost boys, failed learning; toxic with the perverted knowledge that originated in Saturninus and Bassianus (but not in *them*, in the books they'd read): sibling rivalry, sexual competition, ritual humiliation, fratricide, rape, violence as adult game and infantile indulgence; perversions played out to grotesque consequence in Chiron and Demetrius, who are there, with all the other 'boys', in the play's last scene, changed – that final Ovidian joke – into meat.

What sense do we make of these 'lost' boys in *Titus Andronicus?* Like me, interested in the books that inform Shakespeare's play, Jonathan Bate sees Chiron and Demetrius as sensational demonstrations of the failure of humanist education – 'the stupidity of the idea that rote learning of the classics is preparation' for *integer vitae*, 'a noble life'. Imagining that 'intriguing off-stage character', Chiron and Demetrius's 'Gothic schoolmaster', as a 'kind of perverted Guarino' – to borrow the name of the great Veronese humanist educator – Bate wryly observes, 'The triumphs which these alumni owe to the lessons of his classroom' are 'in the arena of rape and mutilation.'[77]

Quite so. But then, there's no getting round it. In Guarino's grammar school classroom, as in Ascham's *ludus literarius*, rape was on the syllabus. Elizabethan schoolboys studied rape. They read deeply in the subject. *Metamorphoses* kicks off with three rape stories;[78] *Ars amatoria* proposes rape as a tactic of seduction;[79] in the *Achilleid*, it's the turning point in the story; in the *Aeneid*, it's the future the Trojan women are quietly queuing up to endure.[80] There's no getting around it either that, on the syllabus, rape had an instructive point. For little Chirons and Demetriuses (or Kits and Wills) in the early modern classroom, the most significant convention operating on those texts – their 'lesson' – was that rape coded puberty. The adolescent's sexual initiation moved him into adult male sexuality, triggered his metamorphosis from boy to man.[81] Like Achilles.[82] So while you, the schoolboy, were taught to weep like Dido as preparation for becoming human, you were perhaps simultaneously taught to rape like Achilles as preparation for becoming male.[83] Conflicted learning? Indeed. The same educational system seems designed to produce as many Chirons as Luciuses.

Reviewing the 'instruction' that informs the violent, wasted boyhoods of Chiron and Demetrius, we might observe that if Tamora's boys are stupid students of 'moral' Horace, they're savvy readers of Ovid. That is, fancying themselves heroes, they imagine hot-blooded Achilles their 'pattern, precedent and warrant'; or Tereus, though not in his 'fatherly' role. The link is manifestly invited: Chiron remembers his namesake, another Chiron, Achilles's tutor, the centaur who raised him and taught him the art of war. Both boys talk like seducers out of Ovid, and they possess sophisticated insider knowledge out of Ovid's libertine *Ars* handbook, matched to verbal facility in the abuser's habit of translating sexual violence into euphemism: 'easy it is / Of a cut loaf to steal a shive' (1.1.586–7). Suddenly proposed, the 'wooing' of the unattainable Lavinia triggers the brothers' murderous sexual rivalry and casts them improbably in the roles of languishing lovers. But that move marks an anxious shift for the boys (as Tamora habitually calls them) from warriors to chamberers. What will they do in this 'weak piping time of peace' (*Richard III*, 1.1.24)? How now to confirm virility, *esse virum*? Achilles gives them the answer. Seduction (or failing that, rape) fixes masculine self-definition. And if Chiron and Demetrius better the instruction from Tereus, they no less improve the learning from the *Ars amatoria*. Their post-rape wisecracking picks up and reproduces Ovid's predatory woman-wrecking jokes.

In Julie Taymor's *Titus*, Chiron and Demetrius have long since abandoned books for adolescent toys – which provide substitute instruction, inter-active learning in a world where books are definitely dead letters. In their gothic rumpus room somewhere in the bowels of Saturninus's palace they stoke up on speed, shoot pool, flourish out-of-service weapons wrapped in Latin epigrams they struggle to read, and play video games that double as training films, virtual reality scenarios on screen that feature a grotesquely over-endowed cartoon 'Daphne' in motorcycle leathers roaring away on her bike, wanting pursuit, wanting the chase, wanting violence, wanting 'it', over and over as, mind-deadened, the boy players hit the 'replay' button. Adopted Roman, these adolescent Goth barbarians have shed their animal skins and scrubbed their faces of battle-field filth in preparation for plastering them with cosmetics. They're dressed in 'the heighth of fashion' – as another juvenile delinquent 'hero' puts it – where 'goth' meets 'glam' on the dark side of punk, a style melange pastiched from Jarman's punk fantasy *Jubilee* (1976), Ridley Scott's futuristic-gothic *Blade Runner* (1982) and Todd Haynes' 1998 *Velvet Goldmine* (where Oscar Wilde meets David Bowie and Iggy Pop, and where Taymor's Chiron and little Lucius – the actors, Jonathan Rhys Meyers and Osheen Jones – both feature). Chiron, the decidedly effemi-nate looking, high cheek-boned, long haired 'little' brother, represents the rubbish of glam in *faux* snakeskin trousers, a silver leather suit, scarves and David Bowie makeup; Demetrius is brutish, a leftover punk (where punk codes exaggerated masculinity). But with scalp-cropped bleached hair, in black leather or simulated tiger skin, behind a Rabelais-sized codpiece, he winds up looking more camp than his androgyne brother.

Failed soldiers transformed by default into monstrous lovers, their phallic aggression simply retooled, Tamora's boys are grotesque refigurations of the masculine self, never more explicitly than when they turn up at Titus's 'disguised' as Rape and Murder, looking outrageous like drag queens in women's knickers, suspender belts, stockings and Doc Marten boots. They gaze out from behind trademark dark-goth 'female' faces: painted death-white with black lips (Chiron's a pout, Demetrius's a slash) and exaggerated black eyeliner layered on like a mask. These boys inhabit a pair of paradoxes. Their violence is simultaneously shocking and infantile – sudden, lethal, mindless, and absurd, like temper tantrums, unconnected either to pain or consequence, the kind of violence the adult mind recoils from. Their violence is a form of child's play. They move through rooms like a pair of young gorillas, aping their elders, trashing the furniture, groping food – and each other. Their first shot at rape has Demetrius simulating anal sex on his brother – ritual humiliation to 'girl' the brat and keep him in his place. Later, when Aaron drags them apart by the scruff of their necks and starts to school them in seriously grown-up forms of abuse – he is the true 'magister' Guarino of this film – the boys continue larking about miming sex with phallic bolsters on their molly-house bed. The proposed 'grown-up' rape of Lavinia wipes the smirks off their faces. But the rape itself is most horrific not for the sexual crime but for the perversely childish mutilation of her body, the way, having cut off her hands, the boys make parallel play with her, imaginatively replacing them with 'pretend' ones, shoving twigs into the stumps, turning her into a grotesque toy. Paradoxically, the more conventionally masculine they become through atrocity, the more effeminate they appear, a reverse metamorphosis of their heroic model: Achilles-the-warrior fixed as Achilles-the-drag-queen.[84]

Trying to make sense of these lost boys, we can reread Lucius's school texts. Or the parallel visual texts Taymor offers. But to figure out how the kind of violence that Chiron and Demetrius study in their textbooks and practice in their ugly lives might ultimately, paradoxically, produce *integer vitae*, we need also to reread a text of our recent time, Anthony Burgess's *A Clockwork Orange* (1962). This is a novel that rewrites *Titus Andronicus* from the boy's point of view; that 'looks like' Chiron and Demetrius; that offers, with uncanny prescience, a 'pattern, precedent, and warrant' for a culture where anarchic youth roams the streets and where adults are on the run. The 'malchicks' who hang out at the Korova Milkbar are all adolescent Shakespearean Goths. Alex and his 'droogs' dress 'in the heighth of fashion' ('which in those days,' says the narrator-as-pop-cultural-aesthete, was neo-Elizabethan, 'a pair of black very tight tights with the old jelly mould, as we called it, fitting on the crotch'[85]). They lace their 'moloko' with 'synthemesc' before cruising a dystopian urban wasteland, 'tolchocking', 'crasting', 'fillying about'. Gleefully, Alex puts in front of readers – and the victim's writer-husband – the gang rape that Chiron and Demetrius conduct out of sight:

> So he did the strong-man on the devotchka, who was still creech creech creeching away in very horrorshow four-in-a-bar, locking her rookers from the back, while I ripped away at this and that and the other, the others going haw haw haw still, and real good horrorshow groodies they were that then exhibited their pink glazzies, O my brothers, while I untrussed and got ready for the plunge. Plunging, I could slooshy cries of agony …. Then after me it was right old Dim should have his turn …. Then there was a changeover … Then there was like quiet and we were full of like hate, so smashed what was left to be smashed – typewriter, lamp, chairs … The writer veck and his zheena were not really there, bloody and torn and making noises. But they'd live.[86]

Alex is wrong. The 'devotchka' doesn't live. And this tolchocking punk only learns to understand violence when he's forced to look at it like a child, when he's made to undergo therapy, strapped to something that looks like a highchair, his eyelids clipped to the skin of his forehead, 'pulled up and up and up' so that, he says, 'I could not shut my glazzies no matter how I tried'.[87] In this new 'clockwork' regime, science has replaced humanist education and 'Ludovico's Technique', Cato's book. But in Burgess, memorising texts is still seen as the right way to construct a model human being. It's a kind of rehabilitation where aversion, not positive reinforcement, is the aim and imitation through representation is the method. Alex is forced to watch scenes of violence with eyes wide open, the optic nerve connected straight to the heart and brain. He's forced to go to the movies. To 'learn of us' by watching versions of himself:

> And then you could viddy an old man coming down the street, very starry, and then there leaped out of this starry veck two malchicks dressed in the heighth of fashion … You could slooshy his screams and moans, very realistic, … and the krovvy flowed beautiful red.[88]

Alex notices something curious about this 'translation' exercise: 'It's funny how the colours of the like real world only seem really real when you viddy them on the screen.' And when his therapy starts to bite, he grows increasingly anxious about the relationship between the represented and the real: 'This was real, very real, though if you thought about it properly you couldn't imagine lewdies actually agreeing to having all this done to them in a film'.[89] He wants to stop watching. But he can't. 'I could not shut my glazzies.' Simulation acts like the real thing. In Burgess, it appears that somewhere in the back of its mind Science remembers Erasmus's dictum: 'even those fictitious examples invented by the great poets' can 'serve as lessons to the world.'[90] 'I knew it could not really be *real*,' writes Alex of those 'fictitious examples' that are his therapeutic 'lessons'; 'but that made no difference.'[91]

Plenty of Burgess's *Orange* (probably via Stanley Kubrick's film) appears in Taymor's *Titus*, but then, plenty of Shakespeare ('Will the English') appears in Burgess. A big difference is that adults have abdicated authority in Alex's world; in Rome, they still rule. In Rome, then, they get their revenge. And they get it by killing children. Inside the Korova Milkbar, children miraculously survive. They grow up. And Burgess's *A Clockwork Orange* (the novel, not the Kubrick film) produces a Shakespearean comic ending that anticipates Taymor's *Titus*. Surrounded by a new assortment of 'droogs', his 'therapy' apparently a failure, Alex looks like he's picking up where he left off. But these days he's strangely puzzled by 'all that horrorshow' that used to interest him. He gets up to go. Something falls out of his pocket:

> I couldn't explain how it had got there, brothers, but it was a photograph I had scissored out of the old gazetta and it was of a baby. It was of a baby gurgling goo goo goo ...[92]

Snarling 'Give me that,' he tears the photograph 'into tiny teeny pieces' while the 'droogs' laugh. But then he has a chance encounter with his 'old droogie', Pete. He's in a suit. He's married. Has a job. With an insurance company. And a flat. And he's speaking real English. In short, he's 'like grown up now, with a grown-up goloss and all.' And then the stunning actuarial fact falls: Pete's 'nearly twenty.' He knows all about the 'terrible experiences' that sent Alex to prison and rehab three years earlier and comments, 'But, of course, you *are* very young still.' 'Eighteen,' Alex replies. 'Eighteen, eh?' says Pete. 'As old as that.' Thinking back to the ripped up photograph Alex suddenly recognises who it must be, the baby in his desiring imaginary: 'my son. Yes yes yes, brothers, my son.' And then he knows what's happening: 'O my brothers. I was like growing up.'[93] There it is. The remedy for adolescence. A slow cure. But it works.

Chiron and Demetrius don't get that far. They never get to 'learn of us' the saving perspective. They never learn 'to melt'. The therapy Titus proposes is 'real, very real'. It kills them. Harsh looking, this, at the beginning of young Will the English's playwriting career. But then, Shakespeare didn't write a (semi) happy ending for childhood until *The Winter's Tale*. There, the Old Shepherd wishes for a world clear of adolescents, a world where 'there were no age between ten and three-and-twenty, or that youth would sleep out the rest; for there is nothing in the between but getting wenches with child, wronging the ancientry, stealing, fighting' (3.3.58–62) – lines that Burgess quotes to preface his dramatised version of *A Clockwork Orange*.

Aaron, however, comes some of the way. Aaron picks up his baby, and like Alex, imagines his future: 'I'll make you feed on berries ... / And fat on curds and whey ... / And cabin in a cave, and bring you up / To be a warrior and command a camp' (4.2.179–82). 'My son, my son,' writes Alex, 'When I had my son I would explain all that to him', even though he knows that his boy 'would do all the veshches I had done'.[94] Like Alex clinging to the shredded baby in the photograph, Aaron hugs his 'Sweet blowze', his 'beautous blossom': he'll 'keep safe' this 'treasure in mine arms' 'maugre all the world' (4.2.74, 112, 175). In *Titus*, there is no more stunning metamorphosis than this of Aaron into father.

'Behold the child,' says Lucius, at the end. And Aaron: 'save my boy' (5.1.84). How will Rome look at Aaron's boy – and he at Rome? What stories will he learn? Will he repeat all of his father's 'veshches'?[95] Or is there somewhere in *Titus Andronicus* a story for the child that saves?

Chapter 3

Curing Thought in *The Winter's Tale*

> Go, play, boy, play: thy mother plays, and I
> Play too …
>
> *The Winter's Tale*, 1.2.187–8

> He makes a July's day short as December;
> And with his varying childness cures in me
> Thoughts that would thick my blood.
>
> *The Winter's Tale*, 1.2.169–71

> … the great law that presides over the rules and rhythms of the entire
> world of play [is]: the law of repetition. We know that for a child repeti-
> tion is the soul of play, that nothing gives him greater pleasure than to
> 'Do it again!' The obscure urge to repeat things is scarcely less powerful
> in play, scarcely less cunning in its workings, than the sexual impulse in
> love … And in fact, every profound experience longs to be insatiable,
> longs for return and repetition until the end of time, and for the rein-
> statement of an original condition from which it sprang.
>
> Walter Benjamin, 'Toys and Play', 1928

Preliminary play: Take I

In early spring 1856 there was a knock on the door for eight-year-old
Ellen Terry. Delivered to the child in rooms that her parents had taken at
the top of a house around the corner from Gower Street: a book, 'Bound
in green American cloth'. She remembered the object fifty years later in
The Story of My Life as 'more marvellous than the most priceless book' had
'ever looked since'.[1] It was her first professional acting part, Mamillius in
Charles Kean's Princess Theatre production of *The Winter's Tale*.[2] 'Tried'
for the role along with 'five or six other children' by the formidable Mrs

Kean, who would play Hermione to her husband's Leontes, she, like the others, had been dismissed from the audition with, 'That's very nice! Thank you my dear. That will do.' Now, the book in her hands, 'a real Shakespeare part', Ellen 'danced a hornpipe for joy'. Had she known better, she might have conserved her energies.

Kean was exacting. 'Rehearsals lasted all day, Sundays included, and when there was no play running at night, until four or five the next morning!' The grown-up Terry remembered her child's legs aching, her eyes heavy with exhaustion, her weary body creeping 'when my scene was over' 'into the greenroom' to fall into 'a delicious sleep'. She also remembered – 'as though it were yesterday' – the 'little red-and-silver dress' she wore as Mamillius. And that her debut (with Queen Victoria and Prince Albert in the audience) was something of a fiasco:

> Besides my clothes, I had a beautiful 'property' to be proud of. This was a go-cart, which had been made in the theatre by Mr Bradshaw, and was an exact copy of a child's toy as depicted on a Greek vase. It was my duty to drag this little cart about the stage, and on the first night, when Mr Kean as Leontes told me to 'go play', I obeyed his instructions with such vigour that I tripped over the handle and came down on my back! A titter ran through the house, and I felt that my career as an actress was ruined for ever.[3]

It wasn't. Not only did Mrs Kean, the following day, give the child 'a pat on the back'. For years afterwards she lavished upon her a mother's attention. Her 'patience and industry were splendid', wrote Terry. 'No woman ever gave herself more trouble to train a young actress.' 'How I admired and loved and feared her!' Even so, this mentor, this female god who, for little Ellen, was compounded of 'fire and genius' (nothing compromised by the fact that 'she wore a white handkerchief round her head and had a very beaky nose'), was the beguiler who tempted Terry-the-child-actor into her original theatrical sin. The 'first wicked thing I did in a theatre', Terry confessed in her *Life*, was to 'borrow a knife from a carpenter' and use it – as Ellen? Or as Mamillius? – to cut 'a slit in the canvas' backdrop of Thomas Grieve's painted scenery. Whatever for? 'To watch Mrs Kean as Hermione!'[4]

I begin with this history, this brief tale about performance remembered across a 'wide gap of Time', because its surface activity traces the deep business of *The Winter's Tale*. Like the play's generic shape, the trajectory of Terry's anecdote is tragicomic. She tells of trial, of elation and exhaustion, tyrannical rigour and kindness, sweet innocence and mortifying experience, falls literal and symbolic. There's a 'loss of Eden' story here, the child as mini-hooligan vandalising theatre property, but worse, as naughty voyeur or peeping Tom getting, as children do, perhaps more than she bargained for. For what could the child have been watching through the slit she made in the canvas? Only the scene of Hermione's trial. Or the statue scene. The first scene stages the appalling shaming of Mamillius's mother. Mere 'conceit' of Hermione's 'speed' (3.2.144–5) – that is, merely imagining his mother's shame in thought – is traumatic enough to kill the boy-child, off-stage.[5] So what effect would it have had on the watchful child actor? The second is a 'play' scene, exquisitely beautiful but pitched in a minor key. It's a scene about lost Perdita found, about a stone-cold body that's warm to the touch – a scene that the voyeuristic child had to know was predicated on the 'real' death of Mamillius who wasn't going to be found miraculously saved.

Terry's reminiscence displays a complicated, cross-gendered story of desire and longing that mimics the profound and troubled familial relationships that Shakespeare's play exposes. Backstage, Ellen fixed on Nelly Kean is Mamillius-behind-the-scenes yearning for Hermione and *like* Mamillius-in-Leontes's-court, trying to catch his mother's eye. Peering through the canvas, the Victorian girl in the boy's part was seeing an uncanny premonition of her adult self: this Mamillius would grow up to play Hermione, opposite Charles Warner in Beerbohm Tree's 1906 revival (and the adult knew it: Terry's autobiography was published two years after Tree's *Winter's Tale*). Interestingly, in Terry's telling, as in Shakespeare's play, child looking alternates with adult interpretation. The comment about 'fire and genius': that's a perception that belongs to the adult's knowing. The white handkerchief, the beaky nose: those were horrors the child saw.

The moves Terry makes between selves, between looking and interpreting, prompt questions that also disturb the surface of Shakespeare's *Winter's Tale*. Can the adult remember childhood without contaminating it with adult knowingness, without evoking adult fantasies of childhood or adult memories of being a child? Are stories that 'seem to have children as their subject' always, as Blake Morrison writes, 'really stories about grown-ups'?[6] Certainly Terry's anecdote is concerned with child's play – or looks like it is: playing is both what Ellen is doing on stage and what Mamillius is doing in the narrative, with a toy, a cart, that authentic copy borrowed from a Greek vase. This toy marks the space of childhood, indeed, is the salient 'property' of childhood; but it's also dangerously, unexpectedly (to the unsuspecting child) implicated in adult games that can trip up childhood (authenticity being one of those adult games). Toys,

From The Play Pictorial, No. 51. "The Winter's Tale"

Plate 10 1906 *Play Pictorial* advertisement for Beerbohm Tree's *The Winter's Tale* with Ellen Terry as Hermione. By permission of the Shakespeare Birthplace Trust.

after all, as Walter Benjamin writes, are really only scaled-down adult tools, 'cult implements'[7] put in childhood's way, Roland Barthes insists, '*literally* [to] prefigure the world of adult functions'.[8]

That said, what interests me most about Terry's remembering is the way it puts the child squarely downstage-centre in the scene that her memory restages: the way it *forgets*, blanks out a whole 'world of adult functions'. And what a busy adult world it was! Charles Kean thought of *The Winter's Tale* as a Greek play (and accordingly cut the script of its non-Greek inconsistencies).[9] And he also thought that Shakespeare's opening act was dull: 'Can anything be flatter than these four people stalking down the stage to say "goodbye"?' So Kean introduced 'attraction', setting the opening as an 'authentic' Victorian version of ancient Greek hospitality, circa 330 BC. There was a hymn to Apollo, an elaborate wine mixing ceremony, a banquet served to Leontes and Polixenes as they reclined on couches, the one, dressed 'like the Lycian King, Jobates' as he appeared on a 'vase in the

Hamilton collection', the other 'like a tragedian at a dress rehearsal in a vase from Naples', with Hermione at the visitor's foot in a chair. And to cap it all, a 'warlike Pyrrhic dance'.[10] Slightly agog, *The Times* reviewer published an eyewitness account three days later:

> Three dozen ladies of the *corps de ballet*, attired in glittering armour as youthful warriors, go through all the mazes of Terpsichorean strife, in the course of which occurs a group representing a scene of victory and death that might have been copied from some ancient frieze.[11]

A contemporary illustration of this moment shows the stage crowded, besides, with eight musicians, a dozen servants, and the royal spectators.[12] But no Mamillius. How telling, then, that Terry recalls none of this teeming world, remembers instead the mother, the father, the toy – and the child at play. (How telling, too, that what's lost in the clutter of Kean's scenic invention is his clear-eyed understanding that Shakespeare's opening act is about 'four people' who have 'to say "goodbye"'. Four. For Kean, Mamillius counts. And for Terry, the opening scene of *The Winter's Tale* was *all about Mamillius*.

Preliminary play: Take 2

In spring 2005, another son and heir to a famous English theatrical name began work on *The Winter's Tale* – a play that reviewers, noticing it turning up in repertoires more and more frequently, had taken to calling 'millennial Shakespeare'.[13] Like Charles Kean (son of Edmund), Edward Hall (son of Peter) introduced 'attraction'. Cannily, he set the play – like Julie Taymor in her filmed *Titus* – in a space that worked like a three-dimensional palimpsest, where the ancient past wasn't 'elsewhere' but in front of us, its traces surfacing through the visual materials of the early-modern and post-modern present, a space that could be occupied, with no sense of incongruity, by Delphic oracles, Giulio Romano sculptures, Warwickshire shepherds playing Whitsun pastorals, Ovid's myths and the language of the Elizabethan Book of Common Prayer. The kings – Bohemia and Sicilia – wearing modern dress, suits and ties, smoked cigars, drank brandy, ran fingers through moussed hair. Leontes entertained in an oak-panelled Jacobean hall, renovated from something much older into a gentleman's snug (complete with upright piano and bearskin rug). Remnants of ruinous Greek columns, now only decorative, holding up fragments of white marble masonry, 'remembered' a past when oracles were consulted – and believed.

This production, wrote Sam Marlowe in *The Times* (28 January 2005), began 'like a twisted children's game'. Or perhaps like experience remembered in a child's dream. On the dark stage, a single candle flared, took hold, burned. A beam of blue-grey light picked out a slight boy in pyjamas (Tam Williams) crouched on a nursery floor among toys, silently playing with wooden dolls, his eyes screwed up 'against the terrors of night-time' (Paul Taylor, *Independent* 4 February 2005).[14] Just beyond him, in the shadows, distorted by the candlelight into monster shapes: the stuff of adult culture – a desk, a chair. Beside him, like a visitor from *Alice in Wonderland*, an oversized hourglass. Music tinkled in the background. A clock tick-tocked. And, surreally, sand spilled from a hole in the ceiling. It fell into the child's toy wagon as though escaped from a playground or a sack of shells brought home from a day at the sea – or from the cracked glass of some cosmic timepiece.

This wordless play scene, a kind of 'time out', ended when the adults burst in, when court life surged around Mamillius and took up most of the standing room, when grown-up games – and Shakespeare's text – began. The boy moved to the edge, curious, alert, patrolling the margins and surveying the adult world 'with a haunted horrified look', as though, wrote Dominic Cavendish, 'the whole thing' were 'a midwinter night's dream, in which the latent anxieties of a boy about what will be expected of him as a man' were 'feverishly played out' (*Daily Telegraph*, 1 February 2005).[15] But was he dreaming? Or was he, naughty, eavesdropping? Those pyjamas said the kid was supposed to be in bed.

Setting *The Winter's Tale* as a story seen through the eyes of a child, a story all about a boy, Hall, consciously or not, was tapping in to ideas recently put on general release in popular culture by Taymor's film.[16] ('The arc of the story is the child's,' she'd said of *Titus*; the story was 'brought to life by the boy's vision.'[17]) But Taymor, who called Shakespeare's *Titus Andronicus* 'the greatest dissertation on violence ever written', was interested in investigating that violence as one function of masculinity – ritually performed, recruiting children, indoctrinating and acculturating them through practices so powerfully over-determining that, in Titus's Rome, the warrior class subsumed all other ways of being male (father, brother, husband, emperor). And she was interested, too, to know whether the child had power to dismantle adult culture, or to avoid it, to walk out of the killing field. By contrast, Edward Hall in *The Winter's Tale* was concerned with what the child cannot avoid: growing up. Becoming adult. Becoming, in this case, Leontes. (For if Ellen Terry's Mamillius was going to grow up to be Hermione, Tam Williams's Mamillius, it seemed in the opening scene, was just as certainly headed for Leontes.) The toy, the doll that he could pick up and put down, master of its movements and its meanings, might indeed *literally* prefigure 'adult functions'. But it might also, like the toy gladiator the Boy retrieves from the mud in the opening sequence of *Titus*, work like a psychic prompt or cosmic wormhole to let in the adult play. Beguilingly, then, Hall's opening 'attraction' admitted two readings: regression; premonition. This *Winter's Tale* was a nightmare, a remembering, repeating and working through of traumatic experience. This *Winter's Tale* was a fantasy, imagining anxiety as a prophylactic, a hedge against what otherwise would kill.

Seeing childhood under siege from adults and the nursery as a place of terror where time was running out, Hall, however, had more to go on than Taymor. He had the news – both in the theatre and in the media. Martin McDonagh's *The Pillowman* (National Theatre, November 2003) was touring England; Philip Ridley's *Mercury Fur* was in preview and reminding audiences of Deborah Warner's gut-wrenching *Medea* with, at the end, the smear of drying infant blood, splattered the length of the perspex corridor that backed the production when the mother killed the children, running like rain down the surface (2001, US tour 2002–3). Michael Moore's *Bowling for Columbine* was out on DVD, and, on TV, day after day, the awful stories of child murder in Soham (August 2002) and child massacre in Beslan (September 2004).[18]

But he also had the past: most significantly, the past thirty-five years of *The Winter's Tale* on stage. It was Trevor Nunn in 1969 – Nunn had taken over as Artistic Director of the Royal Shakespeare Company from Peter Hall a year earlier, when Edward was two years old – who first saw *The Winter's Tale* as a play about children: the innocent child, scrabbling about in a toy chest; the residual child, a fugitive (or saboteur) trapped inside an adult body; the child who was the 'prisoner to the womb', waiting to be born. Stunningly, Nunn was the first director ever to put a visibly pregnant Hermione on stage at the RST.[19]

Nunn set the opening scene in a white box, a nursery, but a nursery, writes Dennis Bartholomeusz, 'evoked, rather than literally established', such as 'one might meet in dreams'.[20] A white rocking horse big enough for Leontes (Barrie Ingham) and Mamillius (Jeremy Richardson) to ride piggyback stood centre stage. White boxes – like giant-sized building blocks – were set in the space. One of them turned out to be a toy chest. From it emerged objects 'dredged up from the play's images'[21]: a yo-yo, a plastic Mickey Mouse, a kaleidoscope, a top, a doll whose face was half ripped off, toys that the play would recognise retrospectively as proxies for its adult anxieties.

Plate 11 In Trevor Nunn's 1969 RSC *The Winter's Tale*, Leontes (Barrie Ingham) sits astride his son's rocking horse while Polixenes (Richard Pasco) hugs Mamillius (Jeremy Richardson) and Hermione (Judi Dench) looks on. (*Source:* Tom Holte photograph. By permission of the Shakespeare Birthplace Trust.)

Into this 'dreamlike, childhood world' the royals made their first entrance, like children, running, 'laughing, light-hearted, unaware of terrors to come',[22] playing a game of tig, with Mamillius 'it'.[23] Like Edward Hall's royals, they belonged to the present, dressed, 1960s style, off Carnaby Street, Leontes in cream flares, high-heeled boots, a regency-style frilled shirt and high-collared jacket; Mamillius, his design copy in miniature; Polixenes (Richard Pasco), his double in pink; and Hermione (Judi Dench) in a pure white empire-style gown that a Jane Austen heroine would have felt comfortable in and that Twiggy had made (again) the 'groovy' fashion rage. On The Waif the empire dress fell flat. On Hermione, gathered tight under her breasts, it spread, curved, emphasised the swell of the baby so close to term.

This production's opening image was not, however, the royal entrance in white, but a preview in the dark. From blackout, the stage went into strobe-light effect. The 'scrambled, bewildering' flickering, wrote Ronald Bryden in *The Observer* (18 May 1969), flashed across spectators' retinas the image of a man. Perhaps he was Leonardo's Renaissance man, man drawn in perfect proportions; or perhaps he was Leontes, those arms outstretched posed him as man crucified. Whichever, he was enclosed in a revolving box made of mirrors, a weird version of an early modern 'perspective' or optical game, while, in voice-over, Time spoke lines from his Act 4 soliloquy, 'I that please some, try all ....' (4.1.1). When the lights came up, the box was gone, shrunk to a toy-sized version of itself, a tiny glass box, a tiny figure inside, revolving, and Camillo playing with it. How you see, what you see – and whether it's a monster or a miniature – was the original idea spectators took from Nunn's opening scene, an original idea that would play back later when Leontes saw something tiny – a gesture between his wife and friend – and understood it as monstrous.

Reviewers saw in Nunn's nursery disquieting images, images that triggered thoughts far beyond the play, and captured them for interpretation. For Ronald Bryden, the strobe lighting, the 'frantic flickering' that reduced 'the stage's characters to puppets scurrying through an antique silent film', and the slow-motion sequences, when 'the air darkens', when 'gestures are frozen', when the play-world's heart skips a beat as Leontes's sick fantasies lurch into consciousness: all this made Bryden think of 'those photographs of the Dallas crowd lining Deeley Plaza when the first bullet flung Kennedy's hand in the air'. And the way, 'In that pause, the world looks different' (*The Observer*, 18 May 1969). It was a telling association, this almost Leontes-like tripping of a switch in the reviewer's brain between performance and recent memory, and it gives an insight into the immediate ways Shakespeare was being read politically in late-1960s Britain, the way that global borrowings were turning up on Stratford's stage, and the way childhood was being politicised, on the street and on stage. If, for many, Kennedy's assassination in 1963 had marked the end of America's childhood, in the years since, America had not grown up. Indeed, American youth was refusing to – since growing up in Lyndon Johnson's America, Richard Nixon's America meant turning into capitalist pigs, lackeys to the military industrial complex, pawns in the international cold war chess game, napalm-dropping stooges in an undeclared war in Vietnam. The new knowledge was 'Trust no one over thirty.' And the official motto, 'Make love, not war.' In the spring of 1969, it was good advice. Better to join the student protesters, the hippies, the flower children. (Nunn's bohemian sheep-shearing was staged to look like a flower-power love-in.) The adults in Washington, in the Pentagon, were wrecking the world. (Of course, to those tax-paying adults, the sit-ins, the bank bombings, the draft-card and flag burnings, the attacks on property, the riots on university campuses and inner-city ghettoes looked less and less like childish temper tantrums, more and more like anarchy, calculated to destroy civilisation as they knew it. And not just in Chicago and Los Angeles; in Paris, London, Madrid. Worldwide, the children were revolting.)

Like Bryden watching Nunn's *Winter's Tale* in Stratford and thinking about Dallas, J.W. Lambert, The *Times* theatre critic, sat in the theatre in *Lear* mode, thinking about history – and, bleakly, history's 'promised end'. He was facing, he wrote, a 'Now' when 'a whole culture seems to be disintegrating, when destruction is, if not the joy of millions, at any rate the staple diet of the mass media.' Could Shakespeare make the centre hold? Back in 'the Fifties and Sixties', Lambert observed, Stratford had 'rehabilitated the history plays', so showing, 'in the days of Britain's decline … the bitter foundation of England's greatness.' Now Lambert seemed to be counting on the children to rehabilitate the future, 'the young Royal Shakespeare Company' ('young' because it had become the RSC only a year earlier), 'under its young director, Trevor Nunn' (who wouldn't hit thirty for another year) turning to Shakespeare's plays about childhood, 'in which the theme is the possibility of redemption through courage, endurance and patient love' (18 May 1969). And adult wish-fulfilment?

It took a year for the shock of the new to settle in – though for some reviewers, it never did. One critic, with devastating sarcasm but no sense of the prim 'child' self he was revealing, commented sourly that, 'Right from the start', watching this *Tale*, he 'had a shrewd idea that this was not the Shakespeare of my boyhood'.[24] Performance ideas that looked radical when Nunn proposed them in 1969 travelled into a shared, international vocabulary as the RSC took this production on a world tour the following year. Not least, radical ideas like his white box. Borrowed (perhaps, originally) from Granville Barker's 1912 Savoy Theatre production of *The Winter's Tale*, Nunn's 'baby' was cradle-snatched by Peter Brook for *A Midsummer Night's Dream* the following year who, adopting a nursery, adapted it into what reviewers would see as a different kind of play space, a squash court.[25]

After Nunn, it no longer surprised or bewildered spectators to see *The Winter's Tale* as a play about childhood. In 1976, Ian McKellen's Leontes – in an RSC production that John Barton set in a legendary Lapland where every indoor surface was totemically inscribed with a primitive image of a bear – played at bear hunting with Mamillius (Richard Porter). In 1986, in Terry Hands's RSC production, Mamillius (Martin Hicks) had forced the grown-ups out-of-doors – to play. Seen through a scrim in slow motion as though in a dream while, over the top of the scene, the pure, unbroken voice of a boy chorister soared, the royals all in white stood up to their ankles in winter – the thick fur of a massive white

Plate 12 In Terry Hands's 1986 RSC *The Winter's Tale*, Leontes (Jeremy Irons) observes Polixenes (Paul Greenwood) telling Hermione (Penny Downie) tales of childhood while Mamillius (Martin Hicks) makes mouths at himself in the mirror-walls, behind. (*Source*: Joe Cocks photograph. By permission of the Shakespeare Birthplace Trust.)

bearskin rug – throwing snowballs. In 1990, Michael Bogdanov's English Shakespeare Company *Winter's Tale* opened in a Victorian parlour, a schoolboy standing in front of a crackling fire singing 'In the Bleak Midwinter'.[26] When someone called for a story and the child replied, 'A sad tale's best for winter', the scene went to blackout, the *Christmas Carol* prologue was flown out, and Shakespeare's *Tale* began – a tale called up by adults, but framed by a child, told by a child. The following year Simon Usher's mafioso *Winter's Tale* at the Leicester Haymarket – a production, wrote Peter Smith, imbued 'with the intellectual despair of Modernism' but also with 'some of the Modernists' fierceness'[27] – stripped child's play of cosiness. Sweltering under hot light, the royals – 1930s Sicilians – relaxed after an *al fresco* dinner, smoking, conversing, while upstage a guard with a snub-nosed machine gun patrolled. Mamillius (Oliver Payne) played with something in a box. He poked it with a stick, lifted it out, presented it to his mother (Valerie Gogan). A snake. (How did spectators read this? Typical boy's stuff? More? Was

Hermione Eve? Was Mamillius, was *childhood*, the serpent in the garden, the snake with the beautiful face of a boy – as in Michelangelo's 'Adam and Eve'?)

Adrian Noble's opening at the RSC in 1992 was kinder – and crueller. Mamillius (Marc Elliott), in a turn-of-the-century blue sailor suit, was the only child attending his seventh birthday party. Far downstage centre, just visible in the dark before the lights came up, he sat on his own, on the floor, playing with a snow scene in a toy globe – like the one that drops from Citizen Kane's dying hand, the one that conjures up Kane's childhood and 'Rosebud'. Shaking it, then holding it high over his head so that it caught the light as he watched the snow settle, it seemed his play was summoning up another trapped world. Behind Mamillius, lights came up to reveal, enclosed inside a white gauze box that stretched up into the flies, his parents' court. Twenty adults sat talking, laughing, celebrating – his party – in formal dinner clothes, the gilt chairs tied with red, blue, and yellow balloons. Seen through the gauze, their shapes lacked definition, fuzzy, like hallucinations, their motions slightly out of synch, spasmodic,

Plate 13 Adrian Noble's 1992 RSC *The Winter's Tale*. Mamillius (Marc Elliott) plays alone while the grown-ups stage his birthday party. (*Source:* Donald Cooper photograph. © Donald Cooper.)

his mother (Samantha Bond) bending forward, whispering something into Polixenes's (Paul Jesson) ear, his father (John Nettles), standing, stiff, behind her chair. Twisting, the solitary little boy gazed at them. Or was he imagining them – shaking the snow scene, watching it settle? Was this *Winter's Tale*, as Michael Billington wrote in the *Guardian*, 'A child's darkling fantasy' (3 July 1992) brought to life when the gauze box rose and the adults spilled out into the child's space? The birthday present Mamillius lifted out of the red tissue paper from the splendidly wrapped box presented to him, teasingly, by Polixenes was a top. On the forestage, the boy pumped it, set it spinning. It whirled and whirled – and whirled. The adult world froze. Time stopped.

In the opening scenes of Gregory Doran's *Winter's Tale* at the RSC and Cheek by Jowl's on tour from the Maly Theatre, St Petersburg (both 1999), the boy-heirs were damaged products of their culture. Leontes (Antony Sher), in Doran, was a Romanoff, a lookalike Czar Nicholas II. His imperial court wasn't a nursery but a whispering gallery where one of the topics of gossip was his son: a child dressed in military uniform, like him, but confined to a wheelchair, his whole space of play the wooden tray clamped to its arms. Was the Tsarevich (Emily Bruni) a haemophiliac? Evidence in the flesh, which no one could ignore, that the past matters, that the sins of the fathers are visited on the children?[28] Theatre Maly's *Tale* (performed in Russian with English surtitles) was set in a Russia thirty years later, the uniforms, Stalinist, the gowns, 1940s, the public speeches broadcast through clumsy microphones, the totalitarian regime ensconced in apartments originally decorated for the czars (which would give way, in the pastoral scenes set sixteen years later, to the shoddy pirate capitalism of an on-the-make fake-American Russia, post-Yeltsin). Seven-year-old Mamillius (Nikolai Zakharov), stiff, gravely danced with his mother (Natalia Akimova), another little boy-as-toy-soldier in a sailor suit, a pint-sized stand-in for his dad (Pyotr Semak).

Altogether more precocious, evidently hothoused by pushy parents (or maybe just their mothers), the boys in Nicholas Hytner's *Winter's Tale* at the National Theatre (2001) and Matthew Warchus's at the RSC (2002) didn't play. They *performed*. Hytner opened with Mamillius (Thomas Brown-Lowe), spookily spotlit, dressed like death as a Lilliputian Father Time, complete with scythe and wings, reciting *Shakespeare*. (Sonnet 12, 'When I do count the clock that tells the time …', a poem that ends with the poet urging the youth he's addressing to counter Time's depredations with 'breed' – that is, children – 'to brave him'.) When the lights came up on a chic, ultra-modern penthouse apartment and adults in Armani applauding his party-piece, the boy retired upstage to play Schumann on a grand

Plate 14 Gregory Doran's 1999 RSC *The Winter's Tale.* Leontes (Antony Sher) examines Mamillius's (Emily Bruni) 'smutched' nose. (*Source*: Heritage Theatre in association with the RSC.)

piano. But you had to wonder: was this artful Mamillius his father's son? Behind the sleek sofas, tables cluttered with executive toys and a cabinet crammed with sports trophies, a series of photographs on a wall showed two schoolboys – not Mamillius, but kids his age from a former time. Tousled, grubby, they posed in their muddy sports kit, grinning.[29] (Those same 'boys', bigger, older, still mates, still tossing rugby balls, were currently draped over the leather furniture: Sicilia, Bohemia.) But just as Hytner's Leontes (Alex Jennings) clearly hadn't grown up – his courtiers were in grown-up suits, but he was still in jeans and a sweater that he might have worn at nets, and he nursed that rugby ball like a surrogate teenage pregnancy – his over-accomplished Mamillius wasn't quite a child. He had plenty of expensive toys – but they were carpet soldiers, for indoor play. This kid growing up in a penthouse was never going to get dirty, wasn't built for the scrum, fumbled the ball his father threw to him.[30] In Warchus, too, precocious performance hijacked real play. Into a dimly-lit space set with tables and chairs for after-dinner entertainment, guests arrived – like Usher's Sicilians, they looked like 1930s mafiosi, but they were 'family' who'd cut ties with the old country, relocated to Chicago (or maybe New Orleans), lived at all hours in evening dress, and saw themselves on screen in films starring Edward G. Robinson. The lights dimmed. The guests watched a magic act, conducted by a kid (Toby Parkes) in top hat and tails, aided by a 'Glam Assistant'.[31] He'd chosen interesting material, Mamillius.

Plate 15 Gregory Doran's 1999 RSC *The Winter's Tale*. Leontes (Antony Sher), mimes, in play, the cuckold's horns, and tells his crippled son Mamillius (Emily Bruni) to 'go play, boy, play'. (*Source:* Heritage Theatre in association with the RSC.)

Voodoo. The 'dead woman in the box' routine. He placed 'Glam' in a coffin. Made her disappear. Then, as torches whirled, smoke billowed, and trad-jazz accompaniment reached a screaming crescendo, the coffin opened. The body rose from the dead. The lady returned. Little Mamillius had beaten the Big Sleep. The adults clapped.

From this scan across forty years of theatrical beginnings, re-performing performance, I want to observe the obvious. Theatre knows more about Shakespeare's play than criticism does – or perhaps better said, knows *differently*.[32] Criticism of *The Winter's Tale*, from F.R. Leavis and Wilson Knight to J.H.P. Pafford and Wilbur Sanders to Brian Gibbons and beyond, habitually starts with the adults.[33] Theatre knows the play starts with the child. And not just one child – a crowd of them, residual, actual, notional, imminent.

To explore what I'm calling obvious, I want to return to the opening of *The Winter's Tale* to reread Shakespeare's text, a text remarkable both for its explicitness and its opacity – and for the gaps it leaves; a scene resonant with what is *left unsaid*, with what is entirely at the disposal of performance. Thinking of the text (following W.B. Worthen) as 'material for labor, for the work of production'[34] and a playground for Mamillius, I want to examine 'childness' in the scene, how adults construct it, the language they use to frame it, the expectations they have of it, and the identity crises it brings them to, all this, before seeing 'childness' as it performs itself: the theatrical fact, throughout 1.2, of Mamillius, playing. (So at the beginning of *The Winter's Tale* the kinds of questions I asked at the end of *Titus Andronicus* about the boy Lucius occupy me again – but differently.) As Catherine Belsey has observed, *The Winter's Tale* 'constitutes Shakespeare's most detailed depiction of the affective nuclear family.'[35] More than that, though, it produces the longest, hardest look Shakespeare takes at childhood – at the child's small body, the contextualising of that body in adult scenarios, fantasies, nostalgia. 'In Shakespeare,' says Russell Fraser, 'the meaning of the play is the play.'[36] Watching Mamillius, I want to argue that in *The Winter's Tale* Fraser's claim is literally true. We have in Shakespeare's play a demonstration of Joseph Roach's notion of performance as 'surrogation', a process of cultural memory, of cultural reproduction and recreation that traces 'the doomed search for originals by continuously auditioning stand-ins' – only here, the search isn't doomed.[37] Miraculously, 'originals' return. Saying, 'Do it again! Do it again!', *The Winter's Tale* plays with rhythms Walter Benjamin would recognise: its 'profound experience' 'longs for return and repetition until the end of time', longs 'for the reinstatement' of the 'original condition from which it sprang'.[38]

Boys eternal

As a kind of prologue or curtain raiser to things to come, in the opening scene of *The Winter's Tale* two courtiers stand exchanging formal pleasantries. They talk about children. They discuss affairs of state. And talk about children. They consider the future of the kingdom. And talk about children. The royals enter – Bohemia and Sicilia, raised together in childhood; the prince, a child; the queen, with child. She's nearly nine months pregnant. Visibly so, on stage. But no one mentions the expected child.[39] And nothing in the playtext notices her 'condition' – unless we count, wiser after the fact, references that snagged our attention without making us really think twice about them when we first heard them: 'Nine changes of the watery star ...'; 'burden'; 'breed'; 'a cipher ... in rich place'; 'a prisoner, / ... a guest'; 'issue' (1.2.1, 3, 12, 6–7, 52–3, 188).[40] Seemingly picking up where the gossiping courtiers left off, the queen (who holds a 'prisoner' – or is the baby a 'guest'? – in her 'womb') talks to her guest (not her 'prisoner') about children. (Somewhere in the scene, the child-prince occupies himself.) The king joins in – and talks about children. Intently, he scans the face of his child. Two of the grown-ups exit to the garden – leaving the king talking to the child.

As I'm framing it, 'childness' is the matter of this opening (a word Polixenes invents and no one else in Shakespeare uses, a word that contains meanings far beyond 'childish' or 'child-like'). 'Childness' is what people talk about in Sicilia. It's their subject matter. But 'childness' is also the matter *with* this opening. Something happens to Leontes in 1.2. He's suddenly infected, overwhelmed with sick thought, 'diseas'd opinion' (1.2.297). And that disease is 'childness'. Paradoxically, however, 'childness' is also the cure.

Initially, the tropes that duck and dive across each other in this opening rise out of the backstory Camillo tells to account for what Archidamus finds 'rare' (1.1.12). It's really no wonder, says Camillo, that Leontes's generosity to his guest has been magnificent. Sicilia cannot 'show himself over-kind' to Bohemia (where 'kind' means more than 'courteous' or 'solicitous': it means 'family', 'kin'). 'They were trained together in their childhoods, and there rooted betwixt them then such an affection which cannot choose but branch now' (1.1.21, 22–4). Leontes (we will see) calls Polixenes 'brother'; Polixenes says he and Leontes were 'twinn'd' (1.2.15, 67).

Talk of these now grown boys turns the conversation to another boy. Archidamus ventures, 'You have an unspeakable comfort of your young prince Mamillius: it is a gentleman of the greatest promise that ever came into my note.' Camillo agrees: Sicilia's 'hope'-ful boy is 'a gallant child; one that, indeed, physics the subject, makes old hearts fresh' (1.1.34–9).

Two powerful and connected metaphors for thinking about childhood are produced in this exchange, metaphors that are going to persist, echo and accrue extraordinary significance across the play: the growing child as plant, the healing child as medicine. 'Trained together', Polixenes and Leontes were not just boys schooled in the same classroom – one kind of training. They were plants cultivated in the same potting shed. Not grafted to each other – the horticultural art of improving nature by marrying a 'gentler scion' to 'the wildest stock' (4.4.93), the pros and cons of which, echoing this originating moment across a wide gap of time, will be argued out at the sheep shearing in Act 4.[41] Leontes and Polixenes were 'rooted' together, then trained, as by a gardener, *en espalier*, to grow, flourish, 'branch'. Separation here is connection. Growing in different directions is continuity. (But submerged meanings lurk in 'branch' too, troubled suggestions lying in wait to ambush the immediate future. A 'branch', if it's a fork in a road, takes you away from your beginnings, your roots. A 'branch', if it's on a deer's head, is an antler, so also a euphemism for the cuckold, he who is 'o'er head and ears a fork'd one' (1.2.186).)

What interests me about this history is that, rooted in the past and remembering organically, it figures childhood not as something over, gone or lost. Taking the sense of Camillo's metaphor, childhood isn't a place or a time or a set of things that define it, like toys. Childhood persists. It's a 'then'-boy preserved in a 'now'-man: located in, visible in the deep structure of his growth. Peer beneath the foliage, the adult's 'rough pash' (1.2.128), you'll see the smooth brow of the little boy.

Perhaps extending this initial metaphor, Camillo first refers Mamillius to a range of conventional tropes – he is Sicilia's 'hope', 'promise', 'comfort'. But he's much more than this. This child, says Camillo, 'physics the subject'. This child, then, is one we'll have to track through the early modern plant bible, John Gerard's compendious *The Herbal* (1597), for one, because Mamillius is like the wild flowers, the weeds and herbs which the herbalist cultivates and gathers, distils to simples, turns into 'physic', applies to cure – Friar Lawrence in *Romeo and Juliet*, or Gerard de Narbonne in *All's Well That Ends Well*, or, indeed, like the Queen of Summer, Mamillius's sister, later, with her 'Hot lavender, mints, savory, … marigold' (4.4.104–5): all of these plants owning 'vertues' described Gerard.[42] Like them, Mamillius's property, Camillo claims, is 'physical'. He's medicinal. And as a restorative, he's supposed to be universal: to physic 'the subject' is to physic all Sicilia. This child-cordial (terming him such, we hear the pun that connects the cure to the disease) miraculously 'makes old hearts fresh'. He is heart's-ease – Gerard's 'Harts ease' or (another name for it) 'gilloflower' – in a court that, we will see, suffers *tremor cordis*, heartache, broken hearts.[43] At least, that's the claim.

These metaphors of Camillo's infiltrate the next scene where, uncannily, we have the sense of a *nature mort* coming to life. Boyhoods past, boys unbreeched, boys in men's clothing, boys remembered, boys inspected: they jostle for attention. How smart of Nick Hytner in 2001 to set his modern-dress version of this scene against a wall of photographs, 'what *was* in what *is*',[44] making present boys from twenty-odd years past, still in each other's company – and in their sons' company.

Hermione wants to talk about boyhood. Flush from her triumph, winning the concession Leontes couldn't get from Polixenes – 'Your guest then, madam' (1.2.56) – she turns the conversation, midline, to this:

Come, I'll question you
Of my lord's tricks, and yours, when you were boys.
You were pretty lordings then?

                                                                1.2.60–2

And again:

> Was not my lord
> The verier wag o' th' two?
>
> 1.2.65–6

Hermione is the mother of a boy, a son who, perhaps, is just the age now that Polixenes and Leontes were when last together; a mother (we will see) who plays with her son, wearies of her son, pulls him back to her lap, indulges him, knows exactly the kinds of 'tricks' waggish boys get up to ('do your best / To fright me with your sprites: you're powerful at it' (2.1.27–8)). Perhaps, wanting a tale of boyhood, wanting to revisit her husband's past, wanting insider knowledge of scrapes and wildness (the stories, so to speak, behind the photographs on the wall), Hermione is anticipating the baby so soon to come. Will the child be like the dad? What she gets from Polixenes is more than her light-hearted questions bargained for. Something heart-stopping:

> We were, fair queen,
> Two lads that thought there was no more behind,
> But such a day to-morrow as to-day,
> And to be boy eternal [...]
> We were as twinn'd lambs that did frisk i' th' sun,
> And bleat the one at th' other: what we chang'd
> Was innocence for innocence: we knew not
> The doctrine of ill-doing, nor dream'd
> That any did. Had we pursu'd that life,
> And our weak spirits ne'er been higher rear'd
> With stronger blood, we should have answer'd heaven
> Boldly 'not guilty', the imposition clear'd
> Hereditary ours.
>
> 1.2.62–5, 67–74

This takes childhood out of the schoolroom, out of the potting shed, out of the footling, promotes it, awesomely, to a theological scheme of things, exposes it to different metaphors, tests it in a divine court of appeal. Boyhood in Polixenes's remembering is a kind of Eden: innocent, unthinking, without the knowledge of Good and Evil, without sin or guilt – or conscience. There are no bad dreams in this space of being boy. And no time: past and future are all 'to-day', God's time, the infinitive, 'to be' – 'boy eternal'. The lambs that 'frisk i' th' sun' of this Eden are signs of immaculate innocence – but also its loss: they're the animals marked for sacrifice to pay 'the penalty of Adam' (*As You Like It* 2.1.5);

ultimately, they signify the 'second Adam' returned incarnated as 'the lamb of God'.[45] They are us; or more properly, we are they: in the 'generall confession' at daily 'Morninge prayer' in the 1559 'Boke of common praier', we – the 'whole congregacion' – acknowledge that 'we haue erred and strayed ... lyke loste shepe'.[46] (With these lambs and the theology that underpins Polixenes's speech, it's no coincidence that we're going to wind up at a sheep shearing in the second half of this play. That's how Shakespeare's theatrical imagination, literalising metaphor, works.)

Even as Polixenes cites Eden, we know that Eden is lost. And we know that he knows it. A profound sense of nostalgia hangs over this speech: a longing for the home the boy can never return to; a longing, too, for himself, the lost boy. For Polixenes to remember childhood, then, is always to remember 'a text of loss'[47] – and to experience anguish, the adult knowledge that 'we are sinners all' (*2 Henry VI* 3.3.31), that, as sinners, we are (as the confession has it) sick: that 'there is no health in vs'.[48]

But what about that bold answer, 'not guilty'? Is it a tenable position? Or is it grave doctrinal error – if not heresy? (Wilbur Sanders writes with comic indignation at Polixenes's line that he 'speaks as if Original Sin were somehow avoidable!'[49] Of course it isn't, to the early modern Catholic, Calvinist, or Anglican. But what about 'remissible'?) In a play that consults Delphic oracles, performs Whitsun pastorals, and (in Polixenes's speech) has just started using the language of the Elizabethan Book of Common Prayer, it may be daft to offer to pin down doctrine. But it's just as well to try – and the fact that the word itself surfaces in Polixenes's speech invites the attempt. For shortly, *The Winter's Tale* is going to take us from Polixenes's figurative trial to a real one where Hermione, accused of 'falling', will stand in the dock answering 'not guilty' to a version of that crime 'hereditary ours'. Is she right to stand out against false accusation? After Eden, are we mortals ever justified to enter the plea, 'not guilty'?[50]

What 'doctrine' supports the plea? In the 1559 Book of Common Prayer, the Nicene Creed – which begins 'I Beleue in one God, the father almightye' – ends acknowledging 'one Baptisme, for the remission of synnes'. Reminding the congregation that 'all men be conceiyued and borne in synne' – original sin, the 'imposition ... hereditary ours' – the service of 'Publique Baptisme' instructs them that 'None can entre into the Kyngdome of God excepte he be regenerate, and borne a new of water and the holye Ghoste'.[51] That's why we need baptism. Locating baptism historically in a series of flood narratives (Noah, Moses leading Israel through the Red Sea, John the Baptist), the Prayer Book understands water thereby sanctified to the 'misticall washing away of sinne' and prays that God 'wylt mercifully loke vpon these children, sanctifie them & washe them with thy holy ghost'. (King Edward's Prayer Book of 1549 petitioned for the infant's sins to be 'washed clean away' 'by this wholesome laver of regeneration'.[52]) So 'receyued into the Arke of Christes Church' and 'deliuered from [God's] wrath', the child will 'enioye the euerlastinge benediction' of God's 'heauenly wasshinge' and 'come to the eternall Kyngdom', attaining everlasting life.[53] Later in the service, godparents are required to answer in the faith on behalf of the infant: 'Doest thou belieue in ... the remission of synnes ...?'[54] Once the child has been dipped three times in water and signed with 'a crosse vpon the chyldes forehead', he is declared 'regenerate & grafted into the body of Christe's congregacion', made God the Father's 'own chyld by adopcion', and, 'dead vnto sinne', 'lyuing vnto righteousnes'.[55]

Elizabethan polemicists and theologians might argue the toss about the precise relationship between original sin and the remission of sins in baptism, but for the early modern parishioner listening to this language at the font, the Book of Common Prayer seems to be offering, for the baptised infant, a 'grace' period (and 'grace' is a word that keeps turning up in *The Winter's Tale*) when, 'laved', 'regenerate', he is 'clean', innocent.[56] (Indeed, the 1549 rite created a space where the child was symbolically dressed in the part of grace, where the godparents put upon him the chrisom, a 'white vesture for a token of the innocency ... by God's grace in this holy sacrament of baptism is given' him.[57]) Baptism, then, 'cleared' the 'imposition ... hereditary ours'. A child – Polixenes, perhaps – so 'laved' and innocent might justifiably plead 'not guilty'. Not insignificantly, this is business attended to in *The Winter's Tale*, first when Paulina carries his newborn daughter to Leontes telling him she's come for 'needful conference / About some gossips' – that is, godparents – 'for your highness' (2.3.40–1) and then when the baby is left on the shores of Bohemia wrapped in 'a bearing-cloth', a baptismal shawl (3.3.114).

But that's not the end of it. For this 'grace' period is terrifyingly brief. Born in sin, the baptised child still carries the residue of original sin, the tendency to sin. The word for it is 'concupiscence'. So even though the stain of original sin is removed in baptism, the effects linger on. Liable to sin, children must shore themselves up against their inevitable slip. As soon as they 'come to the yeres of discrecion', they must 'ratifie' 'wyth their owne mouthe' the promises made by their godparents on their behalf. They must be confirmed in the faith. Although the 1559 Prayer Book rubric on 'Confirmacion' states definitively that 'children beyng baptised, haue all thynges necessary for their saluacion, and be vndoubtedly saued', it still institutes Confirmation as a spiritual booster shot, 'defence againste all temptacions to sinne, and the assaultes of the worlde & the Deuil'. To this end, the sacrament is 'most mete to be ministred when children come to that age, that partly by the frailtie of their owne flesh, partly by the assaultes of the worlde & the Deuil, they begyn to be in daunger to fall into sondry kindes of synne'.[58]

For the early modern child, the age of 'discrecion' (which is also the age of the onset of frail flesh) comes when he can, in his 'mother tongue' say the articles of the faith, the Lord's prayer and the ten commandments and can answer a 'shorte Catechisme'. Age seven, perhaps? The age when boys started learning Ovid by heart in the grammar school. The age when they achieved the biblical 'age of accountability' (Romans 14:12). The age when Elyot in *The Boke of the Governour* thought it 'expedient' that boy children 'be taken from the company of women'. The age Hamlet was when Yorick died. The age when boys were changed out of gowns and long coats and 'breech'd'; visibly marked off, for the first time, from girls, by clothing which instantiated, even drew exaggerated attention to, the difference of their 'fleshe'. And marked this change perhaps precisely at the moment boys first became aware of their body's 'frailtye' – a 'frailtye', paradoxically, that a boy experiences when his flesh is 'higher rear'd / With stronger blood' (1.2.72–3): tumescence. Age seven. Perhaps the age Polixenes was when he discovered himself locked out of Eden. Perhaps the age Mamillius – who's still in coats, unbreeched – will be next birthday (and Florizel, too, Polixenes's son, born within a month of Leontes's boy (5.1.115–18)).[59]

Alert to the past conditional mood of Polixenes's reminiscence ('Had we … we should have'), Hermione impishly concludes: 'By this we gather / You have tripp'd since' (1.2.75–6). And Polixenes soberly agrees:

> O my most sacred lady,
> Temptations have since then been born to 's: for
> In those unfledg'd days was my wife a girl;
> Your precious self had then not cross'd the eyes
> Of my young play-fellow.
>
> 1.2.76–80

No longer 'not guilty', he has slipped, tripped, and fallen – from bleating boyhood innocence into roaring masculine full-bloodedness; into, that is, sex. The initiation which, in the classical model (Achilles, say) publishes virility's robust coming of age, in the Christian scheme of things returns man, ashamed, to Adam's original condition, to his 'hereditary imposition', his disobedience – misled by Eve. We can't duck it: that's the point

Polixenes's remembering reaches. There are, in fact, plenty of ways to sin. As the Prayer Book inventories, there's the 'vain pomp and glory of the world', the 'covetous desires of the same'. But like Angelo (in *Measure for Measure*'s licentious world of lapsed laws) who fixates, finally, on only one crime, fornication, Polixenes sees only one sin: the 'carnall desyres of the fleshe'.[60] (Call them 'Eve'. For the serpent in Polixenes's garden is what Eve tropes: sex.) The 'temptations', the 'devils' that lost the 'twinn'd lambs' their paradise and the 'lads' their 'boy eternal', are those repositories of carnality, those invitations to strong blood, those daughters of Eve, the women they married. How very Adam is Polixenes at this moment, pointing the finger: 'The woman … did' it (Genesis, 3:12)! How very childish. Yet, also, how astonishingly conflicted: for what he figures as 'temptations' that 'cross'd' them he also terms 'sacred', 'precious'. We hear the boy's nostalgia for paradise lost fighting (at some subliminal level of adult consciousness) with awareness of the 'heaven' he's found in 'a lady's lap' (*3 Henry VI* 3.2.148).

The issues that Polixenes's remembering makes current and releases into play in *The Winter's Tale* establish what G.K. Hunter might call the 'framework of assumptions' about childhood in this imagined culture – or Pierre Bourdieu, 'the universe of what is taken for granted', how adults see the child.[61] If we take Polixenes at his word, the pre-sexual child isn't reprobate. The child doesn't need 'th'offending Adam' 'whipped … out of him' (*Henry V*, 1.1.30). Even more miraculously, the boy lost when Polixenes discovered self consciousness, body consciousness, time consciousness – when, that is, he answered his 'blood', not 'heaven' – returns, regenerate, in a surrogate, another boy, his son. ('Do it again!', says the play. 'Do it again!') A place-holder for adult memory, the child stakes the adult's residual claim in Eden. He's a way of remembering. But also a way of lingering there, a stand-in for the original boy – his father – who was himself a stand-in for a previous original boy. The child, then, is a means of cultural reproduction twice over. He is the next generation, but also the next *re*generation. His role is to play his father's boy on the way to becoming his father.

In Polixenes's scheme, you treasure your child because your child remembers you: watching him play, you see yourself. The child occupies the adult, entertains the adult, is grist to the adult's mill; he mirrors the adult, participates the adult,[62] rehearses a world of adult functions, waywardly spells the adult backwards:

> He's all my exercise, my mirth, my matter:
> Now my sworn friend, and then mine enemy;

My parasite, my soldier, statesman, all.
He makes a July's day short as December.

1.2.166–9

But most of all, Polixenes finally observes, you treasure your child because his 'lively' innocence is your hedge against the killing disease of your own flesh. He is prophylactic. 'With his varying childness,' says Polixenes of his son, he 'cures in me / Thoughts that would thick my blood' (1.2.170–1). (Thick blood: the condition doesn't show up in the medical treatises – or in the herbals, those early modern encyclopaedias of homeopathy.[63] But Shakespeare's spectators may have heard of it: 'Make thick my blood,' Lady Macbeth bids the spirits who tend on mortal thoughts: 'Stop up th'access and passage to remorse', block, that is, the arteries to the heart (*Macbeth*, 1.5.42–3).) Curing thought, the child is medicinal, 'physics the subject'. So Camillo's original metaphor returns, recalled.

And not a moment too soon. For as we're listening to Polixenes's life-darkening 'winter's tale', we're watching a scene grow thick with diseased speculation, sick thought. One moment Leontes is well, hearty, enlisting his wife to persuade his friend to stay in Sicilia longer; the next, the moment she's done the business, he's struck down with an 'infection of my brains' (1.2.145) that's already attacked his heart: 'I have *tremor cordis* on me,' he says, 'my heart dances, / But not for joy – not joy' (1.2.110–11). What triggers it, this infection that pierces his eyes and courses along the optic nerve straight to the brain and heart, like a ghastly inversion of love-at-first-sight? Leontes looks at Hermione – and sees a monster. He sees her, suddenly and with a terrible clarity, as what Polixenes's 'twinn'd lamb' speech has made her semantically, a marked woman; and, now, performatively, a body *between men*. He sees her, his 'dearest', under his very nose, take 'a friend' (1.2.88, 108) – a word, as innocent as other words exchanged in the scene, like 'blood' and 'tricks' and 'love', that reaches Leontes's ears 'as an obscene euphemism'.[64] What gesture has Hermione made to accompany those lines about speaking 'to th' purpose twice': 'The one, for ever earn'd a royal husband; / Th'other, for some while a friend' (106–8)? Has she held out a hand to Leontes, another to Polixenes, a gracious gesture that Leontes instantly degrades to 'paddling palms, and pinching fingers' (115)? The free, open, joyous and playful 'liberty', the royal generosity and abundant warmth, the unselfconsciousness that Hermione has performed throughout the scene – the way, belly bulging, she wonderfully invites her husband to 'cram's with praise', 'make's / As fat as tame things' (91–2) – sick Leontes reinterprets as its lewd double. 'Liberty' – that is, princely liberality – becomes sexual 'entertainment'. Every insight gets infected: Hermione's delicious comment on patriarchal power – that husbands 'may ride's' wives 'With one soft kiss a thousand furlongs ere / With spur we heat an acre' (94–6) – will return, perverted, as 'My wife's a hobby-horse' (276). This is Iago-speak: 'Courtesy'? 'Lechery' (*Othello*, 2.1.256–7). Making him an Iago, a pornographer, the infection of Leontes's brain spills out of his mouth: 'Too hot, too hot!' (1.2.108).

Catherine Belsey writes of 1.2 that, 'in this instance', there's 'no external cause, not even a Iago or a Iachimo to blame for the sudden reversal of emotion ... [T]he murderous passion of Leontes ... wells up at a moment of supreme harmony between the couple ... at a time when the meaning of the family as parenthood is most clearly evident in Hermione's pregnancy.'[65] But this is to miss what else is 'most clearly evident' here: the visual problem, the interpretative conundrum posed, for the early modern spectator, by the gravid female body. A double body, one lodged inside another, the pregnant woman is a body that reads 'double', that materialises duplicity. She's anamorphic; from one angle, one thing, from another, a very different 'thing'. Pregnant, she bears upon her body the sin of Eve. But also the grace of God. Swelling, spreading, she's marked as carnal woman, actively sexual: her 'entertain-ment', in terms that *Measure for Measure* provides, is 'writ' upon her body with 'character too gross' to hide (1.2.143). But what she 'shows' is matter for rejoicing: Elizabethan families celebrated news of pregnancies by lighting bonfires. Because she wrecked Eden, she's punished: her 'con-ception' is in 'sorrow' and her childbirth in pain (Genesis 3:16). But her labour is itself the sign of 'a covenant of sanctification, mercy and eternal comfort'.[66] If she's lost by transgression, she's 'saved in childbearing' (Timothy 2:15). Her ripening body is figured as a vine, a tree, a garden, her offspring, the fruit of her womb: 'A man's yard' – that is, his penis – is 'the plough wherewith the ground is tilled, and made fit for production of fruit.' So Jane Sharp writes in *The Midwives Book: Or the Whole Art of Midwifery Discovered* (1671): Man 'is the agent and tiller and sower of the ground, woman is the patient or ground to be tilled.'[67] 'He ploughed her, and she cropped,' says Agrippa of Caesar and Cleopatra (2.2.235). And Lucio of Claudio and Julietta:

> As those that feed grow full, as blossoming time
> That from the seedness the bare fallow brings
> To teeming foison, even so her plenteous womb
> Expresseth his full tilth and husbandry.
>
> *Measure for Measure* 1.4.40–4

But this fruitful garden may be figured instead as a wasteland, a midden. Lucio's gorgeous imagery, which imagines the woman's body as blessed 'patriarchal territory',[68] Leontes degrades to a public commons (even as Hermione exits to attend him 'i'th'garden'): polluted, despoiled, trespassed, poached, his 'gates open'd', his 'pond fish'd', 'sluic'd' 'by his next neighbour', 'Sir Smile' (1.2.194–7). Property can be fenced, the *hortus conclusus* walled, towns fortified. But there's 'No barricado for a belly': the belly 'will let in and out the enemy, / With bag and baggage' (1.2.204, 205–6). And leave behind – what? Infection? The 'filthiness' John Donne preached of?[69] The question is pertinent, because if for Richard Hooker, Robert Hill and Christopher Hooke 'The fruit of marriage is birth'; if a child is the 'pledge of love' between husband and wife, 'a blessing, an inheritance, a crown, a reward unto us of the Lord',[70] pregnancy (in early modern childbirth texts) is a disease, a 'sickness of Nine Months'. Bleakly, 'the greatest disease that can afflict women, is that of the Nine moneths'.[71]

This ambiguity inscribed on the woman works potentially (some would say, inevitably) to confound the man. For him, pregnancy is proof of good husbandry – or its opposite. It shows his 'wondrous kind'-ness (as Helena tells Bertram in *All's Well That Ends Well* (5.3.312)). Or it gives the game away – it's the writing on the wall that discovers dalliance, 'our most mutual entertainment' (1.2.142), as Claudio puts it. It's forensic evidence of fornication that will haul a man up before a church 'bawdy' court or, in *Measure for Measure*'s Vienna, put his head on the block. Pregnancy confirms potency, confers paternity, makes a man a man – or maybe not; instead, a dupe, a cuckold. It produces legitimacy, an heir – or the cuckoo in the nest, a bastard. It settles a man's sense of self – Aaron in *Titus Andronicus*, King Edward at the end of *3 Henry VI* – or throws him into sexual panic, masculine crisis, self-doubt. For how does the man know the child in the womb is his, or that no trespass of his property has been committed?[72] 'It's a wise father,' says Launcelot Gobbo, son, significantly enough, of a blind man who at that very moment is trying to recognise him, 'who knows his own child' (*The Merchant of Venice*, 2.2.66).[73] From which angle does the husband view the anamorph? Does he see his wife as her 'precious self' – or a 'hobby-horse'?

If I'm right, and Hermione's pregnant body is the 'bug' (a word the play uses at 3.2.92) that infects Leontes, this scene shows him catching her 'sickness' – a sickness that participates in the universal disease Polixenes has already diagnosed. (And we see the stage filling up like a hospital ward.) It's as if her body is suddenly, momentarily picked out in a shaft of light or held fleetingly in a pose that discovers something of it always before hidden; or as if it's viewed, for the first time, through one of those newfangled optical instruments Galileo was experimenting with, 'perspectives', that, 'eyed awry', 'distinguish form' (*Richard II*, 2.2.18–20). Hermione's body provokes a crisis of knowledge. Leontes *sees* something. And what he sees – is sick thought. Of course, by now, the 'ocular proof' he has in front of him – gross, bulky, in the flesh – is so coercive that he's stopped listening.

Shakespeare's dramaturgy in 1.2 is astonishing. This is a public, social scene, a crowded court scene full of activity and movement. But Shakespeare constructs it out of what I want to think of as a series of textual gaps, blackouts covered by noisy talk, or air pockets of silent interiority wedged up against outcrops of court chit-chat. Writing like this, Shakespeare finds a way of staging the fevered mind coming into and out of consciousness, into and out of focus. So we *hear* Polixenes, but we *watch* Leontes *watching*, that talk of lost innocence working like a kind of voice-over to Leontes's sickening speculation, captioning his dementia. Bizarrely, Sicilia goes missing, gets lost to the proceedings (slips into an air pocket, so to speak) between 'Tongue-tied our queen?' (27) and 'Is he won yet?' (86). ('Won': another loaded word.) He drops out of the playtext into – what? Into performance. But what, exactly, is he performing? Distraction? (Antony Sher's Leontes in 1999 unfolded wire-rimmed *pince-nez* from their case, balanced them on his nose, and busied himself with state papers.) Hallucination? (Barrie Ingham's Leontes in 1969 stood downstage, in half-darkness, while behind him, as in a dream exploding in a mind illuminated by flashes of strobe-lighting, Hermione and Polixenes in slow motion acted out his sexual fantasies.) Dangerous surveillance? (Pyotr Semak's Leontes in 1999 stalked a court momentarily frozen into statues, eye-balling them, twisted, grinning, an 'in-yer-face' brute.) Meanwhile, Polixenes's voice speaking 'over' Leontes's textual absence elicits from Hermione the key text for interpreting it, her mocking 'conclusion' that all women 'are devils' casting herself in exactly the role Leontes will assign her (ll. 81–2). But that word she uses so lightly in jest – 'slipp'd' (l. 85) – we watch nudge Leontes's slide into the obscene chain of associations that will end two hundred lines later with 'My wife is slippery' (1.2.273).

Then, just as suddenly, Shakespeare's scene switches point of view. Like a camera cutting from shot to reverse shot and zooming in, 'Too hot, too hot!' (108) brings Leontes into sharp focus, into close-up. Words, phrases, come out of him like a man retching. He's a voyeur describing to us, whom he's recruited to his voyeurism, the sex act he sees (as it were, in long shot) Hermione and Polixenes performing:

> This entertainment
> May a free face put on, …'t may, I grant:
> But to be paddling palms, and pinching fingers,
> As now they are, … – Still virginalling
> Upon his palm!
>
> 2.111–16, 125–6

(But now Hermione and Polixenes have dropped out of the text, and Leontes is acting the voice-over to *their* performance. So what are they doing? What are spectators looking at? That 'paddling', 'pinching', 'virginalling'. Is impudence caught in the act – or is a contaminated imagination in meltdown?)

I return to the observation I made earlier. Something happens to Leontes in 1.2. Something signalled textually by 'Too hot, too hot'. It's more than an acute attack of sexual jealousy, more than 'a libidinous invasion' (Molly Mahood's phrase), more than 'thwarted erotics' (Lawrence Danson's) – although it absorbs all of these.[74] It's beyond the misogynistic revulsion Posthumus experiences or the rage Othello feels: 'I will chop her into messes. Cuckold me!' (4.1.195). Leontes, by constrast, despite the headache he feels coming on with the 'hard'ning' of his 'brows' (1.2.146), is almost comically philosophical about wearing the cuckold's horns: 'Should all despair / That have revolted wives,' he quips, 'the tenth of mankind / Would hang themselves' (1.2.198–200).

What happens to Leontes is *more* because Shakespeare intensifies this scene with what he touches on in none of his other jealousy scenes, the matter of childness: the 'issue' that's in front of Leontes. His crisis is a crisis of masculinity swollen to existential crisis. For catching the curve of Hermione's belly Leontes catches doubt. (We're caught in one of those wordless air pockets of interiority here: there's no script for this performance.) Leontes needs to know, and knows he can't. Needs to know not just the child: himself. For if the father makes the child, the child, too, *makes* the father. (I think of Ben Jonson's elegy upon his son, dead, aged seven, called 'Ben Jonson his best piece of poetrie', a line that plays upon 'poet' as 'maker' and upon 'poetrie' as that which makes the poet a maker.[75]) 'Am I I?,' the theatre of this scene asks. And answers: 'I am I if she is me, if hers is mine.' But what if 'it' isn't? What if 'it' is Polixenes's? The trauma Leontes is suffering attacks him in every office of masculine selfhood's triumvirate: husband, father, friend. Needing to know Hermione's heart, Leontes scans her body. It remains inscrutable. We're reminded of Bosola, the court spy, in John Webster's *The Duchess of Malfi*, needing to know, needing a 'whirlwind' to 'strike off these bawd farthingales' so he can see what he suspects, 'the young springal' he thinks the Duchess is carrying 'cutting a caper in her belly' (2.1.148–51). But Leontes needs to see deeper, beneath the flesh, into the womb, as into one of Vesalius' gynaecological anatomies. Failing that – and in the writing, Shakespeare produces for Leontes physical spasms like waves of sickness – he forces his gaze to turn elsewhere. He grabs (like the last desperate clutch of a mind going over the edge or the wounded body reaching for the morphine injection, right at the end of the iambic pentameter line) *his child*. To physic the subject:

> ... and then to sigh, as 'twere
> The mort o' th' deer – Oh, that is entertainment
> My bosom likes not, nor my brows. Mamillius ...

1.2.117–19

And he interrogates the boy, asks *him* the tormented question he needs answered by the reticent belly, the question that only now appallingly, retrospectively, reveals what's on Leontes's mind when he puts it to the proxy:

> Mamillius,
> Art thou my boy?

1.2.119–20

Leontes hangs on to the evidence, the faithful witness, of that little body – a kid with a grubby nose who looks like him:

> I'fecks:
> Why that's my bawcock. What! hast smutch'd thy nose?
> They say it is a copy out of mine. Come, captain,
> We must be neat; not neat, but cleanly, captain:
> And yet the steer, the heifer and the calf
> Are all call'd neat. – Still virginalling
> Upon his palm! – How now, you wanton calf!
> Art thou my calf?

1.2.120–7

We feel in these lines the queasy play of vacillation, the tug of attention from the 'dirty' picture he's been looking at to the clean surface of his boy's face – which he finds 'smutch'd' with the clean dirt of child's play, an accident that draws him into double entendre ('neat', 'cleanly'), then into euphemism ('neat'), and then, irresistibly, back into sick sight. It's as if his whole world – the imaginary and the real – is slippery, coated with a greasy miasma while the coercive but undecipherable female body explodes his mind, forces him constantly to take bodies apart, to see hands, faces, fingers, brows, arms, ears, noses, bellies bizarrely disintegrated.

Horribly, the nursery discovers itself pitched upon a shambles. The language of dandling intimacy that Michel de Montaigne so objected to in adult chat to children, which makes your darling child exclusively your own by naming him something *else* in a secret language that only you can access – 'bawcock', 'captain', 'calf' – imperils innocence, and adult sanity, by putting it in dangerous proximity to its opposite.[76] The child is made precociously adult: 'captain'. The child is made a pet: 'beau coq'. The child is babied, made 'wanton'. In jest. In play. But here, as we will see, play itself becomes an obscene euphemism. And the particular ugliness of this scenario is the physical juxtaposition of the child with lewdness, the way he's inserted into an act of pornographic voyeurism gazed at over the top of his head while his body is made the object of the father's performance – Leontes searching the face, Leontes wiping the nose. Leontes needs the child to clean up his mind. Instead, contamination washes across the child as Leontes searches Mamillius's face for likeness:

> Thou want'st a rough pash and the shoots that I have
> To be full like me: yet they say we are
> Almost as like as eggs; women say so,
> (That will say any thing): but were they false
> As o'er-dy'd blacks, as wind, as waters; false
> As dice are to be wish'd by one that fixes
> No bourn 'twixt his and mine, yet were it true
> To say this boy were like me. Come, sir page,
> Look on me with your welkin eye: sweet villain
> Most dear'st, my collop! Can thy dam? – may't be? – …
>
> 2.128–37

From here, Leontes's eyes again swerve back to fix on dirty pictures – every 'saving' consideration undone by cultural 'knowledge': 'women … will say any thing'; property will be trespassed. His over-driven language seems to have burned up all its fuel. It sputters, conks-out, tail-spins, nose-dives into what Mark van Doren has called 'the obscurest passage in Shakespeare'[77] – a passage that, to my mind, mimics *Othello* 4.1, where the Moor's mind, rubbed raw, rubbed *thin* with what it 'would most gladly have forgot' (4.1.19), finally breaks, felling him in an epilepsy. The sick seizure, the spasms we see Othello perform we hear Leontes speak:

> Affection! thy intention stabs the centre:
> Thou dost make possible things not so held,
> Communicat'st with dreams; – how can this be? – ...
>
> 1.2.138–40

And the crux of the matter is that question: 'Art thou my boy?' For if he is, then maybe the baby in the belly is his too, and life is sane. But how does he know? And what can the child answer? Here, the adult *looks for himself* in his boy: 'like me', 'like as eggs', and more than 'like', 'my collop': a piece of my own flesh. That is, the child serves as a kind of theatrical prop for adult identity.

Simultaneously, though, Leontes turns Mamillius into another kind of object, tries to read him like a book, searching for a 'copy' of an earlier, authorising text whose 'lines' written in the child's features reproduce the original – and the original's original history. Guided by the metaphors of writing and imprinting, Leontes again *looks for himself* in his boy:

> Looking on the lines
> Of my boy's face, methoughts I did recoil
> Twenty-three years, and saw myself unbreech'd,
> In my green velvet coat; my dagger muzzl'd
> Lest it should bite its master, and so prove,
> As ornaments oft do, too dangerous:
> How like, methought, I then was to this kernel ...
>
> 2.153–9

This effort to scrutinise, to read 'copy', to recognise your own work by recognising yourself – your hand – in it will return, urgently, when Paulina presents to Leontes his newborn child and, against his accusations that the 'brat' is a 'bastard', the 'issue of Polixenes', forces the 'matter' to be scanned (2.3.92, 73, 93, 98). In 2.3 Paulina examines the baby like a duodecimo reprint of the father:

> Behold my lords,
> Although the print be little, the whole matter
> And copy of the father: eye, nose, lip;
> The trick of's frown; his forehead; nay, the valley,
> The pretty dimples of his chin and cheek; his smiles;
> The very mould and frame of hand, nail, finger.
>
> 2.3.97–102

Figuring the child as a copy, a print, a book expands upon Camillo's original repertoire of metaphors for imaging (and imagining) paternal relationship. But if printing offers a ready model of that relationship (we think of Titus forging family connections over books, and Theseus in *A Midsummer Night's Dream* declaring a daughter to be 'a form in wax' 'imprinted' by the father (1.1.49–50)), it is a vexed model – as Louis Montrose and Margreta de Grazia have shown.[78] For while *The Winter's Tale* 'demonstrates a cultural link between the fantasies of authentic paternity and identical printed copies', writes Aaron Kitch, it also 'stages the defeat of both models by exposing the flaw of print as an authorizing institution': 'the structure of authority imbedded within print as an ideal of fixity unravels through the circulation of identical copies whose appearance seems to buttress their truth value while their iterability actually transforms the authoritative structure they enact'.[79] In short, printing can't control the circulation of copies. It can't control illegitimate form. Printing produces pirating, forgery, counterfeiting, plagiarism ('plagiarius': literally, 'a kidnapper'). And 'bastards'.[80] And given that children, unlike printed texts, are always collaborations, the notion that one can be the exact 'copy of the father' is nonsense. When, sixteen years hence, Leontes's 'little' 'print' returns, he still won't recognise her as his. For Perdita won't look anything like him. She'll be the double of her mother.

More to the point, however, in performance terms, is the fact that Leontes's speech – 'Looking on the lines ... / Methoughts I did recoil' – is itself doing 'bastard' work. For if, textually, this speech is a nostalgic fantasy of parental return to his lost boyhood, performatively, it's staging an alibi. Leontes's distraction, which has staggered him, bouncing off interior walls of self-absorption ('Can thy dam? – ... infection of my brains / And hardn'ning of my brows' (137–45)), has been noted by his wife and his guest. But when Polixenes asks, 'how is't with you, best brother?', Leontes insists he's not 'mov'd': 'No, in good earnest' (148, 150). And then spins a cover story to prevaricate his distraction, a story about 'Looking' at 'my boy's face' that recoils his own past, takes him back, twenty-three years, to his childhood, to his own 'boy eternal', to see himself in Mamillius, 'unbreech'd', his dagger 'muzzl'd', the phallic weapon turned into a toy. As alibi, the child puts the father 'elsewhere', in another place where he can be 'like' 'this gentleman', a sanctuary place where his mind is evacuated of disease. It's this reminiscence, which replays the 'twinn'd lambs' speech, that prompts Leontes to invite Polixenes to think about *his* 'home' life: 'Are you so fond of your young prince, as we / Do seem of ours?' (64–5) And Polixenes summons into the scene that distant son who 'makes a July's day short as December', that son who, 'with his varying childness cures … / Thoughts' – blood-curdling thoughts like those that are running through Leontes's mind, mental rehearsals for the appalling violence Sicilia will direct against the baby not yet born, the 'Perdita' not yet given up for 'Lost'.

The 'fond' father (as Leontes figures himself in 1.2) already knows that his mind needs medicine: 'Look on me with your welkin eye' (136), he implores Mamillius, 'welkin' meaning not just 'sky blue', but 'celestial', 'heavenly', 'life-giving', 'true', 'providential'. But this 'fond' father will metamorphose into ranting child-killer in 2.3. He'll be Herod ordering the slaughter of the innocents: 'see it' – the baby – 'instantly consum'd with fire', he roars; 'bear it / To some remote and desert place' and 'leave it' (2.3.133, 174–6).[81] He will be offered physic, 'words as medicinal as true' to 'purge him of that humour' that's infecting him, words from Paulina 'who professes' herself the king's 'physician' (2.3.37–8, 53, 54). He'll be offered a baby as cure: 'a daughter'; 'Here 'tis' (2.3.65, 66). But Leontes will throw physic to the dogs – to the 'kites and ravens', the 'Wolves and bears' (2.3.185, 186). Can this mind be cured after it has killed 'childness'?

'Go play, boy, play'

Exploring the semantic field Shakespeare lays down in *The Winter's Tale*'s opening act, I have been observing its deep investment in childhood, how the adult imaginary it puts on view builds itself upon the materials of child-hood. Nothing that happens here happens without childhood as its refer-ence point. From the first, childhood (remembered, reviewed, represented by adults) proposes the counter-text to adulthood that adults must measure up to, knowing they can't. The story of the adult, then, is a story of 'a falling off' (*Hamlet* 1.5.47), a pattern theologically proposed that we see literally performed. The 'slippery' wife, the 'tripp'd' friend, the 'hox[ed]' husband: by slander, by mistaking, by delusion, one after the other they fall from grace, the 'flatness' of their 'misery' (3.2.122) unutterable. Monosyllables understate their tragedy, lines like Hermione's reacting to her arrest for adultery, 'You scarce can right me throughly, then, to say / You did mistake' (2.1.99–100). And what intensifies the experience, makes it unbearable, is that these Eden-sized falls are played out against the very spectacle of innocence which the desiring adult imaginary has so insistently called to mind. For we're not just dealing in semantics here; 'Childness' is put squarely in view in *The Winter's Tale* – staged. Fixing our eyes on Mamillius, we see all the complicated adult scenarios of the opening act written around the child and played off his small body.

He is listed in the Folio stage direction at the top of 1.2 – 'Enter Leontes, Hermione, Mamillius, Polixenes, Camillo'; but thereafter, textually unnoticed until line 119 when his father suddenly calls out his name. At line 187, he is just as abruptly dismissed: 'Go, play, boy, play,' his father tells him. Then again, at line 190: 'Go, play, boy, play.' And *again* at line 211: 'Go play, Mamillius.' By now, of course, 'play', the occupation of the child, has been reframed as something adults do too – only different. 'Thy mother plays,' the father tells the son:

> and I
> Play too; but so disgrac'd a part, whose issue
> Will hiss me to my grave: contempt and clamour
> Will be my knell.
>
> 1.2.187–90

Child's play gets caught up with sexual dalliance, then theatrical dissembling, bad acting – which is also sexual activity: acting bad. 'Part' connects actor's script to cuckold's role; 'issue' is both 'performance' and 'bastard'. And all of this sophisticated 'play of wit' conducted in the tortured adult mind works ultimately to hijack 'play', to re-route it through adult concerns. What is Mamillius doing before 1.2.119? Is he disciplined by the scene, held in check – like Greg Doran's Mamillius in 1999, trapped in his wheelchair unable to move, so that, effectively, the stage belongs to Leontes?[82] Or is he given free rein to roam, as unpredictable as an animal, so that spectators, somewhere in their line of vision, are aware of him negotiating adult space – like Noble's Edwardian Mamillius in 1992 or Propeller's stalker Mamillius in 2005? How does he stand his father's scrutiny – and where is he at line 187? Is he following the skids and swerves of his father's punning? Is he precocious, a sexual ally recruited to his father's side, becoming knowing as he hears child's 'play' (in those increasingly disconcerting repetitions) smeared with innuendo: play as dalliance, play as dissimulation, hypocrisy, the actor's art of lying; play as sport: the angler playing out the line that will hook the catch? Or, unknowing, is he the 'witty' adult's stooge here, carried along by the playful story of a family at play, hearing no trouble until Leontes lands the 'but' that makes play 'disgrac'd' – *that* word, 'disgrac'd', baffling the child, telling him something more is meant by 'play' than he can comprehend? 'Thy mother plays': in its nasty suggestiveness, this is monstrous knowledge to dump upon the child. It's the knowledge (we know from Polixenes) that will lose him Eden. Appallingly, then, we (adult spectators) can see in this scene a father spoiling the imagination, corrupting the son, a black joker prematurely wrecking childhood – Leontes Iago-ing Mamillius. Or we can see the child somehow safe from soiling – his mind not taken, tainted by what it can't absorb. What the scene means, finally, will depend on how it's played.

And that's the crucial observation. What use the child's body is put to in 1.2, how that body 'plays', and the discrepancy played out between adult knowingness and child innocence: *that's* what gives the scene its particular charge. Mamillius is a near blank textually. He has only four lines in the scene. So Mamillius is one of Shakespeare's parts – and we can name dozens of others from mutilated Lavinia to dead Ophelia – that 'means', has always 'meant', and continues to 'mean', entirely in performance. He's the 'theatrical body' Anthony Dawson writes about, a body *of* the text (a body made by what Camillo, Leontes, Hermione say of him) that *exceeds* the text (because while not speaking, he's *doing* in the scene). He's a site of 'fundamental ... signifying power' whose significance must be teased out of the silences Shakespeare wraps around the lines; whose significance must be discovered in the theatre – where every time *The Winter's Tale* is performed Mamillius will mean again and mean differently.[83] ('Do it again! Do it again!' says the play.) Mamillius, played, will tell us about *The Winter's Tale*. But also about 'childness' and what it means as a cultural construction in the 'now' of every subsequent performance. To think about the issues I'm raising here, I return to the theatre, to actual Mamilliuses on actual 'play grounds', to review some of those productions I scanned earlier, looking at the work Mamillius performed in them.

In 1969 Trevor Nunn imagined a Sicilia imagined by Mamillius: Alice in Wonderland in its sense of scale; utopian in its vision. The court was his gigantic toy box where the child was king and held court astride his magnificent, life-sized rocking horse – the *real* king riding pillion *behind him*! (How different was this child-centred world from the Sicilias of earlier RSC *Winter's Tales* – 1937, 1948, 1960 – formal, even hostile spaces, grown-up territory where a child was a starched visitor, to be seen and not heard.) Nunn's Sicilia wrote the importance of children visibly on the surface of this culture, and Mamillius roamed freely across the space, connecting the adults, sharing physicality, touching, holding, hugging. The game of tig the court played as they entered emerged as a metaphor. Mamillius sat on Polixenes's knee. He leaped into the arms of his father ('art thou my boy?') who swung him through the air. He endured his father's handkerchief ('hast smutch'd thy nose?') and his mother's shirt-tail tucking ('We are yours i'th'garden'). Busy, he searched his toy chest, found his kaleidoscope, and when his father took it from him and peered through it to investigate whether 'this boy were like me', Mamillius put his own eye to the other end.[84] (This toy – kaleidoscope: literally, 'beautiful form'. You turn it – like a top? – and it delights you by shattering images then reconstituting the broken bits into new shapes: a resonant metaphor, perhaps, for recombinant DNA.) Gravely, the boy shook his father's hand – the apprentice statesman learning court etiquette – and exited when the king dismissed him, 'Go play' (so he wasn't exposed to Leontes's nastiest speculations), but re-entered running on 'How, boy?', needing something more from his toy box but using his father's question as an excuse to tell him what was on his mind: 'I am like you, they say' (1.2.208).

This was a Sicilia where, if children were prematurely grown up, dressed like miniature adults, adults could still act like children, still had permission to play – to pick up a top, as Polixenes did, and set it in motion ('We were ... twinn'd lambs'); and in play, in the whirring hum of the spinning top, to simulate the 'boy eternal' – until the adult Polixenes stopped it. This lovely, laughing scene, putting 'childness' in view in spotless white, showed what would be wasted by Leontes's 'muddy, ... spotted', sickened imagination (1.2.325, 328). Yanked out of the arms of his mother in 2.1 as he sat whispering his tale into her ear – 'There was a man ...' (29) – Mamillius dropped his toy. It registered as innocence fallen. But the fall wasn't unanticipated. For this utopia had been pre-emptively disturbed by the preview scene that came before it: the strobe-lit nightmare; the man in the spinning box; the voice of Time telling us that, in this mortal life, even if we build a world arrested in childhood, there's no 'boy eternal'.

Seventeen years on – time enough for a Perdita to grow up and for English society to begin to understand what its post-60s infatuation with 'yoof' meant for grown-ups – Sicilia in Terry Hands's 1986 *Winter's Tale* at the RSC was an edgier place, schizophrenia built into its physical geography. Upstage, perspex panels threw back mirror reflections of every image they caught, a design that staged duplicity – or a mind splitting. Everything in Sicilia looked double. A gigantic polar bear rug covered most of the stage, its eyes glaring balefully out at the audience, softness and savagery in one skin. (And for anyone who knew what was coming, a horrible premonition: the monster was there, lying in wait under everyone's insensible feet.) For Mamillius, the bear was nursery furniture: he sat on its head, rode it like a horse, used it as a launch pad to jump into his father's (Jeremy Irons) arms – or into Polixenes's (Paul Greenwood), who held the lad as he spoke the 'boy eternal' speech. This child might have been either man's son, dressed identically to both of them in frock coats which could have been period or modern, original or retro. He moved easily between them, one moment playing with the visitor, then squiring his father, helping him off with his outdoor clothes, his boots before moving upstage to play a ball game with an obliging courtier.

Mamillius was a little 'man's man'. The problem was that in this Sicilia the men were oversized boys who'd never grown up: one of the doubles that was caught in the perspex was the uncanny image of Leontes shrunk to the size of a child. (Indeed, for Nicholas de Jongh, one of the dead give-aways of Leontes's arrested development was the way he gave 'himself over entirely to playing with his son' (*Guardian*, 2 May 1986). And as things deteriorated under his crazed petulance, Leontes threw temper tantrums, stamped his foot, stammered – ''tis true. / It is: you lie, you lie: / I say thou liest, Camillo, and I hate thee' (1.2.298–300) – and regressed, infantilised. He put a blanket over his head to escape Paulina (Gillian Barge), and the crown he wore for Hermione's (Penny Downie) trial slipped down over his eyes, like a party hat pulled from a Christmas cracker. Mamillius, by constrast, acted his age: his play was *serio ludere*, the deeply serious stuff Erasmus wrote about and early modern schoolmasters like Ascham and Brinsley thought important to a boy's development. In 2.1, Mamillius bridled one of his mother's gentlewomen with ribbons, turned her into his galloping horse, and rode in, reins lashing, a pint-sized knight in a gorgeously plumed helmet, to offer his sword in humble service to his 'lady', his mother. Roles were reversed: in this *Winter's Tale* the child comforted the father while the father leaned upon the child as confidant. He burdened Mamillius with his rancid discovery – 'Too hot, too hot!' – and when the child, wonderingly, moved upstage toward his mother, as if to examine her for evidence of his father's devastating accusation, Leontes shrieked hysterically, 'Look on *me* with your welkin eye!' (1.2.136).

Just at a time when new historicism was making a massive impact on academic writing on Shakespeare, the souvenir programme for this production offered views of childhood as cultural construction, historically constituted: the seventeenth-century child (Sir Walter Raleigh and his son from the National Portrait Gallery); the nineteenth-century child (a Mary Cassat painting of a nude baby); the Edwardian child (a Shepard illustration of Christopher Robin); the late Victorian child surviving in post-Edwardianism (an extract from J.M. Barrie's 1917 fantasy play, *Dear Brutus*, quoting Dearth's observation that 'Sons are not worth having', that 'Daughters are the thing', for 'The awful thing about a son is that never, never – at least from the day he goes to school – can you tell him that you rather like him. By the time he is ten you can't even take him on your knee.'). But the cultural work these citations did in the programme – any one of which taken up and translated into design, might have located, for spectators, 'a world in which such things, Shakespeare's things, can happen'[85] – was merely decorative. The citations, it turned out, had nothing to do with the production. For Hands sedulously avoided locating his *Tale* anywhere in 'real' time. Was that because it was meant to be a timeless fairy tale? Maybe. But as the programme demonstrated, citing *Peter Pan*, fairy tales too are embedded in their histories.

More generally (because 'naturally'?), tangled male rivalries (including psychic dependency) were on display here – brother v. brother, father v. son. Leontes's conflicted need for his son was real and frightening. Mamillius had to be peeled out of his crushing embrace by Hermione and Polixenes when they saw Leontes 'unsettled' (1.2.147), and the child was privy to every word of his father's tortured observation – 'Affection! … / Thou dost make possible things not so held' (1.2.138–9). Still, the really killing male rivalry here was internal, the one between the perpetual boy and the stunted man *in Leontes*. Mamillius was a measure of what the father might have been had he grown up. (For Irving Wardle in *The Times*, 2 May 1986, this 'feverish and furtive' Leontes for whom nothing existed 'outside his own fantasy' was 'no more a king than a child playing the tyrant with his toy animals'.) Significantly, before he exited, Mamillius had to stand, hand outstretched, until Leontes realised what he wanted and handed his ball back. Fearing himself usurped as husband, the father in this *Winter's Tale* in fact usurped the role of child.

Six years later at the RSC, the radical shift of perspective Adrian Noble offered on this play registered up front, in the production's publicity material – and the contrast with 1986 was total. What featured on the earlier production poster were headshots of Hermione and Leontes (to capitalise, no doubt, on the pull power of Jeremy Irons's 'star' face). The programme cover used a rehearsal photo taken in the trial scene, in nightmare purples, Leontes, book in hand, facing out, grim eyes swivelled sideways, under an oversized yellow paper crown, a production, said the image, 'all about' Leontes and his twisted viewing. In 1992, by contrast, Adrian Noble advertised a *Winter's Tale according to Mamillius*. The programme cover illustration gave a close-up on a little boy's wide eyes while the poster reproduced the production's opening image: the solitary child, far downstage, sat playing on the floor, holding his crystal ball, gazing behind him at the adults who were trapped in the gauze box as if caught in the structures of court protocol (or in the child's imagination).[86] This 'world according to Mamillius': how different it was from Nunn's lively, joyous child-centred world of 1969 where adults had delighted in

child's play. In Noble, paradoxically, spectators were both invited to privilege the child, to see everything through his eyes, yet also to see him
marginalised, alienated. This Mamillius was the Edwardian child whose
conversation with the grown-ups was strictly timed to 'The Children's
Hour', or (a cultural novelty in 1992, much on the public mind) he was
the hugely expensive designer baby expensively dressed in period clothes
whose function was to 'accessorise' fashionable modern life.[87]

Noble's inspiration was to set this opening scene ('four people' saying
'goodbye') as Mamillius's seventh birthday party, a coming of age
'breeching party' that would rhyme with Perdita's coming of age
'betrothal party' sixteen years hence at the sheep shearing. Setting
Mamillius on a threshold but stranding his *rite de passage* on the wide
expanse of the vacant forestage, Noble ratcheted up what was at stake in
the scene, childhood wrecked at precisely the moment of symbolic fulfilment – an idea captured proleptically in the scene's original image of loss
(and replayed in Act 4 in the wreck of Perdita's fulfilment). This
Mamillius was a child separated from the grown-ups, a lonely spectator
with no other children to talk to, bereft, but gazing at all those party
balloons bobbing from the backs of gilt chairs. (This poster image was the
one that came to stand iconically for Noble's production – a good choice,
considering some of the other options. Among the archive materials
preserved for this *Tale* there's a portfolio of discarded photographic stills,
evidently specially commissioned as publicity material, that record the
'family life' of King Leontes: shot after shot of John Nettles in rehearsal
clothes – but not in rehearsal – in a dozen different poses playing with
Mamillius, who's dressed in striped pyjamas, suggesting bedtime, dream
time. Even more intriguing is the series of shots of Nettles with a baby –
Perdita? – perhaps nine months old, who's being cuddled, bounced, held
aloft, held outstretched, to view and be viewed. These are images that
evoke a fantasy life; they're faked evidence of a history that never
happens, wish fulfilment. Or maybe sentimental whitewash.[88])

There was something magic about this Mamillius. The top he
unwrapped and set spinning was somehow a physical impossibility: it
should have wobbled, should have run out of spin and toppled. But it
didn't. It kept going through the whole of Camillo and Archidamus's
opening dialogue. This was wonderful! Defying physics, mechanics,
gravity! A bit like childhood. He was far upstage out of earshot during
Polixenes's 'boy eternal' speech, in his father's company, moving among
the guests, formally shaking hands with them, learning to be king. Later,
weary, it seemed, of the party, he wandered downstage and slumped in
his dad's chair, only noticed when Leontes called out for him and then

forgotten until the next spasm made his groaning father kneel before him, hug him. (This Leontes used the audience, not his son, as co-voyeurs.)

For this Mamillius, the nightmare began in the next scene. After the party, on his way to bed hours after he should have been tucked up asleep, he made a cheerful nuisance of himself among his mother's indulgent ladies playing ghost in the sheets they were trying to fold while she, big bellied, leaning back in a chair, tried to catch her breath ('Take the boy to you: he so troubles me, / 'Tis past enduring' (2.1.1–2)). There was something sad about this child who had only grown-ups for playmates. A little monarch lording it in the 'women's room', he seemed like a houseplant grown in the dark, not a lamb among lads who'd ever frisked in the sun, his 'play' restricted to his mother's ladies who 'baby' him and 'kiss' him 'hard' and offer their eyebrows for his precocious study, his knowledge 'learn'd … out of women's faces' (2.1.6, 5,12). (And not just sad: there was something slightly queasy here, like a visit to an antechamber in Ben Jonson's *Epicoene* where the 'Collegiate Ladies' are manhandling the Boy in the boudoir.) At the same time, though, Mamillius was never so bursting with 'childness', never so *present* in the play as at this moment, when, drawn back to Hermione ('Come, sir, now / I am for you again') and asked to 'tell's a tale' (2.1.21–2, 23), he began fashioning himself through his tale. Framing himself as narrative 'copy', so full of the story that he couldn't stand still, he was *playing*. 'Sit by us,' said his mother; 'Come on, sit down, come on.' Then, as he fidgeted and hopped, she, laughing, ordered, '*Nay*, come sit down: *then on*' (2.1.22, 27, 29 emphasis scored from performance). No sooner beginning – 'There was a man – Dwelt by a churchyard' – than he turned the story into a marvellous conspiracy: 'I will tell it softly'; 'Yond crickets' – his mother's ladies – 'shall not hear it' (2.1.29–31).

He was hugging her, whispering his story in her ear, oblivious to everything else – certainly oblivious to the way their intimate 'entertainment', their 'whispering', 'leaning cheek to cheek', 'meeting noses' was unconsciously enacting a pornographic fantasy of his father's (1.2.284–5) – when, inside the gauze box behind them the lights came up on his father ordering the search party for fled Polixenes. Leontes's cold self-diagnosis of his infection – 'I have drunk, and seen the spider' (2.1.45) – played as a voice-over to the silent cinema the boy and his mother were performing: weirdly, the 'surtitles' matched, for real, the mock horror story the boy was telling. Leontes splayed himself against the sagging gauze membrane, leaning toward his family: in weird shadow play, he became a gigantic arachnid. Then the box flew out and he was suddenly in the scene, stopping the story, hijacking the child's tale as earlier he'd hijacked the word 'play'. Curtly, he claimed Mamillius – 'Give me the boy' – and answered Hermione's puzzlement – 'What is this? sport?' with a backhander across the face that felled her (2.1.56, 58). Mamillius shrieked, lunged toward his mother. One of the ladies clamped arms around him, hustled him off – the last he was seen. On the floor, yanking her to a kneeling position and groping her from behind while she froze and listened with rising horror, Leontes simulated his sexual fantasies on Hermione's ripe body, touching the 'foundations' he would 'build upon', her 'centre'. His lewd gestures and the operations they mimed – the prodding, the pumping – cast distortedly back to the birthday present from Polixenes pulled from the red tissue paper, and those actions made spectators review it, weirdly, in their imaginations as a sex toy, Mamillius's 'school-boy's top' made over as phallic machine (2.1.103).

Last seen, Noble's Mamillius was a damaged child. Last heard of, dead. For Michael Billington in the *Guardian* the dead boy 'haunted' the rest of the play (3 July 1992), darkening *The Winter's Tale* into the interrupted ghost story Mamillius was telling. But it was Simon Usher, not Noble, who'd first taken spectators deep into this haunting darkness, with his production at the Leicester Haymarket eighteen months earlier. Childhood's chances in Usher's Sicilia were bleak. His Mamillius was a sick kid – who'd caught something off the adults. He coughed consumptively into a handkerchief and spat up blood. Equally bleak: the ending. There was life, but no restoration. The plaster Giulio Romano statue Leontes and the rest gazed at was just that – plaster. It didn't come to life. There was no miracle – unless you counted Hermione's entrance, behind them. The cripple who hobbled in was nothing like her statute stand-in. Hers was a body that bore the brunt of what Leontes had unleashed: on crutches, one leg in an iron splint, her face disfigured under welts of scar tissue. 'I used to think,' wrote Michael Schmidt in *The Daily Telegraph*, that *The Winter's Tale* was 'a glorious, redemptive romance'. No longer. For Usher had shown him 'that it is a "problem play"' (24 January 1991).

If Usher peered into, probed the heart of darkness he found in *The Winter's Tale*, Declan Donnellan opened up that heart. Bringing the Maly Theatre production he'd first directed in St Petersburg in 1997 to the UK in 1999, Donnellan told reviewers he thought the play was 'about forgiveness, redemption and regeneration' (Kate Bassett, *Daily Telegraph*, 4 May 1999); 'about becoming sane. It is a play that holds out the hope of salvation' (Simon Fanshawe, *The Sunday Times*, 24 April 1999). But if Donnellan told reviewers what *else* he'd discovered about *The Winter's Tale*, they didn't print it: that the play, *before* it arrives at 'redemption', is a devastating and enigmatic story of a double murder, of a father who kills his child – because his child is 'killing' him. For Donnellan, Mamillius is 'The most important character' in *The Winter's Tale*, his death, the 'most important event' in the play. It's the event that the play can never recover from; the event Donnellan's production was directed never to recover from. This death continues to shock Donnellan – the way Cordelia's death shocked Dr Johnson. And he's unsparing on the matter. Mamillius 'doesn't die'; 'he's *killed*': 'Leontes ends up killing him'.[89]

In this production's Stalinist setting where everyone was in uniform, including the boy, Mamillius was a sort of company mascot, a bauble played with casually by one party lackey or the other, then casually daffed aside as they turned to more important conversations, everyone jockeying for attention. Conspicuously, Mamillius spent a lot of time on his own. To begin with, he had his mother's attention. Barely reaching her shoulder, he stood on her feet – the way children at grown-up parties do – and they danced, stiff-legged, while downstage Polixenes tried to make his farewells, and Leontes refused to hear them. This argument between men, which remembered boyhood – a deep, sensual history between them, 'trained together in their childhoods' – was an initial wounding, the first inkling for Leontes that he was 'being excluded from love's order'.[90] And the first inkling of how childhood would be damaged in these men's hands: turning upstage, Leontes caught sight of son and wife in each other's arms.

He and Polixenes were brother officers, brother heads of state, who shared a code, part military, part personal, inaccessible to anyone else. (One of the truths these Russian actors brought on stage with them was physical: their training disciplines the actorly body to hold poses with an intensity of concentration that, between moves, seems almost to turn them to stone, and every move is committed. On the surface, then, there is the muscular precision of ballet; underneath, the emotional ferocity of a volcano erupting. In their stand-off, playing the surface, Polixenes and Leontes revealed the molten depths.) The men's epaulettes, their medals were merely the outward and visible sign of the bond uniting them. But what kind of bond was it? Who loved whom? Who feared whom? Their 'manly' sparring began to discover a twisted love story of uncertain male desire. 'Sir, you speak a language that I understand not', Hermione tells Leontes at her trial (3.2.80). In this production, languages were spoken that men didn't understand either: homoeroticism trying to empty itself of desire and masquerade as homosociability discovered itself ambushed by self-revulsion instead, deeply homophobic. Leontes wanted Polixenes to stay, wanted him to go; saw Hermione as an interloper, coming between brothers; saw Mamillius as an interloper, coming between husband and wife. In his skewed imagination, he feared the brother playing the husband's part as much as he feared the son taking the father's part. ('Listen,' says Donnellan, 'to what people in Shakespeare shout at each other. Then listen to the opposite, to what they *aren't* saying. Some of this "noise": it acts like a verbal torch shone in our eyes to blind us to what it doesn't want us to see – in this case, a terrifying anxiety *in the male*.'[91]) Leontes's talk of love, of his boy, of himself as a boy: all this talk was actually a subterfuge, covering over what else this anxious male scene discovered, an unspoken hatred of his child, his rival, the embodiment of what he'd lost forever – childhood. While Pyotr Semak's Leontes could be wildly nostalgic about his own vanished childhood (for instance, in that speech remembering himself 'unbreech'd', the Russian actor plummeted into sentimentality as down a mineshaft suddenly opening under his feet), he was coldly, observably inattentive to the child in front of him.

When he flipped – 'Too hot, too hot!' – a single bell chimed. The court froze. Then spectators watched Leontes turn on his child, grab him by the hair, shake him, ranting, slamming accusations into the boy's face ('Can thy dam? – may't be?'), before throwing him to the floor. The court unfroze; a thoroughly rattled Polixenes blurted, 'What means Sicilia?'; the child cringed. Later, left behind by his mother, the boy couldn't escape. His father dragged a chair centre stage, pinned him to it, and unleashed the full rage of 'Inch-thick, knee-deep' at him. Mamillius sat, white-faced, too terrified to cry or run – until Camillo saved him, drawing Leontes's attention to his silent entrance with a stage cough. Mamillius fled.

This episode of Leontes savaging Mamillius: were we watching an irrational transfer, generated by an upwelling of emotional chaos, Leontes clutching at the nearest object? Or was Mamillius, after all, Leontes's intended victim? Retrospectively, it became clear that Leontes's rage had many more places to go than this single target; that his abuse of Mamillius was merely a warm-up for what he would inflict upon Hermione. But it became clear, too, that this shocking family violence had been perversely instructive for the child. As Donnellan directed 2.1 – 'Take the boy to you …'; 'Come, sir, now / I am for you again' – Hermione and Mamillius were laughing, dancing – when suddenly the child, like a tamed wild animal remembering the trick of his savagery (or maybe just the boy replaying the assault performed on him minutes earlier), yanked his mother by hair, dragging her to her knees. She screamed, slapped the child hard across the face, then sat, shaken, trying to regain composure while the child was hustled downstage, out of reach. Where had this violence come from? From the father – the child his stand-in, punishing his mother for the pornographic scenarios he'd been forced to witness in imagination? From inside the child himself – having internalised, already, a culture of male violence that made him a 'man'? Or worse, having learned the ugly secret pleasures of physical abuse, yielding himself to complicity with the abuser by abusing?

Helped by the Russian translation, which frequently felt threatening to English ears, but also by cultural difference, which gave access to a kind of violent physical immediacy long since bred out of polite English culture, Donnellan's opening act told a story of a child brutalised and killed by adult awfulness, by the inexplicable, the incomprehensible in adult actions. The father blamed the mother: 'Conceiving' her 'dishonour', he said, Mamillius

> straight declin'd, droop'd, took it deeply,
> Fasten'd and fix'd the shame on't in himself,
> Threw off his spirit, his appetite, his sleep,
> And downright languish'd.
>
> 2.3.14–17

The courtier blamed the king:

> The prince your son, with mere conceit and fear
> Of the queen's speed, is gone ... Is dead.
>
> 3.2.143–5

But the truth of the matter was different. Those adults: broke the child's heart. Usher's consumptively sick kid was no more than a pale premonition of Donnellan's psychically diseased, spiritually ill little boy. After this *Winter's Tale*, after Donnellan and Theatre Maly, the way was prepared for Edward Hall and Propeller.

'Enter ... Babe / ... Exit ... Beare / Enter ... Sheephearde'

The Winter's Tale requires spectators to develop the viewing habits of a sight-damaged Edgar in *King Lear*. Do you think you know the worst? Keep watching. Because just when you imagine nothing can go more wrong, it does. We listen to Hermione at her show-trial (a scene calculated with exquisite irony to reiterate Leontes's notions of 'play', being, the queen says, as if 'devis'd / And play'd to take spectators' (3.2.36–7)). We watch her enumerating her loss, her husband (his 'favour', which she calls the 'crown and comfort of my life'); her son (she says she's 'barr'd' his presence 'like one infectious'); her infant daughter (snatched from her breast, 'The innocent milk in it most innocent mouth', 'Hal'd out to murder'); herself, 'on every post / Proclaim'd a strumpet' (3.2.94, 98, 100, 101–2). 'What blessings,' she wonders, 'I have here alive / That I should fear to die?' (107–8). Were he her counsel, *Lear*'s Edgar might advise: 'If you can ask that question, the worst hasn't yet happened. Just wait, just wait.'

Wait for Antigonus's next move. Last seen in 2.3 picking up the 'brat', the 'bastard', the infant waste that Leontes wants disposed of 'remote' from 'our dominions' (2.3.92, 74, 175, 176), he crosses paths, as he exits, with the servant who enters, bringing Leontes news that the messengers have returned with 'The truth' which 'great Apollo suddenly' wants known from his oracle in Delphos (2.3.199–200). (Stop, Antigonus, stop! listen to the message! But he doesn't; he presses on.) In 3.3 Antigonus stumbles along a beach in Bohemia in a raging storm carrying Leontes's child. Now, Leontes's *only* child. ('*Enter Antigonus, a Marriner, Babe*' says the Folio stage direction, TLN 1438.) The good servant trapped in a corrupt oath knows nothing of events in Sicilia: Leontes's family wiped out, royal service betrayed (Camillo) and brotherhood broken (Polixenes), the kingdom dynastically devastated. Neither does he know that he holds in his arms the only restoration for Sicilia, a kingdom punished in the oracle with futurelessness: 'the king shall live without an heir if that which is lost be not found' (3.2.134–6).

Ignorant of all this, holding the baby he's bound to set down on this desolate shore, Antigonus prepares to leave her trebly lost: lost in space, disowned, abandoned, exposed, cast away to strangeness, as Leontes commanded (2.3.182–3); lost in name, the name that Antigonus, surrogate 'gossip' in a mock baptism where rain stands in for holy water and the mother's cast-off mantle for a bearing-cloth, now gives her: Perdita; lost finally to history in false reckoning, the 'character' he writes of her a wrong account, based on 'rotten opinion', surmises – or on a dream, a ghost story that he takes for a truth ('the spirits o' th' dead', he muses, 'May walk again' (3.3.16–27)). How like Leontes is Antigonus here, supposing Hermione unchaste: 'You had a bastard by Polixenes, / And I but dream'd it!' (3.2.83–4). How like Mamillius, with his 'sprites and goblins' (2.1.26). Antigonus, knowing 'Dreams are toys' (3.3.39), yet credits this one and believes 'thy mother's fault' has 'thus expos'd [thee] / To loss and what may follow!' (50–1).

Antigonus gets so much wrong here.[92] But so much right. Like the storm raging over their heads, which Antigonus calls a 'lullaby too rough', the story he tells the baby is a rough lullaby, its dissonant music composed from his dream-wraith's 'gasping … speech' and 'shrieks', from his own momentary tenderness – 'Blossom, speed thee well!' – and from the clamour of the thundering storm (3.3.55, 25, 36, 46). Acoustically, the play reaches its breaking point in this scene. It's been talking through clenched teeth ever since Leontes's 'Too hot, too hot' in 1.2, and scene by scene, speech by speech, we've listened to a rising crescendo of acrimony, accusation, protestation, bellowing, shouting, blind rage that, if it peaks in textual terms with Paulina's savaging of Leontes in 3.2 ('What studied torments, tyrant, hast for me? …' (175–214)), hits a climax now in 3.3 beyond words, in sound, as the storm – every bit as earth-shaking as the storm in *King Lear* – takes on the voice of cosmic fury in the noise the skies produce, 'present blusters', 'loud weather', that show 'the heavens with that we have in hand are angry' (3.3.4, 11, 5). Visually, too, the play reaches its breaking point. The storm is so big, the space so vast, the wrong so huge, the imputations so ugly, the waste so extravagant – and the 'babe' so small. Here again, we have a scene about 'childness'. Everything in Antigonus's speech addresses the child, focuses on the child, makes the child precious – even as it condemns the child to loss. It's unbearable, beyond tears, and Antigonus knows it: 'my heart bleeds' (3.3.52). Worse still, this is the third time spectators have watched this scene – or a version of it: once when Leontes scanned his wife's belly to decipher its hidden contents, then abandoned the unborn baby to fix himself instead on his son; again when Paulina brought the newborn to be known, named, owned – and a second time abandoned, this time to the stone-hearted 'care' of the illiterate father; finally, now, again, misconstrued and cast away by the proxy doing the father's 'message'. This rhythm of three – 'Do it again!' – is the classic pattern of both stand-up comedy *and* tragedy. It's the Marx brothers negotiating doors – and Christ testing mankind: 'Simon, do you love me?' So which way is this play going? Is there any cure for the sorrows it has loaded on its bleeding hearts – Hermione dead in Antigonus's dream, a 'vessel' of 'sorrow' (3.3.21); Leontes bereft, his only 'exercise' his 'sorrows' (3.2.241, 243)? Can anything go more wrong?

Earlier, commanded 'Take it up' (2.3.182), Antigonus lifted the baby, held her in his arms, and spoke to her of the journey they'd be taking – 'Come on, poor babe' (184) – praying for her a miracle, that the savageness of beasts resident in her father's court might be confounded in the wilderness, where human kindness might be found in animals:

Some powerful spirit instruct the kites and ravens
To be thy nurses! Wolves and bears, they say,
Casting their savageness aside, have done
Like offices of pity.

(2.3.185–8)

Now, buffeted by the storm, bent by the 'loud weather', he hears 'A savage clamour!', turns, and just like on shipboard, faces a nightmare – or a dream come true – that allows him time for only two more half lines – 'This is the chase'; 'I am gone forever' – before he makes a run for it: '*Exit, pursued by a bear*' (3.3.11, 56, 57–78).

Why a bear?

I'll return to that question later. First, I want to think about what Antigonus leaves behind, a silence, his last iambic-pentameter line cut off, midway, five beats left stranded in the air, unfinished, empty; and the way the awfulness of that human silence registers the emptiness of the stage, the tiny bundle Perdita left entirely alone. In that silence, it seems that all the clamour of this play's first three acts is finally exhausted. And Perdita is truly lost.

Enter '*Sheephearde*' begins her 'finding'. The bear is Shakespeare's surprise; the Shepherd, a promise he made to the audience in the opening act, now on its way to fulfilment. Searching for a stray sheep, the Shepherd finds a lost lamb.

A crusty old man, 67 years of age (4.4.454), too old for foolishness, he enters, bearish, grumbling about a world we've seen, a world overcharged with testosterone, short on 'boy[s] eternal', where hare-brained youths perform mad tricks to the exasperation of their elders:

I would there were no age between ten and three-and-twenty, or that youth would sleep out the rest; for there is nothing in the between but getting wenches with child, wronging the ancientry, stealing, fighting – Hark you now! Would any but these boiled-brains of nineteen and two-and-twenty hunt this weather? They have scared away two of my best sheep ….

3.3.59–66

At a stroke, we're in a different world. The Old Shepherd has transformed the acoustic of the play. Since 1.2, *The Winter's Tale* has been speaking in verse, a kind of verse whose surface slipperiness, sliding from image to image, whose instant ability to trip from this to that, to imagine out of the bright materials of the licit daylight world in front of our eyes an illicit anti-world of sordid 'play', has produced the persistent effect of psychic pain; pain, moreover, delivered at hysterical pitch. Wilbur Sanders writes of a Leontes 'gone rag-picking among the ancient garbage of misogynist cynicism', the momentum of his tortured amazement 'given us in the rhythms and cadences of his speech'.[93] Now, the Shepherd's prose demotic puts us elsewhere. Quite literally, the play starts to speak a different language.

Of course, we may hear the Old Shepherd before we see him. Edward Topsell in his 1607 treatise on *The Historie of Foure-footed Beastes* advised shepherds to carry a whistle that their wandering beasts would recognise and respond to[94] – standard equipment among Warwickshire sheep farmers even today, and for numbers of stage shepherds at the RSC (in 1987, 1992, and 1999), a sound that works like an acoustic antidote to Leontes's rage, to the storm's noise, to the braying hunting horns of those boiled brains who are charging about in the weather, to the bear's roar. That whistle: as simple a sound as a baby's cry. As thin. As piercing. As arresting.

Visually, too, the Shepherd turns the play around. Whatever the courtiers of the first three acts look like, the Shepherd invites a double-take, for dressed in his trade – booted, hatted, coated in shaggy sheepskin (James Hayes in 1999; Jeffery Dench in 1992) – he looks more like a bear than an Antigonus. (The return of the bear: this was an effect Terry Hands played *double* in 1987, first with Bernard Horsfall's look-alike-bear-Shepherd, then again with Joe Melia's Autolycus, a fly-weight sheep-in-wolf's-clothing who first came on disguised as a bear.)

The theatrical double take, exactly the right response, keys us in to Shakespeare's strategy here. As Brian Gibbons observes, this is a play whose writing is characterised by a kind of doubleness, 'as when more is meant than meets the ear', a doubleness that extends to the visual writing, where constantly more is meant than meets the eye.[95] I've noticed the play's preoccupation with double bodies, double meanings; and Gibbons draws attention to the way spectators are constantly positioned to see 'events in a double sense', enabled to understand things from 'opposite points of view simultaneously': Leontes both tyrant and victim, murderous psychopath and petulant child; the trial both tragic and grotesque; ditto the domestic game of pass the parcel with the baby. The play keeps proposing twins and body doubles (actual, symbolic, the copied self) that arrive in the wake of those 'twinn'd lambs': Mamillius/Leontes; Perdita/Leontes; later, Florizel/Polixenes, Florizel/Mamillius, Perdita/Hermione, and Hermione herself, a statue performing her own body double in front of the child who's her double.

The double-dealing Autolycus ('littered', he says, 'under Mercury' (4.3.25), patron of assemblies and merchants, of highways, trick wrestling, and most significantly for my purposes, children) is, of course, a real twin, born of a double insemination (as Ovid tells it in *Metamorphoses* XI) by half-brothers, Apollo and Mercury, upon Chione – a distant original of the threesome in Sicilia?

With the Old Shepherd's entrance, we see such doubling extended into the larger metaphoric patterns Shakespeare is exploring. Biblically, the shepherd doubles the king, and if the king, then the king's double, the father. As Topsell reminds readers in his chapter 'Of Sheepe', the idea of the king originated in the ancient sheepfold, and the first kings were all shepherds, like David, summoned from shepherding to rule Israel (I Samuel 16). In these terms, the Old Shepherd is Leontes; and Perdita, the moment she is lost, is found:

> They have scared away two of my best sheep, which I fear the wolf will sooner find than the master: if anywhere I have them, 'tis by the sea-side, browzing of ivy. Good luck, and 't be thy will, what have we here? Mercy on 's a barne!
>
> 3.3.65–9

That exclamation registers something entirely new in *The Winter's Tale*. Immediate delight. And warmth. A thaw. Someone looks at the baby and recognises a wonder – 'A very pretty barne! A boy or a child, I wonder? A pretty one; a very pretty one' – which produces another wonder (or is it only natural?): human kindness (3.3.70–1). Instead of thrusting the baby away, the Old Shepherd gathers her up: 'I'll take it up for pity,' he says, making the lost one a 'finding [...]' (3.3.76, 126). That is, he reacts just as Paulina hoped Leontes would: he 'soften[s] at the sight o' th' child' (2.2.40). To date, Perdita's whole heart-breaking family history has been despised rejection. She's the child not wanted; the child damned by parental sin to be cast into the fire. Now, new adopted by rough graciousness, she tropes a new world of new 'made' men and 'good deeds': 'Thou met'st with things dying,' the old man tells his clownish son as he finishes his report of Antigonus's death-by-bear, 'I with things new-born' (3.3.119, 131, 112–13). 'Adopt': from Latin *adoptare*, the word means 'to choose for oneself'; also, 'To receive a graft, as a tree'.[96] Making Perdita the 'chosen child', grafting her, a 'gentler scion', to his 'wildest stock', the Old Shepherd, unwittingly, returns us to Camillo's original metaphors, begins, in language Act 4 will propose, to 'mend nature' – *human* nature (4.4.93, 96). That he's prepared to save the child is all the more

Plate 16 In Gregory Doran's 1999 RSC *The Winter's Tale*, the Old Shepherd (James Hayes) fusses over the foundling baby Perdita. (*Source*: Malcolm Davies photograph. By permission of the Shakespeare Birthplace Trust.)

miraculous since, just like her real father, this surrogate dad reads the body (*like a book*), and reads it all wrong. 'Sure,' he says, this infant 'issue' is evidence of 'some scape':

> Though I am not bookish, yet I can read waiting-gentlewoman in the scape. This has been some stair-work, some trunk-work, some behind-door-work: they were warmer that got this than the poor thing is here.
>
> 3.3.71–6

So much for 'Too hot, too hot!' Where Leontes railed – 'Shall I live on to see this bastard kneel / And call me father?'; 'No: I'll not rear / Another's issue' (2.3.154–5; 191–2) – the Old Shepherd stoops, takes up the 'bastard', willing to do the rearing, no more 'like' Leontes but rather 'like' the bear that Antigonus wished for earlier, a 'chance' 'nurse' to nurse the foundling (2.3.182). Picking up what's been left 'by strange fortune' (2.3.178), the Old Shepherd is the first of the 'precious winners' this play produces: the one who makes precious winning in Act 5 possible (5.3.131).[97] Exiting with the child – her supposed end, a beginning – he instinctively yields himself to an ancient paradigm. He is the wolf suckling Romulus and Remus; Pharaoh's daughter scooping Moses out of the

Nile; Merlin fostering Arthur; Dis adopting Proserpina.[98] The story of the foundling child allows us to inhabit the myth of return – and thereby to scoff at death. 'Do it again!' says the play. And over the next two acts, that's exactly what *The Winter's Tale* does.[99]

The doubles I see scripted in Shakespeare's playtext have been realised on stage in a number of ways in the productions I focus on: in set design (Terry Hands's mirror panels; Adrian Noble's gauze box and party balloons, later converted to human transport; Greg Doran's silk canopy – that later morphed into the bear – and the trial dock – later the statue's plinth); in costumes (fathers, friends, sons dressed as lookalikes) and props (the bearskin rug, Mamillius's toys); in stagecraft (Nunn's 'freeze frames', and Donnellan's). Even more significantly, the stage realises Shakespeare's textual doubles in theatrical doubling. Judi Dench in 1969 and Penny Downie in 1987 doubled Hermione with Perdita.[100] Antony Sher in 1999 intended doubling Leontes with Autolycus – then didn't.[101] Michael Pennington in 1990 doubled Leontes and the Bear. Placing spectators to 'see double', the theatre teases them with re-viewing: seeing likeness, seeing difference. But it also teases them with re-presentation: recursion, temporal return. For while time is experienced linearly in this play, it's also experienced cyclically. Time acts in his own person in this play, performing as the Chorus to open Act 4 by laying out a sixteen-year-long timeline that brings baby Perdita to a 'now' 'grown in grace'. But 'o'er' – that is, 'over' – is the operative word in his speech, set against 'now': 'I slide / O'er sixteen years … o'erthrow law, … o'erwhelm custom'. And then we watch Time 'turn' his 'glass' – *over* (4.1.24, 5–6, 8, 9, 16). The months altering, flowers shooting, blooming, withering, dying, things 'fresh' turned 'stale', the seasonal work of life on the land performed and remembered in festivals that translate labour into ritual play, into celebration, a sheep shearing, for example: Time passes, turned over, sands running through an hourglass, or measured on a clock, a dial, that times a man from cradle to grave even as it counts his minutes round and round a circle. Cyclical time, as in T.S. Eliot's 'Burnt Norton', makes 'Time present and time past / … present in time future / And time future contained in time past'. Hermione returning as Perdita traces this cycle, is 'natural' and 'right', satisfies generational expectations, expresses the 'Triumph of Time', the consolation that every sixteen years or so, human history gets a chance to 'do it again' and do it better, to repair the appalling mistakes one generation makes in the hopeful issue of the next. If Hermione is dead, she lives in Perdita: so the child 'cures' 'thoughts' that clog the ageing arteries of any parent, thoughts of mortality. Theatrically, for spectators, there's pleasure in watching the actor play her own child, mocking 'nature' with 'art'; narratively, there's pleasure in watching Perdita's performance ('prank'd up' 'Most goddess-like', as if she were playing in some 'Whitsun pastorals' (4.4.10, 134)), accomplishing, salvaging, detoxifying the distant memory of her father's 'Go, play, boy, play: thy mother plays ...'

But there is a much tougher story that can be made out of the materials of theatrical doubling. Declining pleasure for pain, for resistance, Edward Hall in 2005 looked at renewal equivocally, turned the screws on the play: his Mamillius doubled Perdita.[102] Tam Williams went from 'boyhood's pyjamas to a lovely floral frock' (Paul Taylor, *Independent*, 4 February 2005), from the dream-tortured child Mamillius to the blooming girl Perdita. Here, however, there was no 'wonder' in the replacement, no artfulness in the representation, and no metamorphosis. Williams, in a dress, made no attempt to conceal his masculinity. His Perdita never erased Mamillius; rather, harrowingly, showed the brother beneath, the lost in the found, refused permission for the dead child to be restored in the living sister – or forgotten. Mamillius's ghost story weirdly persisted, himself haunting Bohemia, remembering his 'winter's tale' in the sunshine of high summer.

These doubles return me to my earlier question: why the bear?

There's no bear in Shakespeare's source, Robert Greene's *Pandosto*, a prose romance (where the narrative, doing nothing more than *telling* the story, might easily have admitted a bear). *Staging* a bear, Shakespeare introduces a degree of technical difficulty to his play (and players) that reviewers still find remarkable (not least because it's such a wild extravagance in terms of economies of plot and performance: so much simpler to let Antigonus go down with the ship). 'Exit pursued by a bear', reviewers write, is 'one of Shakespeare's strangest stage directions' (Malcolm Rutherford, *The Financial Times*, 3 July 1992); it's 'notorious' and 'notoriously unplayable' (Charles Spencer, *Daily Telegraph*, 3 July 1992; Irving Wardle, *Independent on Sunday*, 5 April 1992); it's 'outrageous', an exit line 'explicitly conceived to test its audience's credulity' (Colin Frame, *Evening News*, 16 May 1969; Robert Shore, *Time Out London*, 22 June 2005). Of course, if you're the director who has to 'do' the bear on *today's* stage – like Greg Doran in 1999 – and if you happen to believe (as Doran does) that Shakespeare, when he invented theatrical difficulty, knew exactly what he was up to, you might see the matter somewhat differently. 'The problem,' says Doran 'isn't "Exit pursued ...". It's "Enter Bear".'[103]

Working on *that* problem, Michael Bristol has told us a great deal about what, symbolically, the Bear brings on stage with him, ideas delivered physically when, performing a stunning theatrical coup, he shambles into view, specifically the Bear's 'carnivalesque' role 'as a significant marker of spatiotemporal form'. 'Androgynous', 'polymorphous', the Bear is a 'figure of winter and of earth', his den is 'both a grave and a womb', and his appearance in rituals attached to Candlemas (2 February) marks, for early modern culture, 'the end of Christmastide leisure and the beginning of the agricultural work year'.[104] Teresa Grant has tracked real bears across the early modern stage (picking up on suggestions first made fifty years ago); Maurice Hunt has exhaustively run to ground bearish wordplay (though, it has to be said, much of the punning Hunt finds in the play works only textually, not theatrically, and only to a knowing reader because it anticipates the bear's entrance, already sees the bear coming).[105] We can deduce from all this that Shakespeare was well versed in bear lore – and ready to exploit the topical. He cites bears in twenty-two plays: hunted, baited, muzzled, encompassed by dogs, tied to a stake, led 'by the chain' through a Windsor crowd; Russian bears, bear whelps, head-lugged bears, cub-drawn bears; the bear as heavenly constellation; as coat-of-arms belonging to the Earls of Warwick (the ragged staff and bear, an insignia Shakespeare knew from home); as troping the 'tricks' 'strong imagination' plays on men: 'in the night, imagining some fear / How easy is a bush supposed a bear!'[106]

The Bear, Bristol argues, is a symbolic double for Leontes (troping not just personal violence but the violence of secular authority). In Bogdanov, he was the actual double: as Antigonus fussed over baby Perdita, Michael Pennington-as-Leontes appeared behind him, drew from behind his back a hand gloved with a massive paw, and felled the courtier with one blow to the head.[107] But if the Bear symbolically and actually tropes destruc-tiveness, he stands, too, for nurture: 'it is receiued in many Nations,' writes Edward Topsell, 'that children haue bene Nursed by beares'; and a woodcut illustrating Henry Watson's 'The hystory of the two valyaunte brethren Valentyne and Orson' (1555) shows just that, a bear carrying away one of the twins, wrapped in his swaddling bands.[108] This nurturing Bear, I've suggested, doubles the play's other equally improbable 'nurse', the Old Shepherd.

But more than that, the Bear doubles Hermione. One of the univer-sally recorded 'facts' about bears passed down from Pliny and Ovid – what everybody 'knew' – was the *post partum* role of the mother, unexam-pled anywhere else in the animal kingdom. She 'framed' the child after birth. Topsell opens his chapter 'Of the Beare' telling readers that 'The Latines call him Vrsus which some coniecture to be *tamquam orsus*, signifieng, that it is but begunne to be framed in the dammes belly, and prefected [sic] after the littering thereof', it being anciently 'beleeued and receiued, that the whelpes of bears at their first littering are without all forme and fashion, and nothing but a little congealed blood like a lumpe of flesh, which afterwarde the old one frameth with her tongue to her owne likenes' – natural history Shakespeare knows in *3 Henry VI*, where the deformed crook-back Richard calls himself 'an unlicked bearwhelp / That carries no impression like the dam' (3.2.161–2).[109] In this scenario, the father cannot recognise the child – 'art thou my boy?' – until the mother licks the baby into shape. 'Frame', 'form', 'impression': these are words that take us back to Leontes's metaphors, 'lines', 'print', 'copy', the child a new edition. The mother bear presses bear-ness onto the 'little' 'lumpe' (like Egeus presses patriarchal-ness onto the soft 'lumpe' that is the unformed wax, Hermia) leaving her 'figure', an 'impression' 'like the dam'. It is no coincidence at all that another name for a printing press is a 'bear'.

In the theatre, this enigmatic suggestion that Hermione tropes the Bear has been realised at least once – and magically, in Noble's *Winter's Tale* (1992). A 'real' animal, shaggy, brown, and bulky padded on stage left as Antigonus, downstage, crouching, tucked more warmth around the baby. Feeling the monster's breath on his neck, the courtier turned, leaped away, lunged back to the child, then stood frozen. The Bear was already straddling the baby, nosing her. Three things happened simultaneously to align incongruity and make spectators 'see' the Bear as maternal avatar: from the flies dropped billowing white silk, the phantasm of Hermione; the baby cried, as if giving her first birth-cry; and the Bear's sniff became a kiss, the rugged animal, swinging *her* head side to side (for spectators saw her as a *she*-Bear) as if perplexed by the sound, or bidding farewell, gently backing off before turning on Antigonus.[110]

That double ultimately combined maximum horror and relief – a recoil of emotions that produced the authentic physical experience editors are trying to tell us about when they describe this play generically as a 'romance'. Much more disconcerting (and deeply disallowing of relief) is one final twinning in productions that bid for a double of the Bear and Mamillius, where the killed child returns, remembering grown-up savagery or metamorphosed into child-killer. At the Goodman Theatre, Chicago, in 1990 this double was opportunistic and proleptic, using standard-issue nursery equipment to anticipate the ruin of childhood: Frank Galati's *Winter's Tale* opened with the sound of a wind-up cymbal-clashing toy bear, Mamillius's property. In Hytner's production at the National Theatre (2001), the double was eerily speculative: dead Mamillius entered and stood momentarily over his baby sister's cradle before exiting the world. In Propeller (2005), it was both nostalgic and nightmarish, a monstrous pastiche: for it was dead Mamillius, holding a teddy bear, who savaged Antigonus.

Perhaps the idea of the Bear as Mamillius – a double our theatre strains to imagine – was directly accessible to Shakespeare's original spectators: perhaps it was as immediately 'seen' as the other symbolic connections Bristol detects. For, to early modern understanding, like the child, like Mamillius in *The Winter's Tale*, the Bear is medicinal. The Bear 'physics the subject', 'makes old hearts fresh' (1.1.38, 39). You don't eat him. You take him, because he belongs to the pharmacy, not the larder. He's 'better', writes Topsell, 'for medicine then food'. Listing the 'very many' 'virtues medicinall' in the 'naturall operations in Beares', Topsell describes a miracle cure for almost everything. The fat, dried and ground to powder, is 'giuen against the palsie, the Kings euill, the falling sickenesse, an old cough, the inflamation of the eies, the running of the eares'. For complications in pregnancy, it's a sovereign remedy for most conditions: a prevention for spontaneous abortion; analgesia in child-birth. 'The stones in a perfume, are good ... that women may go their full time'; 'they make amulets of Bears nails, and cause them to weare them all the time they are with child'; 'if a woman bee in sore trauile of child-birth, let a stone ... which hath killed ... a beare ... be throwne ouer the house wherein the Woman is, and she shall be eased of her paine.' Perhaps most poignantly for my concerns, the bear, given to children, cures thoughts – the kind of thoughts that Mamillius can't cure in himself, the kind that kill him: 'The right eie of a beare dried to powder, and hung about childrens neckes in a little bag, driueth away the terrour of dreames'.[111] The prophylactic bear serves as early modern teddy bear.

The Winter's Tale – or – The Pillowman

The Winter's Tale is Mamillius's story. It's the story he tells in response to his mother's request: 'Come, sir, ... / ... pray you, sit by us, / And tell's a tale.'[112] It's the story he begins, 'There was a man ...'. It's the story his father interrupts, silences: 'Give me the boy' (2.1.21–3; 29; 56). And it's the story that, gone missing in substance, yet lingers across the whole play, remembered, called to mind like the boy it belonged to who was lost when he lost it.

Where was it going to end, Mamillius's tale? What happens to lost stories?

One answer, an 'adult' answer, is that nothing is lost, all is salvaged – that's Prospero's answer in *The Tempest*. In *The Winter's Tale* stories are saved, retold. ('Do it again,' says the play. 'Do it again.') Ovid's tale of Dis and Proserpina finds retelling in Florizel and Perdita; Hermione's 'monstrous' birth tale is retold in Autolycus's ballad of the usurer's wife ('brought to bed of twenty money-bags': the entire litter, just like the dad! (4.4.264)). The story of the slandered mother is repeated in that of the slandered child; of the father whose heart's turned to stone redacted in the mother who stands before him, a statue, but warm; the tragic history of the lost infant is retold in the 'amazedness' of 'the king's daughter … found': 'such a deal of wonder' that 'ballad-makers cannot be able to express it' (5.2.4, 23–5). It's 'like an old tale'; 'like an old tale still' (5.2.28, 62).

Retold stories come round again, admit new endings. Take the one about the 'gallant child', Sicilia's 'greatest promise' and 'unspeakable comfort' (1.1.38, 36, 34). He dies. End of story. End of story? No. Retell the story.[113] Give him a sister. She's born. She lives. She returns – and makes good the 'promised end', Perdita, the 'lost one' found. *She*, it turns out, is the medicinal child; *she* the one who 'physics the subject', 'makes old hearts fresh', takes sixteen years off her father's mind, cures thoughts and quickens the blood.[114] She's the one who saves her mother. Only 'hope' that Perdita was 'in being' 'preserv'd' dead Hermione alive (5.3.127). So the sister picks up where the brother left off.

But is this recuperative story a con? 'Do it again! Do it again!' Is that a story that adults tell adults to cheer themselves up – or to perpetuate the myths that acculturate the abuse of children? (How useful to adults that children should be on hand to cure them. How durable that particular myth – and how destructive of children.[115]) But what about the story the *child* tells?

In the contemporary British theatre, it's playwrights like Martin McDonagh and Philip Ridley who've taken today's grubby, urban-junk Mamilliuses under their wing, and taken protective custody of the stories children tell. Their attempt in *The Pillowman*, *The Pitchfork Disney*, *The Fastest Clock in the Universe*, and *Mercury Fur* is to preserve the integrity of children's stories – distinct from adult stories told *to* children or *about* children, which are really stories for adults. 'Let's get out of Elsinore,' says Ridley's grown-up child Dominic, trying to dodge the adults, the lifestory-police, by running away to the playground to sit on the roundabout and wonder 'what it might've been like', 'when we were kids. Toddlers … If we'd grown up with someone to talk to about all the stuff in our heads …?'[116]

That 'stuff in our heads' – Mamillius-type stuff – is the stuff lost in *The Winter's Tale* but held on to in *The Pillowman* where McDonagh has Katurian tell the story of 'The Writer and his Brother' three times, with three different endings, all of them taking the child's life as the writer's material (literally and horrifically) but twisting and mocking the notion of the adult-imposed 'happy' ending. McDonagh's is a play that's profligate with stories: Katurian has, he claims, written more than four hundred of them (and in the play's rehearsal at the National Theatre, those stories were written – then lost[117]). Of the masses and masses of stories, he insists (and remember, he's being forced to justify his writing to a self-described 'high-ranking police officer in a totalitarian fucking dictatorship') only 'maybe ten or twenty have children in'. Tupolski corrects him: 'Have *murdered* children in.'[118] Under interrogation, it's those stories of murdered children that Katurian is forced to recite: those are the stories the audience hears. But most disturbing among them is the one the interrogators don't hear, the one his brain-damaged older brother (damaged by the systematic, 'scientific' torture inflicted by his parents), the child-like Michal, asks him to tell, the story of 'The Pillowman'.

He's a huge, soft, blobby shape, 'all made up of these fluffy pink pillows'. 'On his head he had two button eyes and a big smiley mouth which was always smiling' – which was good, says Katurian, because 'the Pillowman's job was very, very sad because the Pillowman's job was to get' little children 'to kill themselves'. Why? Well, the Pillowman first meets these children when they're grown-ups – when they're knotting a noose and slipping it around their own necks or kneeling in front of a gas oven, the door open. He stops time. He regresses those wrecked adults to childhood, before any of the awful 'history' ahead of them is their lived story, and he offers them a 'pillow' death right now, so they can 'avoid the years of pain' that are their future. Katurian, narrating, raises the obvious objection. Little kids committing suicide? Who ever heard of a kid killing himself? 'Well, the Pillowman would always suggest they do it in a way that would just look like a tragic accident … Because mummies and daddies always find it easier to come to terms with a five-year-old lost in a tragic accident than they do with a five-year-old who has seen how shitty life is and taken action to avoid it'.[119] The bedtime story – the little face pressed hard against the pillow – tells the 'real' story, the child's story of self-slaughter. But it's immediately recruited by the adult to the process of recuperation.

So what happens to Mamillius? Where was his story going to end? In Shakespeare's playtext, Sicilia owns him memorially, preserves him for posterity like a hero of a fairy tale or a religious monstrance: he's converted to story, rendered a 'Jewel of children' (5.1.116) who, 'when talk'd of', 'dies … again' (5.1.119). That's later – sixteen years later. But even newly dead, Mamillius is recruited for different adult stories: his father's, which transforms him into a prototype Hamlet, killed by his mother's shame; the courtier's, which transforms him into a baby nemesis, punishing tyranny. But is there another story? Has Shakespeare's Mamillius been consulting off stage with McDonagh's Pillowman, the pair of them cutting a hole in the canvas, so to speak, like little Ellen Terry, to peer into the 'adult' world before turning the blade on the kid? Is Mamillius in *The Winter's Tale* a suicide – a child who kills himself with grieving? Does he resist the adult's happy ending?

Whatever Shakespeare's playtext is doing at the end of *The Winter's Tale*, performances of the play on contemporary English stages are now regularly requiring spectators to experience as much the 'numbness' that the ending wants to 'Bequeath to death' as the 'Dear life' it awakes to 'faith' (5.3.102, 103, 95). In 2005, the 'happy ending' unravelled in the final moments of Propeller's *Winter's Tale*. A 'creepy, ghost-like atmosphere' returned, wrote Paul Taylor (*Independent*, 4 February 2005); Hermione pointedly spoke nothing to Leontes, and his courtiers peeled away, leaving him stranded centre stage. Perdita took off her dress. Tam Williams became once again, wrote Taylor, 'the son who is conspicuous by his absence at this reunion'. He stared at his father 'with accruing incredulity' – then blew out the candle. Blackout. End of story.

In 1999, the 'happy ending' was nowhere to be seen in the final moments of Maly Theatre's *Tale*. The parents – reconciled (but to what?) – were old and broken; the daughter, Perdita, at their feet, helpless to help, curing nothing, her childhood squandered in the squalidness of her impoverished, trashy life in Bohemia. A clock chimed. The court froze. Threading his way among them, led by the figure of Time, came the small boy, Mamillius. He paused. He gazed at each parent, a look that was finally uninterpretable. Sad? Reproachful? Forgiving? Or not? His look told a story only the child could tell, and now wouldn't. End of story.

Chapter 4

Precious Motives, Seeds of Time
Killing futures in *Macbeth*

Kill him, Commandant is saying in my ear and lifting my hand high with the machete. Kill him oh ... He is taking my hand and bringing it down so hard on top of the enemy's head and I am feeling like electricity is running through my whole body. The man is screaming, AYEEEIII, ... but it is not helping because his head is cracking and the blood is spilling out like milk from a coconut. I am hearing laughing all around me even as I am watching him trying to hold his head together. He is annoying me and I am bringing the machete up and down and up and down hearing KPWUDA KPWUDA ... there is just blood, blood, blood ... I am not bad boy. I am not bad boy. I am soldier and soldier is not bad if he is killing ... All we are knowing is that, before the war we are children and now we are not.

Uzodinma Iweala, Beasts of No Nation

He has no children.

Macbeth, 4.3.218

Lines written to a son

Late in 1598, troubled that 'the houre of death', 'uncertaine to me (as unto all fleshe)', was upon him, James VI of Scotland composed his 'Testament, & latter wil': a jobbing king's detailed instructions on the day-to-day business of being king. He called it *Basilikon Doron*, the 'kingly gift', a Greek title rather in excess of the treatise's homeliness.[1] Written out in the king's distinctive hand (and in Middle Scots, a choice that registered the work's privacy of address to a single intended reader), and bearing on its surface the marks, Jenny Wormald writes, of 'a mind at work' – 'scribbling, scoring out, scribbling again' – the manuscript was entrusted the following year to the printer Robert Waldegrave who, sworn to secrecy, produced seven copies of the now-anglicised text to be circulated among, or better said, assigned to, seven deliberately chosen textual guardians.[2]

Basilikon Doron belonged to the *speculum principis* genre – in Scotland, an untested genre. Every English king from Edward III to Henry VIII had been addressed with letters of advice to princes (excepting, significantly enough, only Richard III and Henry VII: perhaps the 'wars of the roses' – as Shakespeare would call them – exhausted confidence in such literature). But before *Basilikon Doron*, a princely 'Booke' of 'good advice', a 'mirrour vive and faire' that 'sheweth the shadow of a worthy King' (in short, the job title, description and instruction manual) had never been issued to a Scottish king.[3] Certainly, nothing like it was on offer when James's most distant ancestor needed its urgent instruction: the eleventh-century Fleance, Banquo's child and, in Raphael Holinshed (via Hector Boece's historical myth-making) the dynastic originator of the royal Stuart line. By the time Shakespeare wrote Fleance into *Macbeth*, and Scotland onto the English stage in 1606, however, *Basilikon Doron* was the acknowledged published authority on 'how to' be king. It was a book, I want to argue, that Shakespeare had much in mind as he was writing *Macbeth*. The play, like the book, looks hard at being a king. But more than that, the play, like the book, looks hard at being a child.

King James's remarkable treatise is in three parts that inform 'A Kings Christian Duetie towards God', his 'Duetie in his Office' and his 'behaviour in Indifferent Things': duties Shakespeare's Macbeth would later agonise over in soliloquies and Malcolm would distil into the 'king-becoming graces' (4.3.91).[4] Fathers and sons are everywhere in this text, and the language of legitimate, loving and 'natural' paternity frames James's similes. The good king is a 'naturall father and kindly Master' to his people; the 'vsurping Tyrant', 'a step-father and an vncouth hireling'. The good king's 'greatest suretie' is 'in having [his subjects'] hearts' while 'subjecting his owne priuate affections and appetites to the weill and standing of his Subjects'. A tyrant will 'frame the common-weale euer to advance his particular', 'inuerting all good lawes' and 'building his suretie vpon his peoples miserie'.[5] The good king is generous and self-subjecting but severe. There are some crimes he cannot 'in Conscience' ever forgive: 'Incest …: Sodomie, Poysoning, and false coyne'. And most heinous of all: 'Witch-craft, [and] wilfull-murther'.[6]

By turns deeply serious, jocular, epigrammatic, testy, canny, and calculating (his eye is clearly fixed on the English throne), James in *Basilikon Doron* discourses on big ideas and minutiae. He writes about how to deal with 'these … verie pestes in the common-weill', 'these Puritanes' who would put down kings in Scotland and 'fantasie to themselves a

Democraticke forme of government'; how to handle fractious clergy, arrogant, blood-feuding nobility, avaricious merchants and slack crafts-men; how to conduct foreign policy, and when it fails, how to conduct war – but James, the self-styled 'Rex Pacificus', clearly wasn't struck on war. He covers the subject in three paragraphs – while it takes him thirteen pages in Waldegrave's printed text to describe how to choose the right wife. 'Mar-riage,' he writes, 'is the greatest earthly felicity or miserie, that can come to a man'. 'Treate [your wife] as your owne flesh: Command her …: Cheerish her …: Rule her …: Please her in all thinges reasonable': but do not 'pride you that yee wil bee able to frame & make her as ye please: that deceiued Salomon the wisest King that euer was.'[7]

The busy, intimate discourse of *Basilikon Doron* has the power almost to persuade us that, as the conceit has it, we are, if not talking, then listening to the dead.[8] The king seems to be sitting at our elbow, his confi-dential voice in our ear. (Dismissing calumniators he briskly advises 'feare not their orping' but 'bang it out bravely'.[9]) But reading James's instruc-tion book, what arrests my attention is not the lively argument at its centre, the 'matter' relevant to *Macbeth* that I'll return to later, or even the urgent theatricality of its performance, the way the king is so very obviously staging himself in this writing.[10] Rather, it's the domestic circumstance that frames the text, the fact that *Basilikon Doron* was a book written for a child: written for James's 'Dearest Sonne' and 'nat-ural and lawfull Successor', Prince Henry, who, in 1599, was just four years old. As it proceeds – one long soliloquy (or perhaps better said, a duologue engaging a silent partner) – it emerges as a book written *about* a child: about James himself and a childhood bereft of parents and their instruction, a childhood heir to their mistakes. *Inter alia*, it is a book that discovers how dangerous it was to be a child in the Scotland of King James – and the Scotland of his ancestors which *Basilikon Doron* informs, the Scotland of *Macbeth*.

We can hardly imagine a four-year-old, even a precocious one, the reader of *Basilikon Doron*, yet this book was evidently the child's property,[11] and it was meant, as the prefatory '*Epistle*' informed the prince, to fill an absence, his father's absence, to be 'a faithfull praeceptour and coun-sellour', a 'resident faithfull admonisher', to stand in the father's stead 'because my affaires will not permit me ever to be present with you' (something of an understatement, given that the king supposed himself to be dying). So the book was offered as a surrogate father. That aside, the 'Testament' perhaps aimed also to fill another, longer-standing and deeply-felt gap: for it published the guide book to monarchy that James himself had needed as a child – and wasn't provided with.

He was thirteen months old and virtually an orphan when he came to the Scottish throne in July 1567. His father, the 'witless drunkard' Lord Darnley,[12] had been murdered in February, seemingly in reprisal for his participation a year earlier in the assassination of David Riccio, Mary Queen of Scots's Italian secretary, imputed to be the queen's lover and supposed father of the child she was then carrying – baby James, born three months later. One of Riccio's murderers, a Gowrie (of the clan that would cause James so much future trouble), allegedly held a dagger to Mary's pregnant belly, threatening both the 'good queen' (anticipating *The Winter's Tale*) and the unborn 'bastard'. Six weeks after Darnley's death, Mary married the Earl of Bothwell – the man who'd master-minded Darnley's murder (a gunpowder plot: cue for another in the family's future); who'd taken custody of the infant James; and who'd dealt with Mary's first refusal to marry him by raping her. This marriage was an outrage too far. Within a month, Bothwell was on the run, Mary was taken captive and forced to abdicate (by the by, miscarrying Bothwell's twins), and baby James was king. He never saw his mother again.

It has to be said, however, that if James wasn't issued the rule book to go with the crown, his mother – who acceded in 1543, one week old – wasn't either; or his grandfather, who inherited in 1513, at eighteen months.

I want to suggest, then, that one way of reading *Basilikon Doron* is as a riposte to this failure of legacy, an attempt to fill the silence of a childhood missing paternal conversation, to answer the child's need to speak with the dead, and the father's, to influence the living, to pass on his knowledge. King James's book says 'Remember me'. It talks in a voice as direct, as nostalgic but as controlling, as 'child-authoring', as old Hamlet's to his son, 'I' to 'you', where 'you' is always 'my sonne', and not just in the formulaic opening line of the dedicatory sonnet at the head of the book – 'Lo here (my Sonne) a mirrour ...' – but on page after page thereafter, conversationally, familiarly: 'Take heede therefore (my Sonne) ...'. It is this address that makes it a key text for understanding *Macbeth*: *Basilikon Doron* stands proxy for the book Fleance will need and Banquo can't provide.

James fills the silence he consciously anticipates 'after my death ...' with writing that, as it defines kingship, figures a particular relationship between father and son, based on reciprocal duties underwritten by authority but animated by love (the father's, to 'provide for your trayning up'; the son's, to 'heare' and 'leare', child-duties we will see imposed upon young Fleance).[13] In James's writing, 'king', 'father', 'son' are terms annealed to each other that inform each other: the very idea of the king, of his legitimacy and succession, is bound up with paternity, with the idea

of the child. It's the mark of a usurper (like Shakespeare's Richard Gloucester) to have 'had no father', to be 'like no father' (*3 Henry VI*, 5.6.80),
and the usurper's crime will finally be punished by failure of succession:
'He has no children' (*Macbeth*, 4.3.218). By contrast, the legitimate king is
'A louing Nourish-Father', '*communis parens* to all your people'.[14] Not insignificantly, however, if this book is, as its title makes it, a present, a 'kingly
gift', it is also a contract that carries with it a penalty clause that bears
down fearfully on the child, framed as a father's curse, a renunciation of
paternity:

> I charge you [James writes, in the concluding lines of the prefatory
> '*Epistle*'] (as euer ye thinke to deserue my fatherly blessing) to follow
> and put into practise (as farre as lyeth in you) the precepts hereafter
> following: and if yee follow the contrair course, I take the greate
> GOD to recorde, that this booke shall one day be a witnes betwixt
> me and you, and shall procure to bee ratified in Heaven, the curse
> that in that case here I giue you; for I protest before that great God, I
> had rather be not a Father and child-lesse, norbe [i.e., than be] a
> Father of wicked children.

Equally sobering is the understanding lying unspoken in the text, that
as *Basilikon Doron* offers the small boy a whole household-full of proxy
fathers in textual form – 'admonisher', 'counsellour', 'trusty friend' and
truth-teller, 'lesson', 'guide', constant companion (like 'the *Iliades* of *Homer*
to Alexander') – the child is going to need them.[15] If we wonder how suffi-
cient a substitute writing will be for the flesh-and-blood father, James
offers an oblique answer, instructing Henry, as he himself learns to be a
writer, to craft his 'Enregistrate speech' attentively, for 'Your writs will
remaine as true pictures of your mind to all posterities'.[16] Clearly, *Basilikon
Doron* is 'posterity writing', a 'true picture' perpetually at the child's side,
set to 'remaine', even as, sub-textually, it imagines the author absent and
the child a paternal orphan.

Filling the silence he anticipates, James not only maps the mental world
of the full-grown Stuart king. He tells his own past and gives glimpses of a
childhood that endured, that suffered into, the knowledge he's passing
on, offering cautionary tales – first told him, as it seems they must have
been, by adults, guardians, tutors – from a traumatised family history. His
grandfather turns up several times in the text, a man who probably
deserved 'the honorable stile' given him 'in being called *The poor mans King*'
(an epithet James may have heard from his tutor, George Buchanan, who
knew James V personally) but also a man given to what Malcolm in

Macbeth will call 'stanchless avarice' (4.3.78), to 'lighlying and contemning [his] Nobilitie': 'Remember,' James advises his son, 'how that errour brake the King my grand-fathers hearte'.[17] More grievous was his addiction to 'summer-seeming lust' (*Macbeth*, 4.3.86). James V fathered numerous bastards on nine mistresses.[18] But he was grievously punished: 'the reward of his harlotrie' was 'the suddaine death at one time of two pleasant yong Princes' – his legitimate sons, in 1541 – and 'a daughter only borne to succeed him'. And he dumped a heap of misfortune posthumously on that daughter – saddling her with all the lusty illegitimates, boy-bastards and half-brothers of his promiscuity, trained up to aspire to her throne. 'Have the King my Grand-fathers example before your eies,' James advises his son, 'who by his adulterie, bred the wrak of his lawful daughter and heire'.[19] It's not just enough, then, for a king to have 'issue'. To succeed with succession, that issue must be legitimate.

Remembering not just his grandfather but his grandmother, his mother, his father, his cousin-Queen Elizabeth (whom he addressed in letters as 'dearest sister' and 'mother' while he always called his own mother 'Madame'), James in *Basilikon Doron* makes memory alive by writing its absence – and locates himself, a child, inside the turbulent history that rocked his cradle. He cites his (childish) over-clemency as an example of 'ouer-deare cost experience'. Having decided, just short of his twelfth birthday, that he was old enough to rule without a Protector, he thought '(by being gracious at the beginning) to winne al mens hearts to a louing and willing obedience' – but soon enough 'by the contrarie founde, the disorder of the cuntrie, and the tinsell [that is, the loss] of my thankes to be all my rewarde'.[20]

Writing his absent family, James sets himself inside a wider nexus of father and son relationships, biblical, classical, mythic: Abraham, Isaac, David, Absalom, Solomon, Alexander, Anchises, Brutus. And as he packs his vacant narrative with their histories, he captures for himself what his writing in *Basilikon Doron* endows upon his child: all this knowledge that is his is his son's to own. Even more intriguing, however, is a rebarbative act of *disowning*. Laying out Henry's reading list, instructing him to be 'wel versed' 'specially in the Chronicles of al nations', James, in a sudden, near-hysterical outburst, bans the 'infamous inuectiues' of '*Bvchanans* or *Knoxes* chronicles' – and he imagines 'their authours' appallingly 'risen againe' in 'them that hoardeth their books', monstrous *revenants* who will haunt his son's reign.[21] So:

> if any of these infamous libels remaine while [i.e., until] your daies, vse the law vpon the keepers thereof, for in that poynte I would haue

> you a Pythagorist, to think that the Spirits of these arch bellowces [i.e., ringleaders] of rebellion, ar flitted into them that hoardeth their bookes, or maintaineth their opinions, punishing them, euen as it were their authors risen againe.[22]

John Knox couldn't have been much of a presence in the boy's life: he was dead by the time James was six. How very different, George Buchanan. Humanist, political theorist, slanderer of James's mother. And sadist: a man so terrifying to James that, when he appeared to him years later in a dream ('risen againe'), the king woke up trembling.[23] In 1570 this Buchanan, aged sixty, was appointed the little boy's tutor – James was four, exactly Henry's age in 1599 – and he continued directing the king's studies for at least the next ten years, probably the most influential daily presence in the child's life. The academic regime was formidable – 'they gar me speik Latin ar I could speik Scotis,' James famously reported – and the physical regime, brutal: thrashing 'the Lord's Anointed' was not just a matter of discipline for Buchanan but of satisfaction.[24] No wonder, then, that James, leaving his 'kingly book' to Henry, was providing a very different kind of tutor.

From such brief citations in *Basilikon Doron* – all those family names mentioned once or twice, whole histories alluded to glancingly in half sentences, the injunction to Henry to 'remember' stories the child can't possibly know but that, like readers four hundred years later, he'll have to recover to make sense of – we get some very restricted access to a particular culture of Stuart childhood. We see the child imagined as a conduit of the past; the child as forfeit for parental sin; the child needing 'th' offending Adam' beaten out of him (*Henry V*, 1.1.30); the child as valued object of love, learning and devotion; the child as bearer of aspiration; the uncertainty of childhood and its waste. Only one of James IV's six royal babies survived, all but one of James V's legitimate children died in infancy, and James VI was the only royal child of his generation to live. Given such insecurity, it is no wonder that he sent his orphan manuscript to Waldegrave, the printer, with instructions for those 'onely ... seven' further copies to be made, copies, he writes, 'I dispersed amongst some of my trustiest servants, to be keeped closely by them lest in case by the iniquitie or wearing of time, any of them might have beene lost, yet some of them might have remained after me, as witnesses to my Sonne.'[25] Iniquity of time, loss, remains, witness: powerful terms for imagining writing – and imagining also a child.

Of course, that explanation of the seven copies wasn't attached to the 1599 Waldegrave printing. It was written 'To the Reader' of the English edition published in 1603, an edition that turned into a runaway best-seller.[26] By then, James knew that much of what he'd feared in 1599 hadn't happened. He hadn't died. His manuscript hadn't been lost. He hadn't missed out on the inheritance he most dearly desired – the English crown. That was the good news. The bad news was that, as things were turning out, most of what he'd provided for in *Basilikon Doron* wasn't going to plan – not least, the boyhood of that 'Dearest Sonne'.

Prince Henry had been the object of parental dispute since birth, his Danish mother, Anna, never reconciled to the Scottish practice of delivering royal babies, immediately *post partum*, into the protectorship of guardians.[27] A little over a year after Henry's birth in March 1595, the twenty-one-year-old queen attempted to break the guardianship. It was reported that 'the Queen speaks more plainly than before and will not cease till she has her son'; 'No good can come between the King and Queen till she be satisfied anent [about] the Prince'.[28] Her every act of opposition to her husband and king – including her alleged involvement in the Gowrie plot of August 1600 – can be traced back to the claim 'that herself should have the education of the Prince'.[29] In England, it wasn't just Elizabeth's ministers in Whitehall who knew how matters stood in Scotland, where the king, on the one hand, periodically threatened to imprison Anna for her 'rebellion', and on the other, was 'so "syllid" in love'[30] that he couldn't control her. These matters were common gossip, circulated on the streets of London. In February 1603, John Chamberlain, that tireless letter writer who seems to have viewed all London from his lodgings next door to St Paul's, wrote of 'New troubles' arising 'dayly in Scotland', 'the worst of all' being 'the domesticall daungers and hartbreaking that the Kinge finds in his owne house'.[31] (We remember those lines from *Basilikon Doron* about the futility of trying to 'frame' a wife 'as ye please'.)

A month later, things in Scotland reached a final crisis. Elizabeth died on 24 March; within days, James received news that he was Elizabeth's heir; acceding to the English throne, he began his progress south in April; Anna – pregnant with their sixth child – was to follow in May. From Edinburgh, James wrote a last letter to his eldest son at Stirling Castle, apologising 'That I see you not before my parting' but promising that his dereliction 'shall (by God's grace) shortly be recompensed by your coming to me shortly and continual residence with me ever after' – lines hard to interpret since James left without making any provision for the (now eight-year-old) child to join him. Maybe the king's intentions are revealed by his sending, with his farewell letter, his surrogate, a copy (*another* copy) of *Basilikon Doron*, in its newest edition – 'my book lately printed' – with instruction to Henry to 'study and profit in it as ye would deserve my blessing'. 'It' is no longer a 'Testament', exactly; more of a Hoyle's Rules: 'there can nothing happen unto you whereof ye will not find the general ground therein (if not the very particular point touched)'.[32]

Anna, however, had other plans. She travelled to Stirling Castle to demand custody of her son. When it was refused, she 'flew into a violent fury', and, as the Venetian ambassador reported to his Doge, 'four months gone with child as she was, she beat her own belly, so that they say she is in manifest danger of miscarriage and death'.[33] This was a woman evidently capable of living lines Shakespeare would later write for Lady Macbeth, a mother who'd dash a baby's brains out to prove a point. Anna aborted, sickened; James, far away in England, frantically negotiated – then capitulated. Henry travelled into England with Anna, manifestly his mother's, not his father's 'Dearest Sonne', a son who would be raised in the English court as a thoroughly English Prince of Wales.

Perhaps even more vexing to the father, this 'English' Henry showed little inclination to grow into the 'scholar prince' James had modelled in *Basilikon Doron*. 'Be diligent and earnest in your studies,' he'd instructed the boy in his farewell from Edinburgh, but later complained that he longed 'to receive a letter from you that may be wholly yours', that is, one not just copied out from a pattern but 'as well formed by your mind as drawn by your fingers.' And then the disappointed father is off again, Polonius-wise with advice, thrusting *Basilikon Doron* onto the child one more time: 'For ye may remember that in my book to you ....'[34]

The boy, however, seems to have had other priorities. His interest was arms, not books. Let his little brother Charles be the swot. Henry was cut in his great-grandfather's cloth. He wanted to be a warrior: 'I know what becomes a Prince. It is not necessary for me to be a professor, but a soldier and a man of the world.'[35] For such a child, an apprentice soldier-king whose prototype might be Banquo's Fleance, *Basilikon Doron* was largely irrelevant – the wrong instruction manual.

By April 1603, however, the text itself had taken on another life, no longer the private 'witness' between 'two conjunct persons'[36] but a public broadcast, an English, then an international, best-seller that, within weeks, generated eight editions and circulated in as many as 16,000 copies – one for perhaps every seven Londoners.[37] Six months earlier, when Elizabeth was still alive, John Chamberlain had heard that 'the Scottish king' was 'printing a little peece of worke christened with a Greeke name'.[38] In April, the rush on the booksellers shows English readers wanting direct access to their new king's opinions. Edward

Alleyn, the great tragedian and lead player with Nottingham's Men, bought a copy of the book.[39] Chamberlain sent one hot-off-the-press to Dudley Carleton, secretary to the English ambassadors in Paris, at the end of March.[40] And whether or not he owned it, William Shakespeare undoubtedly read it, and read it attentively: *Basilikon Doron* is a text that haunts *Macbeth*, a play that, we remember, at its climactic moment materialises on stage the originating metaphor of James's book: it produces that significant prop, a looking glass, a 'mirrour vive and faire'. *Macbeth*, I want to argue, can be read as English William's Scottish *speculum*, and like that other mirror, its gaze is turned on children.

If it's possible to read Holinshed's *Chronicle of Scotland* and see how the playwright's mind has moved across it like a magnet picking up iron filings, finding in Boece's accounts of eleventh-century Duff and Duncan scenarios, images, exchanges, chance remarks that snagged in his memory and that returned in *Macbeth*, it's possible to observe that same adhesive mind reading *Basilikon Doron* – and raiding it. King James's book was, after all, a 'history text', its subject Scotland, which brought the story up to date as it rehearsed newer recapitulations of the oldest controversies that, from time immemorial, had troubled the country. For Shakespeare, reciting the past was always a way of writing the present, and there was plenty in the bloody chronicle of Holinshed's 'Makbeth' to put spectators in mind of contemporary horrors in the 'Stuart England' that James had aspired to in *Basilikon Doron* and that he'd now achieved. Most immediately, there was the gunpowder plot of November, 1605. This act of sedition represented attempted regicide at its most ideologically audacious, for it encompassed not just king-killing but child-killing: ten-year-old Henry was to accompany his father to the state opening of Parliament that day. The plotters were tried and executed ('unseamed ... from the nave to th'chaps' (*Macbeth*, 1.2.22)) the following year, among them, the 'equivocator'-conspirator, Father Garnet. Clearly, Shakespeare was writing James into *Macbeth*. The 'shew of eight kings' in 4.1 'and Banquo last, with a glasse in his hand' (Folio S.D., TLN 1657) that 'shows ... many more' (4.1.119) takes in James (and Prince Henry?) as it presents a Stuart line that, from its murdered first father, will 'stretch out to th'crack of doom' (4.1.116). This is a genealogy that Holinshed lists and that John Leslie (commissioned by the king) publishes in *De Origine ... Scotorum* (1578) as a flowering rose tree hung with heraldic shields, twisting up from Banquo and Fleance through numbers of Walters, Roberts and Jameses, topping out at James VI.[41]

Writing the king into *Macbeth*, Shakespeare writes the king's writing into the play. Images from *Basilikon Doron* seem to have burrowed their way under the skin of *Macbeth*: the 'cauterised conscience', the conscience 'become senselesse of sinne, through sleeping in a careless securitie' is one.[42] The tyrant's feast is another.[43] And the mirror – remembered five times in the king's text. Things that matter deeply to James as political problems in *Basilikon Doron* turn up in the play, as performance: the intractability of wives, the absolute evil of witchcraft, the spuriousness of prophetic utterance, the divinity of kings and indefensibility of regicide (an ideology that is troubled by the problematics of the 'bad king' conundrum), the cancer of tyranny that diseases the mind, the advisability of kingly equivocation, the political iconography of banquets, the care one should take with words. If the material Shakespeare scripts in 4.3, the England scene, is lifted straight from Holinshed, it's also the case that those 'king-becoming graces' are as much the theme of *Basilikon Doron*'s second chapter. And it may be that the whole method of the king's treatise is reproduced (as homage?) in Macbeth's self-interrogation: the book's theatrical urgency, scripted as argument that reveals the king's appetite for discourse, for debate, may be remembered in that other king and his tortured mind, obsessed with abstract thinking: 'If ill, / Why …?'; 'If it were done …'; 'wherefore could not I pronounce "Amen"?' (1.3.130–1; 1.7.1; 2.2.34).

More significantly for my purposes, however, I see *Basilikon Doron* reaching into *Macbeth* its dedicated attention to the child. These are two texts that think themselves, imagine themselves through the idea of the child, and in ways that Holinshed simply doesn't. Holinshed gives Shakespeare the raw historical data: he recounts Macbeth killing Duncan – in battle, not bed – and years later his growing fear of Banquo (who aided him in the war). He names Fleance. He cites the murder of Macduff's family. But Shakespeare raises the stakes, at every turn 'childing' his play.[44] Holinshed tells of prophecies. Shakespeare imagines them surfacing in the Weird Sisters' cauldron as children – a bloody babe, an infant crowned – performed by children (who surely double the other children in the play, Fleance a proxy for the child-king Malcolm; Macduff's boy a bloody surrogate for the father ripped from the mother's womb). Holinshed mentions Siward. And five more adult males. Shakespeare gives them all sons (all, of course, except Macbeth), and he gives Siward a boy, a child-soldier who, in the heroic act of being killed, achieves manhood (a theatrical statement set against the killing of other children in the play?). Holinshed's Lady Macbeth goads her husband to murder. Shakespeare has her, appallingly, trump regicide with infanticide: 'I have given suck …' (1.7.54). Holinshed puts Fleance in the scene of ambush and murder; Shakespeare locates the lad much earlier in the story, in a scene he invents, just after the banquet, when the apprentice boy-soldier on sentry duty with his dad acts as his father's squire, takes the sword Banquo hands him – and 'that too', whatever 'that' is (2.1.4, 5). And he listens to his father's confession, 'A heavy summons ... / ... I would not sleep; merciful powers, / Restrain in me ...' (6–8). Shakespeare makes spectators know the slaughter of Macduff's 'Wife, children, servants, all / That could be found' (4.3.213–14) by doing what Holinshed doesn't. He puts squarely in view the killing of the boy, making the death of that 'egg' (4.2.80) the crisis the play has been driving at since Duncan's murder, a killing that completes the king's death with the child's: the first, symbolically, understood regicide as the hacking down of the tree of life; the later figures something worse, the sickening destruction of nature's 'germen' (4.1.58), the killing of the 'seeds of time' (1.3.56). And if that weren't horror enough, Shakespeare puts in front of spectators another scene Holinshed doesn't produce. He sets Macduff in 4.4. (reversing the sequence in Holinshed) to *hear* the news, a hearing we must watch: 'All my pretty ones? ... All? / What, all my pretty chickens ...?' (4.3.218–20). Then numbly, dumbly: 'He has no children'.

Child images are everywhere in the poetry of the play: 'issue', 'seed', 'line', 'breed', 'fry', 'posterity', 'germen', 'copy', 'cherubin', 'firstlings'. And so are infant body parts: baby's 'brains', a 'baby-brow', 'the eye of childhood', the finger of a 'birth-strangled babe', the body of 'a naked newborn babe', manhood transformed to 'The baby of a girl'. More than that, childhood sits at the very nerve centre of Shakespeare's plot. Macbeth's tragedy, unlike Holinshed's history, is slowly, terribly to unpack the calculation that puzzled him as he brooded upon the murder of the king, 'If it were *done* when 'tis done': whether killing is the end of it, and 'th'assassination' will 'trammel up the consequence and catch / With his surcease, success' (1.7.1–4, my italics) – whether, that is, he'll get away with it, evade 'consequence'; whether 'surcease' (doing it, making an end) will mean 'success' (good outcome). Only later does Macbeth recognise that 'consequence' is one of those riddle words in his world that 'palter with us in a double sense' (5.8.20). It's not 'surcease' that delivers 'success'; it's *succession*, succession that fails him. 'He has no children'. In Shakespeare's play, tyranny is not the motive force, Macbeth's need to cover his back, to keep the past at bay by committing greater and greater atrocity. Tyranny is merely the accessory. The motive is barrenness: Macbeth's appalled, delayed, recognition of the black joke that mocks his dynastic project. Having no children, he has no future. To keep that future at bay, he must kill it – by crushing the 'seeds of time' (1.3.56) that are the future. The children.

This play, then, of all the tragedies, has Shakespeare most focused on 'consequence', on a nightmare vision of a kingdom cleared of children devastating in its bleakness. But like James's lines written to a son in 1599 that, published abroad in 1603 somehow missed their mark (lines that, as the reign went on, ironically 'return[ed] to plague the inventor', documenting the squandering of idealism in the king's increasingly profligate English rule), so Shakespeare's 'apocalypse now' play of 1606 almost immediately began to lose its dangerous edge. By the time *Macbeth* was first printed in the 1623 Folio, song and dance routines from Thomas Middleton's *The Witch* had entered the text, along with a serio-comic hocus-pocus Hecate (who, in Middleton's play, hands over to her flunkey some human booty, an 'unbaptised brat', with the ludicrous jingle-jangle instruction to 'Boil it well, preserve the fat' (1.2.18–19)). At the Restoration, William Davenant introduced more 'divertisement' – a full chorus of flying witches played as *opera buffa* – a show that Samuel Pepys in 1666 called 'one of the best plays for a stage, and variety of dancing and music, that ever I saw.'[45] But Davenant cut the ultimate theatrical point of Shakespeare's play: the onstage killing of Macduff's child. In 1847 Samuel Phelps tried to restore it – that is, two hundred years later. But succeeded only briefly. Spectators objected. The killing of the boy, they protested, was too painful to watch. His death wasn't staged again until 1909[46] – five years after A.C. Bradley's magisterial *Shakespearean Tragedy* (1904) argued the 'great importance' of the child-killing (which Bradley had never seen, it being, as he wrote, 'usually omitted in stage representations'). Its 'chief function', Bradley thought, was 'to touch the heart with a sense of beauty and pathos, to open the springs of love and of tears'[47] But aestheticising, sentimentalising, even idealising this local scene of a boy's beautiful death, Bradley (who elsewhere asked 'real' questions of fictional 'lives': 'Where was Hamlet at the time of his father's death?'; 'Why has the Ghost waited nearly a month since the marriage before showing itself?'[48]) made the death all about the audience. He didn't investigate what work that death might be doing in the play.

Bradley was, after all, an eminent Victorian, and heir to his culture's habits of mind. The Shakespeare child-scene that thrilled Victorian nerves was little Arthur in *King John* pleading so sublimely with Hubert to defy the king's orders to put out his eyes (a part always played on the Victorian stage by a girl – Ellen Terry for one). Clearly *that* was a scene 'to touch the heart with a sense of beauty and pathos, to open the springs of love and of tears'.[49] But writing of *Macbeth*, he remained curiously incurious of how the child's killing connected to Shakespeare's bigger thematic and theatrical concerns in that play. He elided its ugly brutality, its active cruelty. And most significantly to me, Bradley (youngest child in a family of twenty-one; a bachelor all his life; a man who had no children) was utterly incurious of the Macbeths' children. 'Whether Macbeth had children or ... had none,' he wrote, was 'quite immaterial'; 'Lady Macbeth's child (I.vii.54) may be alive or may be dead ... We cannot say, and it does not concern the play.'[50]

For three hundred years, then, *Macbeth*'s children behaved like good Victorians, unseen, unheard, 'immaterial' – until 1932, when a young man not long down from Cambridge looked set to recall them to public view and to critical scrutiny with a paper read to a meeting of the Shakespeare Association. Its title: 'How Many Children had Lady Macbeth?'

So remind me: how many children *had* Lady Macbeth?

The title, it turned out, was a spoof. Dropping the question on his unsuspecting audience, L.C. Knights wasn't interested in *Macbeth*'s children. And he didn't want an answer.[51] He wanted a revolution. Thirty years after the event (in a comically self-deprecating mood), he recalled the lecture. He remembered himself 'comparatively young'. (Comparatively? At twenty-six, this Young Turk was barely post-adolescent.) And he remembered himself 'dissatisfied with the prevailing academic approach to Shakespeare', specifically, the kind of 'character' criticism which disciples of Bradley had been writing for the past thirty years: criticism that observed the discrepancy between Lady Macbeth's Act 1 assertion, 'I have given suck and know / How tender 'tis to love the babe that milks me' (1.7.54–5), Macbeth's traumatised meditation on his childlessness in Act 3 (3.1.60–73), and Macduff's desolate cry in Act 4, 'He has no children' (4.3.217), and, worried by apparent inconsistencies, tried to account for the Macbeths' missing babies. Impatient with Bradley and his acolytes, Knights was 'excited by the glimpses I had obtained of new and it seemed more rewarding approaches' – modernist criticism, a criticism framed by T.S. Eliot and G. Wilson Knight that read Shakespeare's plays as dramatic poems, 'imaginative constructions mediated through the poetry', a criticism that found useful analogies with music; that looked for *leitmotivs* and themes rather than motives and character-development; that attempted to account for the complex structures of Shakespeare's verse – and to find the plays' meanings – in what Wilson Knight termed 'the logic of imaginative correspondence' rather than the 'logic of plot'. For young Lionel Knights this was bracing stuff. As he wrote, he 'welcomed the opportunity of proclaiming the new principles in the very home of Shakespearean orthodoxy, whilst at the same time having some fun with familiar irrelevancies of the kind parodied in my title, *How Many Children had Lady Macbeth?* Fired up for war, or at least a few bloody noses, he gave his paper 'and waited expectantly for the lively discussion that would follow this rousing challenge to the pundits'. Only, 'nothing happened':

> except that after a period of silence an elderly man got up at the back of the room and said that he was very glad to hear Mr Knights give this paper because it was what he had always thought.

'The revolution was over,' wrote Knights, 'and I went home.'[52]

Part of the 'fun' Knights's paper had with its original audience – and its subsequent readers – was its mandarin refusal to address, never mind to answer, the question it posed. Evidently, Knights didn't see *Macbeth*'s child-imagery as one of those 'imaginative constructions mediated through the poetry' that shaped dramatic meaning. And he certainly wasn't interested in the play in performance, though just as he was graduating from Cambridge, Barry Jackson's Birmingham Rep *Macbeth* was making news by putting the play in modern dress and restoring the onstage murder of Macduff's boy – killed over a cup of afternoon tea by assassins who climbed in through a casement window. Like a beached whale (or red herring) 'How Many Children had Lady Macbeth?' lay rhetorically stranded at the top of the paper. Ignored, nothing further was needed to demonstrate its concerns as among those 'familiar irrelevancies' modernist criticism wanted mocked.

But 'Jesters', as we know, 'do oft prove prophets' (*King Lear*, 5.3.64). Something that one critic sees as a 'familiar irrelevancy' turns out to be of 'deepest consequence' to another (not least because such categories prove culturally sensitive, historically implicated). On the one hand, in 1932 Knights was perfectly able to see the urgent dramatic relevance of material which the blockheaded editor (so he became, retrospectively) of the 1912 Arden *Macbeth* had thought was 'magnificently irrelevant' to the play: Lady Macbeth's sleepwalking scene and Macbeth's Act 5 soliloquies.[53] But on the other, in 1932 he couldn't see the point of Lady Macbeth's (absent) children. It took Cleanth Brooks in 'The Naked Babe and the Cloak of Manliness', published in Great Britain in 1949, to despoof Knights's question, to show Knights why 'How Many Children had Lady Macbeth?' was no 'familiar irrelevancy' but exactly the right question to be asking, why counting heads in Scotland's nurseries was not some 'pseudo-critical investigation' but utterly to the point – and opened up the play's complex poetic structures to the very scrutiny of close reading that Knights was proposing.[54]

For Cleanth Brooks, the child in *Macbeth* was 'perhaps the most powerful symbol in the tragedy'.[55] Framed sometimes as characters (Fleance, Macduff's boy), sometimes as materialised symbols (the apparitions raised by the Weird Sisters), sometimes as metaphors ('pity' is 'a naked newborn babe / Striding the blast' (1.7.21–2); 'duties' to Duncan's 'throne and state' are 'children and servants' (1.4.24–5); murderous inspirations are 'firstlings', and 'noble passion' is integrity's 'child' (4.1.147, 4.3.114–15)) the image of the child draws together the play's stake in history, its yearning aspirations for 'tomorrow, and tomorrow, and tomorrow' (5.5.18), its frustrated desires for 'blessèd' yesterday (2.3.84), a time of grace before 'memory' (5.3.42) came to figure as waste-ground rooted only with sorrow. From the Weird Sisters' opening utterance – 'When?' – *Macbeth* is concerned with futures, prophetic, dynastic, domestic, metaphysical, eternal, and the child is the material embodiment of these futures. But nostalgically the child represents a longing for the adult's past: his innocent selfhood, the time cited by Polixenes in *The Winter's Tale* as belonging to the 'boy eternal' (1.2.65), before corrupted nature in the grown man falls prey to 'cursèd thoughts', invasive 'in repose' (2.1.8–9). Ironically, Macbeth wants both to possess the future – the one the Weird Sisters 'gave' him – and to destroy it – the one they 'promised' Banquo. But as children fail Macbeth, Macbeth's future fails: 'unlineal', he wears a 'fruitless crown' and grips a 'barren sceptre' (3.1.64, 62, 63). 'It is the babe that betrays Macbeth,' Brooks remarks, ' – his own babes, most of all.'[56] 'If't be so', 'Nought's had, all's spent' (3.1.65, 3.2.4). And Macbeth is left groping line by line after terrible knowledge:

> For Banquo's issue have I filed my mind;
> For them ...
> Put rancours in the vessel of my peace
> Only for them ...
> To make them kings, the seeds of Banquo kings.
>
> 3.1.66–9, 71

His recourse is to make war on the future – a 'war on children'.[57]

Putting children back at the centre of Shakespeare's poetic (if not theatrical) composition (for, I need to observe, Brooks had nothing to say about *Macbeth* performed), what sense did the American critic make of A.C. Bradley's adamant opinion that 'Lady Macbeth's child ... does not concern the play'? What did he do with the rogue datum, 'I have given suck ...'? Was it 'immaterial'? A 'familiar irrelevancy'? Or an 'integral part of a larger context'?

Macbeth's most recent Cambridge editor, A.R. Braunmuller, writes that *Macbeth* is a play that thinks through metaphor – an acute observation, and one surely indebted to Cleanth Brooks.[58] It helps interpret Lady Macbeth's claim – to know 'How tender 'tis to love the babe that milks me' – for that's a claim that seems to have as much force as metaphor as personal history. The line comes at the end of a pair of speeches whose objective is to make a man of Macbeth. He has decided against the 'business'. Honoured by Duncan, he is opinion's golden boy, dressed in glittering approval that is to be worn 'now', he says, in its 'newest gloss', not 'cast aside so soon' (1.7.31–5). She counters by turning the rhetorical tables on him, recasting his definitive statement, 'We will proceed no further', into a series of relentless questions, souring 'the hope ... / Wherein you dressed yourself' (35–6) as merely a drunkard's dream and slighting the crown as an 'ornament' (42) that, his valour mightily desires but his cowardice feebly fears to catch even when it's thrown into his lap. She makes him a cat, a beast, a sot sick on ambition's fantasies. And a man? She constructs him manly – but only, tantalisingly, in one of those hypothetical past-futures this play is constantly imagining: 'When you durst do it, then you were a man' (1.7.49). Killing, it appears, is what makes a man a man. And it is as she is juggling these terms – 'make' and 'unmake', 'more', 'much more' – that she slips in her stunning *non sequitur*, 'the babe that milks me' (52, 54, 50, 51, 55). A logic of association may be working here, analogising gender: that is, childbirth *makes* a woman like killing *makes* a man. Or perhaps the child is instanced as another degrading comparative – 'less than' a man as the beast or drunkard is 'less than' a man. But whatever the anecdote's status as 'real' history, its force here is rhetorical, to set up, through a syntax of conditionals, a terrifying equation on a hypothetical scale of personal investment:

> I would, while it was smiling in my face,
> Have plucked my nipple from his boneless gums
> And dashed the brains out, had I so sworn
> As you have done to this.
>
> 1.7.56–9

To make Macbeth a man, Lady Macbeth produces the death of the child.

Paradoxically, while Cleanth Brooks enabled just this sort of close textual reading, he never attached it to theatre reading: in his seminal essay, he considered none of the scene's performance work. Like Knights, then, entitling Lady Macbeth's history then ignoring it, Brooks read her poetry without probing its authenticity. In his writing, there was never an

actor in the part speaking the speech and occupying the space of its experience. 'I have given suck' was a poetic conceit that operated merely to
index Lady Macbeth's 'quite sincere' 'rationalism': 'She knows what she
wants; and she is ruthless in her consideration of means.'[59] But consideration of Lady Macbeth performed, of her child or the self that might be
deformed by the loss of her child? Brooks did not make that enquiry. If for
Knights, then, the children were irrelevant, for Brooks they were purely
notional.

Missing children

Some questions refuse to go away. And some questions go AWOL from
their fixed domains and set up independent lives. Fifty years on, readers
who knew nothing of the original modernist controversy – or of the original essay, or that it was meant to be a joke – could still quote Knights's
question. Criticism continued to brood upon it.[60] And it might have
struck the by now rather elderly Young Turk as deeply ironic that in the
theatre (where every actor who plays Lady Macbeth must interpret 'I
have given suck', and every actor who plays her husband must interpret
what he hears), 'How Many Children had Lady Macbeth?' was *the* question actors wanted answered. Sinead Cusack made it so – in 1986 – by
putting its serious interrogation at the top of her performance agenda in a
Royal Shakespeare Company production directed by Adrian Noble.[61] By
insisting that performance give weight to the images she heard the
playtext activate, Cusack, I want to claim, effected a major shift in the
theatre, reconnecting *Macbeth* to its early modern origins – to its children.[62] As significantly, her performance redirected the play's post-
modern afterlife: since Cusack, subsequent Lady Macbeths from
Amanda Root to Cheryl Campbell, Brid Brennan, Harriet Walter (who
kept a photograph of a 'missing' baby in her script [63]), and Emma Fielding
have made it a matter of urgency to account for the missing child. Indeed,
locating the 'missing child' has become the crucial performance trope
defining the Macbeths' partnership. ('We ... decided,' wrote Derek
Jacobi of his 1992 RSC *Macbeth*, 'that somewhere in the past of their relationship they had lost a child.'[64] And Tony Sher (RSC, 1999): 'Most
crucial is the baby ... They're a couple whose baby has died. It's a taboo
subject, we decided, never mentioned. And then suddenly it is.'[65])

   Simultaneously, however, something else was happening to *Macbeth* on
stage in England in the 1980s. Its poetry was being politicised, its imaginative reference recruited to 'do' cultural work of the kind Martin Esslin
alludes to when he writes that the theatre is the place 'where a nation

thinks in public in front of itself'.[66] As the 1980s moved into the 1990s, *Macbeth* emerged as the Shakespeare play which the British theatre was going to use to think through the nation's current and ongoing cultural crisis in 'childness', a site where the nation would search its deep anxieties about relatedness and separation, about authority and autonomy, about locating the child in contemporary culture, about valuing the child's life – or not: claims I want to examine by looking first at Noble's 1986 RSC *Macbeth* and Penny Woolcock's extraordinary contemporary film adaptation for BBC television, *Macbeth on the Estate* (1997), then across three more *Macbeth*s – Gregory Doran's (RSC, 1999), Dominic Cooke's (RSC, 2004), John Caird's (Almeida, 2004) – to Out of Joint's *Macbeth* (2004) directed by Max Stafford-Clark.

In the 1980s Britain became child-centred, the 1960s 'me' generation producing babies that absorbed them, 'mini-me's' lavished with almost profligate care and attention. The royal family – Charles and Diana, most conspicuously – produced royal infants, the next Prince of Wales, the next heir to the throne, the nation's 'future'. The politicians produced legislation that saw 'the value of children recognised in unprecedented ways' as the very concept of childhood was 'redefined' to emphasise 'its prerogatives and importance'.[67] Bastardy was removed from the law books (1989), and caning outlawed in schools (1982); child abuse entered public consciousness via the sensational Cleveland crisis (where, across six months in 1987, hundreds of children who were suspected victims of sexual abuse, the allegation made against their parents on the basis of an unproven medical diagnosis, were removed from their families, often from bed in midnight or dawn raids, and placed in foster and residential homes); children's rights were publicly debated via the 1985 Victoria Gillick case, taken eventually to final appeal in the House of Lords (which found against the mother of ten who initiated the litigation, judging that minors were competent to give consent to their own medical treatment and therefore that contraception could be prescribed to under sixteens without parental consent). Between them, Cleveland and Gillick provoked radical reforms that altered the status in law of Britain's children.

But in the same year – 1989 – in which Parliament passed the Children Act and the United Nations declared its Convention on the Rights of the Child, rights that could only be guarded by social responsibility, Britain's Prime Minister seemingly voided the very notion of social responsibility by declaring that (at least in the UK) there was 'no such thing as society'. For Maggie Thatcher, there were 'individual men and women' – and 'there [were] families'.[68] Her government's economic policies, however, were turning the screws on the family, impoverishing children and putting them – as the opposition party in Parliament argued – at risk. After ten years of Thatcher government, the numbers of people living on Income Support in the UK had doubled, to nearly 4.5 million, piggybacking another three million dependents, of whom two million were under 16.[69] Four major inquiries into child abuse and a number of sensational individual cases showed the traditional British family to be terminally dysfunctional, children its victims: the House of Windsor told this story at a national level. So did the working-class houses raided in Cleveland. And out of the tangled mass of accusation and counter-accusation published almost daily in the newspapers (Charles vs. Diana, social workers vs. parents) came national self examination. What kind of adult could perpetrate child abuse, we wondered.[70] And, more anxiously, the questions we almost didn't dare to ask, What kind of child could participate in it? What kind of child was its product? Were children innocents? Or delinquents? Virtuous – or iniquitous? For some of us, early modern Shakespeare converged with contemporary culture and politics to give us terms we could use to frame the debate – or at least keep our anxieties corralled. In Shakespeare, we could see 'childness' as a 'medicine' that 'cures' adults of 'thoughts that would thick [the] blood' (*The Winter's Tale*, 1.2.170–1). Equally, we could see the child as a 'disease', a 'plague-sore' in the parent's flesh (*King Lear*, 2.2.395, 397), a reprobate needing 'th' offending Adam' 'whipped … out of him' (*Henry V*, 1.1.30). The redemptive child vs. the child of loss: at least there seemed to be two possibilities.

Then, in February 1993, the nation watched on the news replay after replay of some grainy CCTV footage, security images captured in a Liverpool shopping precinct that showed a small boy being led away by two bigger boys, his little hand in one of theirs. That night, Jon Venables and Robert Thompson used bricks and an iron bar to batter two-year-old James Bulger to death; nine months later, they were convicted of his murder. Both were ten. Sitting in the courtroom then writing about the Bulger case in a book called *As If*, Blake Morrison needed Shakespeare to supply a language big enough to comprehend the unimaginable 'deed that's done'. He set out lines from *Macbeth* as the book's epigraph:

> … from this instant,
> There's nothing serious in mortality.
> All is but toys, renown and grace is dead,
> The wine of life is drawn.

2.3.85–8

And *Macbeth* kept surfacing in his writing, as if the play's language hung suspended in his imagination just below consciousness:

> In that spring of cold fear, it was as if there'd been a breach in nature: the tides frozen; stars nailed to the sky; the moon weeping far from sight. Those nameless boys had killed not just a child but the idea of childhood.[71]

As a nation, we agreed. From this instant, childhood was tainted, children, evil. But demonising childhood as a way of making it possible for us adults to explain the inexplicable was an invention that returned to plague us. For demonising the child was the very defence put up by the aunt of eight-year-old Victoria Climbié and the aunt's boyfriend to 'explain' why they'd tortured her to death in February, 2000. She was 'possessed by witches', said the aunt. She must have been, said the boyfriend, for even when he beat her with a bicycle chain, she never cried. They had arranged an exorcism – but she died first.[72]

Remembering loss

In William Worthen's terms, performance is 'an act of memory and an act of creation' that 'recalls and transforms the past in the form of the present'.[73] When it opened in late 1986 Adrian Noble's *Macbeth* seemed to be remembering Britain's recent collective past and, uncannily, to be anticipating 'horrible imaginings' (1.3.137) we would wait a decade or more to see played out. This production took a long look at desecrated childhood, perverse parenting, assembling fragments from culture at large into a form that, resonating against the Shakespeare text, interrogated the present.

The production poster, a cartoon by Pollock, was a Spitting Image portrait of the Macbeths (recognisably the actors, Jonathan Pryce and Sinead Cusack) as the (Un)Holy Family done in sick greens and vomit yellows: Macbeth, his face lugubriously stretched like a Giacometti figure, his arm around his wife's shoulder; she, thin-lipped and hatchet-faced staring out of the frame.[74] In her arms, she cradles a baby built by Dr Frankenstein. It's armless, neckless; its legs are mismatched. Seven strands of Adolf Hitler hair are combed across its forehead; and below the folded fat of its blobby jowls, clearly visible is a line of sutures where the head is sewn on. This monster infant with its bloodshot *Rosemary's Baby* demon eyes looked like it might have emerged from the Weird Sisters' cauldron. Indeed, Pollock's family portrait of 'We Three' weirdly anticipated those other three weirdnesses who would present themselves in the play's opening line: 'When shall we three meet again?' Somehow the baby looked both real and fake, a repulsive *putti*, or a voodoo fetish, or perhaps a *memento mori*, a doll dragged around by a deranged mother as a surrogate for a lost child. As the production's publicity 'image', plastered on hoardings outside the RST and in the theatre foyer, it constructed for spectators a memory carried into the auditorium of a past life for the Macbeths, he a father, she a mother – and the child, a grotesque. As it quoted and mocked holy portraits by Michelangelo and Raphael, it was blasphemy. But it also, proleptically, inscribed the narrative with a backstory that would transform *Macbeth* into what Barbara Hodgdon calls a 'text of loss': only in the foyer, only in the poster portrait could spectators see the whole family, the 'complete' picture.[75] Once the play began, the Macbeths whom spectators saw on stage were amputated, their arms empty of the absent child, their narrative, pre-emptively cut. Of course, too, Pollock's poster offered an interpretive frame for reading *Macbeth*: it was, after all, a cartoon. It made a joke of sentimental family poses.

For Sinead Cusack the child-loss experienced in her fantasised, sub-textual history was the biological datum that directed her performance. Childless, indeed now barren, her Lady Macbeth invested all her energies in her husband, charging her obsessiveness with an eroticism that mocked its own redundancy. As Cusack came to understand 'the evil' her Lady Macbeth was 'drawn down into', she named it 'loss' – 'the loss of him', 'the loss of hope', 'And such a loss of innocence. But mainly the loss of hope of anything' – a loss she connected to the lost child: 'We [were] never going to have any more children'.[76] Paradoxically, then, her loss conflated innocence *and* evil in the symbolic body of the baby, since by a perverse logic the death of her child was the motivation for child-killing, the death of other mothers' children.

Like Cusack, Jonathan Pryce keyed his performance to a pretext – but his came from 'real' history. He 'talked a lot to Adrian Noble' in the year before rehearsals began about 'an atrocity that [had] stayed with [him]' since he was a teenager – the Moors murders, committed between 1963 and 1965 by the 'butcher', Ian Brady, and Myra Hindley, his 'fiendlike queen', whose 'gratification', thought Pryce, came 'through power over children'.[77] Their youngest victim was 10; the oldest, 17 – the same age as Hindley's brother-in-law who shopped them; and only two years younger than Hindley, herself little more than a child when her partnership with Brady began. The children they abducted were sexually abused by the much older Brady before he killed them – gross acts of perverse parenting. But at least one of their victims, little Leslie Ann Downey, saw herself as a bad child. Her last minutes, sadistically caught by Brady on the brand new home technology, the tape recorder, were played out in court. She was heard pleading to be let go – she had to get home – she was late – 'me mam'll kill me'.[78]

Noble's production found in these histories narratives that helped his actors translate *Macbeth*'s evil (a metaphysical category that was largely unavailable to a culture formed by 1980s Thatcherite materialism) into scenarios to appal materialist minds. The last taboo, the practice Britain still called 'evil', was the violation of the child, and it was the violation of a child that Noble staged as the originating action of his production. As the stage lights came up on a scene of carnage, dimly, through fog mixed with gun smoke seemingly made greasy with burning flesh, three shapeless figures scavenged a battlefield, looting bodies. Rolling over one corpse, they discovered what it had been sheltering, the filthy, half-naked body of a wild child, a bloody babe who stirred, then rose from the dead. Its hair was knotted in 'glibs' – marking it as one of the 'meere Irish', those 'kerns and galloglasses', who, as the bloody Captain would report in 1.2, swarmed into Scotland 'from the Western Isles' (1.2.12, 13) to swell the rebellion against Duncan, 'in hope', according to Holinshed's *Chronicle*, 'of the spoile'.[79] As described both by King James in *The trew law of free monarchies* and by William Harrison in his *Description of Britaine*, the Scots came originally from the Irish, 'a people,' wrote Harrison (growing increasingly ethnically challenged as he proceeded), 'mixed of the Scithian and Spanish blood', a 'barbarous nation, and longest without letters' 'which were given to the eating of mans flesh, and therefore called Anthropophagi': 'those Irish … are none other than those Scots … who used to feed on the buttocks of boies and womens paps, as delicate dishes'.[80] The 'meere Irish', then, were kin to Shakespeare's Weird Sisters. It was supposed that among these 'meere Irish' was 'vsed a damnable superstition': 'the right armes of their infants' were left 'vnchristened' – that is, their fighting arm – 'to the intent it might giue a more vngratious and deadlie blow'.[81]

On Noble's stage, the child who rose from the carnage faced spectators as an oxymoron. He was a miracle, birthed from death as though 'Untimely ripped' (5.8.16) from Mother Earth's womb. He was a survivor; hopeful.

But he was also an abomination. For, literally tainted by war's filth, and tainted by early modern racist 'history' that demonised him as 'vngratious', this child was made filthy by association, kidnapped by the Weird Sisters, booty, hustled off never to be seen again – unless, of course, it was *he* who returned, dismembered into the body parts that were tossed into the cauldron in 4.1 and re-membered in the near-life-sized effigy they carried around with them. Or maybe it was the child's blood that ringed the mouth of the Sister who answered 'Where hast thou been?' with significant dark irony, 'Killing swine' (1.3.1–2). His abduction located evil in this *Macbeth*. Evil here was fixed on the archetypal moment of trust betrayed, the moment when the innocent child is taken in hand and led away. Only, the scene itself troubled any such obvious Manichean reading. *Was* the child good? If so, why didn't he recoil from the Weird Sisters? Instead, he was fascinated by the tinkling bell one of them produced from her sack and held out to him. He reached for it. Was it a prize in a game, or was it a seductive lure? Was it a child-sized version of the bell Macbeth would later hear? A summons? Or an alarm? Watching him turn to follow the bell, spectators saw the child enact a turn to the bad.

In this production Jonathan Pryce's Macbeth enjoyed the company of children because he enjoyed clowning. When young Fleance, a ten-year-old bored with all the hanging around waiting for the new king's entrance in 3.1, perched himself on the big chair that he didn't know was the throne and stared into space, blank to his father's urgent signals, Macbeth tip-toed up behind him and dropped his huge crown over the boy's head. He watched it fall onto the boy's shoulders as Fleance's shocked face spun round to meet his grin – Macbeth roaring with laughter. But the joke – and Macbeth's jokes were always edgy – strangely fulfilled the Weird Sisters' prophecy. In play, spectators saw the 'seeds of Banquo' king. Simultaneously, however, they saw Fleance contaminated with a future that put him suddenly at risk even as, ambiguously, the moment figured him as dangerous. For wearing Macbeth's crown, he was, like Macbeth wearing Duncan's, a usurper. Held in the physical metaphor of this performance moment, he was both potentially the wrecker and the wrecked. That the crown didn't fit merely emphasised the deferred punchline to this joke: this Fleance was the infant prodigy who would ultimately strip 'the dwarfish thief' of those 'borrow'd' titles that hung 'loose about him like a giant's robes' (5.2.21–2).

Articulating evil through the body of the child, seeing the child recruited by 'the instruments of darkness' (1.3.123) and the sacred preserve of child's play contaminated by black jokers, Adrian Noble's production saw children enlisted as foot soldiers in Macbeth's war on the future – but also as saboteurs. Chillingly, in 4.1 children took on the role of the apparitions. At the end of the banquet (3.4), Macbeth was left smoothing the tablecloth, picking up cutlery to reset scattered places. As he exited, the Weird Sisters invaded his pitch, looting materials for a second sitting, a desecrated Lord's Supper that they weirdly fed back to him when he reappeared demanding to know, 'What is't you do? ... answer me / To what I ask you' (4.1.48, 59–60).[82] Drenching a cloth in the mess they'd brewed in a chalice and thrusting him onto a chair, they blindfolded Macbeth. The hell-broth absorbed through the eyes went straight to the brain, producing hallucinations that walked and talked, 'sights' possessing the bodies of children. Three of them entered giggling, children in white nightgowns (dressed to 'murder sleep'?), carrying a basket of toys, playing a game of tig that changed to blind man's buff as they dodged Macbeth's blindly groping hands. They looked like angels. And it was they who 'became' the apparitions; they who delivered the predictions to his muffled ears. The second child, a little girl, popped up behind him like a jack-in-the-box; the third and smallest solemnly climbed up on Macbeth's knee, a pint-sized toy crown on his head, and whispered in the big man's ear what Macbeth, in a reversal of roles, scale and perspective, spoke aloud like the ventriloquist's dummy.

They vanished when Macbeth tugged off the blindfold – when he started roaring after other children, those 'firstlings of [his] heart' that he would deliver as the 'firstlings of [his] hand' (4.1.146, 147). 'Be it thought and done' (148) he instructed himself, and it was. Weirdly, those 'firstlings' materialised in the space he'd just vacated! The apparitions returned in the next scene as Macduff's children, in those same night-gowns, with those same toys, to play at their mother's feet, golden-haired as if they wore halos. They *were* angels. Weren't they? And 'bright still', 'though the brightest fell' (4.3.22)? But they couldn't help infecting this scene with toxic residues from the last. When the 'young fry' ran at the 'shag-haired villain' who called his father 'traitor', then flatly announced 'He has killed me mother' (4.2.81, 80, 79, 81), the audience laughed. This was a game; the child, tigged 'out'. Then they saw the blood. Lady Macduff's scream filled the theatre; blackout blinded spectators whose ears were filled with the sound of slaughter.

Abusing childhood, Noble's production put up on stage the representation of a violation that shocked to the core because it expressed 'present fears' that contemporary Britain wanted denied and 'horrible imaginings' that it wanted ignored, and it made terrifyingly present a category many modern Britons thought obsolete. It instantiated evil. And it understood fear. It forced spectators to look at culture's sentimental clichés, its standard tropes of innocence, as hypocritical cover-ups – whiteness, brightness, blondness. (Or maybe not. Because of course you really couldn't tell, there being in this play, in this production 'no art to find the mind's construction in the face' (1.4.11–12).) Contaminating childhood's allotted space, the playground, and poisoning it with the image of the

Plate 17 In Adrian Noble's 1986 RSC *Macbeth* the Apparitions (Andrew Bailey, James Macaro, Hannah Young) play blind man's buff with the king (Jonathan Pryce) while the Weird Sisters watch, aloof. (*Source:* Joe Cocks photograph. By permission of the Shakespeare Birthplace Trust.)

abuser's groping hands, this production made children equivocal, saturated signs of the equivocations the *Macbeth* text everywhere produces: foul and fair; not ill, not good; 'honest trifles' who 'betray' the credulous 'in deepest consequence' (1.3.124, 125). When the 'shag-haired villain' called Macduff's son an 'egg', spectators had to wonder. Was he the 'egg' of the serpent – or the miraculous phoenix?

Knowing children

Like Noble's *Macbeth* on stage, Penny Woolcock's 1997 television film, *Macbeth on the Estate*, opened on what looked like an urban battlefield – Sarajevo, perhaps. Across a grey expanse of cratered, rubble-strewn devastation walked a single man, not a looter, like Noble's Weird Sisters, but seemingly a war reporter, a huge man, like the television news anchorman Trevor MacDonald, but twice his bulk, except that unlike MacDonald, this man wore trainers and an American football jersey, and when he turned to talk to the camera as it moved in for the close-up, he exposed a gold tooth and a West Indian Brummie accent – so, not just a reporter, but a combatant whom spectators would later recognise as

Plate 18 'Macbeth shall never vanquish'd be,' the third Apparition (Andrew Bailey) promises Macbeth (Jonathan Pryce) in Adrian Noble's 1986 RSC *Macbeth*. (*Source*: Joe Cocks photograph. By permission of the Shakespeare Birthplace Trust.)

Macduff (David Harewood). By the time the opening camera pan had finished its sweep across the horizon, taking in grey tower blocks sticking up like amputated limbs in the distant background, spectators were aware that this urban landscape wasn't Bosnia. It was Birmingham. And it was now.[83] Macduff, in lines borrowed, updated, from Holinshed, told 'of a time, not long past, when Duncan, de King, held d'power on dis estate – *and we loved him well.* We was men o' war!' who 'punished offenders and gathered all finances due to de King' – 'offenders'; 'finances': a nice pair of euphemisms. But this perfect 'republic' didn't last. 'Duncan grew fat, slack, and many misrule men took occasion dereof to trouble d'peace wid seditious commotion.' Challenged by usurpers and 'Fearful of his crown', Duncan charged his cousin, 'de ever-loyal Macbeth, to take up arms and lead us into battle against de rebels'. From this first prologue, the film cuts to still shots, seven of them, that compose a second prologue, framing a portrait of 'dis estate' in exposures that educate the eye to urban blight: through a broken window, derelict flats; through a dank, water-puddled doorway, a rat nosing the sill; abandoned corridors and graffitied high-rise balconies, a grass-stunted space, once a playground, now parking an industrial skip spilling junk. Over the images comes a high metallic sound and the cries of gulls – or maybe kids, calling something that sounds like 'Macbeth'. Then two children, in high long shot, run across the frame. In the next shot, catching up a third child to pass across the desolated open space, they vanish. As if triggering the action, the passing of these children throws the film footage into fast forward. A montage cut together of short clips shows bursts of violence stopped in freeze frames to pick out close-ups and name the players: Macbeth (James Frain) kicks down a front door and beats to a pulp a druggie he drags from sleep; Banquo (Andrew Tiernan) shoots aerosol into some guy's eyes then slams fists into his groin; Malcolm (Graham Bryan) leaps up and down like a gorilla, smashing heads with a baseball bat. Cuts from frenzy to inertia show Duncan, in mid-shot, counting time at his table in the Community Centre, chain-smoking, ignoring his pint, massaging his forehead as though trying to keep his anxieties from cracking open his skull. Unlike the fit youths who do his dirty work, Duncan (Ray Winstone) is a bloated slob, a superannuated skinhead with 'LOVE' tattooed on his knuckles and an unbuttoned Indian-dyed shirt that exposes a beer belly draped with gold chains.

Shot on Birmingham's notoriously deprived Ladywood Estate by a director known as a documentary filmmaker who works in an experimental style that mixes realism with hyperrealism, even surrealism, and who casts professional actors alongside local amateurs, *Macbeth on the Estate* tapped into a language of violence that restored to Macbeth's story the primitiveness, rawness and thuggery recounted in Holinshed and dramatised by Shakespeare – the brutality that was stripped out of the Restoration play and absent from the 'noble' *Macbeth* when it was subsequently captured for 'high' tragedy.[84] On Woolcock's estate, Duncan is a gross parody of a Thatcherite entrepreneur running drugs, sex and protection rackets, and the estate is a dystopia, ugly, brutal and brutalising, that functions as an 'Other' to the culture it despairingly mimics, but only mutely. 'Dis estate', unlike the Scotland of Shakespeare's play, never gets a scene set 'elsewhere', let's say at Civic Hall, or Whitehall, where cultural difference (call it the Establishment, or cultural supremacism) is interrogated, as in Shakespeare's England scene (4.3). Instead, the estate is a quarantined no-go area, a place, in Bea Campbell's terms, 'colonised' by male criminality. It's an anti-structural space regulated by an illicit patriarchy that has put in place inverted versions of the same codes and hierarchies, including, of course, gender, that organise the licit world.[85]

But that means that besides brutalising its occupants the estate also, bizarrely, infantilises them. It's a 'nanny' estate where grown men are stunted adolescents in dependency relationships with their dole-queue social security 'father', and where all the adults are needy children dependent on handouts, 'estate benefits'. Or more pathetically, because more childishly credulous, they're pinning their hopes on fate, on the one-in-a-zillion chance that the golden finger of fortune will point at them. The National Lottery is big on this estate. (Still a novelty in the UK, the first draw in November 1994, the lottery had already created a new class of 'instant' millionaires – and 'wannabes'.) Watching the balls fall on the TV draw is what the glass-eyed junkies are doing when Macbeth smashes in the screen, and a billboard, promising 'More winners every week than seconds', sits on one of the estate's prime locations. The big fluffy cloud on the hoarding codes 'heaven', but the finger of fate stretching out from the cloud belongs not to some higher divinity but to the god of consumerism who's always, like Duncan on this estate, running a sleight-of-hand racket. Depressingly, the only 'sure thing' this post-capitalist, post-scientific culture can put its money on is chance, fate, the come-on that – as the lottery slogan has it – 'It could be YOU'. On an estate like this one, people read palms. And Tarot cards. They 'look into the seeds of time' (1.3.56). And by the time viewers of the film see the lottery advertisement on the billboard, they know that people on this estate are hooked in to witches.

In the film's first prologue and in the opening gang-war sequence that ends with the 'rebel' Cawdor – a thug who's been defying Duncan – thrust into the driver's seat of a stolen car, doused with petrol through the broken window, and set alight, the estate looks like male territory, a war zone where hyped-up masculinity plays out over-determined rituals of aggression. What the adults don't know is that on this estate, they're only squatters. Their power structures have been infiltrated by fifth colum- nists. In Woolcock's version, Macbeth's 'war *on* children' is a guerrilla war conducted *by* children. The adults are only a puppet regime. The real government in this urban anarchy is not Duncan's in-yer-face totalitari- anism. It's behind the scenes. Literally. To get to 'the man' you have to crawl under ventilation access shafts, duck through knocked-out partition walls. And when you get to him, 'the man' turns out to be three children.[86]

In *Macbeth on the Estate*, children overwhelm the visual text. They appear everywhere: on streets, at bus stops, on their father's knee as he plays poker, in their mother's arms as she crosses the grounds. They watch grown-ups get out of their faces on hard stuff – then into each other's crotches. They bellow out the lyrics to 'Babylon's Burning' as the lurching Duncan, acting like a kid, leads the 'community singing' in a karaoke version of the Ruts' punk classic.[87] In the morning, they see the blood-soaked sheets. They mimic adults. Fleance – a fourteen-year-old – deals drugs in the Community Centre toilets and carries away loot from a raided flat. Macduff's eight-year-old boy questions his mother, 'Was my father a traitor …?' (4.2.44) while he drags inexpertly on a fag. Two steps behind Macbeth and his baseball bat that magically opens the estate's locked doors to correction, tiny-tots run along the same balconies, banging on the same doors with tiny-tot baseball bats, chanting 'Hail Macbeth, hail Macbeth!' Children are not, in Woolcock's narrative, innocents initiated or implicated or even corrupted by the adults. They belong to the estate. The estate's norm is criminality, violence. They are 'good' estate children. And they watch adults constantly. But maybe that's what makes these knowing children seem unnaturally old. And in a world where adults behave like children and children like adults, the idea of the child in the abstract vanishes – or becomes a disturbing inversion of itself.[88]

In this emotional consumer economy where homoeroticism codes heterosexist power relations, Duncan is a perverse parent who handles all his sons with a queasy tactility. A kind of one-man race relations drop-in centre, he has a black wife and a black girlfriend, and two mixed-race kids – the 'white' one, a swaggering yobbo skinhead who, when it happens, is dead chuffed at his unexpected promotion; and the barely noticed 'black' one. Racism, on this racially diverse estate, persists.[89] But Duncan also has his surrogate sons. And there's a nasty sexual undertow to his relations with them, the way he offers his own body, thrusting crotch first, as he embraces Macbeth, the way he incestuously touches up his victorious 'cousin', the exchange of glances between them as he tosses over a flashy diamond ring that codes – what, exactly? Has Macbeth just been nominated as Duncan's heir? Has he just been delivered advance payment on some other form of exchange? Watching in the background, Malcolm, in close-up, makes an obscene tongue gesture that Macbeth, catching it, reads as 'ass licker' but shrugs off as the envy of the displaced weaker sibling. Then, out of the blue, Malcolm is named 'Prince of Cumberland' – and Macbeth turns away, clenching a fist around the meaningless ring on his finger, a 'lost son' who confirms rejection by the father by symbolically dropping out of male culture: Macbeth phones his wife.[90]

Leaving a message on the home voicemail telling her of a weird encounter and of what, in that encounter, he'd been promised – 'more than mortal knowledge'; 'the coming on of time'; 'Hail, king that shalt be'

(1.5.3, 9) – is both a compensation for what he's lost and a way of processing that loss. And loss is a psychic territory Susan Vidler's Lady Macbeth knows by heart. When the camera first finds her she's crossing the estate with her best mate, Lady Macduff (Patsi Fox), who's carrying her big-eyed baby daughter in her arms and manoeuvring the empty pushchair while Lady Macbeth holds the smaller Macduff boy by the hand. Lady Macbeth is good with kids – but these black babies clearly aren't hers. At home alone, as she listens to the voicemail message, the camera roams through rooms, compiling a visual text that fills in her lost narrative. There is a framed photograph of a laughing child beside the answerphone – who is nowhere physically present. As Lady Macbeth starts talking to her absent husband by talking to herself ('Glamis thou art, and Cawdor …') her soliloquies are overlaid with reminders of this missing child (1.5.13). Ghostly children's laughter comes from hide-and-seek brats who buzz the flat's intercom and find it hysterically funny to catch the grown-up out with 'knock down ginger'. Then as she escapes further into the interior of her home, moving from the front door up her stairs towards her bedroom, she hesitates on the landing in front of a closed door – and opens it.

Behind that door is a blue room, a nursery, preserved like a shrine, meticulously ordered. Its mass-market clutter, though, belongs to a period of late capitalism that has emptied the commodity of its power to signify, except fetishistically; so it is impossible, in this place where every object is à la mode retro and codes both nostalgia and amnesia, to date the child or his exit securely.[91] (Did he die last week, last year, last decade? Men Macbeth's age have sons who are strapping teenagers, Banquo's Fleance, for one.) In this nursery, though, time doesn't register. There's a cot with a Winnie-the-Pooh mobile playing a 1950s kids' radio signature tune, a duvet with an Aston Villa cover, posters of Noah's Ark and Mickey Mouse, a dresser draped with a Villa scarf, piled with stuffed animals – none of them worn. The room's atmosphere is dense with palpable absence. As Lady Macbeth picks up a photograph and traces her fingers around the image of her child's body, she weeps, but then regains stony composure, her back against the wall, sliding down its surface as she invokes the 'spirits who tend on mortal thoughts' (1.5.39). Her face is caught in a double exposure, full-on by the camera, and obliquely, reflected in a mirror on the dresser. The child's absence seems compounded in the doubled image of the mother, and as she dully calls upon evil's ministers to 'unsex me here' (39), she projects the sense that her child's absence has rendered a part of her, the mother, similarly absent, or caused a split that, cauterised, immunises her to the violence she internalises in these speeches.[92]

Killing Duncan will recuperate her loss, restore not just the lost son but the son lost when Duncan passed over Macbeth to make Malcolm his heir. So when he decides to 'proceed no further in this business', her rage expresses itself in sexual violence. Woolcock shot the marital row as a bedroom scene, Lady Macbeth remembering the 'babe that milk[ed] me' while Macbeth penetrates her, then straddling him, coercing him back into resolution by thrusting herself onto him, urging him, punningly, to 'screw your courage to the sticking place' before bringing him to climax with 'What cannot you and I perform ...?' When he whispers, 'Bring forth men-children only' (1.7.31, 55, 60, 69, 72) she slams face down the bedside photograph of their dead son – hiding the child's eyes.[93] Already absent, the child is doubly lost in the mother's gesture, as if the escalation of the parents' violence is reductive of the child – or as if the new 'baby', the murder they've just conceived, wipes out memories of the loss it's intended to compensate.

But this new 'baby' too is lost – figuratively, when killing brings no 'success' but rather the appalling realisation that 'Nought's had, all's spent' (3.2.6); but literally, too, in Woolcock's adaptation. Earlier, plotting Banquo's death, Macbeth stood behind her at the kitchen sink, staring down at the fingers he'd laced over his wife's flat belly, a look and gesture that coded pregnancy. Later, lying beside her trying to sleep after the fiasco at the feast – a boozy celebration at the Community Centre – when he saw dead Banquo return among the living, Macbeth holds his wife, but she moans, rolls out of bed. A cut to the bathroom shows her reaching for the Tampax – then furiously grabbing the pregnancy kit that's sitting on the shelf next to them, wrenching it open, and trashing the testers. 'All's spent'. From now on, all of her energies go into cleaning – hoovering, dusting, more hoovering. She's picking imaginary fluff off the antiseptic sofa with a strip of Sellotape when Macbeth bursts through the front door, takes the stairs three at a time, grabs the baseball bat from under their bed and, businesslike, informs her that

> From this moment,
> The very firstlings of my heart shall be
> The firstlings of my hand. And even now
> To crown my thoughts with acts, be it thought and done.

But he's only half way through the rest of the plan –

> The castle of Macduff I will surprise;
> Seize upon Fife; give to th'edge o'th'sword

> His wife, his babes, and all unfortunate souls
> That trace him in his line
>
> 4.1.145–52

– when she is down the stairs and belting across the estate, flinging herself through the Macduffs' back door, babbling out Shakespeare's Messenger's speech, 'Be not found here. Hence with your little ones' (4.2.66), trying to herd the boys, assemble the pushchair, strap the baby into it, over Lady Macduff's bewildered protestations, as Macbeth comes through the front door. The man himself commits these killings, and Lady Macbeth watches at the window as her husband pulps the mother and the boys, then she sinks to her haunches, rocking autistically, covering her ears to deafen the baby's wailing. A close up on the baby's face, her eyes magnified by tears and terror, cuts to a close up on Rosse, coming through the Macduffs' back gate, taking in the horror, turning and running, then to a close up of Macbeth, gazing down at the baby girl, muttering 'you egg' (4.2.80) – and raising his knife. Outside, Lady Macbeth tries to rise but her legs buckle. She moves back across the estate like someone sleepwalking, traumatised by images of slaughtered children. She's standing at her own kitchen sink when she notices 'Yet' again, 'here's a spot', 'out damned spot' (5.1.26, 30), and scrubs and scrubs with the vegetable brush as clear water runs down the drain. In this mind-blown trance she plays out the night of the murder. Upstairs, she pulls sheets off the guest bed. Downstairs, she folds them into the washing machine, the camera angle shifting, as in a horror film, to show Macbeth

Plate 19 Macduff's baby wails as the assassin hits in Penny Woolcock's 1997 *Macbeth on the Estate.* (*Source:* BBC2.)

leaning against the fridge, sullen, silent, watching. But when she urges 'To bed, to bed,' (56) she turns – and sees her absent son in the doorway. Taking him by an invisible hand, she tucks him up in his empty bed in his vacant room. And sometime later that afternoon she stands on the roof of her tower block, lifts her head to survey a world beyond the estate – then walks over the edge.

Her hallucination is the last spasm of a hurt mind. Trying psychically to repair the extravagant damage of Macbeth's violence, to restore the lost children that represent an idea of a future, she feels her absent child most acutely present. But the hallucination that presences a blessed time past, that makes the child heart-wrenchingly 'there' in mind and not there in matter, works ironically to intensify his absence, an absence that reads as the annulling of the idea of childhood in the deaths of particular children. There is no bleaker moment in Woolcock's film.

When Macbeth finds his wife dead on the concrete she is ringed by children, little girls, a couple of mothers. He speaks 'Tomorrow, and tomorrow, and tomorrow' (5.5.18) to them, close-ups cutting between his face and theirs, expressionless, maybe numb, or inoculated to horror that has no power any longer to shock their systems. Certainly, they're not demanding; they just aren't reacting. They are beautiful, these little girls, but their folded arms across flat chests make them look like ancient hags. It's appropriate that Macbeth is talking to them. For while his wife dealt with her childlessness by hoovering furrows into the carpet, Macbeth processed his grief by seeking the company of surrogate children – the 'Weird Children'.

Plate 20 Macbeth (James Frain) brings the knife down on Macduff's baby in Penny Woolcock's 1997 *Macbeth on the Estate.* (*Source:* BBC2.)

The most disturbing decision this film made was to see Shakespeare's Weird Sisters as children. Like the estate's 'normal' children, they appear everywhere; but unlike them, they're unattached to adult culture. Adults push these weird kids away, threaten them with raised fists. They roam, a little feral pack of anarchists – doing, and undoing, estate business. But they almost always elude sighting. They're fugitives in a terrain that gives them hiding places. *Literally*, they're the estate's lost children. So it is only retrospectively that spectators realise it's the Weird Children they saw in distant long shot right at the beginning of the film, running through the estate in that second prologue sequence; it's they who triggered the action; they whose shapes appeared through the car window before they smashed it with a brick and stood back to observe Cawdor shoved inside and burned alive; it's they who summon Macbeth to an appointment he doesn't know he's made.

After the gang battle that opens the film, as he and Banquo are making their way across the estate to headquarters in the Community Centre, taking the back route through a condemned stretch of grey concrete and vandalised flats, Macbeth hears this blasted landscape weirdly calling out to him – voices, whispered, shouted, from an empty window, a dark doorway, a vacant hallway, voices like those hide-and-seek voices on Lady Macbeth's intercom, voices that can't be fixed to a source but keep shifting their ground with impossible speed; voices that call out 'Macbeth'. And then through a smashed pane, a child's head, caught long enough for Macbeth to focus on it, disappears; a foot flees down a corridor, a hand on a window frame vanishes. Undaunted by physical violence, Macbeth is spooked by this weird operation of the physical world – but intrigued. Shrugging off Banquo's cautioning hand he starts up the peeling switch-back stairs – a replay of his assault on Cawdor, itself a take on countless suspense-driven action films. At the top, he stoops to peer through grey ventilation ducts that lead him to a hanging curtain, a grey membrane of builder's plastic. Lifting it, he gazes into something astonishing. Across the threshold is a golden world illuminated by dazzling candlelight enclosing a bizarre shrine whose 'strange intelligence', impacting on Macbeth's eyes, makes him shift like a nervy horse while his 'seated heart knock[s] at [his] ribs' (1.3.74, 135). For this shrine focuses strange energies. There's a voodoo mask on a wall, a clothes line pinned with Tarot cards, a curved, milky mirror that warps the images it reflects, the single arm of a mannequin holding up a grinning fetish, a sepia photograph, and at the centre, surrounded by votive candles, a seeming child, a white plastic doll, propped up and staring.

This shrine anticipates and inverts the other shrine, the blue room dedicated to the Macbeths' dead child, its antithesis, but also strangely its double. Both are set apart, perfect utopias, both beautiful, indeed, the only beauty spots on Macbeth's broken dystopian estate. Carefully assembled as memory spaces to fold time in on itself, they each fuse the future and the instant with the past. Bizarrely, too, like the nursery, this space looks like a kid's playground, an almost ludicrously excessive collection of mumbo-jumbo and Halloween frights. But none of this stuff belongs to childhood – it's all hand-me-downs from the adults, like the stuffed toys in the nursery that aim to naturalise an adult-driven fantasy life for the child. Here it seems that objects captured from the grown-ups – the stopped clock, the rosary, Death in the Tarot pack – have been arranged to taunt those grown-ups with a parody of their own fantasy life, their inveterate superstitiousness, their willingness, as adults, to deceive themselves with lies. Or maybe what Macbeth is looking at isn't parody, but pastiche, in Fredric Jameson's terms, 'blank parody' that comes 'without parody's ulterior motive, without the satirical impulse, without laughter': 'parody that has lost its sense of humour'.[94] So maybe this scene isn't a laughing matter. Maybe it's for real – where the 'real' is evil.

Spectators see the scene from Macbeth's point of view. Then a cut shows us, like him, the rest of the picture. And like us, he's stunned by what he sees. For the high priests who officiate at this shrine are standing solemnly by. *And they're just kids.*[95] The biggest one has a beard coming on, but could still play Thisby. The littlest looks like he should be advertising Pears soap. The girl is bony, akimbo, odd, her over-sized National Health glasses on her angular cocked head making her look both earnest and old, like a studious tortoise. All of them weirdly fuse childness with a premature adultness, a sense of having grown 'instant old' (*Hamlet*, 1.5.94): later, when she becomes the apparition and delivers the prediction that 'none of woman born / Shall harm Macbeth' (4.1.79–80), the girl is wearing a white headscarf and red lipstick erratically applied wide of the mark, dressing up like mother, perhaps, or (strangely absorbing in the costume and cosmetic the stereotypes of the virgin and the whore) a compilation that, superimposed upon her still childlike body, somehow turns a quizzical gaze back upon the riddle she's just uttered, of the child not 'of woman born'.

Like Macbeth, looking at these Weird Children – the name the estate knows them by – spectators are faced with a crisis of interpretation, a deep equivocation. Is the hocus-pocus objectified in this secret garden at the heart of Duncan's urban wasteland just a bit of slightly morbid fun – like reading today's horoscope in the *Sun*? Or is what's going on here an

Plate 21 The Witches – Weird Children – in Penny Woolcock's 1997 *Macbeth on the Estate.* (*Source:* BBC2.)

initiation into occult practices that trap the neophyte in a parallel dark universe? Banquo, coming in behind Macbeth, scoffs. And his reaction is surely right. For there is something utterly ridiculous about the excessiveness of this scene that fits its interpretation into the orthodox Christian understanding of evil as grotesque parody – and ultimately comic because doomed to failure. So much effort goes in to evil's bustling, futile projects that it's laughable! The inevitable tragic fall is always a pratfall, as Satan was the first to demonstrate.[96] Of course, this positivistic analysis of evil depends on other orthodoxies, faith in God's omnipotence, the willingness of 'heaven' not just to 'look on' but to 'take [our] part' (4.3.226–7). So where is God on Duncan's estate? Gone missing?

And what if, on this God-forsaken estate, evil isn't a joke? What if the Weird Children aren't offering a parody of adult power that contains the parody while permitting it childishly to mimic adult power, but instead are operatives in an alternative system of power where the adults are the playthings and these children are in control, are 'our masters' (4.1.62)? We're on Macbeth's side when he searches the Weird Children's faces – for their intent. We need to know whether evil can be resident in the bodies of children. We need to know what evil looks like in the child's face – a need that has become urgent since the death of James Bulger. Looking at the police mugshot of the peroxide blond with the morgue-slab eyes from 1965 we *know* Myra is Medusa (don't we?).[97] But those chirpy little boys showing gap-toothed smiles in school photographs blown up into monsters on the front pages of the tabloids in 1993: who are they? How do we understand what they did? How do we give 'A deed without a name' (4.1.48) a name? Was the abduction of little James a playground game gone wrong – or is that a rationalist apology? Were Thompson and Venables intent on evil? After James Bulger, adults have needed to know more about 'knowing children' – what they know, how they know it, how much of their knowledge they are responsible for.

These are things Macbeth wants to know too – but knowledge, in Shakespeare *and* Woolcock, is denied. And *ways* of knowing are catastrophically destabilised. It turns out that these Weird Children are not explicable in mortal terms. They are not what they appear to be, victims of social deprivation and failed welfare programmes, trainee sociopaths whose 'waywardness' should be assigned to a caseworker for remedial action. For they are not finally knowable in socio-secular terms. They traffic in the metaphysical. They have the ability to vanish off the face of the estate. When Macbeth, wanting certainty from the Weird Children, returns to them in 4.1, rips back the curtain that has separated spectator from spectacle and reaches out toward the apparitions, the shrine, its furniture, the candles and the Weird Children themselves are simply gone. He, bewilderedly, walks into their disappearance – and into what they've left behind, a perfectly ordinary 'sight' on the estate, a vandalised, junk-littered room.

If ontology is troubled in these children, so is teleology. They are not innocent of effect. Their child's play evidently produces images that simulate – and *stimulate* – terrible consequences. When Macbeth appears to them that second time (4.1.) they have rearranged their shrine. The icon at the centre – the white doll: Macbeth's child? – has been replaced. With a black doll. Not sitting up, but lying sprawled on its back, eyes staring, while around it are posed dismembered, twisted limbs, an image that almost instantly translates into utterance – and execution. They imagine – or do they plant it? – what next comes into Macbeth's mind, the slaughter of Macduff's sons and baby girl.

In these sequences, the bleak secularism of Duncan's estate is surprised by metaphysics. Ironically, though, Woolcock's Weird Children can deliver on the future not because they can predict it, but because, as children, they *are* it. And the temptation they offer James Frain's Macbeth is so potent because, as children, they complete the circuit that loops his desire through his loss by offering him both 'having' *and* 'hope'. Weirdly, in this film Macbeth's lost child and his dynastic aspirations come together in these lost children.

In the final condensed minutes of Woolcock's film Macbeth sits staring straight ahead, on his sofa, his dead wife sprawled beside him, his baseball bat between his knees, like a morbid re-vision of Grant Wood's 'American Gothic'. 'What's he / That was not born of woman?' (5.7.2–3) he asks the camera. It answers by cutting to Macduff, walking through Macbeth's front door. 'Despair thy charm,' Macduff advises. And 'yield thee coward' (5.8.13, 23). Then he pulls out a gun and shoots. Macbeth, still on the sofa, in a slow zoom backwards is transported to a glade in Birnam Woods where his dead eyes stare up through the trees. A jump cut frames Macduff walking through another door, into the Community Centre. He tosses Duncan's ring on to the table in front of Malcolm. 'Hail king,' he says (5.9.26). Then he turns on his heel and walks out. The 'boy' Malcolm self-importantly swaggers to his feet, delivering his stagy acceptance speech before turning to the bar to order rounds. The kid he elbows aside to get to the drink is Fleance – who, recovering his balance, mimes a gun with his fingers, lines up the sights on the back of Malcolm's skull, and pulls the imaginary trigger. The Weird Children's prediction is proleptically fulfilled as the adolescent king is assassinated by the schoolboy usurper while violence is passed down into ever smaller children's hands; the screen explodes to whiteout.

Like filmed *Macbeth*s before it (Welles's, Polanski's), Woolcock's *Macbeth on the Estate* ends with a return to its beginning. The imagined gunshot triggers a cut to Macduff. The reporter from the opening prologue is finally revealed as the survivor of these events who, all his children wasted, has told this story 'of a time, not long past' as an effort of memory and an act of creation to put before spectators evidence they must process. Standing in long shot on the rubble-strewn waste ground against the skyline of the estate – the estate that tropes the nation – Macduff has only this to say when the camera moves in to close-up: 'Alas, poor country. Almost afraid to know itself' (4.3.166). Then he turns and walks away. It isn't *Macbeth*'s last line. In Shakespeare, it isn't even Macduff's line. Spoken here, by him, the film's last words work like a zoom back, radically adjusting the final focus, opening up the ending, inviting spectators to read this performance as a kind of documentary and this film as a state of the nation address that wonders apocalyptically about the nation's future, a future equivocally predicted in its children. On the estate that is Britain is childhood an alibi – an 'elsewhere' invented by adults to locate (false) memory, nostalgia, and the seductive fantasy of innocence? Has the myth of childhood dissolved, childhood functioning only as a cultural placeholder for (adult) anxieties? Or is it rather that *adulthood* has dissolved, Woolcock's film documenting and critiquing a politics of abdication that spells the collapse of the myth of the grown-up? 'Alas, poor country. Almost afraid to know itself' speaks across this welter of questions. And Macduff's 'almost' is critical, for what Woolcock finally gives spectators is a version of *Macbeth* that is *unafraid* – a medium for this country to 'think [...] in ... front of itself', and by such thinking, 'to know itself'.

Flying Fleance

So what of the child who survives *Macbeth* – whose last shouted instruction from his father before the voice cuts out is 'Fly, good Fleance, fly, fly, fly! / Thou mayst revenge' (3.3.20–1) – who, with no preparation, no instruction manual, must instantly take on the part of 'father to a line of kings' (3.1.61)?

In 1976, Trevor Nunn's Fleance (Zak Taylor) on the blacked-out battlements in 2.1 was a thing of light. Banquo (John Woodvine) gazed long and hard into his luminous, upturned face before turning abruptly aside to murmur a prayer, 'Merciful powers, / Restrain in me the cursèd thoughts ...' (7–8). Banquo was brooding on the witches' predictions – seeing his boy as Scotland's future king – and beginning to wonder how he might hurry the prediction along. (After the ambush scene, spectators saw no more of him: Nunn's Fleance disappeared from the story.) In 1997, Woolcock's Fleance (Shane McDougall) was a human black hole, a desensitised void, and very much in on the end, the next killer. One child was untainted, unwitting, the tool of the adult imaginary, but ultimately protected from consequence (as spectators were too, the child absent at the end); the other, screwed over, clued in, the product of that imaginary, released at the end to 'play'. He only needed tooling up. (In Holinshed, in 'real' history, the 'real' Fleance was closer to Woolcock than to Nunn: fleeing to Wales after his father's murder, he was adopted into the king's protection. But then he seduced the king's daughter. So the king had him killed. It was the unacknowledged bastard child of that illicit affair, Walter, who, now grown up and needing to leave Wales in a hurry after he killed a man who taunted him about his birth, fled to Scotland – where he eventually rose to become Lord Steward of the realm. It was this bastard child who fathered the line of 'steward'/stewart/stuart kings.)

Since 1986, it's the killing of Macduff's children in 4.2 that British productions of *Macbeth*, marking a growing sense of pain and incomprehension at human atrocity on a global scale, have used to focus culture's stunned revulsion to casual violence, to terrorism and to the slaughter of innocents, locating what the Victorians couldn't bear to look at in the

Plate 22 The boy Fleance takes his aim on the future in Penny Woolcock's 1997 *Macbeth on the Estate. (Source:* BBC2.)

violated space of domesticity. Adrian Noble (1986) set the scene under white lights, in the Macduff nursery where the children played before bedtime, one of them fooling with the assassin's black boot straps before being picked up and stabbed. Gregory Doran (RSC, 1999) set the same scene in the household's laundry, the children in the tub at bath time, hemmed in by washing lines strung with white sheets and clotheshorses draped with white towels; Michael Bogdanov (Granada TV, 1997) put the ambush in a white kitchen, the children hunched over bowls of porridge; Calixto Bieito (Theatre Romea, on UK tour from Barcelona, 2002) set it in the Macbeths' urban gangland back garden – one kid was drowned in the paddling pool which the (childless) couple kept filled for when the little Macduffs came round to play; the second was battered to death with a Coca-Cola bottle. The third would have survived if the assassins, on their way out, hadn't heard the little nervous noise of a child's recorder coming from behind the sofa. They hauled him out, and smothered him with his teddy bear. In John Caird's 2004 Almeida Theatre production, Simon Russell Beale's Macbeth, standing silently apart, supervised the killings. He needed to know what the death of a child looked like. The killing of Duncan had been his 'present' to his wife, compensation for the death of their own child. Now, at his rival's house, he observed Lady Macduff's prolonged death throes with detached fasci-nation, as if he were watching a fluttering moth beating itself to death on a window sill. Throughout the whole of the play's final battle sequence

Plate 23 Macbeth (Antony Sher) clowns around with Fleance (Gareth Williams) on the battlements while the moon goes down in Gregory Doran's 1999 RSC *Macbeth*. (*Source*: Channel 4 in association with the RSC.)

Russell Beale's Macbeth sat rooted to his throne. Bizarrely, three stray children ran across his line of vision. Apparitions? Ghosts? A look passed over his face that registered almost comic bewilderment; a look that said, 'But I thought I'd *killed* all the children'.[98]

These deaths appalled, but in today's *Macbeth*, *Macbeth* performed at the turn of a century that has 'supped full with horrors' (5.5.13), the child who *survives* – the child Fleance – may be even more disturbing than the children who die. For in Fleance spectators have to consider the future: a future left in the hands of a damaged kid who's seen too much, who knows too much; a future that's going to have to be endured. He's the child of atrocity, a monster made of adult brutality. He's a kid our culture knows intimately. And he will certainly 'return / To plague th'inventor' (1.7.9–10), for like Macbeth, he just can't wait to get his hands on the future – as Greg Doran, John Caird and Dominic Cooke (RSC, 2004) showed with their final stage pictures. Doran's Malcolm knelt, bent his head to take the weight of the crown, spoke his 'healing benediction' (4.3.158), the final speech of the play. But just beyond the reach of light stood Fleance (Gareth Williams). Impassive. In fatigues. A child-soldier. He held in his hand the fetish his father had grabbed from one of the Weird Sisters at their first meeting – evidence that 'such things [were] here' (1.3.81), even as they vanished. It was a rattle. And as Fleance shook it, its noise – arhythmic, primitive, other, weird – underneath Malcolm's lines about 'grace', about 'measure, time, and place', undid with its menacing anti-acoustic the sound of human forgiveness. Cooke's Fleance (Oliver Hayes) was a fringe spectator on the final kill and, in the mass exit, the last to leave. The boy heard a whine in the air. He hesitated, turned back – saw the witches and froze. For a split second before the scene went to blackout, their sights locked on to each other, settling the future, constructing him the revenger-in-waiting. In Caird, the Weird Sisters not only fingered Macbeth; with Fleance, they took the future in hand – literally. They led him in and out of danger, placed him to watch the action from the edge of the circle, the space of 'play', which they'd burnt onto the ground, and finally, after the ambush that killed his father, escorted him out of the play.

For these directors, Fleance is the final product of *Macbeth*, the final witness. And metaphysics are to blame for him. The damaged, contaminated, brutalised child is Evil's baby.

In 2004, Max Stafford-Clark, like Penny Woolcock before him, took a tougher line, making humans responsible for human history. But where Woolcock saw the tragedy as a national one played out on desolate killing fields at the heart of an identifiable urban Britain, Stafford-Clark looked beyond Britain to killing fields which were perhaps less readily identifiable but which had as immediate a resonance, somewhere on a post-colonial third world map no longer coloured red-for-British-Empire but red with the blood of civil wars fought to 'liberate' this side or that, with weapons profitably supplied by former colonialists. Stafford-Clark put *Macbeth* in the kind of 'Scotland' that might be imagined from Uzodinma Iweala's child-narrated *Beasts of No Nation*, an unlocated African state – Sierra Leone, Uganda, Liberia, Rwanda: so many to choose from – engulfed in civil war where the children, abducted or 'saved' (the only survivors of the slaughter they've witnessed, their entire families and villages wasted), are forced recruits into guerrilla fighting that turns them into butcher-boy Fleances – or corpses.[99] In these new-model Scotlands, 'metaphysics' operates: tribal magic, ju-ju; more regularly, alcohol and drugs, 'gun juice'. But 'metaphysics' is just an excuse, a distraction. It's not the witches, it's the adults – the Charles Taylors, the Joshua Milton Blahyis (*nom de guerre*: General Butt Naked), the Commandants (the only name which the little boy, Agu, knows for the guerrilla leader in *Beasts of No Nation*), the Macbeths, helped of course by the multinationals – who produce the warrior children, who arm them with machetes and AK-47s, who help them to new names ('Bulletbounce', 'Colonel Deathsquad'). And who initiate them in killing: 'Commandant is saying it is like falling in love. You cannot be thinking about it. You are just having to do it, he is

a

b

Plate 24 a 'Was my father a traitor, mother?' asks young Macduff (Graeme Flynn) in Gregory Doran's 1999 RSC *Macbeth*. (*Source:* Channel 4 in association with the RSC.)
b The murderers answer by stabbing him in the back. (*Source:* Channel 4 in association with the RSC.)

saying ... Stop worrying. Soon it will be your own turn and then you will know what it is feeling like to be killing somebody'. It is the adults who capture the children for atrocity:

> Commandant ... is grabbing my neck and whispering into my ear, kill him now because I am not having the time oh ... He is squeezing my hand around the handle of the machete and I am feeling the wood in my finger and in my palm. It is just like killing goat. Just bring this hand up and knock him well well.[100]

Relocating *Macbeth* to present-day Africa, Stafford-Clark linked the play to recognisable histories, to news items flashing across Britain's television screens nightly, to charity appeals, to international debates about arms control and terrorism (state sponsored or privatised), and he made it a play, as Boika Sokolova writes, about 'ambition acting itself out in a recognisably modern world in time of war, where human life has little value, childhood is squeezed out of existence, where "confusion" reigns supreme.' As she observes, the director's decision to render 'Scotland' through a 'completely alien visual text' magnified the play's central problem, translating it from 'a play about murder' into 'a play about genocide' where the past is 'fixed' by settling old scores that endlessly produce new scores to settle – and where the ultimate casualty is the future.[101] But the relocation also released something that mostly gets lost in contemporary English productions of *Macbeth*, something Shakespeare encountered and engaged with in Holinshed's Scottish history: the force of the primitive, the tribal – renegade Irish, feuding clans – warriors pursuing vendettas across a 'blasted' landscape; technicians of violence capable of 'unseam[ing]' a man from 'the nave to th'chaps' (1.2.22); foot soldiers hero-worshipping those who inflict punitive atrocity and significant mutilation, like, at the end, the decapitated head displayed – 'Behold where stands / Th'usurper's cursed head' (5.9.21–2) – shown to 'mean' something. In Stafford-Clark's African setting, tribalism was a cultural idea made instantly available to *Macbeth*. Significantly enough, however, the tribe could only be discerned beneath the layers of colonialist 'civilisation' loaded on top of African bodies, the consumerist impositions that disfigured black bodies like scar tissue: western shirts, shoes, trainers, handbags, sunglasses, headscarves. Western weapons.

Stafford-Clark's 'Scotland' was, as his designer put it, a 'shit heap' spoiled with the junk that litters a war zone: twisted wire fencing, broken ladders and chairs, discarded bits of useless kit.[102] The Weird Sisters, led by a shaman got up in a tribal mask, head rag, body paint and bra, practiced ju-ju and greeted the man they expected in colonial French – 'Salut Macbeth, salut à toi.' He – a huge man (Danny Sapani) – prowled the area of this site-specific promenade production, a predator of space, never more than a machete's reach from spectators whose faces he glared into. (In the various venues where this *Macbeth* played, from an empty stately home to a disused textile factory to conventional theatres broken down to purpose, spectators were herded from room to room, shoved along by gun-toting soldiers.) First a warlord in bloodstained combat fatigues, then, scrubbed-up 'western', in black tie for Duncan's state banquet, Sapani's Macbeth appeared at his coronation in 'borrow'd robes', a kilt, sporran and regimental cap, a ludicrous 'fantasy of exotic sartorial chic' that quoted the mad posturing of Uganda's wannabe-Scot, Idi Amin.[103] This Macbeth's white European wife (Monica Dolan, the *only* white in 'Scotland' except for the white child she had in tow from a previous marriage) was clearly a trophy wife – but one who saw the manipulative value of tribal superstitiousness. In an arbitrarily lawless world where killing was a normal activity of daily life, whatever she could persuade her husband to 'perform upon / Th'unguarded Duncan' (1.7.69–70) 'would be in the *order* of things'.[104]

A whole world separated her chandeliered drawing room from the heaving camp that her husband's hand-to-mouth guerrilla army squatted in. Everyone was on the make. The Porter who came to see about the knocking stopped and jawed with the audience, cracking jokes about 'lethargy in western society', Bob Geldof, and his own black comedy of a family history ('mother died of AIDS, father, landmines') before pitching his deal, inviting spectators to invest in 'amazon.com'. At the end, it was UN peacekeepers who stormed Dunsinane to set the 'time … free' in this Scotland – but as Malcolm was taking over, speaking his final speech through a megaphone, the 'winners' were passing among the audience, handing out copies of a 'trophy' photograph. It showed a grinning 'warrior' in T-shirt and headscarf. He was holding up by its ears a head. It had been macheted from its body.

As gut-wrenching as that image was, the particular ugliness and heartbreak of this *Macbeth* lay not in what the adults were doing to themselves or each other but in what they were doing to the children. Stafford-Clark's thinking on the production began with children, a series of photographs pinned up on a design board: a child (Rwandan? Sierra Leonean?) whose arms had been chopped off; a girl (Ugandan?) whose eyes had been burnt out. And from Liberia: images of Charles Taylor's boy-militia, doped-up fifteen-year-olds in pink fright wigs and tattered wedding gowns, the ubiquitous AK-47 resting on the hip they've jutted out, posing for the camera; others with dainty tote bags and feather boas or opera gloves staring sullenly at the photographer, vacant, deeply dangerous. More images: of a small child swamped in an adult army helmet; of kids dressed in faded T-shirts and a mishmash of oversized Oxfam clothes – and their weapons; of a boy with a teddy bear knapsack on his back, and an automatic cradled in his arms. They were all victims, the mutilated, the kidnapped, the conscripted, the duped. The boys in drag crossdressed to mind-fuck the enemy but also because, transvestite (they'd been told), they were invincible: 'regional superstition' had it that soldiers could '"confuse the enemy's bullets" by assuming two identities simultaneously'.[105] Traditionally, these native kids would have 'crossed' in ritual bush costumes and tribal masks – but the nylon fright wig, the American high-school prom gown were the modern equivalents.

These were children of utter loss. Civil wars had claimed their schools, their fathers, families, their hands and eyes – and also their childhoods. And the common trope in all these images was the gun: for these were children acculturated to violence, and they carried weapons like western kids carry mobile phones.[106]

Seeing them somehow as the doomed outcome of a history that had begun a thousand years back in a brutally tribal Scotland that Shakespeare had given an early modern voice to – prophetically imagined when Banquo wonders about looking 'into the seeds of time' and saying 'which grain will grow and which will not' (1.3.56–7) – Stafford-Clark put Africa's war-hardened children on stage in *Macbeth*. Scrawny youths armed with AK-47s challenged spectators as they entered the playing space, harassed them, demanded bribes, flaunted weapons, gave them a taste of the intimidation – and powerlessness – the kids themselves felt, shoved them through doors and in among the mob that was both a guerrilla army and their 'family': black men in sweat-blood-and-piss soaked fatigues; black women in turbans and charity jumble dresses; black adolescents in adult clothing and T-shirts blazoned with bizarrely inappropriate First World logos. (They were utterly 'other', but also, in clothes we recognised as our casual cast-offs, 'us'. Branded by us, by colonialism-by-another-means, they claimed our complicity in atrocities we'd like to disown.) These deglamorised warriors, did they but know it, were conscripts to a cult of violence stretching back, via the likes of Idi Amin, to King James's son, Prince Henry in his armour posing for Hilliard and Peake. Donaldbain, Fleance, and young Macduff were all children (recruited to the production at each of the touring venues). Not scruffy, not like those other youths, orphans adopted at gunpoint by the big beasts of war who turned them into monsters, but children of the black elite. Fleance, like some latter-day Henry Stuart, affected military uniform – and imported Nikes.

Nothing was spared these children: yanked from bed in the middle of the night, they stood around yawning, unaware of the significance of Duncan's assassination (just another death?). Ambushed, Fleance would have been cut down with his father – if the Porter hadn't intervened, pushed him to safety, and faced the killers. When Macbeth's thugs broke in on Macduff's wife and child, her body wrapped around the boy couldn't save him. But which was more obscene – that he was dragged off to the next room, and after him, his mother, so that spectators had to hear the sounds of him being macheted, and her, first raped then killed? Or what happened next? That Macbeth's young thugs coerced spectators into witnessing the atrocity – and paying for it, lining them up and taking off them their 20 pence viewing fee before filing them into the next room where they saw murder as 'installation art' framed by a cordon of red crime-scene tape: baby toys scattered about, Lady Macduff horrifically

violated, and blood, *so much blood* ('who would have thought …?' (5.1.33))
pooling the wipe-clean fabric that covered the table. It was printed with
nursery motifs.[107]

Spectators were watching 'the endgame of a bloody regime going for
destruction "even till destruction sicken[s]"' (4.1.59). But as the too-
young conscripts ('hard' in 'fear', old 'in deed' (3.4.143, 144)) looked
more and more dead behind the eyes, so Macbeth looked more and more
'childed'. For the final phase he changed out of his tartan 'skirt' into kid's
clothes – T-shirt, baggy trousers, pink fright wig, a single elbow-length
white glove. Thus, writes Sokolova, 'Dressed in the feminine trappings of
a boy-soldier, as if recalling his own war-time childhood', this 'warrior
paragon' Macbeth – the bloody father to all the bloody babes he'd initiated into atrocity – 'visually replayed the cycle of violent childhood into
violent manhood'. He took spectators 'to the very source of the wish to see
"th'estate o'th'world … undone"' (5.5.50).[108] The 'seeds of time' cultivated by war had sprouted into undaunted mystic warriors set on mass
destruction. This Macbeth's end came across, then, 'not as the irrevo-
cable will of evil fatality but as the product of a desecrated childhood
which had begotten its own religion of merciless violence.'[109] So where
was this history going? What of the future?

In *Beasts of No Nation* little Agu – a child whom King James would have
liked: a bookish child, a reader, a boy who knows his Bible – is forced into
Fleance's part. With no preparation, no *Basilikon Doron*. Ambushed,
shouted a final instruction ('Fly, Fleance, fly'), he's made to witness what
no child should see:

> The air is smelling of burning wood and gunpowder and gasoline. I
> am hearing more shouting and then I am hearing my father saying
> run. RUN! RUN! AGU RUN! And … I am just running. I am seeing
> soldier with black face and big white smile. I am seeing bullet making
> my father to dance everywhere with his arm raising high to the sky
> like he is praising God. I am hearing terrible laughing and I am
> running, running, running … I am seeing man running with no head
> like chicken, and I am seeing arm and leg everywhere. Then every-
> thing is just white and all I am hearing is step slap, step slap, step slap,
> and the sound of my own breathing.[110]

Recovered from his hiding place by the Commandant, trained, indoc-
trinated, initiated and brutalised ('Commandant is saying that she is
enemy, she is stealing our food, and killing my family because she is
enemy. I am jumping on her chest KPWUD KPWUD and I am jumping

on her head, KPWUD, until it is only blood that is coming out of her mouth'[111]), Agu sometimes has a feeling he is sleepwalking through the war: 'Time is passing. Time is not passing. Day is changing to night. Night is changing to day. How can I know what is happening?' Other times, he feels 'the future in the instant': 'thing is just flashing by so fast, WHOOSH there is tree, WHOOSH there is house, WHOOSH there is person, and I am thinking that everything is moving so fast, that I will be old man before the war is over.' But he also knows one of the war's casualties is his childhood: 'I am knowing I am no more child so if this war is ending I cannot be going back to doing child thing. No.' Tomorrow produces tomorrow produces tomorrow. When he finally decides 'I cannot be doing this anymore' and puts down the gun – 'My shoulder ... jubilating because it is not having to be obeying gun anymore' – and walks off the war road and into 'heaven', a UN rehabilitation camp, he knows 'I am like old man'.[112] The female American aid worker wants him to 'tell me what you are feeling. Tell me what you are thinking'– to tell his past, what's happened. 'And every day I am telling her the same thing, I am thinking about my future'.[113]

Thinking about the future: that's what Stafford-Clark's *Macbeth* finally did. Underneath the roar of the UN loudspeakers imposing yet another (perishable) peace on 'Scotland' came a bizarre mingle of sound, of music, bagpipes played against African flutes. The living turned to face spectators, the dead rose, or returned; they lined up shoulder to shoulder upstage and began advancing in a slow ritual march upon the audience, all of them playing. Their music expanded to fill all space – gut-wrenching, riveting – music that, as Sokolova saw it, put spectators in mind of 'something precious, African and contemporary: the possibility for a reconciliation in the wake of a bloody history'. Between 'the children without a childhood' and 'the march of the dead and the living' there 'hung in the balance *hope*'.[114] Fragile, but nevertheless hope, expressed in the music the killers and the killed were making together.

At the end, I need to think back over some endings, and having begun this book with images – twentieth-century illustrations of Shakespeare's children – I want to finish with a final image, a Renaissance painting contemporary with Shakespeare's life.

Woolcock's *Macbeth* (using England as its example) ends siting (and citing) waste: that devastated urban landscape, empty of children, the kids trashed. Stafford-Clark's (using Uganda via Mandela's South Africa, with its hopes for truth and reconciliation) ends with children returned, restored, repairing the future. Doran's *Macbeth* ends with the toxic child, holding infection in his hand. Cooke's, with the kid eyeing fear. All of them negotiate Shakespeare's ending without exactly 'doing' the ending he scripts. Because of course Shakespeare, at the end of *Macbeth*, brings on *yet another child* – the boy Siward, who enters 5.7 as if in answer to Macbeth's crowing come-on, 'What's he / That was not born of woman?' (2–3). Twelve lines later, the kid's dead, obviously (laughs Macbeth), 'born of woman' (13). The Folio gives no stage direction to clear the body; it may lie there for the next hundred lines until the end of the play, until the father, Old Siward, hears the news of the death – 'Your son', says Ross, 'only lived but till he was a man'– interrogates it – 'Had he his hurts before?', that is, in the chest, not in the back – and dismisses him to eternity: 'Why then, God's soldier be he' (5.9.5–6, 12, 13). Malcolm balks at such briskness: 'He's worth more sorrow.' But Siward won't have it: 'He's worth no more' (17, 18). The child has fulfilled the promise of his parental investment. The boy has attained manhood. There's no more to be said. But Malcolm wants more said. Malcolm wants remembering. (So the scene says opposite things about childhood simultaneously.) More than that, *Macbeth* leaves us with a deeply troubling final stage picture, a final ambiguous visual statement about this self-contradictory, self-annulling culture that stoically accepts, celebrates and bewails the death of children: if Macbeth is killed on stage at 5.8.34 and his body left lying in view opposite little Siward's, what spectators see at the end is the dead body of the child as mute counter-image to the body of the king-killing child-killer.[115] How do we read that little corpse?

Perhaps the elder Brueghel can give instruction with *The Adoration of the Magi in the Snow* (1567), a painting completed three years after Shakespeare's birth.[116] On the far left of the composition, which shows a distinctly Flemish peasant 'Bethlehem', a dark crowd, huddled in poor clothes against the weather, mills around the open end of a wooden stable, its thatched roof heavy with snow. Just inside, we can see a woman; on her lap, a baby; on the threshold, in the snow, men in dazzling robes – red, gold – kneeling, 'reverently, passionately', celebrating 'the miraculous birth'. In the wider picture, as Auden might observe, the village goes about its 'anyhow' life: peasants collecting sticks, shouldering bundles, driving pack animals, bent double, hurrying to get out of the snow. Down on the river – frozen solid – a hole has been chopped in the ice; two men are exchanging buckets, drawing water, their backs to the scene. Just beyond them, far right, balancing in the composition the precious baby who, far left, sits safe in the mother's lap, there's another child. Well-bundled against the cold. Playing. On the ice. Sitting on a little sledge. Driving himself blindly backwards with two sticks. Towards the hole. One more push and he'll be over the edge. Is the woman who's leaning over the low parapet crying out to the child? Or is she just busy – wanting water for her washing? And what of the child – so busy with life? So close to the brink?

So there they are, two children: the precious, the adored; the ignored, the 'expendable' (*pace* Ariès) caught in the same frame, a visual gloss (as I want to make it) on the world of extremes and contradictions that Shakespeare's children inhabit. Like Brueghel, Shakespeare makes spectators see both children simultaneously. But unlike the painter's work, the playwright's isn't finished. *Titus Andronicus*, *The Winter's Tale*, *Macbeth*, Lucius, Mamillius, Fleance are parts, are plays still in the making, and as our theatre plays these parts, these parts, culturally, turn out to be playing us. Erasmus in *The ciuilitie of childehode* writes that 'The nature of the child is knowen in playe.'[117] I'd say further that the nature of the early modern child is 'knowen' in Shakespeare's child's play. And finally, that in our continuous re-performances of Shakespeare's children – re-performances constituting acts of memory as acts of creation that recall and transform the past in the form of the present – we are 'knowen' to ourselves 'in playe'.

Notes

1 'Behold the Child' or Parts for Children

1 For Laslett see *The World We Have Lost – Further Explored*, London, 1983, 108. For Geertz see *The Interpretation of Cultures*, New York, 1973, 10.

2 Anon. (attributed to Richard Mulcaster) STC 7590, 'The passage of our most drad Soueraigne Lady Quene Elyzabeth through the citie of London to Westminster the daye before her coronacion Anno 1558.' Incorporated into Holinshed, *The Third Volume of Chronicles*, STC2 13569, 1172–80. For readings of the progress that interpret Mulcaster as writing propaganda rather than public record, see Manuel Gómez-Lara, 'Apocalyptic iconographies and Elizabethan political propaganda' in Homem and Vieira (eds), *Gloriana's Rule: Literature, Religion and Power in the Age of Elizabeth*, Porto, 2006, 83–103, Sandra Logan, 'Making history: the rhetorical and historical occasion of Elizabeth Tudor's coronation entry', *Journal of Medieval and Early Modern Studies* 31, 2001, 251–81, and Wendy Wall, *The Imprint of Gender: Authorship and Publication in the English Renaissance*, London, 1993. None of these accounts notices the role children play in the royal entry.

3 Thus was enacted a public repudiation of Catholic Mary's religious policies. Already Elizabeth had proclaimed that 'the English letanie' was to be 'read … in churches through the citie of London', and within six months of her coronation, the Latin mass was silenced – it 'ceased, and no mass was said any more', STC2 13569. See Carol Chillington Rutter, '"Show me like a queen": Elizabeth among the players' in Homem and Vieira, 2006, 61–81.

4 Holinshed, STC2 13569, 1091.

5 She answered the Commons' petition in January 1559 with canny indirection. She promised she'd make herself a mother: 'a good mother of my countrie.' But as it was 'almightie God' who 'continu[d] her in this mind, to live out of the state of marriage', it was 'almightie God' who would have to deliver England's heir: an heir, she added mischievously, 'peradventure more beneficiall to the realme than such offspring as may come of me. For though I be neuer so carefull for your well doings, and mind euer so to be: yet may mine issue grow out of kind and become vngratious' (Holinshed, STC2 13569, 1181). So: the child is always risky business. The child may grow 'out of kind'. The child may 'turn'. Or worse, he may 'not come'.

6 According to Edward VI's contemporary biographer, 'his birth was violent': 'destituted of the helpes of nature at his entrance, and … faine to haue his way made into the world with a knife'; 'his mothers body was opened for his birth, and … shee dyed of the incision on the fourth day following'. See Barrett L. Beer (ed.), *The Life and Raigne of King Edward the Sixth by John Hayward*, London, 1993, 31–2.

7 Holinshed, STC2 13569, 1123–6. The Commons weren't taking any chances with this geriatric *prima gravida*: they hoped the queen would 'passe well the danger of deliuerance' of the child but, harking back to the 'dolorous experience' of 'inconstant gouernment' during Edward's minority, wanted it confirmed now that 'should … God … call' Mary 'out of this present life', Philip (Spanish, Catholic, and the king-consort) would 'take vpon him the rule, order, education and gouernment' of the child.

8 Holinshed, STC2 13569, 1161.

9 In her failure to produce an heir Holinshed read Catholic devotion unmasked as delusional superstition: 'If their masses' could 'fetch Christ from heauen', he wondered, 'how chanced then they could not reach to the queenes chamber, to helpe hir in hir trauell?', STC2 13569, 1161.

10 See Karen Cunningham, 'Female fidelities on trial: proof in the Howard Attainder and *Cymbeline*', *Renaissance Drama* XXV, Evanston, 1994, 5–6, and M. Lindsay Kaplan and Katherine Eggert (eds), '"Good queen, my lord, good queen": sexual slander and the trials of female authority in *The Winter's Tale*', *Renaissance Drama* XXV, 93–6.

11 I only observe that most of the children had only twelve or sixteen English hexameters to recite; that, since their orations were simultaneously displayed on the face of the scaffold for literate spectators to read, their voices may not have needed to be trained; and that by far the most ambitious of the Latin orations was spoken by a Paul's boy. Their feats of memory were, I'd guess, much less strenuous than their feats of endurance. These children, even where they're noticed, aren't investigated by any of those currently working on Elizabeth's coronation entry: David M. Bergeron, *English Civic Pageantry 1558–1642*, London, 1971; Susan Frye, *Elizabeth I: The Competition for Representation*, Oxford, 1993; Mary Hill Cole, *The Portable Queen: Elizabeth I and the Politics of Ceremony*, Amherst (ed.), 1999; not even by William Leahy, who chides others for failing 'to consider the common people' – then ignores the children. See *Elizabethan Triumphal Processions*, Aldershot, 2005, 11. I'm hopeful that work that Richard Rowland is currently doing on Thomas Heywood's civic performances will help fill our knowledge gap about these London children in the public eye.

12 Though Madden's is as 'true' an account, I'd say, as Stephen Greenblatt's biographic elaborations in *Will in the World*, London, 2004.

13 Richard P. Wheeler, 'Deaths in the family: the loss of a son and the rise of Shakespearean Comedy', *Shakespeare Quarterly* 51: 2 (Summer 2000), 130. Wheeler is particularly interested in Shakespeare post-1596, post, that is, the death of his 11-year-old son (Judith's twin). He observes: 'The death of Hamnet seems likely to have affected the person who wrote the plays deeply'; then asks, 'did it also affect the plays he wrote? How? How would we know?' In the main I agree with Wheeler's close and nuanced readings from the life to the theatre that answer his questions, but I think he's wrong that there is

'nothing in these earlier histories [the *Henry VI* trilogy, *Richard III*] that anticipates the extravagant rhetorical intensity surrounding the death of Arthur in
King John', 141.

14 Quoted in Wheeler, 132.

15 See Katherine Duncan-Jones, *Ungentle Shakespeare*, London, 2001, 15–16.

16 I have more work to do here, to inquire how Marlowe's children in *Edward II*,
Dido Queen of Carthage, and *Tamburlaine Part 2* might have influenced Shakespeare. Was Shakespeare writing for boys 'trained' on Marlowe?

17 Shakespeare makes him a baby for symbolic – and symmetrical – effect.
Historically, Edward York was twelve years old in 1471 when King Henry was
killed.

18 In fact, although she's never mentioned, his mother, Catherine de Valois, was
alive: she married Owen Tudor ca. 1430, had four children by him, and died
in 1437, her grandson, Henry Tudor, Earl of Richmond, appearing in *Part 3*
(see below) and inheriting the English crown as Henry VII in 1485. Henry VI
was crowned king of England in 1429, aged eight years, and crowned again in
Paris, aged ten, in 1431. In the episode of Gloucester going fisticuffs with
Beaufort, he was twelve. His detractors said that Henry's minority accus-
tomed him to dependence.

19 My texts of the three *Henry VI* plays are Michael Hattaway's New Cambridge
editions, 1990, 1991 and 1993.

20 See Kate Chedgzoy, Susanne Greenhalgh, and Robert Shaughnessy (eds),
Shakespeare and Childhood (Cambridge University Press, 2007). Observing the
difficulty of reinserting the agency of the young person into any construction
of early modern childhood, Chedgzoy in her Introduction argues (as she
admits, 'perhaps counter-intuitively') that 'studying dramatic fictions of childhood can be helpful with this task. All the children who appear in Shakespeare's plays are, of course, fictional characters created by an adult – though
not, perhaps, without some indirect input from the boy actors who first played
those roles. Yet through the multivocal, multiperspectival experience of
theatre they can offer us ways of glimpsing situations from a child's point of
view.' On the difficulty of recovering 'the history of children proper', as
opposed to the history of (adult) attitudes toward children, see Keith Thomas
in Gillian Avery and Julia Briggs, *Children and Their Books*, Oxford, 1989.

21 M.H. Curtis, 'Education and apprenticeship', *Shakespeare Survey* 17,
Cambridge, 1964, 53.

22 Desiderius Erasmus, *The ciuilitie of childehode with the discipline and institucion of children*, 1560, STC2 10470.3, Sigs. Fv^r, Fv^v. As Norbert Elias writes in *The Civilizing Process*, '*De civilitate morum puerilium* (On civility in boys), which appeared in
1530 ... immediately achieved an enormous circulation, going through
edition after edition ... [I]n the first six years after its publication it was
reprinted more than thirty times', London, 2000, 47.

23 See Wheeler, *Deaths in the Family*.

24 Henslowe's 'ne' has never been conclusively interpreted; but it's usually taken
to indicate a new play, one requiring a licence from the Master of the Revels
(so occasionally an old play so substantially revised as to require re-licensing).
See R.A. Foakes and R.T. Rickert, *Henslowe's Diary*, Cambridge, 1968, xxxiv.

25 For these accounts, see Foakes and Rickert, 16–19.

26 See Katherine Duncan-Jones's account of the 'upstart Crow' in *Ungentle Shakespeare*. Arden 2001, 43–8. But see also John Jowett, 'Johannes Factotum: Henry Chettle and Greene's Groatsworth of wit', *Papers of the Bibliographical Society of America* 87, 1993, 453–86.

27 On the maternal side, Richmond's uncle, who promotes him in this scene, was Edmund Beaufort, Duke of Somerset; it's through Somerset that Richmond claimed the throne.

28 *OED* sb1.

29 On the Court of Wards (established by statute in 1540, Henry VIII's attempt to modernise and formalise the feudal relationship of tenants to the crown) see Joel Hurstfield, *The Queen's Wards: Wardship and Marriage under Elizabeth I*, Cambridge MA, 1958. Those who inherited during their minority, succeeding to lands and estates, were 'adopted' by the Court of Wards, which then farmed the wardship to overseers responsible for maintaining the estate in trust for the heir while, in the meantime, benefiting from its profits. While the ward was a minor, the guardian also held the absolute parental right to dispose of the child in marriage.

30 Quoted in Ivy Pinchbeck and Margaret Hewitt, *Children in English Society* vol. 1, London, 1969, 27. In any case, as Master of the Wards, Burghley would have been assigned the guardianship of the boy – which Essex, in his letter, recognises. But the father is registering that it's what he *wishes* as well as what he knows is allotted.

31 The Devereux children were kin to the Huntingdons: their grandmother had been a Hastings before she married Walter's father. And Katherine Hastings had been a Dudley – so she was also related by marriage to the Sidneys: she was little sister to Ambrose Dudley (Earl of Warwick), Robert Dudley (Earl of Leicester, who, two years after Walter Devereux's death, married his widow, Lettice), and Mary née Dudley (who married Henry Sidney, and was the mother of Philip, Robert, Mary and Thomas: it was this favourite nephew, Thomas, whom Katherine later fostered). We see in this kinship by birth and marriage the intricacy of familial relationship built up through the interested exchange of children. Edward Russell, heir to the earldom of Bedford, was given to the Huntingdons in 1585, a thirteen-year-old, after his father was killed in a skirmish on the Scots borders just hours after his grandfather's death. That grandfather had been an intimate of William Cecil. The boy's aunt was Countess of Warwick, wife to Ambrose Dudley.

32 See *Cultural Aesthetics: Renaissance Literature and the Practice of Social Ornament*, Chicago, 1991, 36–44.

33 STC2 10470.3 Sigs. Aiv^v, Av^r, Ciii^r, Di^v, Diiii^r, Diii^v, Ev^v.

34 See Joanna Moody (ed.), *The Private Life of an Elizabethan Lady: The Diary of Lady Margaret Hoby 1599–1605*, Stroud, 2001, 31, 149, 186–7.

35 Edmond Henslowe was 14 when his father died in 1593. Originally, his mother 'ded desyer to haue the bordinge & bringyn vp of her owne iij chelldren', but after her decease, 'they came al vp to me to London to kepe', wrote Henslowe in February 1595. He paid £5 to apprentice his niece Mary 'vnto John gryges' – the carpenter who'd built the Rose – 'to Learne to sowe al maner of workes & to Lerne bonelace' in June 1595 (Diary f. 123, 228); the following year, he apprenticed Edmond 'to mr newman dier'. (See Foakes and Rickert, *Henslowe's Diary*, 78–9, 81, 140, 226, 228–30.)

36 Philippe Ariès, *Centuries of Childhood*, translated by Robert Baldick, London, 1962, 366. On apprenticeship, see Curtis, 'Education and apprenticeship', *Shakespeare Survey* 17, 1964, 53–72.

37 On the Statute, see Curtis. See also David Kathman's work on apprentices and players: 'How old were Shakespeare's boy actors?', *Shakespeare Survey* 58, Cambridge, 2005, 220–46, and 'Grocers, Goldsmiths, and Drapers: Freemen and apprentices in the Elizabethan theater', *Shakespeare Quarterly* 55: 1 (Spring 2004), 1–49. Kathman, however, doesn't acknowledge that adult males, sharers in the company, also played women's roles, while it's clear from Henslowe's accounts that they certainly did. See Foakes and Rickert, 72, 85 ('bornes womones gowne').

38 See Foakes and Rickert, 282–3.

39 It's also one of the only surviving letters of its kind – not a schoolboy exercise, nor the letter of an elite child like Elizabeth Tudor or James Stuart.

40 Foakes and Rickert, 73, 318, 321, 323.

41 From the Facsimile of *The Henslowe Papers* vol. I, R.A. Foakes (ed.), London, 1977, I read the signature on f.61^v as autograph. Learning his 'mystery' as a player, Pig would also have been serving Alleyn as a personal servant – like Downton's 'biger boy' who ran messages for his master and 'feched' loans for him. See Foakes and Rickert, 75, 77.

42 Foakes and Rickert, 328–33.

43 *Frederick* uses ten boy players, *Alcazar*, eight, *I Tamar Cam*, nine. No such plot survives for a Shakespeare play to show us the distribution of players in the actual production script, but no doubt many more boys appeared on his stage than we imagine from a modern edition or list of *dramatis personae*. How many fairy 'oofs' does Parson Evans assemble in the final scene of *The Merry Wives of Windsor*? How many pages turn up with the two speaking parts alongside Touchstone singing 'hey-nonny-no' in the Forest of Arden (*As You Like It*, 5.3)? How many children might enliven Capulet's ball in *Romeo and Juliet*? How many boys attend Henry V's army – the baggage boys killed offstage in 4.7? Parts the modern theatre casts as adults – servants, pages, 'boys' – were, I think, played by children on Shakespeare's stage.

44 Fumerton, 39–42.

45 He wasn't the first director to bring on 'the changeling' child at the RST. That was Ron Daniels in 1981, followed by John Caird in 1989. But they cast child actors. Doran's puppet was made by the Little Angel team. See too the TV film version (1996) of Adrian Noble's 1994 RST *Dream*, a *Dream* dreamed by a child, discussed in Carol Chillington Rutter, 'Looking like a child – or – *Titus*: the comedy', *Shakespeare Survey* 56, Cambridge, 2003, 4–10.

46 Christopher Marlowe, *The Jew of Malta*, 1.1.37.

47 Contemporary reviews of Rackham's illustrated *A Midsummer Night's Dream*, 1908. See James Hamilton, *Arthur Rackham: A Life with Illustrations*, London, 1990, 167–71.

48 See the illustration facing, 24 in the 1908 edition.

49 In 1981 Daniels's fairies were all puppets, manipulated by visible operators in black who spoke the lines, which gave the production an Angela Carter quality – not least because many of the toys in fairyland were broken. Puck had a 'little Puck' who was exactly like him (and who waved 'bye bye' at the end). Shadowed by puppets, this production's central fairy characters were in

a sense haunted by their child-selves; they finally regained, at the end, a kind of lost innocence once their adult passions – which had turned so intolerably sour – were worked through. I owe these observations to Tony Howard.

50 I have in mind the murder of the two-year-old, James Bulger, in 1993. His killers were two ten-year-olds. Memories of this murder were also triggered by the fairies' dolls, deliberately reminiscent of Chucky, the child-killing doll of the video nasty, *Child's Play 3*, who was supposed to have 'inspired' the Bulger killing.

51 This production toured the UK throughout 2006, appearing as part of the RSC's Complete Works festival in September. I'm grateful to Kneehigh and Emma Rice for giving me a copy of their working script and permission to quote it.

52 Later in the run the typewriter was cut, but the gag still worked: spectators remembered Posthumus's stubby pencil and frantic scribbling.

53 See www.uk.missingkids.com.

2 The Alphabet of Memory in *Titus Andronicus*

1 My text is the Arden 3, *Titus Andronicus*, Jonathan Bate (ed.), London, 1995. I am silently passing over a number of editorial cruces relating here to speech prefixes. See Bate's notes, 274. Later, I am silent on debates about the authorship of the play's opening scene, making 'Shakespeare' a theatrical shorthand for writing that may be a collaboration with George Peele. On this matter see Emrys Jones, *The Origins of Shakespeare*, Oxford, 1977, and Brian Vickers, *Shakespeare, Co-Author*, Oxford, 2002. All other Shakespeare citations are from *The Complete Works*, Wells and Taylor (eds), Oxford, 1986.

2 Following Bate, I see 3.2, the fly killing scene, which doesn't appear in the 1594 Q1 text, as a later addition to Shakespeare's original play. The 1623 Folio is the first printed text to include the scene. In Quarto, then, the boy Lucius first appears in 4.1; in Folio, in 3.2.

3 I owe this reading of the speech as an exercise in logic to Peter Mack.

4 In *Renaissance Rhetoric*, Peter Mack (ed.), London, Macmillan 1994, 103.

5 In *Tynan on Theatre*, Harmondsworth, 1961, 120; reprinted from his review, '*Titus Andronicus* at Stratford-on-Avon', *Observer*, 17 August 1955.

6 These are stories, relationships, genealogies every Elizabethan grammar school boy versed in Virgil and Livy would have known.

7 *Ovid's Metamorphoses: The Arthur Golding Translation 1567*, John Frederick Nims (ed.), Philadelphia, 2000, 22.

8 That outrage was thwarted by the metamorphosis. Mourning her loss, Apollo fashions the laurel into something new, a 'found' sign that nostalgically remembers her while simultaneously promoting the god's prestige. The laurel wreath is awarded to triumphant poets as well as conquering generals.

9 See Jonathan Bate in *Shakespeare and Ovid*, Oxford, 1993, 95–9. This is the essential book for understanding these two poets in conversation with each other.

10 E.F. Watling (ed.), *Seneca: Thyestes, Phaedra, The Trojan Women, Oedipus with Octavia*, Harmondsworth, 1966, 167.

11 In Jasper Heywood's 1559 *Translations of Seneca's Troas, Thyestes and Hercules Furens*, H. de Vocht, Louvain (ed.) 1913, Agamemnon in the *Troas* warns

Pyrrhus against insisting on the blood sacrifice of Polyxene. 'The happy sword once staynde with blood / vnsacyable is,' he tells Achilles's son (2.3.917–18). He refuses to sanction what he considers 'furious fransye', not just the killing of a royal princess but Pyrrhus's intention of duping her – like Agamemnon's own daughter, Iphigenia, before her, once 'promised' to Achilles – into believing she's being prepared for marriage:

A virgin borne of princes blood / for offring to be slaine
And geuen be, to staine the tombe / and ashes of the ded,
And vnder name of wedlocke se / the giltles blood be shed,
I will not graunt.

2.3.923–9

If Achilles demands blood, let it be an animal's:

If bloodshed vayle hys ashes ought / strike of an oxes hed,
And let no blood that may be cause / of mothers teares be shed.
What furious fransye may this be / that doth your wyll so leade,
This earnest carefull sute to make / in trauaile for the deade?

2.3.941–8

Seneca's modern translator – E.F. Watling – makes Agamemnon's interrogation of Pyrrhus even more appalled:

If blood must flow to give his ashes rest,
Let there be slaughtered finest Phrygian cattle;
Shed blood for which no mother's eyes need weep.
Where is such custom known? Where is man's life
Poured out in payment to the human dead?

288–92

12 George Puttenham, celebrating the faculty of memory in his 1589 *The arte of English poesie*, G.D. Willcock and Alice Walker (eds), Cambridge, 1936, writes, 'There is nothing in man of all the potential parts of his mind (reason and will except) more noble or more necessary to the active life th[an] memory: because it maketh most to a sound judgement and perfect worldly wisedome, examining and comparing the time past with the present, and by them both considering the time to come.' Memory serves the active life by producing the materials of persuasion: there is 'no kinde of argument in all the Oratorie craft, doth better perswade and more universally satisfie than example, which is but the representation of old memories.' See Book 1, Chapter XIX.
13 See Antony B. Dawson's evocative writing on remembering and forgetting in 'The arithmetic of memory: Shakespeare's theatre and the national past', *Shakespeare Survey* 52, Cambridge, 1999, 54–67. It's this essay that I'm glancing at in my chapter title.
14 Bate, *Shakespeare and Ovid*, 105. *De Copia* went through 150 editions between 1512 and 1572: evidence of its enormous contemporary influence. See, too, Philip Sidney in *An Apologie for Poetrie*, London, 1595, urging 'that a feigned

example hath as much force to teach as a true example' (edited by Geoffrey Shepherd, London, 1965, 110).

15 *Shakespeare and Ovid*, 105.

16 Which hand did Titus send the emperor? The point is debatable. In 3.1 it looks like he sacrifices the right hand – the hand that defended Rome (192); but in 3.2, Titus says 'This poor right hand of mine / Is left to tyrannize upon my breast' (7–8). Act 3 Scene 2, however, is a later addition to the play (see note 2). It makes symbolic sense that Titus would send the right hand to ransom his sons, leaving his sinister hand to commit his acts of revenge.

17 *OED sb* 1, 2, and 7 (which citation quotes *Titus*).

18 *OED sb* 1.*c*, *d*, 2, 4.

19 *OED sb* I, 5, 6, 5.*b*, 8, 10.

20 As Bate glosses it, 267, note 43 – though as he observes, this would be *OED*'s first usage for this sense, *a*. 4c.

21 *The Boke of common praier*, 1559. STC 16284.5 Sig. Ni^v.

22 I owe this observation to Thomas Docherty.

23 This, in Tony Harrison's translation of *The Trojan Women*. Hekabe ponders the women's fate and savours its irony. The magnitude of their desolation is somehow its consolation: for if the Troy-destroying Greeks 'hadn't brought us down so low, / face down in the dust, we'd disappear forever. / Whereas now we are stories everyone will tell.' See *Tony Harrison, Plays 4*, London, 2002, 339.

24 Bate, *Shakespeare and Ovid*, 103. The play's 'classical allusiveness,' he continues, 'relies on sustained involvement with a few sources – Ovid and a little Livy, the most famous part of Virgil, some Plutarch and the odd tag from Seneca that might well be derived at second hand.' Coriolanus and Solon put in fleeting appearances in *Titus* from Plutarch; Virginius from Livy; Ajax from Horace; Hippolytus from Seneca; Pyramus, Orpheus, Phaeton, Alcides from Ovid; and Hector, Priam, and Aeneas from Virgil (and from Ovid).

25 Rape is one of the customary ways the gods communicate with mortals in the classical world. See, for example, the story of Ceny in Book XII of the *Metamorphoses* who, raped by Neptune and offered 'what thou wilt' in payment, asks to be metamorphosed male. That way, she'll 'no more constreyned bee to such a thing' (226): she won't ever have to submit to rape again.

26 *The seuen first bookes of the Eneidos of* Virgill, *conuerted in English meter by Thomas Phaer*, London, 1588, STC2 24799.

27 See too the stories of Arachne in *Metamorphoses* Book VI, Penelope in *The Odyssey* Book II and Clytemnestra rolling out the red carpet for Agamemnon in *The Oresteia* who, as he steps onto it, comments (in Tony Harrison's translation, London, 1981), 'I'll feel that I'm walking the women who wove it', 28.

28 Dawson, 'The arithmetic of memory', 55.

29 *The Culture of Playgoing in Shakespeare's England*, Cambridge, 2001, 138.

30 On texts and textiles see Catherine Bates, 'Weaving and writing in *Othello*', *Shakespeare Survey* 46, Cambridge, 1994, 51–60. Tony Howard, in conversation, finds this moment shocking because 'while Marcus makes the instinctive association of Lavinia with raped Philomel at first sight, it isn't until they read Ovid that Titus does. For Titus, the devastation of her body has no perpetrator and needs no motive until then. It's a shock to realise that he doesn't realise she's been raped, that for two-and-a-half scenes he only sees the mutilations that mirror his.'

31 Bate, *Titus Andronicus*, 30.

32 I make this claim from theatrical experience, having watched Deborah Warner's RSC production of *Titus Andronicus* seven times across the season at the Swan in 1987. On every occasion, there was an audible noise, animal satisfaction, from spectators – all suddenly Prognes – when the boys' throats were cut. On the feminising of this cannibalistic revenge moment, Tony Howard comments that where 'we' (versed in Seneca) 'would *expect* Shakespeare to take us with his initial Titus/Priam connection, to Thyestes's banquet' (that original act of pollution in the House of Atreus which will overwhelm Agamemnon the moment he gets back to Argos from Troy), 'he doesn't. Instead, the patriarchal myth is metamorphosed via Progne.' In conversation.

33 On this Clown, see Francis Barker, *The Culture of Violence: Tragedy and History*, Manchester, 1993.

34 As Jonathan Bate observes, 'By virtue of their reading and imitation of Ovid and other classical authors, the characters in the play come to resemble students in grammar school and university' – not least because the language of the schoolroom 'suffuses the play' (*Shakespeare and Ovid*, 104). School 'talk' is on the tip of everyone's tongue: 'learn of us', 'let me teach you', 'O handle not the theme to talk of hands', 'I was their tutor to instruct them', 'drown my oratory / … break my utterance', 'I do digress', 'well has thou lessoned us'.

35 'Humanist imitation,' writes Bate, 'was based on the premiss [sic] that classical texts were appropriate patterns or models because they embodied fundamental, enduring truths', *Shakespeare and Ovid*, 9.

36 *Shakespeare and Ovid*, 19. Throughout, Bate depends on T.W. Baldwin's magisterial *William Shaksperes Small Latine & Lesse Greeke*, Urbana, 1944. The best short introduction to the grammar school curriculum is Peter Mack's 'Humanism, rhetoric, education' in Donna Hamilton (ed.), *A Concise Companion to English Renaissance Literature*, Oxford, 2006, 94–113. But see too his much fuller account and analysis in *Elizabethan Rhetoric: Theory and Practice*, Cambridge, 2002. Walter Ong's discussion of 'Latin language study as a renaissance puberty rite' in *Rhetoric, Romance, and Technology: Studies in the Interaction of Expression and Culture*, Ithaca and London, 1971, has been widely influential, especially among academics in the US, but Ong (anthropologically unpacking the 'ritual' of male incorporation into the academic community) doesn't actually characterise the English grammar school very accurately. A day-school set inside the local community, the boys living at home and perhaps nipping back to dine at mid-day, the Elizabethan grammar was hardly a 'closed world', a 'male rendezvous'; and it is probably overly-mystifying to describe Latin learning – in Elizabethan England – as an 'initiation' into 'a secret language' (120–1). Then, too, Ong (perhaps because of his own training as a Jesuit) seems overly-fixated on the grammar school's regimes of corporal punishment. He writes extensively about the 'instruments' of 'flogging', seeing the scene engraved in Pieter Brueghel the Elder's 'The ass at school' as typical, but fails to notice elsewhere that, in the classroom illustrated on the title page of the widely used English Latin primer, *The Catechism*, 1571, for example, while the schoolmaster sitting on his form has a bundle of switches on the floor beside him, he has also a huge bowl of apples – and it's one of *these* that he's handing the boy who's standing before him, his book closed, his examination evidently over. Switches may have served as

'mnemonic devices in both the real and the allegorical orders,' as Ong claims (125). But so did apples.

37 I'm using 'invention' here anachronistically to mean 'original thinking'. 'Invention' as it applied to the grammar school syllabus was the first of the five distinct rhetorical skills pupils were taught and involved finding the arguments, stories and ideas of a piece. The other four were disposition (putting the arguments and ideas into the most effective order); style (expressing the ideas in the most striking and effective language); memory (memorising the speech); and delivery (putting the speech across using the most suitable resources of voice and gesture). See Peter Mack in Hamilton, 'Humanism, rhetoric, education', 94.

38 John Brinsley, *Ludus Literarius* (1612), Scolar Press Facsimile, Scolar Press, Menston, 1968, 211. Quintilian defined rhetoric as 'the art of speaking well', *Institutio Oratoria*, 2.15.38; Aristotle called it 'the art of finding the available means of persuasion in any situation', *Rhetoric*, 1355.b.25. (I owe these citations to Peter Mack.) Writing themes seems to have been a terrifying prospect for many schoolboys. Brinsley's 'good' teacher tries to demystify the process by observing that 'The principal end of making Theams' is 'to furnish scholars with al store of the choisest matter, that they may therby learne to understand, and speake or write of any ordinary Theame, morall or Politicall, such as usually fall into discourse amongst men & in practice of life; and especially concerning vertues and vices. So as to work in themselues a greater loue of the vertue and hatred of the vice, and to be able with soundnesse of reason to draw others to their opinion' (175). I'm not sure that schoolboys would have been reassured by this explanation.

39 In the medieval, as in the classical and later the early modern worlds, extreme emotion belonged axiomatically (but certainly not exclusively) to women, tears typically being represented as 'women's weapons' (*King Lear*, 2.4.272) or that which 'disclaim'st / Flinty mankind' (*Timon of Athens*, 4.3.476). In Shakespeare's *Lear, Timon, Antony and Cleopatra*, and *Titus*, tears turn men into women, Timon observing of his servant Flavius, 'What, dost thou weep? Come nearer, then I love thee, / Because thou art a woman' (4.3.475–6), and Lear imploring the gods to 'touch' him with 'noble anger': 'And let not women's weapons, water-drops, / Stain my man's cheeks' (2.2.451–2). Since the emphasis in the classroom was on analysing and depicting emotional states in rhetorically affective language, and since women were typically the conduits of such emotions in the literature they were reading, their rhetorical training meant that boys would have devoted considerable time to 'becoming' women.

40 'Weeping for Dido: epilogue on a premodern rhetorical exercise in the postmodern classroom', in Carol Dana Lanham, *Latin Grammar and Rhetoric: From Classical Theory to Medieval Practice*, New York and London, 2002, 284.

41 Ibid., 284.

42 Quoted in Woods, 'Weeping', 285.

43 Woods, 'Weeping', 286.

44 Ibid., 287. Pico in a letter sets puerile 'questions for debate ... concerning the mother of Andromache or the sons of Niobe' against what he considers to be serious matters, 'things human and divine.' Shakespeare's Hamlet, of course, would take a very different view of Hecuba – 'the mother [in law] of

Andromache' – and Niobe – 'all tears' – and by extension, a different view of at least one of Niobe's (surrogate) sons – for Hamlet sees himself as the son of Gertrude/Niobe.

45 *The Heroycall Epistles of the Learned Poet Publius Ovidius Naso, In Englishe Verse: set out and translated by George Turberville Gent*, London, 1567, STC2 18939.5.

46 See Baldwin's *William Shaksperes Smalle Latine & Lesse Greeke*, 423. Erasmus set *Heroïdes* in his 1522 text on letter writing; Eton used *Heroïdes* for this purpose ca. 1530; and a heavily scribbled-over school text preserved in the British Museum shows that *Heroïdes* was still in use for letter writing after 1566.

47 'Humanism, rhetoric, education', 96. (See notes 36 and 37 above)

48 *Ludus Literarius*, 175.

49 Ibid., 210.

50 Ibid., 210, 250.

51 Ibid., 212–13.

52 And beyond the 'local habitation' of this particular name, Ariadne is the Ovidian woman Shakespeare himself remembers most habitually, making me suspect that the lines of Epistle X were the ones he learned and performed at school, 'imprinting the originals in his hart', uttering the 'dialogue liuely' as if he 'were the person [...] which did speake', and 'imagin[ing]' himself 'to haue occasion to vtter the very same things'.

53 See Woods, 'Weeping', 287–8.

54 *Titus Andronicus* may have been written during 1593, a year when the London playhouses were suffering a continuous inhibition because of plague. In December, Philip Henslowe resumed his list of daily receipts at the Rose playhouse: 'the earle of susex his men' began playing there on 27 December – to huge crowds, happy, perhaps, to have the players back in town. Every play that first week took the kind of receipts Henslowe normally expected only for premieres. Sussex's opened 'titus & ondronicus' (a 'ne', that is, 'new' play) on 23 January 1594, but by April, the company had disbanded: broken, no doubt, by the aftershocks of the year's trouble. In June, 'andronicous' was in the repertoire of the combined 'Lord Admeralle men & my Lorde chamberlen men', who shortly split, the Chamberlain's Men (Shakespeare among them) evidently taking *Titus* with them: the play disappears from Henslowe's records. See R.A. Foakes and R.T. Rickert (eds), *Henslowe's Diary*, Cambridge, 1968, Ff 8ᵛ, 9, 9ᵛ, 20–2. *A Midsummer Night's Dream* is first mentioned in Francis Meres's *Palladis Tamia* (1598) but was probably written in 1594 or 1595, just before, or just after *Romeo and Juliet*.

55 'The purpose of playing: reflections on a Shakespearean anthropology', *Helios*, n.s. 7, 1980, 64. The term is borrowed from the anthropologist, Victor Turner, in *Dramas, Fields and Metaphors*, Ithaca, 1974.

56 But see the Folio text, where it's Egeus, not Philostrate, who, playing Master of the Revels, brings on the 'mirth' in Act 5, perhaps signalling a truce with comedy if not a reconciliation with his daughter.

57 See, for example, *Angela's Ashes, And When Did You Last See Your Father?, A Star Called Henry, The Road to Nab End, Atonement, According to Queenie, Mere, The Bonesetter's Daughter, Once in a House on Fire, The True History of the Kelly Gang, Bad Blood, Let's Not Go to the Dogs Tonight, The Flamboya Tree, At Swim, Two Boys, The True Story of Lucy Gault, The Life of Pi*.

58 On the film's 'post modern aspirations', see Mark Thornton Burnett, 'Impressions of fantasy: Adrian Noble's *A Midsummer Night's Dream*' in Mark Thornton Burnett and Ramona Wray (eds), *Shakespeare, Film, Fin de Siècle*, London, 2000, 89. On intertextuality as 'one of the hallmarks of postmodern cinema', see James Loehlin, '"These violent delights have violent ends": Baz Luhrmann's Millennial Shakespeare' in Burnett and Wray, 124. Burnett's essay aims to 'redress' critical opinion of Noble's film as an 'unmitigated disaster' (*Observer*, 1 December 1996), merely 'a highbrow pantomime' (*The Sunday Times*, 1 December 1996) – but to my mind, doesn't succeed.

59 Nowhere that I have come across does Taymor acknowledge her obvious debts to Howell (or likely ones to Warner). Howell wants spectators to see the story from young Lucius's eyes, and puts him in the frame from the opening shot: a shadow anamorphically cast across the frame materialises as a skull then dissolves into the face of the boy (played by Paul Davies-Prowles) whose looking is thus established as the TV film's point of view. While she dresses Rome in period costume, Howell makes the boy also a modern child, giving him, significantly, a pair of steel-framed spectacles to focus his looking. But she kills all the laughs that Deborah Warner later found in the play and performance, cutting Titus's 'Ha, ha, ha' (3.1.265) – and the cook's costume. In her film, Lucius doesn't keep his promise to Aaron. The baby isn't saved. At the end, young Lucius sits gazing at the infant – a corpse in a child-sized coffin.

60 As laughter, since Aristotle, has been held indecorous in tragedy, so dodging the laughs in *Titus Andronicus* has been held a main – indeed, perhaps *the* main – challenge for the play's contemporary directors. Alan Dessen in *Titus Andronicus: Shakespeare in Performance*, Manchester, 1989, takes it as read that Edward Ravenscroft's Restoration adaptation was finding 'solutions' for 'a series of problematic moments that continue to bedevil today's directors', and 'bedevil' them because they 'elicit unwanted audience laughter', 9. See Dessen on Peter Brook directing *Titus Andronicus* in 1955 as a 'beautiful barbaric ritual', a reading Brook achieved, according to J.C. Trewin in a contemporary review, by cutting every 'offending phrase' that threatened 'mocking laughter', 15, 22. But what if Dessen *et al.* are wrong? What if laughter isn't a risk to be avoided but a risk to be *courted* in the play? Following on from Deborah Warner, Taymor hears laughter as aurally constituting the authentic emotional territory of the tragic grotesque in *Titus*, and cues it to the laughter the play itself elicits in Titus's 'Ha, ha, ha' (3.1.265).

61 Produced by Clear Blue Sky, the film features Anthony Hopkins (Titus), Jessica Lange (Tamora), Laura Fraser (Lavinia), Colm Feore (Marcus), Alan Cumming (Saturninus), James Frain (Bassianus), Harry Lennix (Aaron), Angus MacFadyen (Lucius), Matthew Rhys (Demetrius), Jonathan Rhys Meyers (Chiron), Dario D'Ambrosi (Clown), Tresy Taddei (Clown's Assistant), and Osheen Jones as the Boy/young Lucius. Bah Souleymane played Aaron's baby.

62 The Boy was part of Taymor's original concept both on stage and film. Seeing *Titus Andronicus* as 'the greatest dissertation on violence ever written', its themes 'war, ritual, the domestic, lust, nihilism', she fixed on 'the idea of the child watching his family go at it, watching these bloodlines, these tribes, these religious rites, this whole event' as establishing the film's point of view: 'the arc of the story is the child's' and the story is 'brought to life by the boy's vision.'

(Quoted from Taymor's director's commentary, *Titus* DVD, Clear Blue Sky Productions, 2000.)

63 Don Fleming, *Powerplay: Toys as Popular Culture*, Manchester, 1996, 11, 35.

64 *The Development of Play*, London, 1993, 2nd edition, 63.

65 Quoted in Cohen, 63.

66 I am quoting, of course, the famous opening of L.P. Hartley's *The Go-Between*, London, 1953.

67 Bate, *Titus Andronicus*, 17.

68 Fleming, *Powerplay*, 8.

69 Grace Kelly was Taymor's model for Lavinia. Stylistically, the director was looking for 'defamed, deflowered elegance' – like 'graffiti scrawled on ancient monuments' (Clear Blue Sky DVD).

70 For spectators in the know, there's an intertextual film joke here: the unmasked boy is the very changeling child from Adrian Noble's sugar-coated Edwardian-dress film of *A Midsummer Night's Dream*, Osheen Jones. See Carol Chillington Rutter, 'Looking like a child – or – *Titus*: the comedy', *Shakespeare Survey* 56, Cambridge, 2003, 1–26, esp. 4–10. On Taymor's film see also Peter Donaldson, 'Game Space/Tragic Space: Julie Taymor's *Titus*' in Barbara Hodgdon and W.B. Worthen (eds), *A Companion to Shakespeare and Performance*, Oxford, 2005, 457–77 and Pascale Aebischer, *Shakespeare's Violated Bodies*, Cambridge, 2004.

71 Taymor recognises her debt to the Fellini not of *Satyricon* – though that's the film her wedding and orgy sequences in *Titus* call to mind – but to *Amarcord*: 'I'm a caricaturist, and so was Fellini, and … I share Fellini's love of the human face as well as his interest in puppets, clowns, the carnival and the theatre' (Clear Blue Sky DVD). The film was shot at Fellini's old studio in Rome, Cinecitta, and, in a Fellini-esque move, Taymor used one of his 'real' scenic artists to play the restorer in the workshop scene.

72 In Dessen, Daniel Scuro comments that this change makes Marcus a 'nobler' figure, 22.

73 The 1623 Folio *Titus*, set from Q3, ends with four additional lines: 'See Justice done on Aaron, that damn'd Moore / From whom, our heauy happes had their beginning: / Then afterwarde, to Order well the State, / That like Euents, may ne're it Ruinate.' As Bate explains, these lines made their way into Q3 from Q2, set from a copy of the manuscript from which the bottom of the last page had been torn away, prompting the compositor to invent a replacement for the missing ending (113–14). In his Arden 3 edition, Bate follows Q1's ending – and Taymor follows Bate.

74 Or as the screenplay has it: 'The sound of a baby crying transforms into thousands of babies crying, then into squawking birds of prey and then into the tolling of bells', 170. For Bate in the 'Introduction', Marcus is 'the play's chief spectator figure', 9. As I see it, in Shakespeare's final scene, that role is the child's. See Julie Taymor, *Titus: The Illustrated Screenplay*, New York, 2000.

75 *Titus Andronicus*, 22.

76 Don Handleman, quoted by Cohen, 14.

77 *Shakespeare and Ovid*, 108.

78 See, for example, the stories of Daphne, Io, Europa, Syrinx, Proserpina, and Caenis/Ceny – as well as Philomela, of course.

79 It is proposed as a tactic of seduction, the 'acceptable violence' remembered from Ovid by Ben Jonson's adolescent urban wits in the opening scene of *Epicoene.*

80 The classical world handed down to its humanist students two intertwined lines on 'acceptable' rape: rape as seduction (the woman supposed complicit, her 'no' really 'yes') and 'heroic rape', rape perpetrated by a god or hero.

81 I owe these observations to Marjorie Curry Woods. See her important work on 'Rape and the pedagogical rhetoric of sexual violence' in Rita Copeland (ed.), *Criticism and Dissent in the Middle Ages*, Cambridge, 1996, 56–86.

82 Hiding out in drag – his mother, Thetis's idea – to avoid being drafted to the Trojan war, adolescent Achilles is full of self-loathing, humiliated by his cover: he looks like a girl and is, in fact, sexually a 'maid'. His rape of Deidamia (his unwitting host's unwitting daughter whose room he's sharing) ends his sexual anxiety, breaks his mother's control, launches him into the world of his heroic project (not least by producing the son who, in the guise of the 'Hyrcanian beast', will revenge his death) and, not insignificantly, reassures [sic] his readers as much as himself of his virility by ending the troubling gender ambiguity that has attached to 's/he' Achilles in the Latin text. In *Ars amatoria* Achilles again is a model, Ovid presenting his rape of Deidamia as seduction and constructing *the victim* as the agent of the violence: she is one of 'the girls' Ovid describes who 'wish, through compulsion, to grant' what 'they are delighted to grant'. Rough seduction delights a girl like Deidamia: she 'will struggle at first'; but 'still, in her struggling, she will wish to be overcome'. So it's all right to use force: 'Call it violence, if you like; such violence is pleasing to the fair', *passim*, Book I, Henry T. Riley (ed.), London, 1869, 660–75. As *Ars amatoria* presents him, Achilles cross-dressed in women's clothes is an insult and an absurdity – which Deidamia (unwittingly) manages to fix (Book I: 698–701). In Heywood's translation of Seneca's *Troas*, when Agamemnon tears into Pyrrhus, he cites the youth's beginnings in rape, calls him 'a bastarde of a mayde, / deflowred priuely. / Whom (then a boy) Achilles gate, / in filthy letchery' 1033–6, lines E.F. Watson's modern translation makes an uglier insult: Pyrrhus is a 'Son of a girl raped by a boy Achilles, / A stripling –' (338–9).

83 G.B. Shand thinks I may be right. He cites Thomas Middleton's 'The ghost of Lucrece' (STC 17885.5) which he has edited for *Thomas Middleton: The Collected Works*, Gary Taylor *et al.* (eds), Oxford, forthcoming. The 655-line poem, which 'might even have begun life as a schoolboy exercise', says Shand, has 'a boy voicing a violated girl', speaking throughout as Lucrece (just as 'Sebastian' in *The Two Gentlemen of Verona* speaks as Ariadne). It offers a fascinating 'instance of a youthful pre-theatrical mind taking on the woman's part', and taking on that part by self-consciously theatricalising the subject – as in the early modern classroom. 'Under the base type of Tarquin's name', says the abject ghost of Lucrece, linking her story to the stage:

I cipher figures of iniquity.
He writes himself the shamer, I the shame,
The actor he, and I the tragedy.
The stage am I, and he the history.
The subject I, and he the ravisher,
He, murd'ring me, made me my murderer.

I'm grateful to Skip for sharing his work with me in advance of publication – and for reading mine (more than once).

84 Tamora over-mothers these effeminate 'whelps', her sons, while she infantilises Saturninus, her effete husband. She's a 'handmaid' to 'his desires', 'A loving nurse, a mother to his youth' (1.1.336–7). So while the men occupy a space of feminised self-projection, Taymor's film never allows spectators to forget that in *Titus*, savagery wears a woman's face, is also coded female.

85 Anthony Burgess, *A Clockwork Orange*, London, 2000, 4.

86 Burgess, 19–20.

87 Ibid., 76.

88 Ibid., 77.

89 Ibid.

90 Bate, *Shakespeare and Ovid*, 105.

91 Burgess, 78.

92 Ibid., 135.

93 Ibid., 139–40 *passim*.

94 Ibid., 140.

95 In 1964 Jan Kott, describing a Shakespeare who is 'Cruel and true', theorised that 'If *Titus Andronicus* had six acts, Shakespeare would get at spectators sitting in the first row of the stalls and let them die in agony, because on the stage no one, except Lucius, remains alive' (*Shakespeare Our Contemporary*, London, 1964, 217). I think Kott got it wrong – because he didn't see the child alive at the end. But then, the production he had in mind, Peter Brook's, performed in Kott's Warsaw in June 1957, didn't see the child there either. Brook cut the boy from the final scene. It is perhaps one of the most remarkable shifts in theatrical meaning that this play has achieved since Jane Howell's BBC television production in 1985 that spectators of *Titus* are regularly now left with the child at the centre of the final stage picture – and left imagining that child's Act 6. In Yukio Ninagawa's Japanese *Titus* performed at the RST in the Complete Works season (June 2006), little Lucius (a girl-child cast in the boy's part), stood aside as his father's reconstituted Samurai Rome made its final formal exit in procession. But then he ran after the soldier who was carrying Aaron's infant, plucked him by the sleeve, took the baby out of his arms, and returned to kneel, downstage, facing the audience, presenting history, all of it, here, now. Then, with the baby on his lap, Lucius threw back his head and let out scream after scream: a story of raw pain wordlessly filled the theatre as the lights went down on two small bodies.

3 Curing Thought in *The Winter's Tale*

1 *The Story of My Life*, London, 1908, 12; see also 11–13.

2 Mamillius was always cross-cast on the Victorian stage where, writes Adrian Poole (but without any further comment on the practice), 'all the children's roles were played by girls or young women'. See *Shakespeare and the Victorians*, London, 2004, 51. Terry played Prince Arthur in Kean's *King John* two years after her debut as Mamillius.

3 *The Story of My Life*, 15.

4 Ibid., 13–14.

5 My text is *The Winter's Tale*, Arden 2, J.H.P. Pafford (ed.), London, 1963 (rpt., London, 2003). All other citations are from the Oxford *Complete Works* Wells and Taylor (eds.).

6 *As If*, London, 1998, 24.

7 'Marginal notes on a monumental work' (1928), in *Walter Benjamin: Selected Writings, vol. 2, 1927–1934*, Michael W. Jennings, Howard Eiland and Gary Smith (eds), London, 1999, 115.

8 Quoted in David Cohen, *The Development of Play*, London, 1993, 63.

9 On these script changes see Dennis Bartholomeusz, *The Winter's Tale in Performance in England and America 1611–1976*, Cambridge, 1982, 82. Hellenizing the play, Kean was following John Philip Kemble, whose first production of the play in 1802 restored its tragic first half (which, since David Garrick in the 1740s, had always been cut). Convinced that the oracle of Delphi was the historical marker that dated the play's period, Kean cut every Christian, Renaissance or English allusion – very nearly making *The Winter's Tale* 'a Greek play for Victorian times', 3. Enormously popular, Kean's *Tale* ran for 102 nights, 'one of the longest-running performances of the Victorian era', 3. And Ellen Terry as Mamillius played every performance. (See *The Story of My Life*, 15).

10 I am depending here on Bartholomeusz's indispensable study, *The Winter's Tale in Performance in England and America 1611–1976*, especially 81, 84–5. (Cambridge: Cambridge University Press, 1982).

11 Quoted in Bartholomeusz, 85.

12 Reproduced in Bartholomeusz, 85.

13 Susannah Clapp, *Observer*, 27 May 2001.

14 Hall's Propeller Theatre is an all-male company; Williams, in his twenties but with the look of early adolescence, was an adult 'playing' a child.

15 This may be coincidence, but Michael Billington used the same 'dream' allusion in his review of Adrian Noble's *Tale* in 1992. (See *Guardian*, 3 July 1992).

16 While the film wasn't a commercial success in the US, it achieved almost cult status in the UK, and high visibility on university film and Shakespeare courses. For a brilliant reading of this film as overlaying game, virtual and historical performance spaces, see Peter Donaldson, 'Game Space/Tragic Space: Julie Taymor's *Titus*' in Barbara Hodgdon and W.B. Worthen (eds), *A Companion to Shakespeare and Performance*, Oxford, 2005, 457–77.

17 See above, Chapter 2.

18 Ridley's play has teenagers in a contemporary dystopian England making ends meet by organising 'parties' where the rich can play out their most extreme fantasies of sex and death; the latest victim offered for 'play', a ten-year-old child. Faber, Ridley's publisher, found *Mercury Fur* so disturbing that they declined to handle it, and, ironically enough, notified him of the decision – objecting because of its cruelty to children – during the siege of Beslan in Chechnya. That act of terrorism against children in September 2004 (which the international community watched unfold on television, like a play) left 178 of them dead. Like the Soham murders in England in August 2002 (carried out in the school holidays by the school caretaker, boyfriend of the two ten-year-old girls' favourite teacher), the Beslan massacre additionally shocked and horrified because it constituted a violation of the children's 'sanctuary' space – the school.

19 See, for evidence, production photographs of Hermione in opening scenes of Shakespeare Memorial Theatre productions in 1937 (Joyce Bland), 1943 (Anna Konstan), 1948 (Diana Wynyard) and 1960 (Elizabeth Sellars). According to Roger Howells, stage and production manager at the RSC from 1962 to 1994, in those years, to have shown a pregnant Hermione would probably have been thought 'indelicate'. (But without Shakespeare's visible information, how, one wonders, did spectators know what was at stake in the scene?) Judi Dench tells me that Trevor Nunn took his idea for Hermione's 'look' from recent experience: seeing Leslie Caron (then married to Nunn's RSC boss, Peter Hall, and splendidly pregnant) climb out of Hall's Jaguar in a full-length white empire dress. 'He said he'd never seen anything so beautiful'. (Dench, personal communication, September 2006). The baby Caron was carrying was Edward. In Victorian productions – Nelly Kean's, for instance – dresses (and women) were so generously proportioned that, to modern eyes, Hermione looks pregnant even in the statue scene. I'm grateful to Richard Pasco – Polixenes – for remembering this production for me.

20 Bartholomeusz, 214.

21 Ibid.

22 Ibid.

23 As noted in the promptbook held in the RSC archives at the Shakespeare Birthplace Trust, Stratford-upon-Avon.

24 Colin Frame, *The Evening News*, 16 May 1969.

25 Christopher Morley, Nunn's designer, interviewed in *Plays and Players* (January 1970) could have been offering a design manifesto for Brook's empty space when he said that 'what we have got to do now is to explore the right kind of chamber in which to present Shakespeare's plays to a modern audience ... to develop a house style in which nothing is ever literally represented.' Quoted in Bartholomeusz, 212.

26 See Peter J. Smith's review in *Cahiers Élisabéthains* 39, April 1991, 80–2.

27 Peter J. Smith, review, *Cahiers Élisabéthains* 39, April 1991, 84–6.

28 Other readings of this 'sick' child were available. For example: it was wonderful that the crippled son, feeble, hard to rear, had a life that was precious to Sicilia. But that made it all the more horrific that his 'perfect' newborn baby sister, who was 'lusty and like to live' (2.2.27), could be so casually condemned to the fire.

29 Michael Dobson observes of the 'framed photos of Leontes and Polixenes playing rugby and cricket' that, 'ominously', they were 'just a little larger than those of Leontes and Hermione getting married', *Shakespeare Survey* 55, Cambridge, 2002, 318.

30 Dobson saw a quotation here. The 'wheeled truck on which Mamillius had piled some of the many expensive toys that littered the carpet' was 'a Radio Flyer', 'identical in shape to the little truck Ellen Terry towed ... in 1856, as Hytner probably knew', 318. In fact, the 'Flyer' and the 'exact copy' 'Greek' 'go-cart' look almost nothing alike. I thank him for conceding the point to me – and for commenting on this chapter.

31 As noted in the promptbook, held in the RSC archives at the Shakespeare Birthplace Trust, Stratford-upon-Avon.

32 Putting it this way, I'm self-consciously reversing the question Wilbur Sanders poses on the opening page of *The Winter's Tale: Harvester New Critical Introductions*

to Shakespeare, Brighton, 1987 (still, I think, the best introduction to the play): 'what is it about Shakespeare's text that has made it so difficult for theatre people to give their audiences what the astute critic maintains is simply *there?*', xi.

33 See (for example) F.R. Leavis, 'The criticism of Shakespeare's late plays: a caveat', *The Common Pursuit*, London, 1952; G. Wilson Knight, *The Crown of Life*, London, 1948; J.H.P. Pafford, 'Introduction', *The Winter's Tale*, London, 1963; Brian Gibbons, 'Erring and straying like lost sheep: *The Winter's Tale* and *The Comedy of Errors*', *Shakespeare Survey* 50, Cambridge, 1997, 111–23.

34 See 'Drama, performativity, and performance', *PMLA* 113, 1998, 1098.

35 *Shakespeare and the Loss of Eden: The Construction of Family Values in Early Modern Culture*, Basingstoke, 2001, 89.

36 One of Fraser's mantras in his brilliant graduate Shakespeare seminars at the University of Michigan in the 1970s. And another: 'Gloss Shakespeare with Shakespeare' – instruction that has served me well.

37 *Cities of the Dead: Circum-Atlantic Performance*, New York, 1996, 2.

38 'Toys and play' in Jennings *et al.*, 120.

39 Adulterous sex is noted, the imputation that Hermione, like the unnamed 'wife' of Leontes's imagining, has been 'sluic'd' by a 'next neighbour'(1.2.194–6). But her pregnancy isn't textually recognised until 2.1, the 'women's room' scene, where her ladies observe how the queen 'rounds apace' (16). In Robert Greene's *Pandosto*, Shakespeare's source, the pregnancy isn't part of the original situation. It's not until Greene's Hermione character has been committed to prison that, as 'she lay crossed with calamities' she discovered 'herself quick with child, which as soon as she felt stir in her body she burst forth in bitter tears'. See Pafford, 191.

40 For further allusions to a baby as 'prisoner to the womb' who, born, is 'enfranchised and come to light', see Paulina (2.2.59–61) and Aaron in *Titus Andronicus* (4.2.126–7).

41 'Grafted' implies a relationship of inferior to superior – like Camillo to Leontes, whom the king calls 'A servant grafted in my serious trust' (1.2.246).

42 STC2 11750. Shakespeare's Gerard certainly borrows his name from the famous English herbalist.

43 It is intriguing to observe that this little plant connects Mamillius to Perdita, and that brother and sister meet, across 'a wide gap of time', in the pages of Gerard's *Herbal*. In Chapter 299 Gerard writes 'Of Harts ease, or Paunsies' (703). Also called 'viola tricolor' and 'in French *pensees*' – hence, in *Hamlet*, Ophelia's 'And there is pansies; that's for thoughts' (4.5.174) – heart's-ease is also known in some locales as 'Call me to you' and 'Live in Idlenes' (or 'love-in-idleness' as Oberon makes it in *A Midsummer Night's Dream* (2.1.168). A member of the viola family, heart's-ease shares the family's virtues (particularly marked in its own name), the violet being a flower that is 'cooling' and 'tempereth the sharpness of choler', that is, the 'too hot, too hot' humour that infects Leontes. To cure a patient of Leontes's disease, *tremor cordis*, to 'comfort and strengthen the hart', the herbalist should 'mixe drie Violets with' other herbal 'medicines' (702). Now, another name for 'Harts ease', writes Gerard, is 'gilloflower', under which 'are comprehended many kindes of Violets' (Chapter 114: 372). The 'stock' variety grows 'in most gardens throughout England'. But the 'wilde stocke Gilloflower' is 'not used in

physicke, except [he writes, coyly] amongst certaine Empericks and Quack-salvers about love and lust matters, which for modestie I omit' (373). But these 'Gilloflowers' – also called 'wall flowers' (because, like heart's-ease they flourish in crooks and crannies, on walls and paths) – are related to the 'Carnation Gilloflower' described by the herbalist in Chapters 172 and 173: that is, to the flowers Perdita at the late summer sheep shearing calls 'the fairest … o' th' season', 'our carnations and streak'd gillyvors' (4.4.81, 82). A conserve made of 'flowers of carnation' gillyvors, writes Gerard, 'woonderfully aboue measure doth comfort the hart' (478). For Perdita, though, these are 'nature's bastards', 'their piedness' showing their mixed breeding, and she won't have them in her garden: 'I care not / To get slips of them' (4.4.83, 87, 84–5). Ironically, unwittingly, she's picking up her father's fixations: she will not rear another's bastard (2.3.192–3); ironically, unwittingly, she's engaged in this dialogue with the one man who knows more than anyone about her family's 'slips'; ironically, unwittingly, she's banishing the very 'heart's ease' from her rustic herb bed that will cure her family history. What she doesn't yet know is that, in this herbal economy, reared as someone else's issue, a kind of bastard, a 'slip' that will need transplanting, she herself is the 'gillyvor', the 'Call me to you', who ultimately and 'woonderfully aboue measure' will 'comfort the hart'.

44 The phrase is Siri Hustvedt's. Photographs capture 'a subject in a *real* moment of time' but operate always as 'a sign of disappearance'. See '*Death of Photography*: old pictures and a new book', *Modern Painters* (September 2005), 96–9, esp. 96–7.

45 Edward Topsell, in *The Historie of Foure-footed Beastes*, London, 1607 (STC2 24123) concludes his 'discourse of the Lambe': 'The greatest honour thereof is for that it pleased God to call his blessed Son our Sauiour by the name of a Lamb in the Old Testament, a Lambe for sacrifice; & in the new Testament, styled by John the Baptist, the Lambe of God that taketh away the sinnes of the world' (641).

46 Church of England, STC 16284.5 Sig.Cii^r.

47 The phrase is Barbara Hodgdon's in 'Two *King Lear*s: Uncovering the Filmtext', *Literature and Film Quarterly* 11: 3, 1983, 143.

48 'Morninge prayer', 1559, STC 16284.5 Sig.Cii^r. See also Church of England, *The First Prayer-Book of Edward VI compared with The Successive Revision of The Book of Common Prayer*, Oxford and London, 1877, *passim*.

49 Sanders, 12. Critics focus on what happens to Leontes in this scene. But there's a traumatic discovery for Polixenes here as terrible as his brother's.

50 The play itself makes fastidious distinctions between universal or original sin and specific sins, one Lord insisting that he 'dare' his 'life lay down … that the queen is spotless / I' th' eyes of heaven, and to you' – before withdrawing to the more limited claim: 'I mean / In this which you accuse her' (2.1.130–3).

51 'The Communion', STC 16284.5 Sig. Mviii^r.

52 *The First Prayer-Book of Edward VI*, 289.

53 'The ministracion of Publique Baptisme', STC 16284.5 Sig.Oii^v, Sig.Oiii^r.

54 'Baptisme', STC 16284.5 Sig.Oiv^v.

55 'Baptisme', STC 16284.5 Sig.Ov^v.

56 I'm grateful to Tony Dawson for discussing with me the Reformation doctrines of 'total depravity' and 'sola fide, sola gratia' that inform the process

of grace in *The Winter's Tale*. For more on early modern debates on the child as innocent, reprobate, or regenerate see Leah Marcus, *Childhood and Cultural Despair*, Pittsburgh, 1978, 42–93.

57 *The First Prayer-Book of Edward VI*, 297.

58 'Confirmacion', STC 16284.5 Sig. Piͬ.

59 See Sanders, 22, and Pafford, lxxxii. See also Bruce Smith, *Shakespeare and Masculinity*, Oxford, 2000, 75–7, and Keith Wrightson, *English Society 1580–1680*, London, 1998, 112–26.

60 'Baptisme', STC 16284.5 Sig.Oivͬ.

61 See G.K. Hunter, 'Elizabethans and foreigners' in *Dramatic Identities and Cultural Tradition*, Liverpool, 1978, 4; Bourdieu quoted in Peter Stallybrass, 'Patriarchal territories: the body enclosed', in Margaret Ferguson, Maureen Quilligan, and Nancy J. Vickers (eds), *Rewriting the Renaissance*, Chicago, 1986, 94.

62 On this important Elizabethan cultural and theological concept, see 'Performance and participation' in Anthony B. Dawson and Paul Yachnin, *The Culture of Playgoing in Shakespeare's England*, Cambridge, 2001, 11–37.

63 The condition (or anything like it that several ingenious minds have suggested to me) doesn't show up in Andrew Boorde's *Breviary of Health* (1557) STC 3376; Thomas Becon's *The Sicke Mans Salue* (1572) STC2 1760; Robert Burton's *The Anatomy of Melancholy* (1621); John Harington's *The Englishmans Doctor* (1607) STC2 21605; or Sir Thomas Elyot's *The Castel of Helth* (1534), STC2 7642.5. Gerard in *The Herbal* doesn't mention it. Nor is it an illness Margaret Healy considers in *Fictions of Disease in Early Modern England*, Basingstoke, 2001. It seems pretty clear from *Macbeth*, however, that it's a condition connected to the hardening of the heart – and Gerard *does* treat of heart disease: see above, note 43.

64 Sanders, 20.

65 *Shakespeare and the Loss of Eden*, 102.

66 David Cressy, *Birth, Marriage and Death: Ritual, Religion, and the Life-cycle in Tudor and Stuart England*, Oxford, 1999, 17.

67 Quoted in Cressy, 18.

68 See Peter Stallybrass's seminal article, 'Patriarchal territories' in Vickers *et al.*

69 See for example his sermon on the occasion of Lady Doncaster's churching in 1618: 'Our mothers conceived us in sin; and being wrapped up in uncleanness there, can any man bring a clean thing out of filthiness?' Quoted in Cressy, 19.

70 See *The Works of that Learned and Judicious Divine, Mr Richard Hooker* (1723); *The Pathway to Prayer and Pietie* (1610), STC 13463; *The Child-birth or Womans Lecture* (1590), STC 13702. Quoted in Cressy, 17.

71 William Sermon, *The Ladies Companion; or, The English Midwife*, London, 1671, quoted in Raymond A. Anselment, *The Realm of Apollo: Literature and Healing in Seventeenth Century England*, London, 1995, 49.

72 On the 'pathos and panic of male sexuality' located 'within a marital economy of possessiveness', see Lawrence Danson, 'The catastrophe is a nuptial', *Shakespeare Survey* 46, 1993, 69–79. Early modern man, he argues, is always on a hiding to nothing seeking to manage woman according to the terms (male) culture sets itself. Citing Othello's 'That we can call these delicate creatures ours / And not their appetites!' (3.3.273–4) as a line that

'undoes itself', Danson observes that 'the ideology of marital possessiveness repeatedly undoes itself in Shakespeare', 'not only because "we" can never be sure "we" fully own or control a property [like honour, like chastity] that can't be seen, but also because "we" define a woman's appetite as something always alien, the defining attribute or property of the other, the always not-ours', 70.

73 Launcelot (pertinently) reverses the conventional adage, 'It is a wise child that knows his own father'.

74 *Shakespeare's Wordplay*, London, 1957, 148; 'The catastrophe is a nuptial', 71.

75 Epigramme XLV in C.H. Herford, Percy and Evelyn Simpson (eds), *Ben Jonson*, vol. VIII, Oxford, 1947, 41.

76 'Of the affection of fathers to their children' (*The second Booke*. Chap. 8): 'I cannot receive this passion, wherewith some embrace children scarsly borne, having neither motion in the soull, nor forme well to be distinguished in the bodie, whereby they might make themselves lovely or amiable .... A true and wel ordred affection ought to be borne and augmented, with the knowledge they give us of themselves; and then, if they deserve it (naturall inclination marching hand in hand with reason) to cherish and make much of them, with a perfect fatherly love and loving frendship, and conformably to judge of them if they be otherwise, alwaies yeelding our selves vnto reason, notwithstanding naturll power. For the most part, it goeth cleane contrary, and commonly feele our selves more mooved with the sports, idlenesse, wantonnesse, and infant-trifles of our children, than afterward we do with all their actions, when they bee men: As if we had loved them for our pastimes, as we do apes, monkies, or perokitoes, and not as men', *Essays ... done in English ... by Iohn Florio ... 1613*, STC2 18042. 113–14.

77 Quoted in Pafford, 165.

78 See Montrose, '*A Midsummer Night's Dream* and the shaping fantasies of Elizabethan culture: gender, power, form' in Margaret Ferguson *et al.* (eds), 1986, 65–87; Margreta de Grazia, 'Imprints: Shakespeare, Gutenberg and Descartes', in Terence Hawkes (ed.), *Alternative Shakespeares* vol. 2, London, 1996, 63–94.

79 'Bastards and broadsides in *The Winter's Tale*', *Renaissance Drama* 30, 2001, 43–71.

80 Kitch points out that a bastard may be an illegitimate child – but also a mixed cloth of poor quality (*OED* A.*sb*.5.); a print typeface (*OED* B.*adj*.6.d.a); or an abbreviated or half-title preceding the full title page of a printed book (*OED* B.*adj*.6.d.b).

81 'It' functions as an early modern diminutive – but also as a pronoun of contempt (*OED* I.1.b).

82 And in this production it *did*. Antony Sher needed the whole stage for ranging across: other actors moved to the margins. A Romanoff who clearly had never wiped a child's nose, Sher's Leontes handed his handkerchief to crippled Mamillius and gestured to him, crisply, to clean himself up – changing 'nose' to 'face'.

83 See Anthony B. Dawson, 'Performance and participation: Desdemona, Foucault, and the actor's body' in James C. Bulman (ed.), *Shakespeare, Theory and Performance*, London, 1996, 44, and Carol Chillington Rutter, *Enter the Body: Women and Representation on Shakespeare's Stage*, London, 2001, 1–5.

84 A child actor who made 'Mamillius utterly natural', wrote Gareth Lloyd Evans in the *Guardian*, 17 May 1969.

85 The phrase is Declan Donnellan's, discussing what a designer does for Shakespeare. In conversation, May 2006.

86 But see, for further comparison, the poster for the 1998 RSC *Winter's Tale* – an image that restored the play's 'correct' point of view? Reproduced in blue, black, and grey – shades of *film noir* – it shows Antony Sher's Leontes in profile, the photograph enlarged and cropped to give just a section of the face, from eyebrow to lower lip. He's staring out of the frame at something 'off'. As viewers gradually make sense of the anamorphic puzzle (like a drawing by the elder Brueghel), they begin to see what Leontes is staring at. His horrible imaginings are written on his flesh: absorbed through the eye, they've erupted on the skin. Leontes's face is composed of naked bodies embracing: a woman's bent arm constructs his nose; her nipple is a mole on his cheek, her reclining torso makes the curve of his jaw; a youth's head dissolves into his eyeball, his neck sculpting a cheekbone. Leontes is seeing a monster – that monsters him. The poster aptly captured this *Winter's Tale*: Doran's production was all about Leontes and his perspective.

87 While the actual biotechnology was still in the future, the term 'designer baby' had already been coined; see 'Designer babies', BBC programme #ESBP301T in the 'Short circuit' series screened 13 January 1992.

88 Production photographs held in the RSC archive at the Shakespeare Birthplace Trust, Stratford-upon-Avon.

89 Donnellan, in conversation March 2006. See also 'Directing Shakespeare's comedies: in conversation with Peter Holland', *Shakespeare Survey* 56, Cambridge, 2003, 161–6.

90 Donnellan, in conversation, March 2006.

91 Ibid.

92 This father himself has three little girls and, in an extravagant show of faith, offers them as pawns for Hermione's virtue. 'Be she honour-flaw'd / ... they'll pay for it': because if *she's* false, *no woman can be true*, so 'I'll geld 'em all' (2.1.143, 146). These daughters are also Paulina's. One wonders what she would have to say on the matter.

93 Sanders, 20.

94 *The Historie of Foure-footed Beastes*, 608.

95 'Erring and straying like lost sheep', 111.

96 *OED3*. Adoption, significantly, is the theme of the Collect for 'Christmas daie' in the 1559 *Book of Common Prayer*, which calls the faithful 'generate & made thy children by adoption': chosen by God for himself.

97 Of course, he takes up, too, what else Antigonus has left with Perdita to 'breed' her (3.3.48): aristocratic clothing, a mantle that will turn out to be Hermione's (5.2.33), and a box of 'Gold! all gold!' (3.3.120). But by then, the Shepherd has already decided to 'take it' – the baby – 'up for pity' (76). Besides, he says, 'This is fairy gold' – notoriously tricky to hang on to (121). The sheep he was searching for so anxiously earlier, he now forgets: 'Let my sheep go' (124). But that's exactly right. The 'lamb' in his arms, a lamb of God, is the greater care for the good shepherd.

98 See Barbara L. Estrin, 'Finders keepers: preservation and the legendary foundling', in *The Raven and the Lark: Lost Children in Literature of the English Renaissance*, London, 1985, 27–39.

99 There's the Mopsa, Dorcas, Clown triangle (with its gibe about illicit pregnancy, 4.4.240) that replays Hermione, Polixenes, Leontes. There's the father who goes berserk. There's the play upon print and paternity: 'I love a ballad in print, a life, for then we are sure they are true,' says Mopsa (4.4.261–2). For the 'truth' of 'print', Autolycus offers her the ballad of 'a usurer's wife' who 'was brought to bed of twenty money-bags at a burden' (4.4.263–5): that is, in the monstrous birth ballad, the child looks just like the dad.

100 New to the RSC, this double had been performed at least once before, by Mary Anderson at the Lyceum in 1887 – though Nunn and Dench didn't know it.

101 The (uncorrected) cast list in the promptbook held in the RSC archives at the Shakespeare Birthplace Trust names Sher in both roles.

102 The first director to double these roles was Bogdanov (1990), where the double was primarily functional: the English Shakespeare Company was a touring outfit and had to make casting economies where it could. Doran also doubled the parts (1999) because, he says, 'Tony didn't want to act with a child.' 'Children can't act,' says Sher. 'Why should they be expected to? This is Shakespeare.' (In conversation, 17 June 2006.) Paul Taylor in the *Independent Review*, 8 January 1999, thought Doran had committed a 'big error' making Mamillius 'a pasty weakling in a wheelchair, and to have him performed by the actress (Emily Bruni) who goes on to play … Perdita. The little boy needs to be robust so that his pointless death comes as a harrowing shock, and he should not symbolically metamorphose into his sister, because his demise has to register as a tragedy time cannot redeem.' Propeller Theatre's double offered no such consolation.

103 In conversation, April 2006.

104 See 'In search of the bear: spatiotemporal form and the heterogeneity of economies in *The Winter's Tale*', *Shakespeare Quarterly* 42: 2 (Summer 1991), 159.

105 See Teresa Grant, *The Uses of Animals in English Early Modern Drama 1558–1642* (forthcoming, Cambridge University Press) and 'White Bears in *Mucedorus*, *The Winter's Tale*, and *Oberon, the Fairy Prince*', *Notes and Queries*, n.s. 48: 3 (September 2001), 311–3. See Maurice Hunt, '"Bearing hence" Shakespeare's *The Winter's Tale*', *Studies in English Literature 1500–1900*, 44: 2 (Spring 2004), 333–46. See also Nevill Coghill, 'Six points of stage-craft in *The Winter's Tale*', *Shakespeare Survey* 11, Cambridge, 1958, 31–41; George F. Reynolds, '*Mucedorus*, most popular Elizabethan play' in Josephine W. Bennett, Oscar Cargill and Vernon Hall Jr (eds), *Studies in English Renaissance Drama*, London, 1959, 248–68. See his note on the bear in Pafford, 69. By far the best essay on Elizabethan stage bears is Terence Hawkes's, 'Harry Hunks, superstar' in *Shakespeare in the Present*, London, 2002, 82–106.

106 For these citations, see Marvin Spevack (ed.), *The Harvard Concordance to Shakespeare*, Cambridge, MA, 1973, 94–5.

107   I am indebted to Peter Smith in *Cahiers Élisabéthains* 39 for this production note. He comments: 'even destruction in Nature is a direct result of Leontes's unnatural jealousies', 81.

108   Topsell, *The Historie of Foure-footed Beastes*, 41; Watson, *Valentyne and Orson*, STC2 24571.7.

109   Topsell knows the ancients were wrong. He writes: 'yet is the truth most euidently otherwise, as by the eye witnes … is disproued: onlie it is litterd blind without eies, naked without haire, and the hinder legs not perfect, the forefeet folded vp lik a fist', 36–7.

110   I can witness the audible (and general) gasp in the theatre at this moment. The audience held its breath until the Bear shambled off, then laughed with relief. See also Malcolm Rutherford, *The Financial Times*, 3 July 1992; Benedict Nightingale, *The Times*, 3 July 1992; Charles Spencer, *Daily Telegraph*, 3 July 1992.

111   *The Historie of Foure-footed Beastes*, 39.

112   For a fascinating reading of folk tales as gendered discourse see Mary Ellen Lamb, 'Engendering the narrative act: old wives' tales in *The Winter's Tale*, *Macbeth*, and *The Tempest*', *Criticism* XL: 4 (Fall 1998), 529–3.

113   Is it fanciful to see ghostly traces of Stuart family story in this tale? England's Mamillius – Prince Henry – died suddenly in November 1612; his 'baby sister', Elizabeth, married the Elector Palatine on 14 February 1613; *The Winter's Tale* was performed at her wedding; eight years hence, she would become Queen of Bohemia.

114   As M.M. Mahood writes in *Shakespeare's Wordplay*, Perdita inhabits 'the fertility legend of a child healing an old man and so bringing prosperity to the land', 148. Just how 'effective' she is as quickener can be inferred from Greene's *Pandosto* where the King kills himself in remorse, after experiencing incestuous lust for the stranger to his court who turns out to be his daughter.

115   Currently, a Google search for 'child who cures' take the investigator to AIDS sites in South Africa where sex with a virgin is a promised cure for AIDS-HIV and where young girls, even infants (to guarantee virginity) are evidently being used as 'medicine'.

116   *Philip Ridley: Plays 1*, London, 2002, lix.

117   I owe this point to Harriet Mann in an unpublished undergraduate dissertation at Warwick University that tracked the play's rehearsal process at the National Theatre by reconstructing the promptbook, finding in the process the one rehearsal 'story' that, mistakenly stuck between pages of the prompt copy, missed being destroyed.

118   Martin McDonagh, *The Pillowman*, London, 2003, 23, 26. See, too, Paula Rego's triptych, 'The Pillowman', a response to McDonagh's play, at the Tate Gallery, London.

119   McDonagh, 43–5, 62.

4 Precious Motives, Seeds of Time: Killing Futures in *Macbeth*

1   'The epistle', *Basilicon Doron 1599*, Scolar Press Facsimile, Scolar Press, Menston, 1969.

2 See 'James VI and I, *Basilikon Doron* and *The Trew Law of Free Monarchies*: The
   Scottish context and the English translation' in Linda Levy Peck (ed.), *The
   Mental World of the Jacobean Court*, Cambridge, 1991, 49.
3 'Dedication'. See, too, Wormald in Peck, 47, 38–9.
4 'Epistle'. My *Macbeth* text is A.R. Braunmuller's edition, Cambridge, 1997; all
   other quotations are from the Oxford *Complete Works*, Wells and Taylor (eds).
5 28–30.
6 38.
7 46–7, 49, 67–70, 86–99, 94, 97.
8 The 'desire to speak with the dead' is, of course, Stephen Greenblatt's opening
   conceit in *Shakespearean Negotiations: The Circulation of Social Energy in Renaissance
   England*, Berkeley, 1988, 1.
9 54.
10 'It is a true olde saying,' he writes at the opening of 'The Third Booke' (which
   concerns not matters of state or religion but 'a Kings Behaviour in Indifferent
   Things', that is, his personal habits), 'That a King is as one set on a scaffold,
   whose smallest actions & gestures all the people gazingly do behold', 121. The
   saying *is* 'olde'; but as elsewhere in his treatise, James may have had Queen
   Elizabeth immediately in mind. In her 1586 speech to Parliament at the time
   of the Queen of Scots (Mary, James's mother) execution crisis – a speech
   surely reported to James – Elizabeth observed that 'we Princes are set as it
   were upon stages in the sight and view of all the world' where 'The least Spot is
   soone spyed in our garments, a blemish pre[sent]ly noted in our doings'
   (William Camden, *Annales, or, The Historie of the Most Renowned and Victorious
   Princesse Elizabeth … Translated into English by R.N. Gent*, London, 1635, STC2
   4501, 325. On *Basilikon Doron* as a 'Theatrical manual' and on James's habit of
   ventriloquising Elizabeth see Arthur F. Kinney, *Lies Like Truth: Shakespeare,
   Macbeth and the Cultural Moment*, Detroit, 2001, 89, 75.
11 See Wormald in Peck, 49.
12 I'm depending here on Jenny Wormald's entry on James VI/I in the Oxford
   Dictionary of National Biography Online.
13 'Epistle'.
14 51. James didn't invent this language. See Debora Kuller Shuger, 'Nursing
   fathers: patriarchy as a cultural ideal' in *Habits of Thought in the English Renaissance*, Los Angeles, 1990, 218–49.
15 'Epistle'.
16 140.
17 41, 56.
18 'A notable extension of personality,' as his Oxford DNB Online biographer
   terms his promiscuity.
19 90, 97.
20 37.
21 Buchanan (1506–82) argued for a contractual theory of kingship and the right
   of the people to resist their monarch, ideas to which James was deeply
   opposed; Knox (1505–72) was one of the architects of the Reformation in
   Scotland (who took reform too far for James). He was stridently opposed to the
   'monstrous regiment [that is, rule] of women' – opinions directed against
   Mary Queen of Scots with which James may have had sympathy but opinions
   that endeared him not a bit to Queen Elizabeth. The 'Chronicles' James refers

to here are Buchanan's *Rerum Scoticarum Historia* (1592) and Knox's *Historie of the Reformation* (1587).

22 211–12.

23 For a modern remembering of this scene of terror see the opening of Frank McGuinness's *Speaking Like Magpies*, London, 2005, 6.

24 See Wormald, Oxford DNB Online.

25 'To the reader', *Basilikon Doron*, 1603. See Neil Rhodes, Jennifer Richards and Joseph Marshall (eds), *King James VI and I: Selected Writings*, Aldershot, 2003, 203.

26 Wormald in Peck, 51.

27 I am here relying on Leeds Barroll's excellent account in *Anna of Denmark, Queen of England: A Cultural Biography*, Philadelphia, 2001, 24–35.

28 Barroll quoting Roger Aston (the English agent in Scotland) and George Nicholson writing to Robert Bowes, 23.

29 Barroll, 27.

30 Ibid.

31 Norman Egbert McClure (ed.), *The Letters of John Chamberlain* vol. 1, Philadelphia, 1939, 187.

32 G.P.V. Akrigg (ed.), *Letters of King James VI & I*, London, 1984, 211–12, and Barroll (who doesn't cite the letter), 28–30, 33. In his 1595 'Ordinance for the Nursing and Keeping of Prince Henry', James had strictly specified that 'neither for Queen nor Estates' pleasure' should the prince be delivered from his guardians 'until he be eighteen years of age'. Nor was he to be released 'out of your [his guardian's] hands except I command you with my own mouth'. That is, not even a written message would do. Leaving Scotland without issuing that 'command' from 'my own mouth', James, it appears, intended Henry to remain at Stirling, to be educated as a Scot until his installation as Prince of Wales, some ten years hence.

33 Quoted in Barroll, 29.

34 Akrigg, *Letters*, 211, 219.

35 Quoted in Antonia Fraser, *King James VI of Scotland I of England*, London, 1974, 133. Roy Strong in *Henry, Prince of Wales and England's Lost Renaissance*, London, 1986, 15, cites the perhaps apocryphal story that, rebuked by his father for slack study and compared to his assiduous little brother, Henry replied, 'Then we'll make him archbishop of Canterbury'. The French ambassador, La Boderie, writing on 31 October 1606, reported of Henry that 'none of his pleasures savour the least of a child. He is a particular lover of horses ... He studies two hours a day, and employs the rest of his time in tossing the pike, or leaping, or shooting with the bow, or throwing the bar, or vaulting', 66.

36 Rhodes *et al.*, 203.

37 See Wormald in Peck, who is relying on Peter Blayney's superb study of the printing of *Basilikon Doron*. One copy of Waldegrave's Edinburgh edition was evidently in the hands of the London publisher, John Norton, before Queen Elizabeth's death on 24 March. Four days later, Norton entered the book on the Stationers' Register. By 13 April eight editions were out and two pirate versions. Plague hit London and the book trade in those same weeks; sales slumped; 'after the frenzied printings of the first two and a half weeks of the reign, there was virtually no interest in England for further editions – but some thirty continental translations were subsequently published in James's lifetime', 51–2.

38 McClure, *Letters*, vol. 1, 167.

39 Braunmuller, *Macbeth*, 15, note 1.

40 McClure, *Letters*, vol. 1, 191.

41 Reproduced in Braunmuller, *Macbeth*, 3.

42 Facsimile, 1599, 19.

43 'It is meet and honourable,' James advises Henry, for the king 'to eate publicklie' to 'eschew the opinion that yee loue not to haunte companie, which is one of the markes of a Tyrant', 124. Macbeth, of course, avoids Duncan's feast, which he himself is hosting.

44 How old are the boys in *Macbeth*? In Holinshed's *The Historie of Scotland* (1587), Malcolm is not yet 'of able age' to 'take the charge vpon himselfe' of succeeding his father: that is, he's a minor. (See vol. V, London, 1808, 269.) In Shakespeare, he's not yet a man, still a youth, a 'maid', 'Unknown to woman' (4.3.126). So let's call him 20. Entirely speculatively, we can range the others below him, Donaldbain perhaps 17; Fleance, 12, the same age as Prince Henry in 1607; Macduff's 'egg', maybe 7, still unbreeched and under the supervision of women; Macduff's other 'chickens', toddlers or infants in arms. In professional acting terms, all of these are parts written for the company's apprentices and show how wide the range of roles might be for the 'boys'.

45 *The Diary of Samuel Pepys* vol. 8, Robert Latham and William Matthews (eds), London, 1974, 7 (7 January 1667).

46 The production was William Poel's at the Fulham Theatre (London), 22–26 June 1909. The playbill advertising the production informed spectators that 'The whole play will be given, including the important episode introducing Lady Macduff, who will be restored to the stage for the first time since Shakespeare's death. It is contended that Shakespeare's tragedies were written to be acted neither as grand opera nor as grand tragedy but as domestic tragedy. The incidents of the murder, therefore, will be shown as they would have occurred in an Elizabethan nobleman's mansion, about 1610. This involves a new interpretation of the character of Lady Macbeth, and the abandonment of the conventional stage-business of to-day, which dates not from Shakespeare's time, but from the decadent days of the Restoration.' The 'Boy, son to Macduff' was played by 'Miss Madge Venning'. I owe this citation to Marion O'Connor.

47 *Shakespearean Tragedy*, London, 1957, 329–30.

48 Ibid., 341, 339.

49 See Adrian Poole, *Shakespeare and the Victorians*, London, 2004, 51, and the W.F. Yeames painting, *Prince Arthur and Hubert* (1882), which he reproduces, 52.

50 *Shakespearean Tragedy*, 421–2. That said, Bradley's letters show him continuously interested in the theatre of his day.

51 Subtitled 'An essay in the theory and practice of Shakespeare criticism', the lecture was published in *Explorations*, London, 1946, 1–39.

52 'The question of character in Shakespeare' in *Further Explorations*, London, 1965, 186, 190–2.

53 *Explorations*, 18, note 1.

54 Ibid., 37.

55 In *The Well Wrought Urn*, London, 1949, 31.

56 Ibid., 35.

57 Ibid., 35.

58 *Macbeth*, 17.

59 Brooks, 33.

60 See, for example, in *The Masks of Macbeth*, Berkeley, 1978, Marvin Rosenberg's speculations concerning 'Lady Macbeth's indispensable child', 671–6. And for contrast, see Janet Adelman's 'Escaping the matrix' in *Suffocating Mothers: Fantasies of Maternal Origin in Shakespeare's Plays, Hamlet to The Tempest*, London, 1992, 138.

61 For Cusack, see 'Lady Macbeth's barren sceptre' in Carol Rutter, *Clamorous Voices: Shakespeare's Women Today*, London, 1988, 53–72. For other actors' interpretations see Bernice W. Kliman, *Macbeth*, Manchester, 1992. As Judi Dench remembers from 1976 (RSC), she and Ian McKellen's Macbeth 'never discussed the question' of children (personal communication, June 2006). In the Eric Porter/Janet Suzman BBC television *Macbeth* (1970), writes Kliman, the couple 'have no children, they *had* no children'; the line, 'I have given suck', was 'purely metaphoric, not historically accurate', 70.

62 It should be noted that film has a longer history of telling the Macbeths' backstory. Orson Welles's 1947 film opened on the witches pulling from a bubbling cauldron a foetal lump that they – hag-midwives – began to shape into a child. Cackling, they crowned the 'baby' when they greeted Macbeth. Later, Macbeth took charge of the killing of Macduff's family – and Lady Macbeth, listening outside, turned away, into madness. But one sequence, planned through many revisions, didn't make the final cut: in it, Macbeth wandered through the corridors of empty Dunsinane carrying in his arms one of the dead children, then sat on his throne in the vast, vacant hall, stroking the child's hair.

63 The *memento mori* was a present from her husband. In *Beside Myself*, London, 2001, Antony Sher writes: 'I found a photo of a dead baby in one of my Boer War books – the Victorians photographed their infant mortalities – gave Harriet a copy and stuck another in my script. Our baby. Frozen, white, wearing an embroidered shift, lying in a tiny plank-and-nail coffin. The Macbeth baby', 343–4.

64 See Robert Smallwood (ed.), *Players of Shakespeare* 4, Cambridge, 1998, 201.

65 *Beside Myself*, 343.

66 *An Anatomy of Drama*, London, 1976, 101.

67 Marina Warner, *Into the Dangerous World: Some Reflections on Childhood and its Costs*, London, 1989, 9.

68 Quoted in Warner, 16. The UN Convention was finally signed by the UK government in 1991.

69 The Secretary of State refused to talk about social 'poverty', insisting on calling it 'inequality' instead. Quoted in Warner, 3.

70 I am conscious as I use it that 'we' in Britain is a conflicted term: 'we' might be the 'royal' we; or 'we' might be the 'we' solicited in the headlines of tabloid newspapers. I use it, despite its difficulties (and knowingly mobilising its shades of irony), because it seems to me that over the past twenty years a series of domestic events – from the soap operas of failed royal marriages to the melo-drama of Princess Diana's death and funeral to the tragedies in Cleveland, Liverpool and Haringey that centred on the abuse and deaths of children – have involved the nation in a debate with itself about social cohesion and the future of the family, conducted with serious attention to issues like crime, social violence, childcare, education, single parents, immigration, race

relations, terrorism (and much more) in the broadsheet newspapers and on BBC television and radio. As I use it, 'we' does not register easy consensus; rather, it serves metonymically to stand for the range of opinions and responses 'we' uttered as 'we' faced each new *Macbeth*-sized cultural gorgon.

71 *As If*, London, 1998, 21.

72 BBC News 01/10/2000, www.news.bbc.co.uk/1/hi/uk1035455.stm, accessed on 29 September 2003.

73 *Shakespeare and the Force of Modern Performance*, Cambridge, 1993, 64.

74 The effect was intensified by nail holes – stigmata – visibly perforating Lady Macbeth's hands.

75 In 'Two *King Lears*: uncovering the filmtext', *Literature/Film Quarterly* 11: 3, 1983, 88.

76 *Guardian*, 7 November 1986.

77 Ibid.

78 See 'GO TO HELL', *Daily Express*, 16 November 2002; 'THE DEVIL: At last, Myra is where she belongs – HELL', *Sun*, 16 November 2002. See also obituary articles on Hindley in the *Mirror*, *Guardian*, *Independent* and *Daily Mail* for this date.

79 Quoted in Braunmuller, *Macbeth*, 104, note 13.

80 Ibid., *Macbeth*, 11.

81 This 'record' of the barbaric practices of the 'meere Irish' appears on the last page of Richard Stanihurst's *The Description of Ireland* in Holinshed *et al.*, vol. V, London, 1808, 69.

82 Noble cut 3.5 (the disputed Hecate scene) and moved 3.6 (Lennox's observation that 'Things have been strangely borne') so that 3.4 went straight into 4.1. This meant that Macbeth's exit, 'We are yet but young in deed' (3.4.144), was followed by the Weird Sisters' entrance, 'Thrice the brindled cat hath mewed' (4.1.1).

83 Shot during the last full year of Conservative government in the UK, the TV film was broadcast less than a month before the May election that brought New Labour and Tony Blair to power with a landslide victory.

84 Woolcock's earlier films include *When the Dog Bites*, a profile of Consett after the closure of its steel mills, and her award-winning *Shakespeare on the Estate*, directed with Michael Bogdanov, for BBC2 (1994), shot in inner-city Birmingham. As Susanne Greenhalgh writes, these earlier 'performative documentaries' equipped Woolcock with a repertoire of practices that she reused in her 'fiction film *Macbeth*': 'interview sequences (often filmed in a non-conventional *mise-en-scène*), observational footage with a clear symbolic as well as naturalistic force' and 'innovative and controversial use of dramatization in the form of scenarios improvised by some of the film's subjects'. See '"Alas poor country!": documenting the politics of performance in two British television *Macbeth*s since the 1980s' in Pascale Aebischer, Edward J. Esche and Nigel Wheale (eds), *Remaking Shakespeare: Performance Across Media, Genres and Cultures*, Basingstoke, 2003, 97.

85 See Beatrix Campbell, *Goliath: Britain's Dangerous Places*, London, 1993, 319, 321. 'The word that embraced everything feared and loathed by the new orthodoxy about class and crime,' she writes, 'was *estate*: what was once the emblem of respectability, what once evoked the dignity and clamour of a powerful social constituency, part of the body politic, but which now described only the edge of a class and the end of the city.' I owe this citation to Greenhalgh, 100.

86 In *Goliath*, writes Greenhalgh, Campbell suggests 'that a "new myth about children as criminals" displaced awareness of masculinity as a factor in the riots and estate crime of the early 1990s'. See Aebischer, 112.
87 I owe this identification to Peter Balderstone.
88 I am indebted to Naomi Everall for this observation – and for much that stimulated my thinking on this film.
89 Woolcock consciously located cultural stereotypes of 'black' male jealousy, violence and family neglect in the Macduff plot line – and played out those stereotypes to complex ends. Both the (black) Macduffs and the (white) Macbeths were racially 'pure' families.
90 Banquo, too, emerges as a 'lost son' when, later that night, at the fag end of the victory party hosted by the Macbeths, he recognises Duncan as a loser. Watching his bloated king attempt to stagger to bed and falling on his face, Banquo curls his lip, disgusted at the need to lackey to such clapped-out authority, snarling under his breath, 'Merciful powers, restrain in me the cursèd thoughts that nature gives way to in repose' (2.1.7–9). In Shakespeare, the lines feel like a prayer. In Woolcock, they took Banquo to the brink of his own assassination attempt. Macbeth got there first.
91 I am drawing on Fredric Jameson's theorisations in 'Postmodernism and consumer society', *The Cultural Turn*, London, 1998, 7.
92 More obviously, the sequence of mirror shots codes her duplicity – and worse. In the living room she brushes her hair before a circular mirror as she tells her absent husband, 'I fear your nature'. Twined around its circumference is a tangled pattern of leaves that produces her face as if wreathed with snakes. We see her as Medusa.
93 The camera never moves in close enough to the photograph to establish whether the child is a boy or a girl; spectators perhaps assume a boy-child partly on the evidence of the furniture in the preserved bedroom – though plenty of parents give their daughters football scarves. On the Weird Children's altar the dolls that are being celebrated/sacrificed are girl-children, visually reinforcing the final atrocity in the Macduff family killings, the stabbing of the baby girl.
94 In 'Postmodernism and consumer society', 5.
95 Played by Richard Chinn, Clare Dowling and Lee Williams.
96 See Arthur Lindley, 'The unbeing of the overreacher', *Modern Language Review* 84, 1989, 1.
97 At Hindley's death, Jonathan Glancey wrote of the iconic status that the photograph had achieved in her lifetime: 'Myra, Medusa. Medusa, Myra. No matter what she looked like after she was sentenced to life imprisonment in 1966, Myra Hindley was fixed forever in the public eye as the peroxide-haired gorgon of that infamous police snapshot. Look at her defiant evil eyes, we are meant to say' (*Guardian*, 16 November 2002). Evidently fascinated by the photographic image, Marcus Harvey used a cast of a child's hand to print a wall-sized acrylic version of it for the Royal Academy's 'Sensation' exhibition in 1997 – the same year as Woolcock's *Macbeth on the Estate*. In Harvey's portrait, 'Myra, Medusa' is composed entirely of children's handprints. At its first showing, it was pelted with eggs and ink, and it remains one of the most controversial exhibits on permanent display at the Saatchi gallery in London.

98 I'm grateful to Simon Russell Beale for talking me through his Macbeth.
99 Stafford-Clark's acknowledged source was Daniel Bergner's *Soldiers of Light*. Bergner offers a (white) reporter's 'outsider's' view of the Liberian civil wars. Iweala, a Nigerian, gives us, in *Beasts of No Nation*, a black account, an 'insider's' story, that troubles the heart of darkness it probes by being a story told by a child.
100 Iweala, 12, 20–1.
101 See Sokolova, '"Who's there?" – *Macbeth* on the London stage 2004–5', in Marta Gibinska and Agnieszka Romanowska-Kowalska (eds), *History and Memory* (forthcoming in 2007 from Jagiellonian University Press). Stafford-Clark found historical justification for relocating the play to Africa in Giles Foden's book, *The Last King of Scotland*, a fictionalized account of Uganda under Idi Amin, dictator throughout the 1970s. As spectators were informed in a long programme note, Amin was fascinated with all things Scottish (an enduring legacy of his serving under Scottish officers in the King's African Rifles in his youth). He visited Scotland as a guest of State after he came to power in Uganda (having staged a military coup) – and was even granted military solemnities in Holyrood Palace. As the regime grew bloodier and British support fell off, Amin styled himself the leader of Scottish 'liberation'. He volunteered to reign as Scotland's king, and appointed himself chief-of-staff in a Scottish war on English imperialism. He adopted the kilt as his personal costume signature. This story was released as a feature film starring Forest Whitaker in Britain in 2007.
102 Es Devlin in Education Notes accompanying the production. Downloaded from www.outofjoint.co.uk/education/education.html.
103 The phrase is Sokolova's.
104 Sokolova, 'Who's there?'
105 I take this from Mark Scheffler's 'Scare tactics' (1 August 2003), reprinted in Out of Joint's *Macbeth* programme; available at www.slate.com.
106 A programme note offered stark statistics and asked a question that needs answering: 'Humans spend US$1 trillion a year on war. If you earned $10,000 a day (the going rate for Claudia Schiffer), it would take you almost 300,000 years to make that much money. Governments say military spending is an investment in the future. What could that possibly mean?'
107 In the meantime, Macbeth turned up, dragging in with him a trembling Ross. Somewhere beyond the room where the killings were taking place a baby was wailing. Macbeth handed Ross a machete. And with it, he gave this decent guy in a business suit who'd so far managed to keep his hands clean a tacit choice. The baby was still wailing. Ross hesitated, then exited; the wailing stopped. He returned. He stood before Macbeth – but then he buckled at the knees. As he collapsed, Macbeth wiped the machete blade down the front of his T-shirt.
108 Sokolova, 'Who's there?'
109 Ibid.
110 Iweala, 72.
111 Ibid., 51.
112 Ibid., 52, 135–6, 140.
113 Ibid., 141.

114 Sokolova, 'Who's there?' Coincidentally, on 5 July 2006, the day I finished this chapter, an amnesty was announced to the Lord's Resistance Army in Uganda, and an end to the twenty years of civil war, a day when 25,000 Agus could start the journey home.

115 For a 'Note on the Ending(s)' to the play, see my 'Introduction' to G.K. Hunter (ed.), *Macbeth*, London, 2005, lxix–xi.

116 We might put alongside this painting, too, Brueghel's 'Children's Games' (1560) and 'The Massacre of the Innocents' (1565) – and gloss them with Auden's 'Musée des Beaux Arts'.

117 *The ciuilitie of childehode with the discipline and institucion of children ... translated ... by Thomas Paynell*, London, 1560, STC2 10470.3. Sig. Eiiiiᵛ.

Bibliography

Adelman, Janet (1992) *Suffocating Mothers: Fantasies of Maternal Origin in Shakespeare's Plays, Hamlet to The Tempest* (London: Routledge).

Aebischer, Pascale (2004) *Shakespeare's Violated Bodies: Stage and Screen Performance* (Cambridge: Cambridge University Press).

Akrigg, G.P.V. (ed.) (1984) *Letters of King James VI and I* (London: University of California Press).

Anselment, Raymond A. (1995) *The Realm of Apollo: Literature and Healing in Seventeenth Century England* (London: Associated University Press).

Ariès, Philippe (1962) *Centuries of Childhood*, Robert Baldick (tr.) (London: Cape).

Baldwin, T.W. (1944) *William Shaksperes Small Latine & Lesse Greeke* (Urbana, Ill.: University of Illinois Press).

Barker, Francis (1993) *The Culture of Violence: Tragedy and History* (Manchester: Manchester University Press).

Barroll, Leeds (2001) *Anna of Denmark, Queen of England: A Cultural Biography* (Philadelphia: University of Pennsylvania Press).

Bartholomeusz, Dennis (1982) *The Winter's Tale in Performance in England and America 1611–1976* (Cambridge: Cambridge University Press).

Bate, Jonathan (ed.) (1995) *Titus Andronicus* Arden 3 (London: Routledge).

—— (1993) *Shakespeare and Ovid* (Oxford: Clarendon Press).

Bates, Catherine (1994) 'Weaving and writing in *Othello*', *Shakespeare Survey* 46 (Cambridge: Cambridge University Press): 51–60.

Beer, Barrett L. (ed.) (1993) *The Life and Raigne of King Edward the Sixth by John Hayward* (London: Kent State University Press).

Belsey, Catherine (2001) *Shakespeare and the Loss of Eden: The Construction of Family Values in Early Modern Culture* (Basingstoke: Palgrave).

Bradley, A.C. (1957) *Shakespearean Tragedy* (London: Macmillan).

Braunmuller, A.R. (ed.) (1997) *Macbeth* (Cambridge: Cambridge University Press).

Brinsley, John (1968) *Ludus Literarius* (1612), Scolar Press Facsimile (Menston, England: Scolar Press).

Bristol, Michael D. (1991) 'In search of the bear: spatiotemporal form and the heterogeneity of economies in *The Winter's Tale*', *Shakespeare Quarterly* 42: 2 (Summer): 145–67.

Brooks, Cleanth (1949) *The Well Wrought Urn* (London: Dennis Dobson).

Burgess, Anthony (2000) *A Clockwork Orange* (London: Penguin Books).

Burnett, Mark Thornton (2000) 'Impressions of fantasy: Adrian Noble's *A Midsummer Night's Dream*', in Mark Thornton Burnett and Ramona Wray (eds), *Shakespeare, Film, Fin de Siècle* (London: Macmillan), pp. 89–101.

Camden, William (1635) *Annales, or, The Historie of the Most Renovvned and Victorious Princesse Elizabeth … Translated into English by R.N. Gent*, STC2 4501 (London).

Campbell, Beatrix (1993) *Goliath: Britain's Dangerous Places* (London: Methuen).

Chedgzoy, Kate, Susanne Greenhalgh, and Robert Shaughnessy (eds) (2007) *Shakespeare and Childhood* (Cambridge: Cambridge University Press).

Church of England (1559) *The Boke of common praier*, STC 16284.5 (London).

Church of England (1877) *The First Prayer-Book of Edward VI compared with The Successive Revision of The Book of Common Prayer* (Oxford and London: James Parker and Co).

Coghill, Nevill (1958) 'Six points of stage-craft in *The Winter's Tale*', *Shakespeare Survey* 11 (Cambridge: Cambridge University Press): 31–41.

Cohen, David (1993) *The Development of Play* (2nd edn) (London: Routledge).

Cressy, David (1999) *Birth, Marriage and Death: Ritual, Religion, and the Life-cycle in Tudor and Stuart England* (Oxford: Oxford University Press).

Cunningham, Karen (1994) 'Female fidelities on trial: proof in the Howard attainder and *Cymbeline*', *Renaissance Drama* XXV (Evanston: Northwestern University Press): 1–31.

Curtis, M.H. (1964) 'Education and apprenticeship', *Shakespeare Survey* 17 (Cambridge: Cambridge University Press): 53–72.

Danson, Lawrence (1993) 'The catastrophe is a nuptial: the space of masculine desire in *Othello*, *Cymbeline* and *The Winter's Tale*', *Shakespeare Survey* 46 (Cambridge: Cambridge University Press): 69–79.

Dawson, Anthony B. (1996) 'Performance and participation: Desdemona, Foucault, and the Actor's Body', in James C. Bulman (ed.), *Shakespeare, Theory, and Performance* (London: Routledge), pp. 29–45.

—— (1999) 'The arithmetic of memory: Shakespeare's theatre and the national past', *Shakespeare Survey* 52 (Cambridge: Cambridge University Press): 54–67.

Dawson, Anthony B., and Paul Yachnin (2001) *The Culture of Playgoing in Shakespeare's England* (Cambridge: Cambridge University Press).

de Grazia, Margreta (1996) 'Imprints: Shakespeare, Gutenberg and Descartes', in Terence Hawkes (ed.), *Alternative Shakespeares* vol. 2 (London: Routledge): 63–94.

de Vocht, H. (ed.) (1913) *Jasper Heywood and his Translations of Seneca's Troas, Thyestes and Hercules Furens* (Louvain: A Uystpruyst).

Dessen, Alan (1989) *Titus Andronicus: Shakespeare in Performance* (Manchester: Manchester University Press).

Dobson, Michael (2002) 'Shakespeare performances in England, 2001', *Shakespeare Survey* 55 (Cambridge: Cambridge University Press): 285–321.

Donaldson, Peter S. (2005) 'Game space/tragic space: Julie Taymor's *Titus*', in Barbara Hodgdon and W.B. Worthen (eds), *A Companion to Shakespeare and Performance* (Oxford: Blackwell): 457–77.

Donnellan, Declan (2003) 'Directing Shakespeare's comedies: in conversation with Peter Holland', *Shakespeare Survey* 56 (Cambridge: Cambridge University Press): 161–6.

Duncan-Jones, Katherine (2001) *Ungentle Shakespeare* (London: Arden).

Elias, Norbert (2000) *The Civilizing Process* (Oxford: Blackwell).

Erasmus, Desiderius (1560) *The ciuilitie of childehode with the discipline and institucion of children*, in Thomas Paynell (tr.) (London), STC2 10470.3.

Esslin, Martin (1976) *An Anatomy of Drama* (London: Temple Smith).

Estrin, Barbara L. (1985) *The Raven and the Lark: Lost Children in Literature of the English Renaissance* (London: AUP).

Fleming, Don (1996) *Powerplay: Toys as Popular Culture* (Manchester: Manchester University Press).

Foakes, R.A. (ed.) (1977) *The Henslowe Papers* vol. 1 (London: Scolar Press).

Foakes, R.A. and Rickert, R.T. (eds) (1968) *Henslowe's Diary* (Cambridge: Cambridge University Press).

Fraser, Antonia (1974) *King James VI of Scotland I of England* (London: Weidenfeld and Nicolson).

Fumerton, Patricia (1991) *Cultural Aesthetics: Renaissance Literature and the Practice of Social Ornament* (Chicago: University of Chicago Press).

Geertz, Clifford (1973) *The Interpretation of Cultures* (New York: Basic Books).

Gerard, John (1597) *The Herbal* (London), STC 11750.

Gibbons, Brian (1997) 'Erring and straying like lost sheep: *The Winter's Tale* and the *Comedy of Errors*', *Shakespeare Survey* 50 (Cambridge: Cambridge University Press): 111–23.

Gómez-Lara, Manuel (2006) 'Apocalyptic iconographies and Elizabethan political propaganda', in Rui Carvalho Homem and Fátima Vieira (eds), *Gloriana's Rule: Literature, Religion and Power in the Age of Elizabeth* (Porto: Editora da Universidade Do Porto): 83–103.

Grant, Teresa (2001) 'White Bears in *Mucedorus*, *The Winter's Tale*, and *Oberon, The Fairy Prince*', *Notes and Queries*, n.s. 48: 3 (September): 311–13.

Greenblatt, Stephen (1988) *Shakespearean Negotiations: The Circulation of Social Energy in Renaissance England* (Berkeley: University of California Press).

—— (2004) *Will in the World* (London: Jonathan Cape).

Greenhalgh, Susanne (2003) '"Alas poor country!": documenting the politics of performance in two British television *Macbeth*s since the 1980s', in Pascale Aebischer, Edward J. Esche and Nigel Wheale (eds), *Remaking Shakespeare: Performance Across Media, Genres and Cultures* (Basingstoke: Palgrave): 93–114.

Hamilton, James (1990) *Arthur Rackham: A Life with Illustrations* (London: Pavilion).

Harrison, Tony (1981) *The Oresteia* (London: Rex Collings).

Harrison, Tony (2002) *Tony Harrison, Plays 4* (London: Faber and Faber).

Harrison, William (1587) *An Historical description of the Iland of Britaine* in Holinshed et al., *The First and Second Volumes of Chronicles*, London, STC2 13569.

Hartley, L.P. (1953) *The Go-Between* (London: Hamish Hamilton).

Hattaway, Michael (ed.) (1990) *The First Part King Henry VI* (Cambridge: Cambridge University Press).

—— (1991) *The Second Part King Henry VI* (Cambridge: Cambridge University Press).

—— (1993) *The Third Part King Henry VI* (Cambridge: Cambridge University Press).

Hawkes, Terence (2002) *Shakespeare in the Present* (London: Routledge).

Healy, Margaret (2001) *Fictions of Disease in Early Modern England: Bodies, Plagues and Politics* (Basingstoke: Palgrave).

Herford, C.H., Percy and Evelyn Simpson (eds) (1947), *Ben Jonson*, vol. VIII (Oxford: Clarendon Press).

Hodgdon, Barbara (1983) 'Two *King Lear*s: uncovering the filmtext', *Literature and Film Quarterly* 11: 3, July 1983: 143–51.

Holinshed, Raphael *et al.*, (eds) (1586) [sic] *The Third Volume of Chronicles … January 1587 …* London, STC2 13569.

—— (1587) *The Third Volume of Chronicles*, London, STC2 13569 incorporating Richard Mulcaster, The passage of our most drad Soueraigne Lady Quene Elyzabeth through the citie of London to Westminster the daye before her coronacion, STC2 7590.

—— (1808) *Holinshed's Chronicles of England, Scotland and Ireland*, vol. 5 (London: J. Johnson).

—— (1808) *Holinshed's Chronicles of England, Scotland and Ireland*, vol. 6 (London: J. Johnson).

Hunt, Maurice, (2004) ' "Bearing Hence" Shakespeare's *The Winter's Tale*', *Studies in English Literature 1500–1900*, 44: 2 (Spring): 333–46.

Hunter, G.K. (1978) *Dramatic Identities and Cultural Tradition* (Liverpool: Liverpool University Press).

Hurstfield, Joel (1958) *The Queen's Wards: Wardship and Marriage under Elizabeth I* (Cambridge, MA: Harvard University Press).

Hustvedt, Siri (2005) '*Death of Photography*: old pictures and a new book', *Modern Painters*, September (London, LTB (UK) Ltd): 96–9.

Iweala, Uzodinma (2005) *Beasts of No Nation* (New York: HarperCollins).

James VI/I (1969) *Basilicon Doron 1599*, Scolar Press Facsimile (Menston: Scolar Press).

Jameson, Frederic (1998) *The Cultural Turn* (London: Verso).

Jennings, Michael W., Howard Eiland, and Gary Smith (eds) (1999) *Walter Benjamin: Selected Writings Volume 2 1927–1934* (London: Belnap Press of Harvard University Press).

Jowett, John (1993) 'Johannes Factotum: Henry Chettle and Greene's Groatsworth of Wit', *Papers of the Bibliographical Society of America* 87: 453–86.

Kaplan, M. Lindsay and Katherine Eggert (eds) (1994) ' "Good queen, my lord, good queen": sexual slander and the trials of female authority in *The Winter's Tale*', *Renaissance Drama* XXV (Evanston: Northwestern University Press), pp. 89–118.

Kathman, David (2004) 'Grocers, Goldsmiths, and Drapers: freemen and apprentices in the Elizabethan theater', *Shakespeare Quarterly* 55: 1 (Spring): 1–49.

—— (2005) 'How old were Shakespeare's boy actors?', *Shakespeare Survey* 58 (Cambridge: Cambridge University Press): 220–46.

Kinney, Arthur F. (2001) *Lies Like Truth: Shakespeare, Macbeth and the Cultural Moment* (Detroit: Wayne State University Press).

Kitsch, Aaron (2001) 'Bastards and Broadsides in *The Winter's Tale*', *Renaissance Drama* XXX (Evanston: Northwestern University Press), pp. 43–71.

Kliman, Bernice W. (1992) *Macbeth in Performance* (Manchester: Manchester University Press).

Knight, G. Wilson (1948) *The Crown of Life* (London: Methuen).

Knights, L.C. (1946) *Explorations* (London: Chatto & Windus).

—— (1965) *Further Explorations* (London: Chatto & Windus).

Kott, Jan (1964) *Shakespeare Our Contemporary* (London: Methuen).

Lamb, Mary Ellen (1998) 'Engendering the narrative act: old wives' tales in *The Winter's Tale, Macbeth*, and *The Tempest*', *Criticism* XL: 4 (Fall): 529–53.

Laslett, Peter (1983) *The World We Have Lost – Further Explored* (London: Methuen).

Latham, Robert and William Matthews (eds) (1974) *The Diary of Samuel Pepys* vol. 8 (London: Bell).

Leavis, F.R. (1952) *The Common Pursuit* (London: Chatto & Windus).

Lindley, Arthur (1989) 'The unbeing of the overreacher', *Modern Language Review* 84: 1–17.

Loehlin, James (2000) '"These violent delights have violent ends": Baz Luhrmann's Millennial Shakespeare', in Mark Thornton Burnett and Ramona Wray (eds), *Shakespeare, Film, Fin de Siècle* (London: Macmillan): 121–36.

Logan, Sandra (2001) 'Making history: the rhetorical and historical occasion of Elizabeth Tudor's coronation entry', *Journal of Medieval and Early Modern Studies* 31: 251–81.

Mack, Peter (ed.) (1994) *Renaissance Rhetoric* (London: Macmillan).

—— (2002) *Elizabethan Rhetoric: Theory and Practice* (Cambridge: Cambridge University Press).

—— (2006) 'Humanism, rhetoric, education', in Donna Hamilton (ed.), *A Concise Companion to English Renaissance Literature* (Oxford: Blackwell): 94–113.

Mahood, M.M. (1957) *Shakespeare's Wordplay* (London: Methuen).

Marcus, Leah (1978) *Childhood and Cultural Despair* (Pittsburgh: University of Pittsburgh Press).

McClure, Norman Egbert (ed.) (1939) *The Letters of John Chamberlain*, 2 vols. (Philadelphia: American Philosophical Society).

McDonagh, Martin (2003) *The Pillowman* (London: Faber and Faber).

McGuinness, Frank (2005) *Speaking Like Magpies* (London: Faber and Faber).

Montaigne, Michel (1613) *Essays written in French ... done in English ... by Iohn Florio reader of the Italian tongue unto the Soueraigne Maiestie of Anna, Queen of England, Scotland, France* (London), STC2 18042.

Montrose, Louis (1980) 'The purpose of playing: reflections on a Shakespearean anthropology', *Helios*, n.s. 7: 51–74.

—— (1986) '*A Midsummer Night's Dream* and the shaping fantasies of Elizabethan culture: gender, power, form', in Margaret Ferguson, Maureen Quilligan, and Nancy J. Vickers (eds), *Rewriting the Renaissance* (Chicago: University of Chicago Press).

Moody, Joanna (ed.) (2001) *The Private Life of an Elizabethan Lady: The Diary of Lady Margaret Hoby 1599–1605* (Stroud: Sutton Publishing).

Morrison, Blake (1998) *As If* (London: Granta).

Nims, John Frederick (ed.) (2000) *Ovid's Metamorphoses: The Arthur Golding Translation 1567* (Philadelphia: Paul Dry Books).

Ong, Walter (1971) *Rhetoric, Romance, and Technology: Studies in the Interaction of Expression and Culture* (Ithaca and London: Cornell University Press).

Pafford, J.H.P. (ed.) (1963) *The Winter's Tale* Arden 2 (London: Methuen) (rpt., London: Thomas Nelson, 2003).

Phaer, Thomas (1558) *The seuen first bookes of the Eneidos of Virgill, conuerted in Englishe meter by Thomas Phaer* (London), STC 24799.

Pinchbeck, Ivy and Margaret Hewitt (1969) *Children in English Society* vol. 1 (London: Routledge).

Poole, Adrian (2004) *Shakespeare and the Victorians* (London: Thomson).

Reynolds, George F. (1959) '*Musedorus*, most popular Elizabethan play', in Josephine W. Bennett, Oscar Cargill and Vernon Hall Jr (eds), *Studies in English Renaissance Drama* (London: Owen): 248–68.

Rhodes, Neil, Jennifer Richards and Joseph Marshall (eds) (2003) *King James VI and I: Selected Writings* (Aldershot: Ashgate).

Ridley, Philip (2002) *Philip Ridley: Plays 1* (London: Faber and Faber).

Riley, Henry T. (ed.) (1869) *Ars amatoria* (London: Bell and Daldy).

Roach, Joseph (1996) *Cities of the Dead: Circum-Atlantic Performance* (New York: Columbia University Press).

Rosenberg, Marvin (1978) *The Masks of Macbeth* (Berkeley: University of California Press).

Rutter, Carol Chillington (1988) *Clamorous Voices: Shakespeare's Women Today* (London: The Women's Press).

—— (2001) *Enter the Body: Women and Representation on Shakespeare's Stage* (London: Routledge).

—— (2003) 'Looking like a child – or – *Titus*: The comedy', *Shakespeare Survey* 56 (Cambridge: Cambridge University Press): 1–26.

—— (2005) 'Introduction', in G.K. Hunter (ed.), *Macbeth* (London: Penguin).

—— (2006) '"Show me like a Queen": Elizabeth among the players', in Rui Carvalho Homem and Fátima Vieira (eds), *Gloriana's Rule: Literature, Religion and Power in the Age of Elizabeth* (Porto: Editora da Universidade Do Porto), pp. 61–81.

Sanders, Wilbur (1987) *The Winter's Tale: Harvester New Critical Introductions to Shakespeare* (Brighton: Harvester Press).

Shand, G.B. (ed.) (forthcoming) 'The ghost of Lucrece', in Gary Taylor *et al.* (eds), *Thomas Middleton: The Collected Works* (Oxford: Oxford University Press).

Shepherd, Geoffrey (ed.) (1965) *Sir Philip Sidney: An Apologie for Poetrie* (London: Thomas Nelson).

Sher, Antony (2001) *Beside Myself* (London: Arrow).

Shuger, Debora Kuller (1990) *Habits of Thought in the English Renaissance* (Los Angeles: University of California Press).

Smallwood, Robert (ed.) (1998) *Players of Shakespeare 4* (Cambridge: Cambridge University Press).

Smith, Bruce (2000) *Shakespeare and Masculinity* (Oxford: Oxford University Press).

Smith, Peter J. (1991) [review], 'Michael Bogdanov (dir.), *The Winter's Tale*', *Cahiers Élisabéthains* 39, (April): 80–2.

—— (1991) [review], 'Simon Usher (dir.), *The Winter's Tale*', *Cahiers Élisabéthains* 39, (April): 84–6.

Sokolova, Boika (2007) (forthcoming) '"Who's there?" – *Macbeth* on the London stage 2004–2005', in Marta Gibinska and Agnieszka Romanowska-Kowalska (eds), *History and Memory* (Wydawnictwo, UJ: Jagiellonian University Press).

Sommerville, C. John (1992) *The Discovery of Childhood in Puritan England* (Athens, GA: University of Georgia Press).

Spevack, Marvin (ed.) (1973) *The Harvard Concordance to Shakespeare* (Cambridge, MA: Harvard University Press).

Stallybrass, Peter (1986) 'Patriarchal territories: the body enclosed', in Margaret Ferguson, Maureen Quilligan, and Nancy J. Vickers (eds), *Rewriting the Renaissance* (Chicago: University of Chicago Press).

Stanihurst, Richard (1808) *The Description of Ireland* vol. V, in Holinshed *et al.* (eds), (London).

Stone, Lawrence (1977) *The Family, Sex and Marriage in England 1500–1800* (London: Weidenfeld and Nicolson).

Strong, Roy (1986) *Henry, Prince of Wales and England's Lost Renaissance* (London: Thames and Hudson).

Taymor, Julie (2000) *Titus: The Illustrated Screenplay* (New York: Newmarket Press).

Terry, Ellen (1908) *The Story of My Life* (London: Hutchinson & Co).

Thomas, Keith (1989) 'Children in early modern England', in Gillian Avery and Julia Briggs (eds), *Children and Their Books* (Oxford: Clarendon Press): 45–77.

Topsell, Edward (1607) *The Historie of Foure-footed Beastes* (London: William Jaggard), STC 24123.

Turberville, George (tr.) (1567) *The Heroycall Epistles of the Learned Poet Publius Ovidius Naso, In Englishe Verse: set out and translated by George Turberville Gent,* (London), STC2 18939.5.

Turner, Victor (1974) *Dramas, Fields and Metaphors* (Ithaca: Cornell University Press).

Tynan, Kenneth (1961) *Tynan on Theatre* (Harmondsworth: Penguin).

Wall, Wendy (1993) *The Imprint of Gender: Authorship and Publication in the English Renaissance* (London: Cornell University Press).

Warner, Marina (1989) *Into the Dangerous World: Some Reflections on Childhood and Its Costs* (London: Chatto & Windus).

Watling, E.F. (ed.) (1966) *Seneca: Thyestes, Phaedra, The Trojan Women, Oedipus with Octavia* (Harmondsworth: Penguin).

Watson, Henry (1555) *The hystory of the two valyaunte brethren Valentyne and Orson* (London), STC2 24571.7.

Wells, Stanley and Gary Taylor (eds) (1986) *The Complete Works* (Oxford: Clarendon Press).

Wheeler, Richard P., (2000) 'Deaths in the family: the loss of a son and the rise of Shakespearean comedy', *Shakespeare Quarterly* 51: 2 (Summer): 127–53.

Willcock, G.D. and Alice Walker (eds) (1936) *George Puttenham: The Arte of English Poesie* (Cambridge: Cambridge University Press).

Woods, Marjorie Curry (1996), 'Rape and the pedagogical rhetoric of sexual violence', in Rita Copeland (ed.), *Criticism and Dissent in the Middle Ages* (Cambridge: Cambridge University Press): 56–86.

—— (2002) 'Weeping for Dido: epilogue on a premodern rhetorical exercise in the postmodern classroom', in Carol Dana Lanham (ed.), *Latin Grammar and Rhetoric: From Classical Theory to Medieval Practice* (New York and London: Continuum): 284–93.

Wormald, Jenny (1991) 'James VI and I, *Basilikon Doron* and *The Trew Law of Free Monarchies*: The Scottish context and the English translation', in Linda Levy Peck (ed.), *The Mental World of the Jacobean Court* (Cambridge: Cambridge University Press): 36–54.

Worthen, W.B. (1993) *Shakespeare and the Force of Modern Performance* (Cambridge: Cambridge University Press).

—— (1998) 'Drama, performativity, and performance', *PMLA* 113: 1093–107.

Wrightson, Keith (1998) *English Society 1580–1680* (London: Routledge).

Index